369 0246572

D1741125

PUBLIC HEALTH IN THE 21ST CENTURY

FRONTIERS IN SUICIDE RISK

RESEARCH, TREATMENT AND PREVENTION

PUBLIC HEALTH IN THE 21ST CENTURY

Additional books in this series can be found on Nova's website
under the Series tab.

Additional e-books in this series can be found on Nova's website
under the e-book tab.

SOCIAL ISSUES, JUSTICE AND STATUS

Additional books in this series can be found on Nova's website
under the Series tab.

Additional e-books in this series can be found on Nova's website
under the e-book tab.

FRONTIERS IN SUICIDE RISK

RESEARCH, TREATMENT AND PREVENTION

JILL E. LAVIGNE

EDITOR

nova
publishers
New York

Copyright © 2012 by Nova Science Publishers, Inc.

For permission to use material from this book please contact us:
Telephone 631-231-7269; Fax 631-231-8175
Web Site: http://www.novapublishers.com

NOTICE TO THE READER

The Publisher has taken reasonable care in the preparation of this book, but makes no expressed or implied warranty of any kind and assumes no responsibility for any errors or omissions. No liability is assumed for incidental or consequential damages in connection with or arising out of information contained in this book. The Publisher shall not be liable for any special, consequential, or exemplary damages resulting, in whole or in part, from the readers' use of, or reliance upon, this material. Any parts of this book based on government reports are so indicated and copyright is claimed for those parts to the extent applicable to compilations of such works.

Independent verification should be sought for any data, advice or recommendations contained in this book. In addition, no responsibility is assumed by the publisher for any injury and/or damage to persons or property arising from any methods, products, instructions, ideas or otherwise contained in this publication.

This publication is designed to provide accurate and authoritative information with regard to the subject matter covered herein. It is sold with the clear understanding that the Publisher is not engaged in rendering legal or any other professional services. If legal or any other expert assistance is required, the services of a competent person should be sought. FROM A DECLARATION OF PARTICIPANTS JOINTLY ADOPTED BY A COMMITTEE OF THE AMERICAN BAR ASSOCIATION AND A COMMITTEE OF PUBLISHERS.

Additional color graphics may be available in the e-book version of this book.

Library of Congress Cataloging-in-Publication Data

Frontiers in suicide risk : research, treatment, and prevention / [edited by] Jill E. Lavigne.
 p. cm.
Includes bibliographical references and index.
ISBN 978-1-62081-373-7 (hardcover)
 1. Suicidal behavior--Diagnosis. 2. Suicide--Risk factors. 3. Suicide--Prevention. I. Lavigne, Jill E.
RC569.F76 2011
616.85'8445--dc23

2012008882

Published by Nova Science Publishers, Inc. † New York

CONTENTS

Preface   ix

Medical Technologies for Suicide Risk Detection and Treatment

Chapter 1   Potential Biomarkers of Suicide Risk   **1**
Lei Zhang, Xian-Zhang Hu, He Li, Xiaoxia Li,
Stanley Smerin and Robert Ursano

Chapter 2   Innovative Drug Delivery and Formulation Designs
to Deter Drug Abuse/Misuse Related to Suicide   **23**
Fang Zhao

Chapter 3   The Comparative Safety of Multiple Prescription Drug Regimens
with Adverse effects of Risk of Suicidal Ideation
or Behavior: A Study Design in Bipolar Disorder   **35**
Jill E. Lavigne

Chapter 4   Blister Packaging Medication to Increase Treatment
Adherence and Clinical Response: Impact on
Suicide-Related Morbidity and Mortality   **55**
Peter M. Gutierrez, Lisa A. Brenner, Hal Wortzel,
Jeri E. F. Harwood, Rebecca Leitner, Jeffrey Rings
and Stephen Bartlett

Clinical Suicide Risk Assessment and Management

Chapter 5   Advances in Motivational Interviewing to Address
Suicidal Ideation (MI-SI)   **79**
Peter C. Britton

Chapter 6   Traumatic Brain Injury and Suicide: Contributing Factors,
Risk Assessment and Safety Planning   **95**
Gina M. Signoracci, Bridget B. Matarazzo
and Nazanin H. Bahraini

Chapter 7   Interventions to Address Suicidal Behavior in Adults
with Substance Use Disorders   **115**
Kenneth R. Conner

Chapter 8   Older Men and Suicide Risk: Clinical and Research Implications   **123**
                     Alisa A. O'Riley and Phillip N. Smith

Statistical Methods and Issues in the Study of Suicide

Chapter 9   Statistical Methods and Issues in the Study of Suicide   **139**
                     Y. Xia, N. Lu, H. Zhang, D. Gunzler, G. S. Zubenko
                     and X. M. Tu

Population-Based Approaches to Suicide Research and Prevention

Chapter 10   Building Connections: Strategies to Mitigate Suicide Risk
                     in Civilians and Military Veterans Living in Non-Urban
                     and Rural Areas with a Focus on Telecommunication
                     and Internet Technologies   **161**
                     John F. Crilly

Chapter 11   Operation S.A.V.E.: Suicide Prevention Training
                     for Front-Line Employees in the Us Department
                     of Veterans Health Affairs   **185**
                     Deborah A. King, Heather Von Bergen (In Memoriam),
                     Kerry L. Knox, Jane Wood, Krista Stephenson,
                     Lynda Chauncey, Naji Lu, Kimberly Kaukeinen
                     and Janet E. Kemp

Chapter 12   Pharmacist and Pharmacy Staff Knowledge, Attitudes
                     and Motivation to Refer Patients for Suicide Risk Assessment:
                     Lessons from Operation S.A.V.E.   **195**
                     Jill E. Lavigne, Deborah A. King, Nai Ji Lu,
                     Kerry L. Knox and Jan E. Kemp

Chapter 13   Court Perspectives on Addressing Mental Health in the Justice
                     System Through Community-Based Participatory Research   **203**
                     Ann Marie White, Corey A. Nichols-Hadeed,
                     Henry J. Steadman and Catherine Cerulli

The Economics of Suicide and Suicide Prevention

Chapter 14   Determinants of Suicidal Ideation and Behavior, Economic
                     Theories of Suicidal Behavior and the Economics of Prevention   **221**
                     Alper Altinanahtar and Nazmi Sari

International Perspectives on Clinical Approaches to Suicide Prevention

Chapter 15   Suicide: Risk Factors and Prevention   **241**
                     Barbara Schneider

Chapter 16   Suicide Attempters Transferred by Ambulance:
                     Prevention of Recurrent Suicide Attempts   **247**
                     Kaoru Kudo, Kotaro Otsuka and Akio Sakai

Chapter 17   Suicidal Syndrome Rather than Process Related to Suicide in Severe
                 Depression: Evidence from a Controlled Longitudinal Case Study
                 of 100 People Who Died by Suicide   **259**
                 Louise Bradvik and Mats Berglund

Chapter 18   Executive Functioning in Borderline Personality Disorder
                 with and without Self-harming Behaviors   **279**
                 Laurence Claes, Frederique Van den Eynde,
                 Sébastien Guillaume, Caroline Vogels and Kurt Audenaert

Index   **287**

PREFACE

Jill Lavigne
Wegmans School of Pharmacy, St. John Fisher College
Rochester, New York

Suicide prevention has become a stated priority of several US government agencies including the US Surgeon General, the Centers for Disease Control, the Department of Defense and the US Department of Veterans Affairs. The VA established a suicide prevention research and operations center in 2007 as well as a telephone hotline and later a chatline to operate 24/7 specifically for veterans [1]. National Institute of Health support for community based collaborative research in addition to suicide prevention, specifically, has expanded the "laboratory" for suicide risk and prevention research to courts, prisons and schools, for example. Funding in the 2009 US stimulus budget for comparative effectiveness research fueled innovation in the methods used to assess drug safety in large observational data sets including the measurement of adverse effects of suicidal ideation and behavior. In 2009, a consensus conference resulted in the publication of a statement regarding drug development needs in suicide prevention [2]. After years of controversy regarding the association between antidepressants and other classes of prescription drugs and treatment-emergent suicidal ideation and behavior, the US Food and Drug Administration posted its Guidance to Industry, "Suicidality: Prospective Assessment of Occurrence in Clinical Trials," in 2010. [3] Accrediting bodies of health professional schools in the US, including medicine, pharmacy and nursing, are requiring training in the population and public health sciences which encompass prevention broadly and specific public health priorities such as suicide. Finally, in September 2011, the White House recognized the suicide prevention efforts of the National Institute of Mental Health with a "Champions of Change" award [4].

The genesis of this book was the US Department of Veterans Affairs/Department of Defense Second Annual Suicide Prevention Conference: All the Way Home held in Boston, MA in March, 2011. Presenters and attendees from the conference appear as authors, but the book has been greatly expanded to feature topics not covered in that conference, such as drug delivery and pharmacy-based suicide prevention. Contributions from clinicians and scientists in Europe and Japan also appear.

We begin with overviews of the epidemiology and economics of suicide, turning to new science about risk factors and the clinical management of suicidal ideation and behavior. We then consider opportunities to apply current knowledge to better manage suicide risk. For example, in the area of pharmacotherapy, we consider the application of new drug delivery technologies to deter abuse of prescription medications, the generation of new prescribing knowledge about multiple drug regimens from innovative comparative safety studies in existing medical records, the restriction of means through prescription drug dispensing advances using blister packaging and limited days supply, and finally motivational interviewing and referral for suicide screening and treatment in community pharmacy settings.

Innovative delivery systems for suicide prevention programming have emerged in recent years as well. The VA developed a system-wide suicide education and training program in 2007 that continues to encourage all of its employees to view suicide prevention as a job responsibility and to actively direct patients and other employees to screening and treatment. Motivational interviewing techniques have been developed specifically for patients with active suicidal ideation. Acknowledgement of the significant risk differences across population subgroups such as rural, geriatric and substance user populations continues to spur programming targeted specifically to the needs and opportunities in these communities.

I wish to thank the many expert colleagues who have contributed to this book. In my years working as a faculty fellow in the Department of Psychiatry at the University of Rochester Medical School and later as a researcher at the US Department of Veterans Affairs Center for Excellence in Suicide Prevention, I have witnessed a steadfast commitment to ask questions most would rather avoid for dread of the answers, and moreover a determination to measure (and publish) outcomes of clinical care regardless of outcome. I admire the devotion of these clinicians, researchers and administrators who strive to ensure that others live another day.

Personally, my interest in suicide prevention and risk research stretches to 1976 when I was eight years old and my mother received a mysterious phone call that spurred a panicked 250-mile ride to my grandfather's house. The flashing lights of police cars lit up the night as my father went in and my mother cried, head in her hands, my siblings and I frozen and perplexed in the backseat. Grandpa Jack had called his daughter to say goodbye.

The death by suicide of any one individual may remain something that we must face without ever completely understanding it. Yet, population and clinical approaches offer the promise of prevention without first waiting for scientists to span current gaps in scientific knowledge about exactly how the brain develops thoughts of suicide or is spurred to acts of self-harm. My hope is that this book may help those facing suicidal thoughts or behaviors in themselves or others to both understand what is known about suicide and its prevention and also to accept the frontiers of our understanding of suicide and its prevention. As the title implies, this book is not intended to be the definitive text of all that is known with certainty about suicide and its prevention, but rather to share current efforts to push that frontier outward and in doing so, to save lives.

With all the best wishes to you and yours,
Jill E. Levigne

December, 2011

REFERENCES

[1] United States Department of Veterans Affairs. Suicide Prevention website. Last accessed 12.30.2011 at: http://www.mentalhealth.va.gov/suicide_prevention/

[2] Meyer RE, Salzman C, Youngstrom EA, et al. Suicidality and risk of suicide – definition, drug safety concerns, and a necessary target for drug development: A brief report. *J Clin Psychiatry.* 2010;71(8):1040-1046.

[3] Food and Drug Administration. U.S. Department of Health and Human Services. Center for Drug Evaluation and Research (CDER). (September 2010) *Guidance for Industry: Suicidality: Prospective Assessment of Occurrence in Clinical Trials.* Last accessed on 12/29/2011 at: http://www.fda.gov/downloads/drugs/guidancecomplianceregulatory information/guidances/ucm225130.pdf

[4] White House. White House Names NIMH a "Champion of Change" for its Suicide Prevention Efforts. Last accessed 12/30/2011 at: http://nimh.nih.gov/science-news /2011/white-house-names-nimh-a-champion-of-change-for-its-suicide-prevention-efforts.shtml

[5] Defense Centers of Excellence in Psychological Health and Traumatic Brain Injury. 2011 DOD/VA ANNUAL SUICIDE PREVENTION CONFERENCE AGENDA: ALL THE WAY HOME: PREVENTING SUICIDE AMONG SERVICEMEMBERS AND VETERANS. Last accessed 12/30/2011 at: http://www.dcoe.health.mil/ Content /Navigation/Documents/DoDVA_Suicide%20Prevention%20Conference_Draft%20Ag enda_%20NOV%2010.pdf

[6] Office of the Surgeon General. The US Surgeon General's Call to Action to Prevent Suicide. Last accessed on 12/30/2011 at: http://www.surgeongeneral.gov

[7] /library/calltoaction/

MEDICAL TECHNOLOGIES FOR SUICIDE RISK DETECTION AND TREATMENT

In: Frontiers in Suicide Risk
Editor: Jill E. Lavigne

ISBN 978-1-62081-373-7
©2012 Nova Science Publishers, Inc.

Chapter 1

POTENTIAL BIOMARKERS OF SUICIDE RISK

Lei Zhang, Xian-Zhang Hu, He Li, Xiaoxia Li, Stanley Smerin and Robert Ursano

Center for the Study of Traumatic Stress, Department of Psychiatry,
Uniformed Services University of the Health Sciences, Bethesda, United States

ABSTRACT

Suicide is a preventable public health problem. Yet, it represents 1.8% of the global burden of disease, and is expected to rise to 2.4% by the year 2020. In 2002, suicide was the 11th leading cause of death in the young age of the United States. Of those who die by suicide, as many as 90% have been diagnosed with a psychiatric disorder. In fact, those diagnosed with a psychiatric disorder constitute most (47-74%) of the population at risk for suicide. More than half of all those who die by suicide meet established criteria for current depressive disorders. In addition, traumatic events generally increase an individual's suicide risk. There is a significant correlation between post-traumatic stress disorder (PTSD) and suicide risk. The likelihood of suicide attempts among individuals with PTSD is approximately 15 times higher than among those without it. Sixty-two percent of individuals diagnosed PTSD have suicidal ideation.

Suicide prevention requires not only clinical observation but also biomarkers for identification of suicide risk. In this chapter, we briefly introduce the concept of biomarkers for suicide risk. Preliminary results demonstrating the possibility of blood biomarkers for suicide risk encourage the effort to develop a biological tool for the diagnosis and treatment of suicide. We therefore focus on current transitional research regarding suicide risk biomarkers. Specifically, we discuss the results of studies from bench to bedside and from bedside to bench, two research approaches in the development and identification of suicide risk biomarkers, a novel tool for diagnosis and treatment.

INTRODUCTION

Suicidal behavior is a major public health problem. It represents 1.8% of the global burden of disease and is expected to rise to 2.4% of the global burden by the year

2020(Hawton, 2001; Hawton and van Heeringen, 2009; Nock et al., 2008). In the United States, suicide was the 11th leading cause of death in 2002. In addition, 421,200 to 842,400 suicide attempts occur annually in the US among people aged 15 to 24 years old (Department of Health and Human Services, Centers for Disease Control and Prevention. Web-based Injury Statistics Query and Reporting System (WISQARS). Atlanta, GA: Centers for Disease Control and Prevention; 2007).

The causes of suicide are heterogeneous and complex. All major mental disorders are associated with increased suicidal risk (Harris and Barraclough, 1997). Psychiatric disorders are present in about 90% of people who commit suicide and contribute to most (47–74%) of the population at risk for suicide (Cavanagh, Carson, Sharpe, and Lawrie, 2003; Hawton et al., 2009). The incidence of mental disorders in suicide victims at the time of their death has been estimated at between 87.3% (Arsenault-Lapierre, Kim, and Turecki, 2004) and 98% (Arsenault-Lapierre et al., 2004). More than half of suicide victims meet established criteria for current depressive disorders (Cavanagh et al., 2003). A number of risk factors also increase the chance of attempting suicide. They include,,but are not limited to,, multiple hospitalizations, depression, presence of stressful life events, the onset of mental disorders during early youth, the absence of remission between episodes of mental disorder or illness, and high number of previous episodes (Azorin et al., 2009; Rihmer, 2007).

THE CONCEPT OF "SUICIDE"

Suicide is defined to include a spectrum of thoughts and behaviors related to self-harm. The concept of suicide includes suicidal ideation as well as the actual taking of, or attempt to take, one's own life (suicide completion and/or suicide attempts). Suicidal behavior (death and attempts) is usually a complication of psychiatric conditions, most commonly involving mood disorders (Rihmer, 2007)(Azorin et al., 2009). However, it also involves those with schizophrenia, substance use disorders (particularly with alcohol), and personality and anxiety disorders (Azorin et al., 2009; Rihmer, 2007). Only about 10% of those who commit or attempt suicide have no identifiable psychiatric illness. According to the International Classification of Diseases (ICD), the concept of suicide contains operational definitions for both suicide and attempted suicide. An alternative term used by many researchers for attempted suicide is intentional self-inflicted injury.

BIOLOGICAL FACTORS ASSOCIATED WITH SUICIDE RISK

Researchers have for centuries attempted to develop a practical tool for diagnosing suicide risk (Shneidman, 1998), such as lab tests, for detecting increased risk, do not yet exist. Behavioral observation and self-reports are typically used, but lack the objectivity of laboratory tests. After a self-injury or suicide attempt, subjects may not understand what actually happened (Wilson, Deri Armstrong, Furrie, and Walcot, 2009). Most people who die by suicide explicitly deny that they are having suicidal thoughts in their last verbal communications before killing themselves (Busch, Fawcett, and Jacobs, 2003). It is difficult to measure suicidal thoughts and attempted suicide without objective tools, such as biological markers, which have been used in other disease diagnosis; for example, the tuberculosis (TB) skin test for TB.

Biological markers hold promise for suicide risk detection and management because biological factors play important roles in suicide risk. Approximately 43% of the variability in completed suicide is attributable to genetics (McGuffin, Marusic, and Farmer, 2001) and about 57% of variability in completed suicide is attributable to environmental factors. Research has focused on gene polymorphisms. At the protein level, neurotransmitter alterations are implicated in the etiology of suicide risk. Future research may identify the specific genes associated with increased risk.

Serotonergic Functioning

Among the receptors, the serotonin (5-HT) receptors, including the serotonin transporter (5-HTT), have been considered as potential markers for suicide risk (Mann, Brent, and Arango, 2001; van Heeringen, 2001). At the time of this writing, a search of the scientific literature identified 37 articles related to the 5-HT receptor, and 140 articles related to the serotonin transporter. Altered serotonergic function is implicated in the etiology and pathogenesis of several major psychiatric conditions. In particular, there is considerable evidence of an association between reduced serotonergic function and suicidal behavior. Suicide attempters had a 10% smaller right caudate nucleus and a 19% bilaterally smaller globus pallidus compared to controls. In suicide attempters, the volume of the globus pallidus correlated negatively with both previously reported measures of solidity (which are associated with a non-impulsive temperament) and the binding potential of the serotonin transporter (Vang, Ryding, Traskman-Bendz, van Westen, and Lindstrom, 2010). Also, in suicide attempters, but not in controls, low 5-HTT availability was associated with the S allele of 5-HTTLPR and with the 12 repeat allele of STin2, which suggests that polymorphisms in SLC6A4 may influence the expression of the brain serotonin transporter in suicide attempters. (Bah et al., 2008)

There are several studies regarding polymorphisms of the serotonin biosynthetic enzyme tryptophan hydroxylase (TPH; A779C substitution), the 5-HT1B receptor (G861C, C129T substitution) and the 5-HT2A receptor (T102C). For the TPH gene, it has been found that the less common U or A allele variant of the A779C polymorphism was associated with suicide attempts. Also, a 44 base pair insertion/deletion in the 5' flanking promoter region of the 5-HTT gene may result in less 5-HTT expression and less 5-HTT binding (Arango, Huang, Underwood, and Mann, 2003). The density of ^{3}H-paroxetine binding sites tended to be higher in subjects expressing the short (S) allele of 5-HT transporter gene. Furthermore, there was a significant difference in serotonin transporter binding sites between the genotype S/S and combined genotypes S/L and L/L (Du et al., 1999). An alteration in 5-HT1A receptor levels in depressed and suicidal subjects is also found. Gene knockout of the 5-HT1A receptor results in an anxiety phenotype in mice, suggesting that abnormal transcriptional regulation of this receptor gene may underlie depression and suicide (Albert and Lemonde, 2004).

In 5-HT2 receptor research, one study demonstrated that 5-HT2A receptor gene polymorphisms are not significantly associated with suicidal behavior. In contrast, the 5-HT2A receptor itself is reported to be increased in suicidal subjects. Functional polymorphisms involving the promoter region that affect gene expression may explain this discrepancy (Arango et al., 2003). Decreased levels of 5-HT2A serotonin receptor binding in the brain have been reported (Arango, Underwood, and Mann, 1997; Mann et al., 2000), while a higher number of free ^{3}H-imipramine binding sites in serotonergic neurons of the left frontal cortex has been found in those who died by suicide than in control subjects (Arato et al., 1987; Arato et al., 1991; Demeter et al., 1989). Single photon emisson computer tomography (SPET) for the 5HT-2A-receptor ligand ^{123}I-5-I-R91150 in the brains of suicide attempters revealed a decreased binding index (indicating a decreased number of free receptors) in the frontal regions of violent (i.e., not entirely drug-free) suicide attempters (Audenaert et al., 2001; van Heeringen et al., 2003). Also a low level of frontal activation was seen in depressed suicide attempters (Audenaert et al., 2002).

The presynaptic re-uptake (transporter) capacity for monoamines in the brain has been studied with SPECT and the cocaine analogue ^{123}I-2-β-carbomethoxy-3-β-(4-iodomethyl)-tropane(Laruelle et al., 1994). ^{123}I-β-CIT imaging illustrates serotonin and dopamine re-uptake capacity. Tests on non-human primates indicate that the 5HTT uptake of ^{123}I-β-CIT is competitively reduced by increased synaptic concentrations of serotonin or dopamine (Laruelle et al., 1993).

Conflicted findings have been reported concerning depressive disorders. In depressed drug-naïve adults, decreased 5-HTT capacity has been identified in the hypothalamic and the thalamic regions (Laasonen-Balk et al., 1999; Willeit et al., 2000). Newberg et al. (2005), using ^{123}I-ADAM, found decreased 5-HTT capacity in the midbrain region. Parsey, et al. (2006), used positron emission tomography (PET) and [^{11}C]McN 5652 to find decreased 5-HTT capacity in the amygdala and midbrain regions, while in depressive drug-naïve children and adolescents, Dahlstrom, et al. (2000), using ^{123}I-β-CIT, found an increased 5-HTT capacity in the hypothalamic/midbrain region. However, Meyer, et al. (2004), using PET and [^{11}C] DSAB, found no difference in 5-HTT capacity between patients with an ongoing major depressive episode and controls, except for a subgroup with highly negativistic and dysfunctional attitudes. Frankle, et al. (2005), using ^{123}I-β-CIT, found reduced 5-HTT capacity in the anterior cingulate cortex in impulsive-aggressive subjects, indicating a relationship between suicide and 5-HTT, since suicide is connected with increased aggressiveness and impulsivity.

The Dopamine System

Several lines of evidence demonstrate the role of the dopamine system in suicide (Ryding, Lindstrom, and Traskman-Bendz, 2008). Suicide attempters show significantly lowered dopamine metabolite homovanillic acid (HVA) levels than controls. Some studies have suggested a possible association between the DRD4 gene exon III 48 bp repeat polymorphism and novelty seeking behavior. However, Allard and Norlen reported no differences in D_2 binding activity (Allard andNorlen, 2001) and dopamine transport in the brain (Allard and Norlen, 1997) with the exception of a subgroup of subjects with major depression in whom decreased D_2 receptor affinity (increased k_d) was found in the caudate nucleus.

Glutamatergic and GABAergic Systems

In studies of the glutamatergic and GABAergic systems, it was found that global glutamatergic and GABAergic alterations may be associated with suicide and major depression (Sequeira et al., 2009). Evidence suggests global alteration of GABAergic neurotransmission in suicide (Sequeira et al., 2007). In addition, the suicidal subjects showed a significant decrease of peripheral-type benzodiazepine receptor (PBR) density in platelets (Soreni et al., 1999). GABA is the major inhibitory brain neurotransmitter (Nutt and Malizia, 2001) and regulates anxiety, which is associated with acute suicide risk (Korn, Plutchik, and Van Praag, 1997; Rochet et al., 1992). In Caucasians, there are four frequent allelic variants (169 bp was named allele A1, 167 bp allele A2, 165 bp allele A3, and 163 bp allele A4). (Hicks, Johnson, Barnard, and Darlison, 1991). Males have one allele, resulting in four relatively common genotypes (A1, A2, A3 and A4). Females have two alleles, leading to 10 possible common genotypes. Although this gene has been of interest among research and the subject of genetic studies of mood disorders, published findings show no association between this gene and bipolar disorder (Puertollano, Visedo, Saiz-Ruiz, Llinares, and Fernandez-Piqueras, 1995), unipolar depression (Massat et al., 2001), or lithium response in bipolar disorder (Duffy, Grof, Robertson, and Alda, 2000). In addition, there is no association between polymorphic variations in the alpha 3 subunit GABA receptor gene and suicide attempts (Baca-Garcia et al., 2004).

Tyrosine Hydroxylase (TH)

Tyrosine Hydroxylase (TH) is a rate-limiting enzyme in adrenaline, noradrenaline and dopamine synthesis. The human TH gene is located on chromosome 11p15.5, which is reported to be linked to bipolar disorder (Baumann et al., 1999; Gos et al., 2008). It may be a high risk indicator for suicide and involved in biological susceptibility to suicide. A penta-allelic polymorphism consisting of several numbers of tetranucleotide repeats in the first intron and three SNPs that cause the substitutions - Val81Met, Leu205Pro, Val468Met - may alter the functional activity of TH protein. Albanese et al. (2001) reported that allelic variations of the tetranucleotide repeats were involved in quantitative and qualitative changes in the binding of ZNF191, a zinc finger protein, and that the repeats may regulate transcription. Persson et al. (2000) showed that 8 repeats in allele was significantly more common in suicide attempters with adjustment disorders than in controls. Yet, an association study between subjects who died by suicide and TH functional polymorphisms suggested a negative result. The discrepancy of these results might be due to the difference in the samples between those who died by suicide and those who attempted suicide. Orderway et al. (1994) reported higher concentrations of tyrosine hydroxylase in subjects who died by suicide, indicating that locus coeruleus neurons contain higher than average concentrations of tyrosine hydroxylase. It is possible that the expression of tyrosine hydroxylase in the locus coeruleus may be relevant to the pathophysiology of suicide. Among suicide attempters, Persson et al. found a significant variation in the prevalence of carriers of the TH-K3 allele and a tendency toward a variation of the TH-K1 allele (low among all suicide attempters), suggesting that these alleles may reflect vulnerability for psychiatric disorders (Persson, Wasserman, Geijer, Jonsson, and Terenius, 1997). However, Hattori et al. reported that functional polymorphisms (tetranucleotide repeat polymorphism and Val81Met polymorphism) are not involved in a biological susceptibility to suicide (Hattori et al., 2006).

Tryptophan Hydroxylase 1 and 2 Genes

Among the genes involved in regulating serotonin levels, two have received the most research attention: tryptophan hyroxylase 1 (TPH1) and 2 (TPH2). Although several association studies and meta-analyses confirm the involvement of TPH1 and TPH2 as vulnerability genes for suicidal behavior (Bellivier, Chaste, and Malafosse, 2004; Li and He, 2007; Lopez, Detera-Wadleigh, Cardona, Kassem, and McMahon, 2007; Zill et al., 2004), little is known about the regulation of their expression in the brains of suicide victims. Arango et al. (Arango et al., 2001) found no difference in TPH1 mRNA levels in the cortex between those who died by suicide and controls (Zill et al., 2009). In contrast, an increased TPH2 expression was found in the dorsal and median raphe nuclei of depressed subjects who died by suicide (Bach-Mizrachi et al., 2006; Bach-Mizrachi et al., 2008; Boldrini, Underwood, Mann, and Arango, 2005) and in the dorsolateral prefrontal cortex of those who died by suicide (De Luca et al., 2006a). In addition, the association between suicide and a SNP (rs1386483) was examined in the recently identified TPH2 gene. The TPH2 polymorphism is associated with suicide. This genetic marker may be particularly important in measuring risk of multiple suicide attempts (Fudalej et al., 2010). Another SNP (rs7305115) has been investigated in major depressive disorders associated with suicide. Results showed that the G allele frequency was significantly higher in suicidal cases than in a control group, suggesting that hopelessness, negative life events and family history of suicide are risk factors of attempted suicide in MDD while the TPH2 rs7305115A remains a significant protective predictor of suicide attempts (Zhang et al., 2010). The TPH2 gene and its 5' upstream region variants (rs4448731 and rs4641527) are also involved in predisposition to suicide in major depressive disorder (MDD)(Lopez de Lara et al., 2007). However, the finding does not support the hypothesis of TPH2 as a susceptibility factor for completed suicide in males of Estonian origin (Must et al., 2009). No associations were revealed, either on allelic or haplotype levels. De Luca et al. (2006b) found no difference in the mRNA levels of TPH2 between those who died by suicide and controls. Thus, further investigation of TPH2 gene expression is needed to clarify the potential role of this gene in the pathophysiology of suicide (De Luca, Likhodi, Van Tol, Kennedy, and Wong, 2006b).

Catechol-O-Methyltransferase (COMT) Pathways

Catecholaminergic pathways may also be involved in suicide (Rujescu, Giegling, Gietl, Hartmann, and Moller, 2003), although the evidence is mixed. COMT is in the pathway for catecholamine degradation. It catalyzes the transfer of a methyl group to catecholamines and degrades dopamine, norepinephrine, and epinephrine. There is a common functional polymorphism (COMT Val108/158Met), a G to A nucleotide transition, which results in an amino acid substitution from valine (Val) to methionine (Met) at position 158 in the membrane bound or position 108 in the soluble form of COMT (rs4680). The Met form is associated with the lower activity of COMT, whereas the Val form of COMT is related to its higher activity (Russ, Lachman, Kashdan, Saito, and Bajmakovic-Kacila, 2000). The Met/Met genotype leads to a threefold to fourfold decrease in COMT enzymatic activity compared to the Val/Val genotype (Kia-Keating, Glatt, and Tsuang, 2007). The Met and Val alleles act in codominant fashion (Harris et al., 2005). The Met (49%) and Val (51%) alleles of the COMT Val108/158Met are represented similarly in healthy Caucasian subjects of Croatian or similar origins (Nedic et al., 2011; Nedic et al., 2010).

COMT Val108/158Met polymorphism is associated with psychiatric disorders characterized by an increased risk of suicidal behavior. Some studies have found an association between the Met allele and violent suicide attempts in schizophrenic patients (Kotler et al., 1999; Lachman, Nolan, Mohr, Saito, and Volavka, 1998; Nolan et al., 2000; Strous, Bark, Parsia, Volavka, and Lachman, 1997), and with suicidal behavior in affective disorders (Ohara, Nagai, and Suzuki, 1998). However, these results have not been confirmed in other studies. (De Luca et al., 2006c; De Luca, Tharmalingam, Sicard, and Kennedy, 2005; Frisch et al., 1999; Kunugi et al., 1997; Zalsman et al., 2008). The Val/Val genotype is more frequent in suicide attempters than in normal controls (Baud et al., 2007). It is protective against suicide in males without psychiatric disorders (Ono, Shirakawa, Nushida, Ueno, and Maeda, 2004). A meta-analysis of six studies (based on data from a total of 519 cases and 933 control subjects) found a significant association between the COMT Val108/158Met polymorphism and suicidal behavior (Kia-Keating et al., 2007). The significance of the combined results is not strong and is related to gender both in cases and controls (Kia-Keating et al., 2007). Yet, a meta-analysis of 12 independent studies failed to confirm the role of the COMT Val108/158Met polymorphism in suicide (Calati et al., 2011).. Nedic et al., (2010) have investigated the relationship between COMT functional polymorphism (COMT Val108/158Met) and aggressive and suicidal behavior and found that alcoholic male suicide attempters, compared to alcoholic male non-attempters, had a higher frequency of the Met/Met genotype or Met allele, and significantly higher aggression and depression scores. These results confirm the associations among the Met allele, aggressive behavior, and violent suicide attempts in various psychiatric patients.Yet Calati et al. (2011) found that COMT variants may not be directly implicated in suicidal behavior.

Brain-Derived Neurotrophic Factor (BDNF)

The gene for Brain-Derived Neurotrophic Factor (BDNF) may be associated with suicide (Perroud et al., 2008). Neurotrophin BDNF regulates neuronal growth, plasticity, survival, repair, neurodegeneration, mood, cognition, behavior, and stress response, in addition to its role in affective disorders (Russo-Neustadt, 2003). In subjects who died by suicide, decreased levels of BDNF in the hippocampus and prefrontal cortex (Karege, Vaudan, Schwald, Perroud, and La Harpe, 2005) and reduced expression of BDNF in the post-mortem brain (Dwivedi et al., 2003) have been reported. The BDNF Val66Met variant is a functional polymorphism (rs6265), consisting of the substitution of valine ("Val") with methionine ("Met") in codon 66. It has been shown that the Met allele is associated with reduced BDNF activity (Egan et al., 2003). BDNF Val66Met is associated with suicide attempts in depressed patients (Sarchiapone et al., 2008), childhood sexual abuse, and violent suicide attempts in adulthood (Perroud et al., 2008). These findings suggest that childhood sexual abuse may affect brain structures through BDNF dysfunction and thus enhance the risk of violent suicide attempts in adulthood. BDNF Val66Met moderates both (1) the effect of stressful life events and adult depressive symptoms and (2) the effect of childhood adversity on suicidal behavior (Aguilera et al., 2009). Pregelj et al. (Pregelj et al. 2010) reported that the combined Met/Met and Met/Val genotypes of the BDNF Val66Met variant could be a risk factor for violent suicide in female subjects and for suicide in victims exposed to childhood trauma. These results confirm a major role of BDNF in increased vulnerability to suicide (Pregelj et al., 2011). Schenkel et al. reported that the BDNF 66Met allele is an independent predictor of high lethality in suicide attempts of depressed patients (Schenkel et al., 2010). Lee and Kim (2010) have found that BDNF mRNA expression is significantly lower in peripheral blood mononuclecytes (PBMC) of MDD patients with or without a history of suicide attempts, when compared with healthy controls. Their findings suggest that the BDNF mRNA expression is reduced in PBMCs of patients with MDD. Such a decrease in BDNF mRNA might be associated with BDNF protein decrease in serum or plasma and might also correspond to a BDNF decline in the brains of MDD patients (Lee et al., 2010). An epigenetic study found that BDNF promoter/exon IV is frequently hypermethylated in the Wernicke area of the postmortem brain of suicide subjects, indicating that a gene-specific increase in DNA methylation could cause or contribute to the down regulation of BDNF expression in suicide (Keller et al., 2010). These findings indicate that BNDF might be a useful marker in identifiying patients who are at high risk for suicide.

Fk506 Binding Protein 5(FKBP5)

Cortisol response to psychosocial stress is related to early life stress (Heim, Newport, Mletzko, Miller, and Nemeroff, 2008), and gender (Uhart, Chong, Oswald, Lin, and Wand, 2006), as well as to genes that regulate or modulate the function of the hypothalamic–pituitary–adrenal (HPA) axis (Derijk, 2009). Suicidal patients in diagnostically heterogeneous populations exhibit HPA axis abnormalities and resistance to the dexamethasone in suppression tests (DST) (Coryell and Schlesser, 2001). Abnormal DST results are associated with higher suicide risk in affective disorder patients (Targum, Rosen, and Capodanno, 1983)(Jokinen et al., 2007a; Jokinen and Nordstrom, 2009; Mann et al., 2006). Although most people who die by suicide or attempt suicide have a diagnosable psychiatric illness (Shaffer et al., 1996; Vermeiren et al., 2003), not all do. Thus, a diagnosis of mental disease is insufficient as a marker of suicide risk (Szigethy, Conwell, Forbes, Cox, and Caine, 1994; Jokinen, Nordstrom, and Nordstrom, 2007b).

The involvement of the HPA axis in suicidal behaviors is thought to be mediated by stress response mechanisms (Westrin, Ekman, and Traskman-Bendz, 1999). Environmental factors, such as stressful life events, are important components of suicidal behaviors, however genetic components may also play a role in suicide risk. HPA axis reactivity is regulated by feedback mechanisms mediated by the high affinity mineralocorticoid receptor (MR) and the lower affinity glucocorticoid receptor (GR). Functional polymorphisms in genes encoding these receptors most likely will affect HPA axis reactivity, and consequently the stress response (de Kloet et al., 2006; van Leeuwen et al., 2010). GR is a nuclear receptor regulated by co-chaperone immunophilin FK506 binding protein 5 (encoded by FKBP5). GR is regulated by FK506 Binding Protein 5 (FKBP5). Given FKBP5's role as a GR regulator, polymorphisms in FKBP5 might also affect HPA axis reactivity. To determine if the effect of childhood trauma on suicide risk was modified by FKBP5, Roy et al (Roy, Gorodetsky, Yuan, Goldman, and Enoch, 2010) genotyped sixteen FKBP5 haplotype-tagging SNPs in a sample of African Americans. They found that childhood trauma and variants of the FKBP5 gene may interact to increase the risk of suicide attempt.

Corticotrophin-Releasing Hormone Receptor 1 (CRHRL1)

Corticotropin-releasing hormone receptor-1 (CRHR1) is a gene with a major role in HPA axis activation and the modulation of neurocircuits coupled to HPA axis functioning. SNPs in CRHR1 are shown to interact with childhood maltreatment and is associated with dexamethasone non-suppression (Heim et al., 2009; Tyrka, Wyche, Kelly, Price, and Carpenter, 2009). Dexamethasone non-suppression is an indicator of a dysregulated cortisol response and a partial predictor of future suicide (Coryell et al., 2001). One of these SNPs in CRHR1, rs110402, is associated with early onset of the first depression episode (Papiol et al., 2007). Other SNPs, including rs4792887, are associated with attempted suicide, predominantly in depressed males. Some of these genetic effects may be masked in individuals exposed to stressful life events (Wasserman, Sokolowski, Rozanov, and Wasserman, 2008). To additional SNPs, rs16940665 and rs7209436, are associated with suicidal behavior via gene–gene interactions. Additional associations of variants in other HPA axis regulatory genes have been discovered (De Luca, Tharmalingam, and Kennedy, 2007; Roy et al., 2010; Willour et al., 2009).

Limbic System-Associated Membrane Protein (LSAMP)

The limbic system is an integrated brain area involved in the regulation of reward, motivation, emotional expression, and memory, as well as decision-making and predicting the likely outcomes of one's behavior. Neuroimaging studies of the limbic system have demonstrated volumetric abnormalities in the structures of depressive, schizophrenic and suicidal patients (Adler, Levine, DelBello, and Strakowski, 2005; Chua et al., 2007). These findings have been explained by HPA axis hyperactivity, resulting in glucocorticoid neurotoxicity (Bremner et al., 2002). The observed changes in volume of structures may not result from lifetime stress but rather may be caused by an inherited neurodevelopmental defect. Proper development of the nervous system includes formation of specific connections between neuronal populations. The process depends on growth cone guidance molecules that lead to accurate axon targeting. Limbic system-associated membrane protein (LSAMP) is a highly conserved adhesion molecule expressed primarily by cortical and subcortical neurons of the limbic system during the early developmental stages (Zhukareva and Levitt, 1995). It exerts dual effects, attracting limbic thalamic axons while simultaneously impeding nonlimbic thalamic axons from innervating inappropriate cortical regions. Animal studies have revealed that rats with lower exploratory activity have an increased expression of the LSAMP gene in their limbic structures, while LSAMP knockout mice demonstrate behavioral hyperactivity in novel environments, suggesting a behavioral disinhibition in stressful situations rather than diminished anxiety (Catania, Pimenta, and Levitt, 2008).

Thirty SNPs from LSAMP were investigated in 288 males who died by suicide and 327 healthy male volunteers (Must et al., 2008). The investigation found an association between death by suicide and four allelic variants (rs2918215, rs2918213, rs9874470 and rs4821129) located in the intronic region of the gene, with major alleles over represented. Yet, the associations did not survive multiple correction tests. These results suggest that LSAMP may play a role in the etiology of suicidal behavior, but further studies are needed to understand its exact contribution.

Regulator of G-Protein Signalling2 (RGS2)

The family of proteins that serve as regulators of G-protein signaling (RGS) play a key role in modulating intracellular signaling through the G protein pathways. More than 30 mammalian RGS family members have been identified (Ross and Wilkie, 2000). Their primary functions are to act as GTPase-activating proteins that negatively regulate signaling by G protein-coupled receptors, such as serotonin, by accelerating GTP hydrolysis of the Gα subunit. Within this family RGS2 has been reported to be involved in anxiety and aggresson. RGS2-deficient mice displayed increased anxiety and decreased aggression (Oliveira-Dos-Santos et al., 2000). The genetic dissection of a behavioral quantitative trait locus study showed that RGS2 modulated anxiety in mice (Yalcin et al., 2004). Moreover, RGS2 gene polymorphisms are associated with panic disorder (Leygraf et al., 2006), suggesting that RGS2 modulates anxiety. Cui and colleagues (Cui et al., 2008) report an association between the SNPs (C+2971G, rs4606, C-395G and rs2746072) and completed suicides, signifying that RGS2 is genetically involved in biological susceptibility to suicide.

P450 System Genes

Early studies have demonstrated low concentrations of the serotonin metabolite 5-hydroxyindole acetic acid in the cerebrospinal fluid of patients who attempted suicide. Lester (1995) performed a meta-analysis of 27 research reports detailing strong evidence for the involvement of the serotonin system in suicidal behavior, especially in patients using violent methods.

The studies of Isacsson et al. (2005) demonstrated a substantial decrease in suicides in Sweden during the years 1995–2005, in correspondence with an increased use of antidepressants, mainly selective serotonin reuptake inhibitors (SSRIs). These authors discussed evidence supporting the notion that treatment of depression with antidepressants prevents suicide. These data seem to indicate that serotonergic mechanisms are involved in etiology of suicidal behavior.

Zackrisson et al. (2010) describe the remarkable finding that in 262 cases of suicide, the frequency of the cytochrome P450 CYP2D6 gene duplication is 10-fold higher than in the controls who died of natural causes. CYP2D6 gene duplication causes ultrarapid metabolism of antidepressants (tricyclics as well as SSRIs) and neuroleptics. The relationship might have a very simple explanation: as a result of ultrarapid metabolism, antidepressant treatment failed in the subjects who died by suicide. For patients who fail to respond to antidepressants (known to be substrates of CYP2D6), the frequency of CYP2D6 gene duplication has been found to be 10-fold higher than in healthy controls (Aklillu, Herrlin, Gustafsson, Bertilsson, and Ingelman-Sundberg, 2002). The CYP2D6 enzyme is mainly active in the liver and is also expressed in the brain, where its distribution follows that of dopamine nerve terminals, indicating its possible role in the dopamine system (Siegle, Fritz, Eckhardt, Zanger, and Eichelbaum, 2001).

There are several endogenous substrates of CYP2D6. The fact that 5-methoxytryptamine is O-demethylated by CYP2D6 to serotonin is vital in relation to suicidal behavior. Serotonin might be synthesized in dopaminergic neurons by CYP2D6 and act as a false transmitter. The observation of distinct platelet serotonin concentrations in subjects with different CYP2D6 genotypes gives further support for a link. Yet, the mechanism by which CYP2D6 gene expression is related to suicidality is still unknown.

P11 (Annexin II Light Chain)

P11 (annexin II light chain) is a potential biomarker for suicide in PTSD patients. P11 was first described by Gerke et al. (Gerke and Weber, 1985; Gerke, Koch, and Thiel, 1991), and characterized as a member of the S-100 calcium binding protein family. p11 has been shown to be down-regulated in the cortical tissue of patients with depression (Svenningsson et al., 2006), and up-regulated in the prefrontal cortex of patients with PTSD (Zhang et al., 2008).

These contrasting results suggest that p11 may effectively differentiate between the two conditions. The possible role of p11 in depression has been supported by the finding that p11 knockout mice exhibit a depression-like phenotype together with reduced responsiveness to 5-HT1B receptor agonists (Svenningsson et al., 2006; Svenningsson and Greengard, 2007). Furthermore, p11 over-expression was shown to increase localization of 5-HT1B receptors at the cell surface and enhance 5-HT1B receptor activity (Svenningsson et al., 2006). In contrast, patients with PTSD had lower levels of PBMC p11 mRNA than control subjects, while those with major depressive disorder (MDD), BP, and schizophrenia (SCZ) had significantly higher p11 mRNA levels than controls (Su et al., 2009). P11 mRNA levels were positively correlated with scores on the Hamilton Rating Scale for Depression (HAMD) (Su et al., 2009). Most recently, PBMC p11 transcripts have been found to be significantly lower in those who attempted suicide than healthy controls (Zhang et al., 2011).

Serum S100β

Serum S100β may serve as an adjunctive biomarker to assess suicidal risk in patients with mood disorders or schizophrenia. S100β levels have been found to be significantly higher and positively correlated to severity of suicidal ideation in patients with psychosis (Falcone et al., 2011).

Patients with low suicidality subscores of the Brief Psychiatric Rating Scale for Children (BPRS-C) had lower levels of serum S100β values compared to those with patients with high suicidality score of BPRS-C.

CONCLUSION

Emerging evidence for associations between twelve biological factors and suicide risk suggest that the development of biomarkers and laboratory tests to assess suicide risk and treatment response may be possible in the future. Here we defined "biomarker" and presented a brief review of important findings in molecular, clinical, and translational research that have emerged as we search for biomarkers for suicide risk. Biologic factors of particular interest include those related to serotonergic functioning, the dopamine system, glutamatergic and GABA-ergic systems, tyrosine hydroxylase (TH), catechol-o-methyltransferase (COMT) pathways, brain-derived neurotrophic factor (BDNF), FK506 binding protein 5(FKBP5), corticotrophin-releasing hormone receptor 1 (CRHR1) regulator of RGS2, the P450, P11 (Annexin II Light Chain), and Serum S100β. The search for biomarkers of suicide risk has improved our understanding of the pathophysiology of suicide, which may lead to the development not only of biomarkers but also of priorities for drug development.

ACKNOWLEDGMENTS

We thank Ms. Jane Chen and Mr. Berwin Yuan for their assistance in editing the manuscript.

REFERENCES

Adler, C. M., Levine, A. D., DelBello, M. P., and Strakowski, S. M. (2005). Changes in gray matter volume in patients with bipolar disorder. *Biol Psychiatry* 58, 151-7.

Aguilera, M., Arias, B., Wichers, M., Barrantes-Vidal, N., Moya, J., Villa, H., van Os, J., Ibanez, M. I., Ruiperez, M. A., Ortet, G., and Fananas, L. (2009). Early adversity and 5-HTT/BDNF genes: new evidence of gene-environment interactions on depressive symptoms in a general population. *Psychol Med* 39, 1425-32.

Aklillu, E., Herrlin, K., Gustafsson, L. L., Bertilsson, L., and Ingelman-Sundberg, M. (2002). Evidence for environmental influence on CYP2D6-catalysed debrisoquine hydroxylation as demonstrated by phenotyping and genotyping of Ethiopians living in Ethiopia or in Sweden. *Pharmacogenetics* 12, 375-83.

Albanese, V., Biguet, N. F., Kiefer, H., Bayard, E., Mallet, J., and Meloni, R. (2001). Quantitative effects on gene silencing by allelic variation at a tetranucleotide microsatellite. *Hum Mol Genet* 10, 1785-92.

Albert, P. R., and Lemonde, S. (2004). 5-HT1A receptors, gene repression, and depression: guilt by association. *Neuroscientist* 10, 575-93.

Allard, P., and Norlen, M. (1997). Unchanged density of caudate nucleus dopamine uptake sites in depressed suicide victims. *J Neural Transm* 104, 1353-60.

Allard, P., and Norlen, M. (2001). Caudate nucleus dopamine D(2) receptors in depressed suicide victims. *Neuropsychobiology* 44, 70-3.

Arango, V., Huang, Y. Y., Underwood, M. D., and Mann, J. J. (2003). Genetics of the serotonergic system in suicidal behavior. *J Psychiatr Res* 37, 375-86.

Arango, V., Underwood, M. D., Boldrini, M., Tamir, H., Kassir, S. A., Hsiung, S., Chen, J. J., and Mann, J. J. (2001). Serotonin 1A receptors, serotonin transporter binding and serotonin transporter mRNA expression in the brainstem of depressed suicide victims. *Neuropsychopharmacology* 25, 892-903.

Arango, V., Underwood, M. D., and Mann, J. J. (1997). Postmortem findings in suicide victims. Implications for in vivo imaging studies. *Ann N Y Acad Sci* 836, 269-87.

Arato, M., Tekes, K., Tothfalusi, L., Magyar, K., Palkovits, M., Demeter, E., and Falus, A. (1987). Serotonergic split brain and suicide. *Psychiatry Res* 21, 355-6.

Arato, M., Tekes, K., Tothfalusi, L., Magyar, K., Palkovits, M., Frecska, E., Falus, A., and MacCrimmon, D. J. (1991). Reversed hemispheric asymmetry of imipramine binding in suicide victims. *Biol Psychiatry* 29, 699-702.

Arsenault-Lapierre, G., Kim, C., and Turecki, G. (2004). Psychiatric diagnoses in 3275 suicides: a meta-analysis. *BMC Psychiatry* 4, 37.

Audenaert, K., Goethals, I., Van Laere, K., Lahorte, P., Brans, B., Versijpt, J., Vervaet, M., Beelaert, L., Van Heeringen, K., and Dierckx, R. (2002). SPECT neuropsychological activation procedure with the Verbal Fluency Test in attempted suicide patients. *Nucl Med Commun* 23, 907-16.

Audenaert, K., Van Laere, K., Dumont, F., Slegers, G., Mertens, J., van Heeringen, C., and Dierckx, R. A. (2001). Decreased frontal serotonin 5-HT 2a receptor binding index in deliberate self-harm patients. *Eur J Nucl Med* 28, 175-82.

Azorin, J. M., Kaladjian, A., Adida, M., Hantouche, E., Hameg, A., Lancrenon, S., and Akiskal, H. S. (2009). Risk factors associated with lifetime suicide attempts in bipolar I patients: findings from a French National Cohort. *Compr Psychiatry* 50, 115-20.

Baca-Garcia, E., Vaquero, C., Diaz-Sastre, C., Garcia-Resa, E., Saiz-Ruiz, J., Fernandez-Piqueras, J., and de Leon, J. (2004). Lack of association between the serotonin transporter promoter gene polymorphism and impulsivity or aggressive behavior among suicide attempters and healthy volunteers. *Psychiatry Res* 126, 99-106.

Bach-Mizrachi, H., Underwood, M. D., Kassir, S. A., Bakalian, M. J., Sibille, E., Tamir, H., Mann, J. J., and Arango, V. (2006). Neuronal tryptophan hydroxylase mRNA expression in the human dorsal and median raphe nuclei: major depression and suicide. *Neuropsychopharmacology* 31, 814-24.

Bach-Mizrachi, H., Underwood, M. D., Tin, A., Ellis, S. P., Mann, J. J., and Arango, V. (2008). Elevated expression of tryptophan hydroxylase-2 mRNA at the neuronal level in the dorsal and median raphe nuclei of depressed suicides. *Mol Psychiatry* 13, 507-13, 465.

Bah, J., Lindstrom, M., Westberg, L., Manneras, L., Ryding, E., Henningsson, S., Melke, J., Rosen, I., Traskman-Bendz, L., and Eriksson, E. (2008). Serotonin transporter gene polymorphisms: effect on serotonin transporter availability in the brain of suicide attempters. *Psychiatry Res* 162, 221-9.

Baud, P., Courtet, P., Perroud, N., Jollant, F., Buresi, C., and Malafosse, A. (2007). Catechol-O-methyltransferase polymorphism (COMT) in suicide attempters: a possible gender effect on anger traits. *Am J Med Genet B Neuropsychiatr Genet* 144B, 1042-7.

Baumann, B., Danos, P., Diekmann, S., Krell, D., Bielau, H., Geretsegger, C., Wurthmann, C., Bernstein, H. G., and Bogerts, B. (1999). Tyrosine hydroxylase immunoreactivity in the locus coeruleus is reduced in depressed non-suicidal patients but normal in depressed suicide patients. *Eur Arch Psychiatry Clin Neurosci* 249, 212-9.

Bellivier, F., Chaste, P., and Malafosse, A. (2004). Association between the TPH gene A218C polymorphism and suicidal behavior: a meta-analysis. *Am J Med Genet B Neuropsychiatr Genet* 124B, 87-91.

Boldrini, M., Underwood, M. D., Mann, J. J., and Arango, V. (2005). More tryptophan hydroxylase in the brainstem dorsal raphe nucleus in depressed suicides. *Brain Res* 1041, 19-28.

Bremner, J. D., Vythilingam, M., Vermetten, E., Nazeer, A., Adil, J., Khan, S., Staib, L. H., and Charney, D. S. (2002). Reduced volume of orbitofrontal cortex in major depression. *Biol Psychiatry* 51, 273-9.

Busch, K. A., Fawcett, J., and Jacobs, D. G. (2003). Clinical correlates of inpatient suicide. *J Clin Psychiatry* 64, 14-9.

Calati, R., Porcelli, S., Giegling, I., Hartmann, A. M., Moller, H. J., De Ronchi, D., Serretti, A., and Rujescu, D. (2011). Catechol-o-methyltransferase gene modulation on suicidal behavior and personality traits: review, meta-analysis and association study. *J Psychiatr Res* 45, 309-21.

Catania, E. H., Pimenta, A., and Levitt, P. (2008). Genetic deletion of Lsamp causes exaggerated behavioral activation in novel environments. *Behav Brain Res* 188, 380-90.

Cavanagh, J. T., Carson, A. J., Sharpe, M., and Lawrie, S. M. (2003). Psychological autopsy studies of suicide: a systematic review. *Psychol Med* 33, 395-405.

Chua, S. E., Cheung, C., Cheung, V., Tsang, J. T., Chen, E. Y., Wong, J. C., Cheung, J. P., Yip, L., Tai, K. S., Suckling, J., and McAlonan, G. M. (2007). Cerebral grey, white matter and csf in never-medicated, first-episode schizophrenia. *Schizophr Res* 89, 12-21.

Coryell, W., and Schlesser, M. (2001). The dexamethasone suppression test and suicide prediction. *Am J Psychiatry* 158, 748-53.

Cui, H., Nishiguchi, N., Ivleva, E., Yanagi, M., Fukutake, M., Nushida, H., Ueno, Y., Kitamura, N., Maeda, K., and Shirakawa, O. (2008). Association of RGS2 gene polymorphisms with suicide and increased RGS2 immunoreactivity in the postmortem brain of suicide victims. *Neuropsychopharmacology* 33, 1537-44.

Dahlstrom, M., Ahonen, A., Ebeling, H., Torniainen, P., Heikkila, J., and Moilanen, I. (2000). Elevated hypothalamic/midbrain serotonin (monoamine) transporter availability in depressive drug-naive children and adolescents. *Mol Psychiatry* 5, 514-22.

de Kloet, C. S., Vermetten, E., Geuze, E., Kavelaars, A., Heijnen, C. J., and Westenberg, H. G. (2006). Assessment of HPA-axis function in posttraumatic stress disorder: pharmacological and non-pharmacological challenge tests, a review. *J Psychiatr Res* 40, 550-67.

De Luca, V., Hlousek, D., Likhodi, O., Van Tol, H. H., Kennedy, J. L., and Wong, A. H. (2006a). The interaction between TPH2 promoter haplotypes and clinical-demographic risk factors in suicide victims with major psychoses. *Genes Brain Behav* 5, 107-10.

De Luca, V., Likhodi, O., Van Tol, H. H., Kennedy, J. L., and Wong, A. H. (2006b). Gene expression of tryptophan hydroxylase 2 in post-mortem brain of suicide subjects. *Int J Neuropsychopharmacol* 9, 21-5.

De Luca, V., Tharmalingam, S., and Kennedy, J. L. (2007). Association study between the corticotropin-releasing hormone receptor 2 gene and suicidality in bipolar disorder. *Eur Psychiatry* 22, 282-7.

De Luca, V., Tharmalingam, S., Muller, D. J., Wong, G., de Bartolomeis, A., and Kennedy, J. L. (2006c). Gene-gene interaction between MAOA and COMT in suicidal behavior: analysis in schizophrenia. *Brain Res* 1097, 26-30.

De Luca, V., Tharmalingam, S., Sicard, T., and Kennedy, J. L. (2005). Gene-gene interaction between MAOA and COMT in suicidal behavior. *Neurosci Lett* 383, 151-4.

Demeter, E., Tekes, K., Majorossy, K., Palkovits, M., Soos, M., and Somogyil, E. (1989). The asymmetry [correction of asymetry] of 3H-imipramine binding may predict psychiatric illness. *Acta Med Leg Soc (Liege)* 39, 451-2.

Derijk, R. H. (2009). Single nucleotide polymorphisms related to HPA axis reactivity. *Neuroimmunomodulation* 16, 340-52.

Du, L., Faludi, G., Palkovits, M., Demeter, E., Bakish, D., Lapierre, Y. D., Sotonyi, P., and Hrdina, P. D. (1999). Frequency of long allele in serotonin transporter gene is increased in depressed suicide victims. *Biol Psychiatry* 46, 196-201.

Duffy, A., Grof, P., Robertson, C., and Alda, M. (2000). The implications of genetics studies of major mood disorders for clinical practice. *J Clin Psychiatry* 61, 630-7.

Dwivedi, Y., Rizavi, H. S., Conley, R. R., Roberts, R. C., Tamminga, C. A., and Pandey, G. N. (2003). Altered gene expression of brain-derived neurotrophic factor and receptor tyrosine kinase B in postmortem brain of suicide subjects. *Arch Gen Psychiatry* 60, 804-15.

Egan, M. F., Kojima, M., Callicott, J. H., Goldberg, T. E., Kolachana, B. S., Bertolino, A., Zaitsev, E., Gold, B., Goldman, D., Dean, M., Lu, B., and Weinberger, D. R. (2003). The BDNF val66met polymorphism affects activity-dependent secretion of BDNF and human memory and hippocampal function. *Cell* 112, 257-69.

Falcone, T., Fazio, V., Lee, C., Simon, B., Franco, K., Marchi, N., and Janigro, D. (2011) Serum S100B: a potential biomarker for suicidality in adolescents? *PLoS One* 5, e11089.

Frankle, W. G., Lombardo, I., New, A. S., Goodman, M., Talbot, P. S., Huang, Y., Hwang, D. R., Slifstein, M., Curry, S., Abi-Dargham, A., Laruelle, M., and Siever, L. J. (2005). Brain serotonin transporter distribution in subjects with impulsive aggressivity: a positron emission study with [11C] McN 5652. *Am J Psychiatry* 162, 915-23.

Frisch, A., Postilnick, D., Rockah, R., Michaelovsky, E., Postilnick, S., Birman, E., Laor, N., Rauchverger, B., Kreinin, A., Poyurovsky, M., Schneidman, M., Modai, I., and Weizman, R. (1999). Association of unipolar major depressive disorder with genes of the serotonergic and dopaminergic pathways. *Mol Psychiatry* 4, 389-92.

Fudalej, S., Ilgen, M., Fudalej, M., Kostrzewa, G., Barry, K., Wojnar, M., Krajewski, P., Blow, F., and Ploski, R. (2010). Association between tryptophan hydroxylase 2 gene polymorphism and completed suicide. *Suicide Life Threat Behav* 40, 553-60.

Gerke, V., Koch, W., and Thiel, C. (1991). Primary structure and expression of the Xenopus laevis gene encoding annexin II. *Gene* 104, 259-64.

Gerke, V., and Weber, K. (1985). The regulatory chain in the p36-kd substrate complex of viral tyrosine-specific protein kinases is related in sequence to the S-100 protein of glial cells. *EMBO J* 4, 2917-20.

Gos, T., Krell, D., Bielau, H., Brisch, R., Trubner, K., Steiner, J., Bernstein, H. G., Jankowski, Z., and Bogerts, B. (2008). Tyrosine hydroxylase immunoreactivity in the locus coeruleus is elevated in violent suicidal depressive patients. *Eur Arch Psychiatry Clin Neurosci* 258, 513-20.

Harris, E. C., and Barraclough, B. (1997). Suicide as an outcome for mental disorders. A meta-analysis. *Br J Psychiatry* 170, 205-28.

Harris, S. E., Wright, A. F., Hayward, C., Starr, J. M., Whalley, L. J., and Deary, I. J. (2005). The functional COMT polymorphism, Val 158 Met, is associated with logical memory and the personality trait intellect/imagination in a cohort of healthy 79 year olds. *Neurosci Lett* 385, 1-6.

Hattori, H., Shirakawa, O., Nishiguchi, N., Nushida, H., Ueno, Y., and Maeda, K. (2006). No evidence of an association between tyrosine hydroxylase gene polymorphisms and suicide victims. *Kobe J Med Sci* 52, 195-200.

Hawton, K. (2001). Studying survivors of nearly lethal suicide attempts: an important strategy in suicide research. *Suicide Life Threat Behav* 32, 76-84.

Hawton, K., and van Heeringen, K. (2009). Suicide. *Lancet* 373, 1372-81.

Heim, C., Newport, D. J., Mletzko, T., Miller, A. H., and Nemeroff, C. B. (2008). The link between childhood trauma and depression: insights from HPA axis studies in humans. *Psychoneuroendocrinology* 33, 693-710.

Heim, C., Young, L. J., Newport, D. J., Mletzko, T., Miller, A. H., and Nemeroff, C. B. (2009). Lower CSF oxytocin concentrations in women with a history of childhood abuse. *Mol Psychiatry* 14, 954-8.

Hicks, A. A., Johnson, K. J., Barnard, E. A., and Darlison, M. G. (1991). Dinucleotide repeat polymorphism in the human X-linked GABAA receptor alpha 3-subunit gene. *Nucleic Acids Res* 19, 4016.

Isacsson, G., Holmgren, P., and Ahlner, J. (2005). Selective serotonin reuptake inhibitor antidepressants and the risk of suicide: a controlled forensic database study of 14,857 suicides. *Acta Psychiatr Scand* 111, 286-90.

Jokinen, J., Carlborg, A., Martensson, B., Forslund, K., Nordstrom, A. L., and Nordstrom, P. (2007a). DST non-suppression predicts suicide after attempted suicide. *Psychiatry Res* 150, 297-303.

Jokinen, J., Nordstrom, A. L., and Nordstrom, P. (2007b). The relationship between CSF HVA/5-HIAA ratio and suicide intent in suicide attempters. *Arch Suicide Res* 11, 187-92.

Jokinen, J., and Nordstrom, P. (2009). HPA axis hyperactivity and attempted suicide in young adult mood disorder inpatients. *J Affect Disord* 116, 117-20.

Karege, F., Vaudan, G., Schwald, M., Perroud, N., and La Harpe, R. (2005). Neurotrophin levels in postmortem brains of suicide victims and the effects of antemortem diagnosis and psychotropic drugs. *Brain Res Mol Brain Res* 136, 29-37.

Keller, S., Sarchiapone, M., Zarrilli, F., Videtic, A., Ferraro, A., Carli, V., Sacchetti, S., Lembo, F., Angiolillo, A., Jovanovic, N., Pisanti, F., Tomaiuolo, R., Monticelli, A., Balazic, J., Roy, A., Marusic, A., Cocozza, S., Fusco, A., Bruni, C. B., Castaldo, G., and Chiariotti, L. (2010). Increased BDNF promoter methylation in the Wernicke area of suicide subjects. *Arch Gen Psychiatry* 67, 258-67.

Kia-Keating, B. M., Glatt, S. J., and Tsuang, M. T. (2007). Meta-analyses suggest association between COMT, but not HTR1B, alleles, and suicidal behavior. *Am J Med Genet B Neuropsychiatr Genet* 144B, 1048-53.

Korn, M. L., Plutchik, R., and Van Praag, H. M. (1997). Panic-associated suicidal and aggressive ideation and behavior. *J Psychiatr Res* 31, 481-7.

Kotler, M., Barak, P., Cohen, H., Averbuch, I. E., Grinshpoon, A., Gritsenko, I., Nemanov, L., and Ebstein, R. P. (1999). Homicidal behavior in schizophrenia associated with a genetic polymorphism determining low catechol O-methyltransferase (COMT) activity. *Am J Med Genet* 88, 628-33.

Kunugi, H., Vallada, H. P., Sham, P. C., Hoda, F., Arranz, M. J., Li, T., Nanko, S., Murray, R. M., McGuffin, P., Owen, M., Gill, M., and Collier, D. A. (1997). Catechol-O-methyltransferase polymorphisms and schizophrenia: a transmission disequilibrium study in multiply affected families. *Psychiatr Genet* 7, 97-101.

Laasonen-Balk, T., Kuikka, J., Viinamaki, H., Husso-Saastamoinen, M., Lehtonen, J., and Tiihonen, J. (1999). Striatal dopamine transporter density in major depression. *Psychopharmacology (Berl)* 144, 282-5.

Lachman, H. M., Nolan, K. A., Mohr, P., Saito, T., and Volavka, J. (1998). Association between catechol O-methyltransferase genotype and violence in schizophrenia and schizoaffective disorder. *Am J Psychiatry* 155, 835-7.

Laruelle, M., Baldwin, R. M., Malison, R. T., Zea-Ponce, Y., Zoghbi, S. S., al-Tikriti, M. S., Sybirska, E. H., Zimmermann, R. C., Wisniewski, G., Neumeyer, J. L., and et al. (1993). SPECT imaging of dopamine and serotonin transporters with [123I]beta-CIT: pharmacological characterization of brain uptake in nonhuman primates. *Synapse* 13, 295-309.

Laruelle, M., van Dyck, C., Abi-Dargham, A., Zea-Ponce, Y., Zoghbi, S. S., Charney, D. S., Baldwin, R. M., Hoffer, P. B., Kung, H. F., and Innis, R. B. (1994). Compartmental modeling of iodine-123-iodobenzofuran binding to dopamine D2 receptors in healthy subjects. *J Nucl Med* 35, 743-54.

Lee, B. H., and Kim, Y. K. (2010). BDNF mRNA expression of peripheral blood mononuclear cells was decreased in depressive patients who had or had not recently attempted suicide. *J Affect Disord* 125, 369-73.

Lester, D. (1995). The concentration of neurotransmitter metabolites in the cerebrospinal fluid of suicidal individuals: a meta-analysis. *Pharmacopsychiatry* 28, 45-50.

Leygraf, A., Hohoff, C., Freitag, C., Willis-Owen, S. A., Krakowitzky, P., Fritze, J., Franke, P., Bandelow, B., Fimmers, R., Flint, J., and Deckert, J. (2006). Rgs 2 gene polymorphisms as modulators of anxiety in humans? *J Neural Transm* 113, 1921-5.

Li, D., and He, L. (2007). Meta-analysis supports association between serotonin transporter (5-HTT) and suicidal behavior. *Mol Psychiatry* 12, 47-54.

Lopez de Lara, C., Brezo, J., Rouleau, G., Lesage, A., Dumont, M., Alda, M., Benkelfat, C., and Turecki, G. (2007). Effect of tryptophan hydroxylase-2 gene variants on suicide risk in major depression. *Biol Psychiatry* 62, 72-80.

Lopez, V. A., Detera-Wadleigh, S., Cardona, I., Kassem, L., and McMahon, F. J. (2007). Nested association between genetic variation in tryptophan hydroxylase II, bipolar affective disorder, and suicide attempts. *Biol Psychiatry* 61, 181-6.

Mann, J. J., Brent, D. A., and Arango, V. (2001). The neurobiology and genetics of suicide and attempted suicide: a focus on the serotonergic system. *Neuropsychopharmacology* 24, 467-77.

Mann, J. J., Currier, D., Stanley, B., Oquendo, M. A., Amsel, L. V., and Ellis, S. P. (2006). Can biological tests assist prediction of suicide in mood disorders? *Int J Neuropsychopharmacol* 9, 465-74.

Mann, J. J., Huang, Y. Y., Underwood, M. D., Kassir, S. A., Oppenheim, S., Kelly, T. M., Dwork, A. J., and Arango, V. (2000). A serotonin transporter gene promoter polymorphism (5-HTTLPR) and prefrontal cortical binding in major depression and suicide. *Arch Gen Psychiatry* 57, 729-38.

Massat, I., Souery, D., Del-Favero, J., Oruc, L., Jakovljevic, M., Folnegovic, V., Adolfsson, R., Kaneva, R., Papadimitriou, G., Dikeos, D., Jazin, E., Milanova, V., Van Broeckhoven, C., and Mendlewicz, J. (2001). Lack of association between GABRA3 and unipolar affective disorder: a multicentre study. *Int J Neuropsychopharmacol* 4, 273-8.

McGuffin, P., Marusic, A., and Farmer, A. (2001). What can psychiatric genetics offer suicidology? *Crisis* 22, 61-5.

Meyer, J. H., Houle, S., Sagrati, S., Carella, A., Hussey, D. F., Ginovart, N., Goulding, V., Kennedy, J., and Wilson, A. A. (2004). Brain serotonin transporter binding potential measured with carbon 11-labeled DASB positron emission tomography: effects of major depressive episodes and severity of dysfunctional attitudes. *Arch Gen Psychiatry* 61, 1271-9.

Must, A., Tasa, G., Lang, A., Vasar, E., Koks, S., Maron, E., and Vali, M. (2008). Association of limbic system-associated membrane protein (LSAMP) to male completed suicide. *BMC Med Genet* 9, 34.

Must, A., Tasa, G., Lang, A., Vasar, E., Koks, S., Maron, E., and Vali, M. (2009). Variation in tryptophan hydroxylase-2 gene is not associated to male completed suicide in Estonian population. *Neurosci Lett* 453, 112-4.

Nedic, G., Borovecki, F., Klepac, N., Mubrin, Z., Hajnsek, S., Nikolac, M., Muck-Seler, D., and Pivac, N. (2011). Association study of a functional catechol-o-methyltransferase polymorphism and cognitive function in patients with dementia. *Coll Antropol* 35 Suppl 1, 79-84.

Nedic, G., Nikolac, M., Sviglin, K. N., Muck-Seler, D., Borovecki, F., and Pivac, N. (2010). Association study of a functional catechol-O-methyltransferase (COMT) Val108/158Met polymorphism and suicide attempts in patients with alcohol dependence. *Int J Neuropsychopharmacol* 14, 377-88.

Newberg, A. B., Amsterdam, J. D., Wintering, N., Ploessl, K., Swanson, R. L., Shults, J., and Alavi, A. (2005). 123I-ADAM binding to serotonin transporters in patients with major depression and healthy controls: a preliminary study. *J Nucl Med* 46, 973-7.

Nock, M. K., Borges, G., Bromet, E. J., Alonso, J., Angermeyer, M., Beautrais, A., Bruffaerts, R., Chiu, W. T., de Girolamo, G., Gluzman, S., de Graaf, R., Gureje, O., Haro, J. M., Huang, Y., Karam, E., Kessler, R. C., Lepine, J. P., Levinson, D., Medina-Mora, M. E., Ono, Y., Posada-Villa, J., and Williams, D. (2008). Cross-national prevalence and risk factors for suicidal ideation, plans and attempts. *Br J Psychiatry* 192, 98-105.

Nolan, K. A., Volavka, J., Czobor, P., Cseh, A., Lachman, H., Saito, T., Tiihonen, J., Putkonen, A., Hallikainen, T., Kotilainen, I., Rasanen, P., Isohanni, M., Jarvelin, M. R., and Karvonen, M. K. (2000). Suicidal behavior in patients with schizophrenia is related to COMT polymorphism. *Psychiatr Genet* 10, 117-24.

Nutt, D. J., and Malizia, A. L. (2001). New insights into the role of the GABA(A)-benzodiazepine receptor in psychiatric disorder. *Br J Psychiatry* 179, 390-6.

Ohara, K., Nagai, M., and Suzuki, Y. (1998). Low activity allele of catechol-o-methyltransferase gene and Japanese unipolar depression. *Neuroreport* 9, 1305-8.

Oliveira-Dos-Santos, A. J., Matsumoto, G., Snow, B. E., Bai, D., Houston, F. P., Whishaw, I. Q., Mariathasan, S., Sasaki, T., Wakeham, A., Ohashi, P. S., Roder, J. C., Barnes, C. A.,

Siderovski, D. P., and Penninger, J. M. (2000). Regulation of T cell activation, anxiety, and male aggression by RGS2. *Proc Natl Acad Sci USA* 97, 12272-7.

Ono, H., Shirakawa, O., Nushida, H., Ueno, Y., and Maeda, K. (2004). Association between catechol-O-methyltransferase functional polymorphism and male suicide completers. *Neuropsychopharmacology* 29, 1374-7.

Ordway, G. A., Smith, K. S., and Haycock, J. W. (1994). Elevated tyrosine hydroxylase in the locus coeruleus of suicide victims. *J Neurochem* 62, 680-5.

Papiol, S., Arias, B., Gasto, C., Gutierrez, B., Catalan, R., and Fananas, L. (2007). Genetic variability at HPA axis in major depression and clinical response to antidepressant treatment. *J Affect Disord* 104, 83-90.

Parsey, R. V., Oquendo, M. A., Ogden, R. T., Olvet, D. M., Simpson, N., Huang, Y. Y., Van Heertum, R. L., Arango, V., and Mann, J. J. (2006). Altered serotonin 1A binding in major depression: a [carbonyl-C-11]WAY100635 positron emission tomography study. *Biol Psychiatry* 59, 106-13.

Perroud, N., Courtet, P., Vincze, I., Jaussent, I., Jollant, F., Bellivier, F., Leboyer, M., Baud, P., Buresi, C., and Malafosse, A. (2008). Interaction between BDNF Val66Met and childhood trauma on adult's violent suicide attempt. *Genes Brain Behav* 7, 314-22.

Persson, M. L., Wasserman, D., Geijer, T., Jonsson, E. G., and Terenius, L. (1997). Tyrosine hydroxylase allelic distribution in suicide attempters. *Psychiatry Res* 72, 73-80.

Persson, M. L., Wasserman, D., Jonsson, E. G., Bergman, H., Terenius, L., Gyllander, A., Neiman, J., and Geijer, T. (2000). Search for the influence of the tyrosine hydroxylase (TCAT)(n) repeat polymorphism on personality traits. *Psychiatry Res* 95, 1-8.

Pregelj, P., Nedic, G., Paska, A. V., Zupanc, T., Nikolac, M., Balazic, J., Tomori, M., Komel, R., Seler, D. M., and Pivac, N. (2010).The association between brain-derived neurotrophic factor polymorphism (BDNF Val66Met) and suicide. *J Affect Disord* 128, 287-90.

Puertollano, R., Visedo, G., Saiz-Ruiz, J., Llinares, C., and Fernandez-Piqueras, J. (1995). Lack of association between manic-depressive illness and a highly polymorphic marker from GABRA3 gene. *Am J Med Genet* 60, 434-5.

Rihmer, Z. (2007). Suicide risk in mood disorders. *Curr Opin Psychiatry* 20, 17-22.

Rochet, T., Kopp, N., Vedrinne, J., Deluermoz, S., Debilly, G., and Miachon, S. (1992). Benzodiazepine binding sites and their modulators in hippocampus of violent suicide victims. *Biol Psychiatry* 32, 922-31.

Ross, E. M., and Wilkie, T. M. (2000). GTPase-activating proteins for heterotrimeric G proteins: regulators of G protein signaling (RGS) and RGS-like proteins. *Annu Rev Biochem* 69, 795-827.

Roy, A., Gorodetsky, E., Yuan, Q., Goldman, D., and Enoch, M. A. (2010). Interaction of FKBP5, a stress-related gene, with childhood trauma increases the risk for attempting suicide. *Neuropsychopharmacology* 35, 1674-83.

Rujescu, D., Giegling, I., Gietl, A., Hartmann, A. M., and Moller, H. J. (2003). A functional single nucleotide polymorphism (V158M) in the COMT gene is associated with aggressive personality traits. *Biol Psychiatry* 54, 34-9.

Russ, M. J., Lachman, H. M., Kashdan, T., Saito, T., and Bajmakovic-Kacila, S. (2000). Analysis of catechol-O-methyltransferase and 5-hydroxytryptamine transporter polymorphisms in patients at risk for suicide. *Psychiatry Res* 93, 73-8.

Russo-Neustadt, A. (2003). Brain-derived neurotrophic factor, behavior, and new directions for the treatment of mental disorders. *Semin Clin Neuropsychiatry* 8, 109-18.

Ryding, E., Lindstrom, M., and Traskman-Bendz, L. (2008). The role of dopamine and serotonin in suicidal behaviour and aggression. *Prog Brain Res* 172, 307-15.

Sarchiapone, M., Carli, V., Roy, A., Iacoviello, L., Cuomo, C., Latella, M. C., di Giannantonio, M., Janiri, L., de Gaetano, M., and Janal, M. N. (2008). Association of polymorphism (Val66Met) of brain-derived neurotrophic factor with suicide attempts in depressed patients. *Neuropsychobiology* 57, 139-45.

Schenkel, L. C., Segal, J., Becker, J. A., Manfro, G. G., Bianchin, M. M., and Leistner-Segal, S. (2010). The BDNF Val66Met polymorphism is an independent risk factor for high lethality in suicide attempts of depressed patients. *Prog Neuropsychopharmacol Biol Psychiatry* 34, 940-4.

Sequeira, A., Klempan, T., Canetti, L., ffrench-Mullen, J., Benkelfat, C., Rouleau, G. A., and Turecki, G. (2007). Patterns of gene expression in the limbic system of suicides with and without major depression. *Mol Psychiatry* 12, 640-55.

Sequeira, A., Mamdani, F., Ernst, C., Vawter, M. P., Bunney, W. E., Lebel, V., Rehal, S., Klempan, T., Gratton, A., Benkelfat, C., Rouleau, G. A., Mechawar, N., and Turecki, G. (2009). Global brain gene expression analysis links glutamatergic and GABAergic alterations to suicide and major depression. *PLoS One* 4, e6585.

Shaffer, D., Gould, M. S., Fisher, P., Trautman, P., Moreau, D., Kleinman, M., and Flory, M. (1996). Psychiatric diagnosis in child and adolescent suicide. *Arch Gen Psychiatry* 53, 339-48.

Shneidman, E. S. (1998). Perspectives on suicidology. Further reflections on suicide and psychache. *Suicide Life Threat Behav* 28, 245-50.

Siegle, I., Fritz, P., Eckhardt, K., Zanger, U. M., and Eichelbaum, M. (2001). Cellular localization and regional distribution of CYP2D6 mRNA and protein expression in human brain. *Pharmacogenetics* 11, 237-45.

Soreni, N., Apter, A., Weizman, A., Don-Tufeled, O., Leschiner, S., Karp, L., and Gavish, M. (1999). Decreased platelet peripheral-type benzodiazepine receptors in adolescent inpatients with repeated suicide attempts. *Biol Psychiatry* 46, 484-8.

Strous, R. D., Bark, N., Parsia, S. S., Volavka, J., and Lachman, H. M. (1997). Analysis of a functional catechol-O-methyltransferase gene polymorphism in schizophrenia: evidence for association with aggressive and antisocial behavior. *Psychiatry Res* 69, 71-7.

Su, T. P., Zhang, L., Chung, M. Y., Chen, Y. S., Bi, Y. M., Chou, Y. H., Barker, J. L., Barrett, J. E., Maric, D., Li, X. X., Li, H., Webster, M. J., Benedek, D., Carlton, J. R., and Ursano, R. (2009). Levels of the potential biomarker p11 in peripheral blood cells distinguish patients with PTSD from those with other major psychiatric disorders. *J Psychiatr Res* 43, 1078-85.

Svenningsson, P., Chergui, K., Rachleff, I., Flajolet, M., Zhang, X., El Yacoubi, M., Vaugeois, J. M., Nomikos, G. G., and Greengard, P. (2006). Alterations in 5-HT1B receptor function by p11 in depression-like states. *Science* 311, 77-80.

Svenningsson, P., and Greengard, P. (2007). p11 (S100A10)--an inducible adaptor protein that modulates neuronal functions. *Curr Opin Pharmacol* 7, 27-32.

Szigethy, E., Conwell, Y., Forbes, N. T., Cox, C., and Caine, E. D. (1994). Adrenal weight and morphology in victims of completed suicide. *Biol Psychiatry* 36, 374-80.

Targum, S. D., Rosen, L., and Capodanno, A. E. (1983). The dexamethasone suppression test in suicidal patients with unipolar depression. *Am J Psychiatry* 140, 877-9.

Tyrka, A. R., Wyche, M. C., Kelly, M. M., Price, L. H., and Carpenter, L. L. (2009). Childhood maltreatment and adult personality disorder symptoms: influence of maltreatment type. *Psychiatry Res* 165, 281-7.

Uhart, M., Chong, R. Y., Oswald, L., Lin, P. I., and Wand, G. S. (2006). Gender differences in hypothalamic-pituitary-adrenal (HPA) axis reactivity. *Psychoneuroendocrinology* 31, 642-52.

van Heeringen, C. (2001). Suicide, serotonin, and the brain. *Crisis* 22, 66-70.

van Heeringen, C., Audenaert, K., Van Laere, K., Dumont, F., Slegers, G., Mertens, J., and Dierckx, R. A. (2003). Prefrontal 5-HT2a receptor binding index, hopelessness and personality characteristics in attempted suicide. *J Affect Disord* 74, 149-58.

van Leeuwen, N., Kumsta, R., Entringer, S., de Kloet, E. R., Zitman, F. G., DeRijk, R. H., and Wust, S. (2010). Functional mineralocorticoid receptor (MR) gene variation influences the cortisol awakening response after dexamethasone. *Psycho neuroendocrinology* 35, 339-49.

Vang, F. J., Ryding, E., Traskman-Bendz, L., van Westen, D., and Lindstrom, M. B. (2010). Size of basal ganglia in suicide attempters, and its association with temperament and serotonin transporter density. *Psychiatry Res* 183, 177-9.

Vermeiren, R., Schwab-Stone, M., Ruchkin, V. V., King, R. A., Van Heeringen, C., and Deboutte, D. (2003). Suicidal behavior and violence in male adolescents: a school-based study. *J Am Acad Child Adolesc Psychiatry* 42, 41-8.

Wasserman, D., Sokolowski, M., Rozanov, V., and Wasserman, J. (2008). The CRHR1 gene: a marker for suicidality in depressed males exposed to low stress. *Genes Brain Behav* 7, 14-9.

Westrin, A., Ekman, R., and Traskman-Bendz, L. (1999). Alterations of corticotropin releasing hormone (CRH) and neuropeptide Y (NPY) plasma levels in mood disorder patients with a recent suicide attempt. *Eur Neuropsychopharmacol* 9, 205-11.

Willeit, M., Praschak-Rieder, N., Neumeister, A., Pirker, W., Asenbaum, S., Vitouch, O., Tauscher, J., Hilger, E., Stastny, J., Brucke, T., and Kasper, S. (2000). [123I]-beta-CIT SPECT imaging shows reduced brain serotonin transporter availability in drug-free depressed patients with seasonal affective disorder. *Biol Psychiatry* 47, 482-9.

Willour, V. L., Chen, H., Toolan, J., Belmonte, P., Cutler, D. J., Goes, F. S., Zandi, P. P., Lee, R. S., MacKinnon, D. F., Mondimore, F. M., Schweizer, B., DePaulo, J. R., Jr., Gershon, E. S., McMahon, F. J., and Potash, J. B. (2009). Family-based association of FKBP5 in bipolar disorder. *Mol Psychiatry* 14, 261-8.

Wilson, A. M., Deri Armstrong, C., Furrie, A., and Walcot, E. (2009). The mental health of canadians with self-reported learning disabilities. *J Learn Disabil* 42, 24-40.

Yalcin, B., Willis-Owen, S. A., Fullerton, J., Meesaq, A., Deacon, R. M., Rawlins, J. N., Copley, R. R., Morris, A. P., Flint, J., and Mott, R. (2004). Genetic dissection of a behavioral quantitative trait locus shows that Rgs2 modulates anxiety in mice. *Nat Genet* 36, 1197-202.

Zackrisson, A. L., Lindblom, B., and Ahlner, J. (2010). High frequency of occurrence of CYP2D6 gene duplication/multiduplication indicating ultrarapid metabolism among suicide cases. *Clin Pharmacol Ther* 88, 354-9.

Zalsman, G., Huang, Y. Y., Oquendo, M. A., Brent, D. A., Giner, L., Haghighi, F., Burke, A. K., Ellis, S. P., Currier, D., and Mann, J. J. (2008). No association of COMT Val158Met polymorphism with suicidal behavior or CSF monoamine metabolites in mood disorders. *Arch Suicide Res* 12, 327-35.

Zhang, L., Li, H., Su, T. P., Barker, J. L., Maric, D., Fullerton, C. S., Webster, M. J., Hough, C. J., Li, X. X., and Ursano, R. (2008). p11 is up-regulated in the forebrain of stressed rats by glucocorticoid acting via two specific glucocorticoid response elements in the p11 promoter. *Neuroscience* 153, 1126-34.

Zhang, L., Su, T. P., Choi, K., Maree, W., Li, C. T., Chung, M. Y., Chen, Y. S., Bai, Y. M., Chou, Y. H., Barker, J. L., Barrett, J. E., Li, X. X., Li, H., Benedek, D. M., and Ursano, R. (2011) P11 (S100A10) as a potential biomarker of psychiatric patients at risk of suicide. *J Psychiatr Res* 45, 435-41.

Zhang, Y., Zhang, C., Yuan, G., Yao, J., Cheng, Z., Liu, C., Liu, Q., Wan, G., Shi, G., Cheng, Y., Ling, Y., and Li, K. (2010). Effect of tryptophan hydroxylase-2 rs7305115 SNP on suicide attempts risk in major depression. *Behav Brain Funct* 6, 49.

Zhukareva, V., and Levitt, P. (1995). The limbic system-associated membrane protein (LAMP) selectively mediates interactions with specific central neuron populations. *Development* 121, 1161-72.

Zill, P., Buttner, A., Eisenmenger, W., Moller, H. J., Bondy, B., and Ackenheil, M. (2004). Single nucleotide polymorphism and haplotype analysis of a novel tryptophan hydroxylase isoform (TPH2) gene in suicide victims. *Biol Psychiatry* 56, 581-6.

Zill, P., Buttner, A., Eisenmenger, W., Muller, J., Moller, H. J., and Bondy, B. (2009). Predominant expression of tryptophan hydroxylase 1 mRNA in the pituitary: a postmortem study in human brain. *Neuroscience* 159, 1274-82.

In: Frontiers in Suicide Risk
Editor: Jill E. Lavigne

ISBN 978-1-62081-373-7
©2012 Nova Science Publishers, Inc.

Chapter 2

INNOVATIVE DRUG DELIVERY AND FORMULATION DESIGNS TO DETER DRUG ABUSE/MISUSE RELATED TO SUICIDE

Fang Zhao

Pharmaceutical Sciences, St. John Fisher College,
Wegmans School of Pharmacy, East Avenue, Rochester, New York, US

ABSTRACT

Patients with a history of abuse/misuse of pain and psychotic medications are at high risk for suicide. Novel drug delivery and formulation approaches have been explored to reduce the potential of drug abuse/misuse and to improve patient compliance. This chapter reviews the design and mechanism of five successful products in the opioid and anti-psychotic categories.

Embeda® is an extended release capsule containing morphine pellets with a sequestered core of naltrexone; naltrexone acts as an aversive agent and is released only when the product is crushed. Remoxy® is an extended release oxycodone capsule with a highly viscous liquid fill content which is resistant to most common methods of tampering. Suboxone® is a sublingual tablet or film strip of buprenorphine with naloxone as an aversive agent; naloxone has poor sublingual/oral bioavailability and does not exert its activity unless the product is abused by the injectable route.

Risperidal® Consta®, is a biweekly intramuscular injection of risperidone based on a biodegradable polymer microsphere technology. Invega® Sustenna® is a once-monthly intramuscular injection of paliperidone based on the water insoluble prodrug approach. The review of these five new drug products showcases the novel formulation tools and technologies available to deter drug abuse/misuse in patients who are at high risk of suicide.

INTRODUCTION

Prescription and OTC drugs contribute to suicide in three general ways.

1) Some CNS-active drugs, such as the anti-depressants, have been linked to suicidal ideation and behavior as treatment emergent adverse events.[1]

2) A number of prescription drug classes, such as opioid analgesics, stimulants, and anti-psychotics, have high potentials for abuse/misuse. Drug abusers and non-compliant psychotic patients are at high risk for suicidal ideation and behavior. [2,3]

3) Prescription and OTC drugs are often used directly and intentionally in suicidal attempts via overdosing [4]

This chapter provides a review of recent innovations in drug delivery and formulation designs to address issue 2, i.e. the abuse and misuse of prescription drugs. Selected new products are discussed as examples to showcase the novel drug delivery and formulation approaches. Issue 1 is related to the intrinsic pharmacological properties of the active drugs, which typically cannot be overcome by any drug delivery or formulation approaches. Issue 3 is difficult to address by product design due to the vast availability of prescription and OTC drugs, especially in developed countries. Some long-acting injectable or implantable drug products do reduce their potentials for being used directly in suicidal attempts. However, a determined suicidal patient can simply choose other alternative drug products as a means of suicide. Therefore, this chapter will focus solely on the formulation innovations intended to deter drug abuse/misuse in patients who are at high risk of suicide.

ORAL OPIOID PRODUCTS

Opioid medications play an essential role in the management of moderate-to-severe pain in patients. The number of prescriptions for opioid medications has increased significantly over the last two decades [5-7] Due to this increased accessibility, especially for the oral dosage forms, the opioid products are often abused by patients and channeled into illicit distribution chains. Most opioid drug abusers prefer intense and rapid onset of action, and they often choose products which have high drug contents and can be tampered easily to attain rapid drug release and exposure. Many novel formulation designs have been explored to reduce the potential for misuse/abuse and diversion [7-9] Currently the most promising approaches can be classified in two general categories: (i) physical barriers are introduced to prevent tampering, such as crushing and solvent extraction; (ii) a deterrent or aversive ingredient is incorporated in the formulation, and it remains inactive unless the product is being misused or tampered. Three new opioid products are discussed below to illustrate the utility and application of these novel formulation designs.

1. Embeda®, an Extended Release Capsule of Morphine Pellets with Sequestered Naltrexone

Morphine is a pure opioid receptor agonist, and it has been used for over a century as the gold standard to treat moderate-to-severe pain [10-11] It is available commercially as both injectable and oral dosage forms [11] Due to the increased accessibility, the oral products present high potentials for abuse, especially the extended release capsules and tablets which contain a high drug content in each product unit [12-13] The individuals may chew the capsules or tablets to destroy the extended release mechanism and attain a quicker and higher exposure of the drug. Another common way of abuse is to extract the drug in a solvent followed by injection.

A new abuse deterrent formulation, Embeda®, was developed by King Pharmaceuticals (now Pfizer) and approved by US FDA in 2009.[14,15] Embeda® is an extended release capsule formulation containing pellets of morphine and naltrexone at a ratio of 100:4.[14] Naltrexone is an opioid receptor antagonist, and it is normally well absorbed via the oral route. In Embeda® capsules, however, naltrexone is sequestered in the pellet core. When used as directed, the Embeda® capsules deliver morphine over an extended period of time similar to the previous extended release capsule products, and the naltrexone remains sequestered within the core. Tampering with the capsule pellets by crushing or chewing (still swallowed orally) leads to rapid release and absorption of naltrexone which counteracts the euphoric effect of morphine [14-16] If the crushed pellets are dissolved or extracted followed by injection, the naltrexone is also released into the systemic circulation which achieves the same deterrent effect [16]

While the Embeda® product design reduces the potential for abuse/misuse, it does not completely eliminate it. For example, the sequestered naltrexone has no deterrent effect if the patient takes extra capsules as prescribed to get an increased drug exposure. It is also unknown whether naltrexone is effective (bioavailable) if the crushed pellet powder is snorted via the nasal route.

2. Remoxy®, an Extended Release Oxycodone Capsule with a High Viscosity Matrix

Oxycodone is an opioid agonist with an abuse liability similar to morphine, and both are classified as CSA (Controlled Substances Act) schedule II.[17] The first generation extended release oral tablet, OxyContin®, was developed by Purdue Pharma and approved by FDA in 1995.[11] OxyContin® was launched in 1996, and many patients responded well to this extended release opioid formulation. Initially FDA and Purdue Pharma did not expect OxyContin® to have high potential for abuse due to the controlled release formulation design [18] By 2001, the product grew to be the most prescribed brand name narcotic medication for treating moderate-to-severe pain. Ironically, this product also became extremely popular among opioid abusers [18] Aside from the increased accessibility, the drug abusers also realized that OxyContin contained high drug content in each tablet and that the controlled release formulation could be easily manipulated to obtain a rapid release of drug for the oral or injectable route.

Purdue Pharma reformulated the OxyContin and obtained approval from FDA in April 2010.[19] However, the new formulation appeared to offer only incremental improvement on abuse deterrent features, based on the limited technical information available [19,20] The company stated that "there is no evidence that the reformulation of OxyContin is less subject to misuse, abuse, diversion, overdose, or addiction" [21]

A separate effort has been undertaken by King Pharmaceuticals (now Pfizer) to develop an abuse deterrent extended release capsule of oxycodone. The new drug application (NDA) of this product, Remoxy®, has been filed to FDA and is currently under review [22] The Remoxy® capsule formulation employs a novel proprietary Oradur™ sustained release gel cap technology. [23-25] The oxycondone is suspended in a water-insoluble, highly viscous, and hydrophobic fluid matrix, which is subsequently filled into the regular capsule shells. This unique fluid matrix is designed to deter the four common routes of abuse - oral ingestion, snorting, injection, and inhalation. [23-25] In an aqueous medium, such as the gastrointestinal fluid, the viscous liquid transforms into an elastic matrix, which maintains the controlled drug release but prevents rapid drug extraction. The viscosity of the Oradur™ fluid matrix is extremely high (~ 60,000 centipoise), which renders it impossible for direct injection. This high viscosity also serves as a barrier for volatilization of the drug by heat for inhalation. The matrix remains as a liquid even at subzero temperatures. Therefore, it cannot be frozen to facilitate crushing or grinding to obtain solid powder for snorting. The tamper resistance features of Oradur™ have been demonstrated by several *in vitro* studies. [23-25]

A recent clinical study also showed that the abuse potential of Remoxy when taken whole or chewed was much lower than the regular immediate and extended release dosage forms of oxycodone [26]

Similar to the limitation of Embeda™, the Remoxy® product design does not reduce the potential of an abuser to overdose the product via the intended oral route.

3. Suboxone®, a Sublingual Tablet or Film Strip of Buprenorphine with Deterrent Naloxone

Buprenorphine is a partial agonist at the mu-opioid receptor [27] It was first approved as an injectable analgesic in 1981. [11] The tablet formulations, Subutex® and Suboxone®, were later developed by Reckitt Benckiser and approved in US in 2002 for office-based treatment of mild-to-moderate opioid dependence.[11,27] Subutex® and Suboxone® are sublingual tablets, which means that the drug is absorbed through the veins under the tongue. Subutex® contains only buprenorphine at 2 mg and 8 mg strengths; it is used during the induction phase of the treatment. [27] Suboxone® contains a combination of buprenorphine/naloxone at 2 mg /0.5 mg and 8 mg/2 mg strengths; it is used for the maintenance phase of the treatment [27].

Based on its unique pharmacological properties, buprenorphine has a less abuse potential than full mu-opioid agonist [28] and hence a CSA schedule III status.[17] However, Subutex® and Suboxone® are prescribed to patients with existing opioid dependence and are therefore subjected to high risk for potential misuse. There were also concerns that these sublingual tablets dissolve rapidly in aqueous media and can be manipulated easily to allow abuse via injection. The second ingredient naloxone in Suboxone was specifically added as a deterrent for potential abuse by injection [27, 28] Naloxone is a potent antagonist at mu-opioid receptor. It has no clinically significant effect when administered sublingually or orally due to poor bioavailability [27, 28] However, if an abuse attempts to extract the active ingredient buprenorphine by a solvent vehicle, the deterrent naloxone will also dissolve in the vehicle. Once injected, naloxone will exert full antagonist activity, attenuate the buprenorphine effect, and lead to withdrawal in patients with opioid dependence. As expected, the withdrawal effect depends on the ratio of buprenorphine/naloxone. Several clinical studies were conducted to identify the optimal dose ratio in patients with existing full agonist opioid dependence. In a pivotal clinical study using morphine stabilized subjects, IV injections of

2:1 and 4:1 ratios resulted in the most intense withdrawal effect [27,28]. Hence, the ratio of 4:1 buprenorphine/naloxone was chosen for the final product.

Since the launch of Subutex® and Suboxone® tablets, encouraging clinical results have been reported and published [28-31] The buprenorphine/naloxone combination tablets, Suboxone, were found to offer a safe and effective treatment for opioid dependence with similar or better outcomes than methadone or clonidine, respectively. Moreover, Suboxone tablets were available through office based treatment with patient friendly dispensing frequency, which improved the overall patient accessibility and retention. Both Subutex and Suboxone had documented abuse cases, but the numbers were low relative to the number of prescription dispensed [29] The incidence for abuse/misuse were reported as 0.08 and 0.16 abuse cases per 1,000 prescriptions dispensed for Subutex® and Suboxone®, respectively [29] The higher rate of abuse for Suboxone® over Subutex® was not expected. A few possibilities were proposed as follows: Suboxone was prescribed to a broader spectrum of patients; Suboxone® was diverted and used by non-opioid dependent abusers via the sublingual route; the deterrent effect of naloxone for the iv route of abuse is only partial and short-lived in nature [29,10]. Most recently a new formulation, Suboxone® sublingual film strip, was approved and launched in US in late 2010 [11,32] The buprenorphine and naloxone strengths are kept the same as in the tablets. The pharmacokinetic behavior of the film is similar to that of the tablet, although not all doses are bioequivalent [32]. Interestingly, the company decided not to pursue the single ingredient buprenorphine film product. Only the combination buprenorphine/naloxone film is marketed.

Several new features have been incorporated in the Suboxone film product to further address the abuse/misuse and diversion issues [32,33] Suboxone film strips are individually packaged as unit-dose child-resistant pouches. In contrast, the previous sublingual tablet products are packaged as 30 tablets per bottle [27] This unit-dose pouch packaging also reduces the potential for being used directly as a means for suicide, serving as a primary prevention mechanism similar to the blister packaging approach described in Chapter 4 of this book. A 10-digit code is printed on each pouch which facilitates medication counts and deters diversion [32,33] The manufacturer also states that the film formulation makes it difficult to be crushed into a powder for snorting [33]

In addition to reduced potential for abuse/misuse, the film strips offer several improved product attributes over the tablets, which should aid in patient compliance. In short, the films adhere better to the oral mucosa in the sublingual region, dissolve faster, and taste better than the tablets. Unfortunately, neither the sublingual tablet nor the film reduces the potential for overdosing via the intended sublingual route. Naloxone has poor oral bioavailability. Even when overdosed orally, the amount of naloxone in Suboxone does not result in the necessary systemic concentration to elicit the antagonist effect. The Suboxone tablets or films also do not deter the non-opioid dependent abusers from taking the product via the sublingual or oral route.

LONG-ACTING INJECTABLE ANTI-PSYCHOTIC PRODUCTS

Psychotic disorders, such as schizophrenia and bipolar disorder, are a major risk factor for suicide [2,34] Studies also suggest that 25 – 60% psychotic patients do not take their medications as prescribed; some are non-adherent, some partial adherent, and some excess fillers [35-37]. All these non-compliant behaviors of antipsychotic drug treatment are strongly linked to relapse, rehospitalization, and potentially suicide. In addition to strengthening the social support and medical supervision, much effort has been directed to novel formulation designs to improve patient compliance.

The long-acting injectable antipsychotics have been recognized as an effective approach to address the non-compliance issue for psychotic patients who require long-term medications [38]. These injections are administered via the intramuscular route by the health care providers. Upon injection, the product forms an *in situ* depot of drug, which is released slowly over an extended period of time, typically 2 – 6 weeks. In comparison to the oral product, the long-acting injectable formulation reduces the fluctuation of plasma drug concentration, which can improve the safety and efficacy of the antipsychotic medication. In addition, the long-acting formulations eliminate the need for patients to keep large quantity of pills for maintenance therapy and reduce the potential for these oral products to be used as a means of suicide. Some early generation of depot injection products were formulated in oil which could lead to undesired side effects over time, such as nodules at the injection site. Two recent products with distinct mechanisms of depot formation and drug release are described below.

1. Risperidal® Consta®, Extended-Release Microspheres of Risperidone

Risperidone is an atypical (second generation) antipsychotic drug, and it is one of the most commonly prescribed medications to treat schizophrenia and bipolar disorder [39-41] This drug was first approved by FDA in 1993 as an immediate release oral tablet [11] An oral solution and orally disintegrating tablets were later developed and approved to for patients who cannot swallow tablets or are resistant to taking medications [11]

A long-acting injection formulation, Risperdal® Consta®, was developed by Janssen Pharmaceuticals and approved by US FDA in 2003. This was the first long-acting atypical antipsychotic product on the market. Risperdal® Consta®, is a twice-monthly intramuscular depot injection. The drug is encapsulated in poly(lactic-co-glycolic acid) (PLGA) microspheres at a concentration of ~38% w/w.[39] PLGA is a biodegradable and biocompatible polymer excipient. Prior to injection, the microspheres are suspended using an aqueous diluent provided in a pre-filled syringe. Once injected, the microspheres form a depot in the muscular tissue at the injection site. The PLGA copolymer undergoes hydrolytic degradation progressively and releases risperidone over several weeks. According to the prescribing information from the manufacturer, [39] significant release of risperidone from the microspheres starts at week 3, is maintained from week 4 to week 6, and subsides by week 7. Therefore, supplemental oral antipsychotic medication should be given to the patient during the first 3 weeks of treatment with Risperdal® Consta®. Steady-state plasma concentrations are achieved after 4 biweekly injections.

The hydrolysis of PLGA gives back the lactic acid and glycolic acid monomers. These two acids are normal by-products of various metabolic pathways in the body. Therefore, the PLGA microsphere depot injections are generally safe and well tolerated with low incident rate of injection site pain or irritation.

The efficacy and tolerability of Risperdal® Consta® were investigated in a number of clinical studies in schizophrenic and bi-polar patients [39-42]. The data suggested that the Risperdal® Consta® treatment regimen offered similar efficacy as the long-term oral dose regimen with minimal increase in injection related adverse effects. As the first long-acting atypical antipsychotic product, Risperdal® Consta® offered a new mode of treatment with improved patient compliance and long-term outcomes.

2. Invega® Sustenna®, Extended-Release Injectable Suspension of Paliperidone Palmitate

Paliperidone is an active metabolite of risperidone discussed above [43,44] This drug was first approved by FDA as an extended release oral tablets in 2006 for treating schizophrenia and in 2009 for schizoaffective disorders [11] Paliperidone has improved pharmacokinetic properties over the parent drug risperidone, which reduces the risk for hepatic drug-drug interactions [44] The unique OROS® tablet formulation technology also provides steady drug release rate and smooth drug plasma level, which allows once-daily dosing with no need for dose titration [43,44]

In 2009, a long-acting injectable formulation, Invega® Sustenna®, was approved by FDA for once-monthly dosing [11,45] Invega® Sustenna® is also an intramuscular injection which serves a depot function similar to Risperal® Consta® described above. However, it employs a prodrug approach instead of the microsphere approach [43] Invega® Sustenna® contains paliperidone palmitate, which is an ester prodrug of paliperidone. In the body, the palmitate prodrug is converted to paliperidone via hydrolysis catalyzed by esterase. The product is formulated as a ready-to-use aqueous based suspension, so it does not require a reconstitution step as Risperal® Consta® prior to injection. Paliperidone palmitate is extremely insoluble in water. Therefore, the prodrug particles form an *in situ* depot after the intramuscular injection, and the prodrug dissolves slowly to provide the extended release mechanism. The dissolved prodrug is rapidly hydrolyzed to the parent drug paliperidone and absorbed into the systemic circulation [45]. Following a single intramuscular dose, the drug plasma concentration rises gradually to reach a maximum at day 13. The drug release starts as early as day 1 and lasts for as long as 126 days. Even though Invega® Sustenna® is intended for once-monthly injection, an initial regimen of two injections on day 1 and day 8 is recommended to rapidly attain the steady-state drug concentration without the use of oral supplementation [45]. As a relatively new product on the market, there are limited clinical data on Invega® Sustenna® in the literature besides the studies conducted by the manufacturer for registration. It remains to be seen whether this long-acting depot product provides any improvement in efficacy, safety, and patient compliance over the long-term oral therapy and/or the risperidone long-acting depot product.

In theory, the long-acting injectable product designs can also be applied to opioids (discussed earlier in this chapter) to reduce abuse/misuse. However, this approach is not applicable to all drugs, especially the ones with high doses and/or undesirable physicochemical properties. In addition, opioid drug therapy requires careful dose titration, and there are sometimes needs to switch drugs for the same patient to improve outcomes. There are also concerns about dose dumping from some of these long-acting formulations, which can lead to life threatening adverse effects. On a positive note, several injectable and implantable products of buprenorphine have been developed and are currently in different stages of clinical trials [9] One of these products, Probuphine, is a 6-month sustained-release implant and has recently demonstrated positive results in Phase 3 clinical studies [46]

CONCLUSION

This chapter provides a review of recent innovations in drug delivery and formulation designs to reduce drug abuse/misuse in patients who are at high risk of suicide. These include the use of aversive agents, unique physical properties to resist tampering, and long-acting depot injections. All these approaches provide exciting opportunities for the development of future abuse deterrent drug products. Meanwhile, each approach has its limitations and needs to be balanced with the potential benefits.

REFERENCES

[1]   Meyer RE, Salzman C, Youngstrom EA, et al. Suicidality and risk of suicide – definition, drug safety concerns, and a necessary target for drug development: a brief report. *J Clin Psychiatry.* 2010;71(8):1040-1046.

[2]   Risk Factors for Suicide. American Foundation for Suicide Prevention Website. *http://www.afsp.org/index.cfm?page_id=05147440-E24E-E376-BDF4BF8BA6444E76.* Accessed Aug 15, 2011.

[3]   Borges G, Walters EE, Kessler RC. Associations of substance use, abuse and dependence with subsequent suicidal behavior. *Am J Epidemiol.* 2000;15:781-789.

[4]   Suicides Due to Alcohol and/or Drug Overdose. A Data Brief from the National Violent Death Reporting System. Centers for Disease Control and Prevention Website. *http://www.cdc.gov/ViolencePrevention/pdf/NVDRS_Data_Brief-a.pdf.* Accessed Aug 15, 2011.

[5]   Wick JY. Drug abuse: a far-reaching reality. Pharmacy Times Website. *http://www. pharmacytimes.com/publications/issue/2010/september2010/counselingdrugabuse-0910.* Accessed Aug 25, 2011.

[6]   Compton WM, Volkow ND. Abuse of prescription drugs and the risk of addiction. *Drug Alcohol Depend.* 2006;83(Suppl 1):S4-7.

[7]   Schneider JP, Matthews M, Jamison RN. Abuse-deterrent and tamper-resistant opioid formulations. *CNS Drugs* 2010;24(10):805-810.

[8]   Schuster CR. History and current perspectives on the use of drug formulations to decrease the abuse of prescription drugs. *Drug Alcohol Depend.* 2006;83(Suppl 1):S8-14.

[9]   Fudala PJ, Johnson RE. Development of opioid formulations with limited diverion and abuse potential. *Drug Alcohol Depend.* 2006;83(Suppl 1):S40-47.

[10]   Golan DE, Tashjian AH, Armstrong EJ, Armstrong AW. *Principles of Pharmacology.* 3rd ed. Philadephia, PA: Lippincott Williams and Wilkins. 2011:273-275.

[11]   Drugs@FDA. FDA Approved Drug Products website. *http://www.accessdata.*
fda.gov/scripts/cder/drugsatfda/index.cfm. Last accessed on Aug 31, 2011.

[12]   Sloan P, Babul N. Extended-release opioids for the management of chronic non-
malignant pain. *Expert Opin Drug Deliv.* 2006;3:489-497.

[13]   Katz NP, Adams EH, Benneyan JC, et al. Foundations of opioid risk management. *Clin
J Pain.* 2007;23:103-118.

[14]   Embeda [Prescribing Information]. King Pharmaceuticals, Bristol, TN. June 2009.
http://embeda.com/. Accessed Aug 25, 2011.

[15]   Johnson F, Setnik B. Morphine sulfate and naltrexone hydrochloride extended-release
capsules: naltrexone release, pharmacodynamics, and tolerability. *Pain Physician.*
2011;14(4):391-406.

[16]   Raffa RB, Pergolizzi JV. Opioid formulations designed to resist/deter abuse. *Drugs.*
2010;70(13):1657-1675.

[17]   US Drug Enforcement Administration. Drug scheduling. *http://www.justice.gov*
/dea/pubs/scheduling.html. Accessed Aug 26, 2011.

[18]   US Government Accounting Office. Report to congressional requesters. OxyContin
abuse and diversion and efforts to address the problem. Dec 2003.
http://www.gao.gov/new.items/d04110.pdf. Accessed Aug 26, 2011.

[19]   FDA News Release. FDA approves new formulation for OxyContin. Apr 2010.
http://www.fda.gov/NewsEvents/Newsroom/PressAnnouncements/ucm207480.htm.
Accessed Aug 26, 2011.

[20]   OxyContin [Prescribing Information]. Purdue Pharma, Stamford, CT. Nov 2010.
http://www.purduepharma.com/pressroom/news/OxycontinPI.pdf. Accessed Aug 26,
2011.

[21]   Dear healthcare professional letter. Purdue Pharma. Oct 2010. *http://www.purdue*
pharma.com/pdfs/DearHCPLetter.pdf. Accessed Aug 26, 2011.

[22]   Pfizer pipeline – our medicines in development. Pfizer Website. *http://www.pfizer.com*
/research/product_pipeline/product_pipeline.jsp. Accessed Aug 21, 2011.

[23]   Zamloot M, Chao W, Kang LL, Ross J, Fu R. Remoxy: a novel formulation of
extended-release oxycondone developed using the Oradur technology. *J Appl Res.*
2010;10(3):88-96.

[24]   Durect Corporation. Oradur oral delivery technology. May 2010. *http://www.durect*
.com/pdf/ORADUR_Brochure_July2010.pdf. Accessed Aug 26, 2011.

[25]   NDA 22-324- Remoxy advisory committee briefing materials. Oct 2008.
http://www.fda.gov/ohrms/dockets/ac/08/briefing/2008-4395b1-02-PAIN.pdf. Accessed
Aug 26, 2011.

[26]   Setnik B, Roland CL, Cleveland JM, Webster L. The abuse potential of Remoxy, an
extended-release formulation of oxycodone, compared with immediate- and extended-
release oxycodone. *Pain Med.*2011;12(4):618-631.

[27]   Suboxone and Subutex sublingual tablets [Prescribing Information].Reckitt Benckiser
Pharmaceuticals, Inc. Richmond, VA. Sep 2006. *http://suboxone.com /pdfs/ Suboxone*
PI_tablet.pdf. Accessed Aug 26, 2011.

[28]   Orman JS, Keating GM. Buprenorphine/naloxone, a review of its use in the treatment
of opiod dependence. *Drugs.* 2009;69(5):577-607.

[29] Smith MY, Bailey JE, Woody GE, Kleber HD. Abuse of buprenorphine in the United States: 2003 – 2005. *J Addict Dis.* 2007;26(3):107-111.

[30] Polsky D, Glick HA, Yang J, Subramaniam GA, Poole SA, Woody GE. Cost-effectiveness of extended buprenorphine-naloxone treatment for opioid-dependent youth: data from a randomized trial. *Addiction.* 2010;105(9):1616-1624.

[31] Maremmani I, Gerra G. Buprenorphine-based regimens and methadone for the medical management of opiod dependence: selecting the appropriate drug for treatment. *Am J Addict.* 2010;19(6):557-568.

[32] Suboxone sublingual film [Prescribing Information]. Reckitt Benckiser Pharma ceuticals, Inc. Richmond, VA. Aug 2010. *http://suboxone.com/pdfs/ Suboxone PI.pdf.* Accessed Aug 26, 2011.

[33] Suboxone film key benefits. Suboxone product website. *http://suboxone.com/ hcp/ about_suboxone/key_benefits.aspx.* Accessed Aug 27, 2011.

[34] Suicide: risk and protective factors. Centers for Disease Control and Prevention Website.*http://www.cdc.gov/ViolencePrevention/suicide/riskprotectivefactors.html.* Acc essed Aug 27, 2011.

[35] Gilmer TP, Dolder CR, Lacro JP, et al. Adherence to treatment with antipsychotic medication and health care costs among Medicaid beneficiaries with schizophrenia. *Am J Psychiatry.* 2004;161(4):692-699.

[36] Becker MA, Young MS, Ochshorn E, Diamond RJ. The relationship of antipsychotic medication class and adherence with treatment outcomes and costs for Florida Medicaid beneficiaries with schizophrenia. *Adm Policy Ment Health.* 2007;34(3):307-314.

[37] Velligan DI, Wang M, Diamond P, et al. Relationships among subjective and objective measures of adherence to oral antipsychotic medications. *Psychiatr Serv.* 2007;58 (9):1187-1192.

[38] Patel MX, Taylor M, David AS. Antipsychotic long-acting injections: mind the gap. *Br J Psychiatry.* 2009;195(52):S1-S4.

[39] Risperidal® Consta® [Prescribing Information]. Ortho-McNeil-Janssen Pharmaceuticals, Inc. Titusville, NJ. Apr 2011. *http://www.janssencns.com/risperdal-prescribing-information.* Accessed Aug 27, 2011.

[40] Kane JM, Eerdekens M, Lindenmayer JP, Keith SJ, Lesem M, Karcher K. Long-acting injectable risperidone: efficacy and safety of the first long-acting atypical antipsychotic. *Am J Psychiatry.* 2003;160(6):1125-1132.

[41] Möller HJ. Long-acting injectable risperidone for the treatment of schizophrenia: clinical perspectives. *Drugs.* 2007;67(11):1541-1566.

[42] El-Hage W, Surguladze SA. Emerging treatments in the management of bipolar disorder – focus on risperidone long acting injection. *Neuropsychiatr Dis Treat.* 2010;6:455-464.

[43] Invega® [Prescribing Information]. Ortho-McNeil-Janssen Pharmaceuticals, Inc. Titusville, NJ. Apr 2011. *http://www.janssencns.com/invega-prescribing-information.* Accessed Aug 28, 2011.

[44] Gahr M, Kölle MA, Schönfeldt-Lecuona C, Lepping P, Freudenmann RW. Paliperidone extended-release: does it have a place in antipsychotic therapy? *Drug Des Devel Ther.* 2011;5:125-146.

[45] Invega® Sustenna® [Prescribing Information]. Ortho-McNeil-Janssen Pharmaceuticals, Inc. Titusville, NJ. Dec 2010. *http://www.janssencns.com/sustenna-prescribing-infor mation.* Accessed Aug 27, 2011.

[46] Press Release. Titan pharmaceuticals provides additional positive results in confirm atory phase 3 trial of probuphine. Titan Pharmaceuticals, Inc. South San Francisco, CA. May2011.*http:/.titanpharm.com/press/110816-phase3-probuphine-positive-results.htm.* Accessed Aug 28, 2011.

In: Frontiers in Suicide Risk
Editor: Jill E. Lavigne

ISBN 978-1-62081-373-7
©2012 Nova Science Publishers, Inc.

Chapter 3

THE COMPARATIVE SAFETY OF MULTIPLE PRESCRIPTION DRUG REGIMENS WITH ADVERSE EFFECTS OF RISK OF SUICIDAL IDEATION OR BEHAVIOR: A STUDY DESIGN IN BIPOLAR DISORDER

Jill E. Lavigne
Wegmans School of Pharmacy, St. John Fisher College,
Rochester, New York, US

ABSTRACT

Bipolar disorder is a relatively rare disease associated with the highest known risk of suicidal ideation or behavior of any disease or disorder. Untreated bipolar disorder is estimated to have a suicide risk of 100 times that of the general population. The disease is challenging to treat for variety of reasons, particularly the cyclical nature of mood states which may be difficult to detect and impossible to predict, prescription medications that are indicated during some states of the cycle (or episodes) but contraindicated in others, and very limited empirical evidence about the effectiveness of routinely administered multiple drug regimens. A number of prescription drugs routinely used to treat bipolar disorder are labeled for risk of adverse effects of suicidal ideation or behavior by the FDA, but the warnings are so general as to be of limited use to prescribers, patients and families. The greatest potential for new breakthroughs in the treatment of bipolar disorder may come from comparative safety studies using electronic medical records at the population level, but the value of these studies will depend on the quality of observational data, particularly with regard to suicidal ideation and behavior outcomes.

INTRODUCTION

In this chapter we identify questions about the comparative safety of prescribing guidance and routine prescribing patterns for the treatment of diseases and conditions associated with elevated risk of suicide. Throughout the chapter, we use bipolar disorder (BD) as an illustrative example.

Bipolar disorder is one of several conditions associated with an elevated risk of suicide. Any psychiatric diagnosis is associated with an increase in suicide risk of 5.18 for women (95% CI 4.08-6.58) and 2.50 (2.38-2.64) for men [1] Yet, all of the following conditions are associated with higher suicide rates among both men and women veterans: bipolar disorder, depression, post-traumatic stress disorder (PTSD), other anxiety, substance abuse and schizophrenia. Untreated bipolar disorder is associated with a suicide risk about 100 times that of the general population [2]

Here we use BD as an illustrative example for 6 reasons: (1) It is the diagnosis associated with the highest burden of suicidal ideation and behavior, [1] (2) BD treatment is characterized by a wide variety of prescription drug regimens, many of which have limited supporting evidence and conlfictingclinical guidelines, [3] (3) many of the drugs and drug classes in these regimens are labeled with warnings for potential serious adverse effects of suicidal ideation and behavior, [4] (4) yet, BD is a cyclic disease and medications indicated at one stage in the cycle (called an "episode") may be contraindicated during other episodes, [5] and a second generation atypical anti-psychotic, clozapine, has FDA approval for the prevention of suicidal ideation and behavior in schizophrenia, but its effect in BD is unknown [6]

PRESCRIBING GUIDANCE IN BIPOLAR DISORDER

Bipolar disorder is a chronic condition that may be disabling even in the presence of access and adherence to evidence-based medicine [7] The disorder is characterized by episodes of depression, mania or hypomania and/or mixed episodes. Identification of transitions between episodes is based on the emergence of symptoms specific to each episode but may vary significantly by individual patient. Evidence-based clinical practice guidelines (CPGs), such as the US Department of Veterans Affairs/Department of Defense (VA/DoD) Bipolar Disorder Guidelines (2010), [6] provide for the timing of assessments and an assortment of medication regimens from which prescribers may select any number of combinations. (For a summary of this Guideline see Appendix A.)

Regimens recommended for a manic episode may be contraindicated for a depressive episode and vice versa (Table 1). Therefore, agile detection of emerging signs and symptoms and management of drug regimens is imperative. Guidelines typically recommend that prescribers choose from a variety of drugs in each class to create a "designer" drug regimen that is customized to each patient and titrated over time.

Clinical guidelines rate medical evidence based on a commonly accepted rating scale for the quality of evidence. (For detailed information about how various pieces of scientific evidence are "graded" during the guideline development process, see: The Grading of Recommendations Assessment, Development and Evaluation (short GRADE) Working Group at http://www.gradeworkinggroup.org/index.htm.) Yet, guidelines are only as good as the evidence on which they are based. limited Evidence about the use of prescription medications for the management of bipolar disorder is limited (Table 1) and sometimes conflicting for drugs within the same class (Table 2).

Table 1. Drugs Recommended in VA/DoD Guidelines for the Treatment of Bipolar Disorder by BD Episode Type and Level of Evidence (2010)

Drug (Class)	Effectiveness of Medication			
	Likely (SR)	Trade-off Between Benefit and Harm	Unknown	Unlikely/May be Harmful
Clozapine (Atypical Antipsychotic-A)		Mania (I), Mixed Episode(I)	Depression (I), Remission (I)	
Quetiapine (Atypical Antipsychotic-B)	Depression (A) Mania (A) (Monotherapy –A, Adjunct to lithium or valproate - A) Remission (with lithium or valproate) (B)	Mixed Episode (I), Depression (with SSRI, SNRI, Bupropion and MAOI) (C)		
Antidepressant Monotherapy				Mania (C) Depression (D) Remission (D)
Lamotrigine (Anti-convulsant)	Depression – with Lithium(A), Remission –prevention of depression (B) Remission – prevention of mania (C)	Depression (B), Depression (with lithium, SSRI, SNRI, Bupropion and MAOI) (C)		Mania(D), Mixed Episode (D)
Oxcarbazepine (Anti-convulsant)		Mania (I), Mixed Episode(I)	Depression (I) Remission (I)	
Valproate (Anti-convulsant)	Mania (A)	Remission (C)	Depression (I)	
Lithium (Mood stabilizer)	Mania (A) Depression (B) Depression – with lamotrigine (A) Remission-Prevention of Depression(B) Remission-Prevention of Mania (A)	Mixed Episode (I) Depression (with SSRI, SNRI, Bupropion and MAOI) (C)		
Carbamazepine (Anti-convulsant)	Mania (A)	Remission (C)	Depression (I)	

Table 1. (Continued)

Drug (Class)	Effectiveness of Medication			
	Likely (SR)	Trade-off Between Benefit and Harm	Unknown	Unlikely/May be Harmful
Aripriprazole (Atypical Antipsychotic-B)	Mania (A) (Monotherapy –A, Adjunct to lithium or valproate - A)	Remission – Prevention of Mania (B)		Depression (D) (Monotherapy)
Olanzapine (Atypical Antipsychotic-A)	Mania (A) (Monotherapy –A, Adjunct to lithium or valproate - A) Remission – Prevention of Depression (C), Remission – Prevention of Mania (B) Remission (with lithium or valproate) (C)	Depression (C)		
Risperidone (Atypical Antipsychotic-B)	Mania (A) (Monotherapy –A, Adjunct to lithium or valproate - A)		Depression (I) Remission (long-acting injection) (I)	
Ziprasidone (Atypical Antipsychotic-A)	Mania (A)		Depression (I) Remission (I)	
Gabapentin (Anti-convulsant)			Remission (I)	Mania (D) Mixed Episode (D) Depression (D)
Topiramate (Anticonvulsant)			Depression (I) Remission (I)	Mania (D) Mixed Episode (D)
Olanzapine/Fluoxetine (Atypical Antipsychotic/SSRI)		Depression (B)	Remission (I)	
Haloperidol (Typical Antipsychotic)			Depression (I) Remission (I)	

SR = Strength of Recommendation.

Table 2. Atypical Antipsychotics Recommended in VA/DoD Guidelines for the Treatment of Bipolar Disorder by Type, BD Episode and Level of Evidence (2010)

Drug (Class)	Effectiveness of Medication			
	Likely (SR)	Trade-off Between Benefit and Harm	Unknown	Unlikely/May be Harmful
Atypical Antipsychotics-A				
Clozapine		Mania (I), Mixed Episode(I)	Depression (I), Remission (I)	
Ziprasidone	Mania (A)		Depression (I) Remission (I)	?? Depression (Adjunctive)? Sachs, et al (2011)
Olanzapine	Mania (A) (Monotherapy –A, Adjunct to lithium or valproate - A) Remission – Prevention of Depression (C), Remission – Prevention of Mania (B) Remission (with lithium or valproate) (C)	Depression (C)		
Atypical Antipsychotics-B				
Quetiapine	Depression (A) Mania (A) (Monotherapy –A, Adjunct to lithium or valproate - A) Remission (with lithium or valproate) (B)	Mixed Episode (I), Depression (with SSRI, SNRI, Bupropion and MAOI) (C)		
Aripriprazole	Mania (A) (Monotherapy –A, Adjunct to lithium or valproate - A)	Remission – Prevention of Mania (B)		Depression (D) (Monotherapy)
Risperidone	Mania (A) (Monotherapy –A, Adjunct to lithium or valproate - A)		Depression (I) Remission (long-acting injection) (I)	
Olanzapine/Fluoxetine (Atypical Antipsychotic/SSRI)		Depression (B)	Remission (I)	

SR = Strength of Recommendation.

Table 3. Comparison of Relative Potential for Suicidal Behavior and Other Serious Adverse Effects of Second Generation Anti-Psychotics

Adverse Event	Aripiprazole	Clozapine	Olanzapine	Quetiapine	Risperidone	Ziprasidone
Anticholinergic Effects	1	4	3	1	1	1
Extrapyramidal Effects	1	0	1	0	2	1
Hyperglycemia	1	4	3	2	1	0
Hyperlipidemia	1	4	3	2	1	0
Hyper-prolactinemia	1	1	1	1	3	1
Neuroleptic Malignant Syndrome	1	1	1	1	1	1
Orthostatic Hypotension	1	4	1	3	2	1
QTc Prolongation	0	2	1	2	2	3
Sedation	1	4	3	3	2	1
Tardive Dyskinesia	0	0	1	0	1	1
Weight Gain	0	4	3	2	2	0
Suicidal Ideation and Behavior	U	U Protective-Schizophrenia	U	U	U	U

0 = unlikely

1 = unlikely-low possible

2 = low-moderate

3 = moderate-high, probable

4 = high, likely

U = unknown, not assessed/included in the VA/DoD 2010 Clinical Management Guideline

(This table is an extension of Table E-7, VA/DoD Clinical Practice Guideline (Summary Guideline) Management of Bipolar Disorder in Adults (2010)).

For prescribers selecting 2 or more drugs to treat the same condition in the community, little evidence-based medicine exists regarding the best combination. As the VA/DoD Bipolar Disorder Guidelines (2010) note:

> A significant percentage of patients will not respond to any one medication approach even when the medication is taken regularly in proper dosages. For these patients the provider will need to try different strategies in order to maximize benefits and obtain remission. Unfortunately, little data exists to guide the provider in the exact sequence of steps. Possible strategies include switching to a different mood stabilizer or combining agents.
> – VA/DOD Clinical Practice Guideline for Management of Bipolar Disorder in Adults (Summary) p. 20.

Factors contributing to limited evidence about the effectiveness of multiple drug regimens in bipolar disorder include the routine exclusion of patients with active suicidal behavior or ideation from clinical trials. Such trials typically include only patients free of comorbidities and/or concomitant medication use. Lack of treatment response or increased illness severity is typically treated with multiple drug regimens, confounding the treatment with suicide risk. Finally, the number of patients in treatment for active suicidal ideation and behavior is relatively small in the general population at any given time. These factors make it difficult to design experimental or observational studies with adequate internal validity and power. Complicating the optimal selection of combination therapy are FDA warnings about potential increased risk of suicidal thoughts or behaviors following exposure to the prescription drugs typically used to treat these conditions. As of October 2010, the FDA had re-labeled 125 prescription medications sold in the US for risk of adverse effects related to suicidal behavior and ideation [4] Of these drugs, the 45 with the highest volume sales represented a total US prescription sales volume of 540.8 million 30-day supply prescriptions in 2009 alone. [4]. Labeling changes may not appear in clinical guidelines, which are written by committees and are updated only periodically. This is the case, for example, with the current US Department of Veterans Affairs/Department of Defense guidelines for prescribing in bipolar disorder which were last updated in 2010. Finally, medications for the treatment of bipolar disorder may have adverse effects related to other diseases and conditions that must be weighed alongside any risk of suicide. For example, second generation anti-psychotics are associated with several serious adverse effects that may pose particular risk to obese or diabetic patients and the likelihood varies by each drug in the class (Table 3). Prescribers must balance these risks as they weigh prescribing decisions. To the best of our knowledge, studies have yet to examine the comparative safety of various multiple drug regimens for the treatment of bipolar disease or other diseases associated with increases suicide risk.

WHAT IS "COMPARATIVE SAFETY"?

Comparative safety is "the likelihood that a given drug will cause a severe adverse event of any type." (Solomon, et al, Arch Intern Med 2010, p. 1968) [14]. In contrast, the randomized controlled trials required as part of the FDA New Drug Application process focus on a specific organ system risk (e.g., cardiovascular risk) rather than on all potential risks. Comparative safety is a relatively new term, first cited in 2008 in the context of a call for mandatory "comparative safety and efficacy" by Wayne Ray in the *New England Journal of Medicine* to accompany the publication of observational studies showing that patients receiving aprotinin, a drug approved to reduce blood loss during coronary artery bypass grafting (CABG), had worse outcomes in both the short and long-term than those receiving older alternative drug treatments [15] The NDA had been supported with drug trials that compared aprotinin to placebo.

Comparative safety studies use large observational datasets to study multiple outcomes of interest across alternative drug treatments for a specific indication. For example, Solomon, et al (2011) used Medicare data to estimate the risk of 15 adverse events associated with the use of three alternative therapies for arthritis analgesia in older adults[14] and to compare opioid therapies for non-malignant pain in older adults [16] In the study arthritis analgesia adverse events were: myocardial infarction, heart failure, stroke, coronary revascularization, out-of-hospital cardiac death, upper GI tract bleeding, lower GI tract bleeding, bowel obstruction, acute kidney injury, falls, hip fracture, humerus fracture, pelvic fracture, radius fracture, and hepatotoxic effects. Medicare patients who initiated therapy with an nsNSAID, coxib or an opioid between January 1, 1999 and December 31, 2005 were matched using propensity scores. (Propensity scores are derived from multiple regression models used to estimate the probability that a particular person will be prescribed a specific drug from the 3 drug choices based on patient characteristics.) nsNSAIDs were associated with lower relative risk for cardiovascular events, but coxibs were associated with lower gastrointestinal bleeding risk. Opioids were associated with an elevated risk of fracture, safety events requiring hospitalization and all-cause mortality. Few comparative safety studies have been published, despite recent efforts by the US federal government to invest more than $1 billion in comparative effectiveness studies as part of the Stimulus bill. Comparative effectiveness studies require significant expertise in statistics and access to large datasets. The pharmaceutical industry has no commercial incentive to conduct such studies, and in fact may face disincentives [15] To improve our understanding of adverse effects of suicidal ideation and behavior in bipolar disorder, we might use existing panel data from US Department of Veterans Affairs (VA) electronic medical records. The VA is the largest single health system in the US, serving approximately 6.1 million patients. Veterans face a relatively higher risk of suicide than the general US population [17-18] In the following section we describe two high priority research questions and the types of methods that might be used to address them. Data specific to the VA are described in the appendices.Prescription Drug Regimens to Treat Bipolar Disorder: Recent Empirical Evidence.

Post-et al (2010) provide a description of the complexity of regimens used in routine outpatient care in the Bipolar Disorder Network (formerly the Stanley Foundation Network).[7] For bipolar disorder patients who were well at entry into the study, the number of drugs used for maintenance of BD ranged from 0 to 5 (mean 1.65). For patients who were not well, but responded to treatment, the number of treatment drugs ranged from 0 to 13, and for those who did not respond, the total number of drugs used after study entry ranged from 0 to 21. These ranges represent a variety of drug treatments tested. The mean number of drugs used and the range were similar for both responders and non-responders at study entry and exit. About one-third (37.9%) of all patients in the study achieved remission, improvement or limited improvement for a mean of 1.5 years. 18.3% of study patients were well at study entry and remained well for the entire period. 43.4% of patients continued to have at least moderately severe manic or depressive symptomology despite treatment. Generalized linear regression models identified several factors that were significantly different in non-responders. At study entry, non-responders were taking more medications for BD than responders. Non-responders were typically older, had a longer history of BD that included more than 20 mood episodes, hospitalizations, dysphoric mania, a diagnosis of Bipolar I and rapid cycling. Non-responders also were more likely to exhibit drug abuse and unemployment and to have a family history of parental alcohol and drug use. Most recently, a handful of new studies from the same research network have drawn into question the clinical effectiveness of agents routinely used to treat BD (and labeled for risk of adverse effects related to suicide). In a randomized controlled trial of adjunctive oral ziprasidone for acute depression in Bipolar I Disorder, Sachs and colleagues (2011) found no benefit over placebo on any primary endpoint and on most secondary endpoints [8]

This study is particularly important given that another atypical anti-psychotic, clozapine, is the only drug labeled for suicide prevention (specifically in schizophrenia) by the FDA. Recent studies of anti-depressants and anti-epileptic drugs suggest no elevated risk of suicide in any drugs in either class [9,10] Yet, these studies maximized internal validity by including only patients with incident diagnoses and initiating monotherapy and followed them for only 12 months or until first event, including switching therapy or the addition of a second therapy in the same class. By design, these studies excluded the patients at greatest risk of suicidal ideation or behavior. In a randomized study of the discontinuation of "modern" antidepressants for the treatment of bipolar depression, Ghaemi, et al (2010) found that rapid cycling patients who stayed on antidepressants, including SSRIs, had worse outcomes than those who discontinued [11] Furthermore, among all BD patients, no long-term treatment benefit was found, including no change in remission rates and no change in robust depressive episode prevention. Antidepressant monotherapy has now been dropped from some clinical guidelines [3] Yet, in the same population of BD patients, Perlis and colleagues (2010) found that the number of drugs in a BD regimen has been shown to be negatively associated with adherence to pharmacotherapy and positively associated with suicide risk [12] This poses challenges for pharmacoepidemiologists designing studies of drug exposures and suicide risk. Patients at higher suicide risk are prescribed more medications, but are also less likely to comply with their regimens. Perlis and colleagues present a risk stratification algorithm for non-adherence that accurately classified 80.6% of patients in an independent validation cohort.

Finally, benzodiazepines were associated with greater risk for recurrence of a mood episode in both bipolar I and II patients followed from 1999 to 2005, according to Perlis, et al (2010). Patients taking benzodiazepines were also more likely than other BD patients to be taking lamotrigine (and less likely to be taking lithium), an antidepressant, an additional anticonvulsant and trazadone.

THE BASICS OF A STUDY DESIGN OF THE COMPARATIVE SAFETY OF PRESCRIPTION DRUG REGIMENS FOR BIPOLAR DISORDER – DEPRESSION UNRESPONSIVE TO MONOTHERAPY

Patients who do not respond to first-line therapies for the treatment of depressive episodes in bipolar disorder are prescribed second-line multiple drug therapies "trading off benefit and harm"(Figure 1) [6] The drugs included in these combination therapies all have an evidence based medicine (EBM) grade of "C" for evidence of effectiveness. (For a discussion of evidence based medicine grades of evidence, please see the Grade Working Group series.) [19-24]

Adjunctive olanzapine (with lithium OR quetiapine (AA-B) OR lamotrigine OR (lithium + lamotrigine))

OR

Any 1 of 7 SSRIs + any 1 of 4 SNRIs + buproprion + any 1 of 4 MAOIs   AND

1. Lithium (mood stabilizer) OR
2. Quetiapine (AA-B) OR
3. Lithium (mood stabilizer) + lamotrigine (AED)
4. Lamotrigine

SSRIs	SNRI	MAOIs
Citalopram	Desvenlafaxine	isocarboxazid
Escitalopram	Duloxetine	Phenelzine
Fluoxetine	Milnacipran	Selegiline
Fluvoxamine	Venlafaxine	Tranylcypromine
olanzapine/fluoxetine		
Paroxetine		
Sertraline		

Figure 1. Possible Regimens for the Treatment of Bipolar Depression Unresponsive to Monotherapy.

The total number of combinations of unique regimens (excluding differences in dosing) is then 196. These regimens include drugs with a range of serious adverse effects, which may vary across a single drug class. (For an example, see the table of the likelihood of various serious adverse effects associated with second generation anti-psychotics (Table 3)). A comparative safety design using VA data might be used to answer the question:

"What trade-offs in suicide-related adverse events (outpatient suicide attempt (SPC), inpatient suicide attempt, admission for psychoses) and known adverse effects (e.g., hyperglycemia, sedation, weight gain etc.) are made among these combination regimens?"

Study Design: A matrix design for comparative safety may be used to address this question. This design is specifically for chronic diseases with multiple exposures and multiple outcomes of interest [14,16,25]

Data: For an overview of VA data that may be useful in studies of comparative effectiveness such as this, see Appendix B.

Subjects: Inclusion criteria may include:

- Prior to the index date, taking only monotherapy lithium or olanzapine (AA-A) (first line therapies for maintenance of BD remission), and
- Partial or complete remission BD, and

- At least a 12-month window of any prescription drug use in the prescription drug file before and after the index date.

Exclusion criteria may include:

- Any history of injectable risperidone (a marker for rapid cycling), or
- Absence of a wash-out period of at least 3 months monotherapy with lithium or olanzapine prior to index date.

Exposure Measurement: The index date, or the date defining exposure to the regimens of interest, may be defined as the first prescription fill date during the study period for the 196 regimens previously described above. Concurrent use of prescription medications will be defined as a 14-day window of overlap in filled medications, with sensitivity analysis to 30 days. To determine adherence to pharmacotherapy for bipolar disorder, we will calculate the Medication Possession Ratio (MPR) for the study period as follows:

$$MPR = \Sigma \qquad \frac{Day\ Supply_i}{n = 1 - i\ Day\ supply Last\ Rx\ date - Day\ Supply\ First\ Rx\ date}$$

The degree of non-adherence to the prescribed regimen may be estimated using Perlis, et al. (2010) who found that 24% of BD patients reported non-adherence on 20% or more of study visits.[12] Non-adherence was associated with greater incidence of suicidal behavior and more prescriptions written. Perlis's risk stratification model using clinical predictors accurately classified 80.6% of visits in an independent validation cohort.

Outcomes Measurement: Outcomes will be represented in a matrix of adverse effects including all serious adverse effects associated with each drug in a regimen. Ideally, these adverse effects would include the spectrum of ideation and behaviors described by the Centers for Disease Control in their Self-Directed Violence Classification System and promulgated by the VA in the Self-Directed Violence Toolkit. [26] For example, the FDA recommends the Columbia Classification Algorithm of Suicide Assessment (C-CASA) in its Guidance for Industry: Suicidality: Prospective Assessment of Occurrence in Clinical Trials [27] C-CASA includes: Suicidal ideation, suicidal behavior (i.e.., suicide attempt, suicide), non-suicidal self-injurious behavior, and accidental injuries.

Investigators using existing data (such as electronic medical records) must limit outcomes to those of high quality in the data. Outcomes with high validity in VA data have appeared in published studies and include inpatient deaths by suicide, inpatient suicide attempts and hospital admission for psychosis, for example. Fields in VA data that may hold promise for measurement of suicidal ideation and behavior outcomes appear in Appendix C.

Composite measures of suicidal thoughts and behaviors may also be used. A composite measure is a dichotomous indicator of the presence or absence of any one or more of suicidal ideation or behaviors identifiable in available data. This type of measure is consistent with the range of thoughts and behaviors included in definitions of suicide as well as recent pharmacoepidemiology and drug safety research [10].

Limitations: The inclusion of only incident users will exclude patients who have been on multiple drug regimens for long periods and have succeeded on those therapies. Censoring data when a patient switches to a new medication regimen will exclude patients who may be unstable. Users who experience little or no therapeutic benefit or who experience significant side effects may quit or switch reigmens within 30 days of first use [14, 28] We measure adherence using the well-accepted MPR, yet this measure describes adherence to filling prescriptions and not necessarily taking medications. Sensitivity analyses should be conducted around the proposed adherence adjustment method using data from Perlis, et al. (2010) [12]

Finally, practice guidelines suggest that the current philosophy in treating BD is that more serious disease or non-response to medication merits more aggressive prescribing, including more medications and/or higher doses. Population-based studies such as comparative safety studies will face the well-known limitations of confounding by prescription and diagnoses. The medication regimen is dependent upon the severity and degree of response to first-line regimens. Therefore, the effects of multiple drug regimens on suicidal ideation and behavior are confounded with the severity of bipolar disorder which is also associated with risk of suicidal ideation and behavior.

FUTURE RESEARCH: CLOZAPINE VERSUS OLANZAPINE FOR SUICIDE RISK REDUCTION IN MANIA OR MIXED EPISODE BIPOLAR DISORDER

An additional question for future research is the comparative safety of clozapine versus olanzapine for suicide risk reduction in mania or mixed episode bipolar disorder. Specifically, is adjunctive clozapine protective against suicidal ideation and behavior compared to adjunctive treatment with other second-generation anti-psychotics (aripiprazole, olanzapine, quetipanine, risperidone or ziprasidone) in patients experiencing mania or mixed episode BD (Diagnostic Statistical Manual DSM 296.0 – 296.05; 296.4-296.45) [29]? Current VA/DoD guidelines for medication management of BD (2010) specify the second-generation anti-psychotic olanzapine as a first-line therapy. Yet, a drug in the same class, clozapine, is FDA-approved for the indication "suicide risk reduction." In a randomized controlled trial, clozapine-treated schizophrenia patients with a history of recent suicidal behavior and/or current suicidal ideation had 25% fewer suicide-related events than olanzapine-treated patients over a 2-year period. A 2010 suicide and drug development consensus statement identified the following target for drug development:

> Do drugs that appear to reduce risk of suicide for patients with onediagnosis (e.g., clozapine in patients with schizophrenia) also lower suicide risk for individuals with other diagnoses? [30]

CONCLUSION

Bipolar disorder is associated with a high risk of suicidal ideation and behavior, likely exposure to multiple drugs labeled for risk of adverse effects of suicidal ideation and behavior, and limited evidence with which to make prescribing decisions. The cyclical nature of the disorder means that prescription medications indicated for one type of episode may be contraindicated in another. Agile prescription drug management is therefore important. Multiple drug regimens are recommended by evidence based clinical practice guidelines for patients in episodes unresponsive to monotherapy, yet relatively little is known about the comparative safety of these combination regimens. For example, 196 regimens are recommended (balancing risk and benefit) for bipolar depression unresponsive to monotherapy. New comparative safety matrix designs applied to panel data (e.g., population-based electronic medical records) may provide the best opportunities to advance prescribing knowledge. Notably, these designs accommodate the study of multiple serious adverse effects. This is particularly important given that medications routinely used to treat bipolar disorder, such as second generation antipsychotics, may have serious adverse effects related to obesity, hypertension and hypercholesteremia in addition to any risk of increased suicidal ideation or behavior.

APPENDIX A. SUMMARY OF BD DRUG REGIMEN RECOMMENDATIONS FROM THE 2010 VA/DOD CLINICAL PRACTICE GUIDELINE FOR MANAGEMENT OF BIPOLAR DISORDER IN ADULTS

Recommended Prescription Drug Regimens by BD Episode

Mania

Monotherapy: Lithium (mood stabilizer) OR valproate (AED) OR cabamazepine (AED) OR aripiprazole (AA-B) OR olanzapine (AA) OR quetiapine (AA-B) OR risperidone (AA-B) OR ziprasidone (AA-A)

2-drug therapy: Lithium (mood stabilizer) OR valproate (AED) plus any 1 of 4 atypical antipsychotics:

- Lithium (mood stabilizer) + ADJUNCTIVE (aripiprazole (AA-B) OR olanzapine (AA) OR quetiapine (AA-B) OR risperidone (AA-B))
- Valproate (AED) + ADJUNCTIVE (aripiprazole (AA-B) OR olanzapine (AA) OR quetiapine (AA-B) OR risperidone (AA-B))

Trade-off between benefit and harm: clozapine (AA-A), oxcarbazepine (AED)

Bipolar Depression

A significant percentage of patients will not respond to any one medication approach even when the medication is taken regularly in proper dosages. For these patients the provider will need to try different strategies in order to maximize benefits and obtain remission. Unfortunately, little data exists to guide the provider in the exact sequence of steps. Possible strategies include switching to a different mood stabilizer or combining agents. – VA/DOD Clinical Practice Guideline for Management of Bipolar Disorder in Adults (Summary) p. 20.

Monotherapy: Lithium (mood stabilizer) OR quetiapine (AA-B)
2-drug regimen: Lithium + lamotrigine (AED)

For patients who fail to respond to the above regimens, adjunctive regimens (trading off benefit and harm) may be used. Additionally, augmentation with agents with unknown effects is possible.

Adjunctive 2-drug regimens for Non-response (trading off benefit and harm):

- Quetiapine (AA-B)+ lamotrigine (AED)
- Lithium (mood stabilizer) + olanzapine/fluoxetine (AA/SSRI)
- Quetiapine (AA-B)+ olanzapine/fluoxetine (AA/SSRI)
- Lithium (mood stabilizer) + olanzapine (SSRI)
- Quetiapine (AA-B)+ olanzapine (SSRI)

5-drug regimen choices for non-response (trading off benefit and harm):

- Lithium (mood stabilizer) + SSRI + SNRI + buproprion + MAOI
- Quetiapine (AA-B) + SSRI + SNRI + buproprion + MAOI

6-drug regimen (trading off benefit and harm): Lithium (mood stabilizer) + lamotrigine (AED) + SSRI + SNRI + buproprion + MAOI
Additional Experimental (I) Adjunctive Therapies (effects unknown) may be added: clozapine, carbamazepine, oxcarbazepine, risperidone, topiramate, valproate, ziprasidone, haloperidol

Bipolar Remission – Maintenance Therapies
First–line maintenance (monotherapy): lithium (mood stabilizer) OR olanzapine (AA-A)
Also acceptable monotherapy: lamotrigine (AED)
Also acceptable *2-Drug Therapies:*

- quetiapine (AA-B) + lithium (mood stabilizer)
- quetiapine (AA-B) + valproate (AED)
- olanzapine (AA-A) + lithium (mood stabilizer)
- olanzapine (AA-A) + valproate (AED)

Patients with frequent recurrences (rapid cycling) should be considered for risperidone long-acting IM injection.
Patients with psychoses are to be given antipsychotics *Alternatives for monotherapy maintenance (but weigh benefits and risks):* valproate (AED), carbamazepine (AED)
Unknown: Clozapine (AA), gabapentin (AED), haloperidol, olanzapine/fluoxetine (AA/SSRI), oxcarbazepine (AED), risperidone (AA), topiramate (AED), ziprasidone (AA)

APPENDIX B. A BRIEF OVERVIEW OF VA DATA SOURCES FOR COMPARATIVE SAFETY RESEARCH

The US Department of Veterans Affairs, Veterans Health Administration (VHA) is the largest health system in the United States.. VHA uses an electronic medical record, abstracts of which are cleaned and maintained in a national research dataset accessible only by VHA employee researchers and their staffs who have access appropriate for only Research Subject Review Board approval for specific research studies. All records are linked across datasets at the patient level. Here we describe the research datasets available to these researchers and appropriate to our research questions.

Prescription drug exposures can be estimated using the VA Pharmacy Benefits Management Database (PBM). The PBM is updated monthly and maintained by VAMed SAFE.

The Medical SAS File (MDP) (I.e., the national administrative data for the VHA) will be used to identify the cohorts, determine psychiatric history and assess suicide attempts and ideation. The MDP includes utilization primarily by veterans, as well as some employees and research participants. SAS data files are provided by fiscal year (Oct. 1 - Sept. 30). For example, the fiscal year 2007 Medical SAS File contains nearly 58 million outpatient visits. As noted in VA documentation: SAS files are complete extracts from the National Patient Care Database (NPCD), maintained by the VHA Office of Information at the Austin Automation Center (AAC), the central repository for VA data. Patients are identified by unique scrambled SSNs. The Medical SAS file consists of dozens of files that cover acute, extended, observation and non-VA care. Within each category there are outpatient and inpatient files already prepared for analysis at the event, visit or episode of care. Access to these files requires an application to ViREC. Analyses are conducted virtually via the Austin Automation Center.

The Decision Support System (DSS) Pharmacy National Data Extracts (NDEs) will be used to identify exposures of interest. The DSS are SAS data available directly to researchers via the Austin Automation host. Variables are listed in the appendix and include: scrambled Social Security number, date of birth, sex, date of prescription, zip code + 4 digits, prescription primary care provider, diagnosis, drug description (including the dose) and days supply. The DSS NDE also includes Rx Risk, a measure of comorbidity shown to be similar to Ambulatory Diagnostic Groups (ADGs) in predicting future healthcare costs (Sloan, et al, 2003). These data will be used to obtain variables for analysis.

The VA Vital Status Master File will be used to determine all-cause mortality for the cohorts. In a validity study comparing the Vital Status Master File to the National Death Index, the Vital Status File was found to have sensitivity of 98.3% and specificity of 100%. The file combines death records from national VA healthcare and benefits (including pension benefits), Medicare records and Social Security Administration records. Cause of death is not available through this file.

Suicides for which death occurs in a hospital are recorded in the inpatient files. The VA Vital Status Master File will be used to determine all-cause mortality for the cohort. The File does not include cause of death.

APPENDIX C. VA DATA FIELDS RELEVANT TO SUICIDE RESEARCH

Suicide, attempted suicide and ideation are coded under the ICD-9-CM codes in national VA research datasets (e.g., Medical SAS File) and linked Medicare files (Table C1). A primary ICD-9-CM Code is assigned for each visit and episode of care including up to 12 secondary ICD-9-CM codes.

Table C1. VA Data Fields for Possible Use in Capturing Suicidal Ideation and Behavior

Outcome	Setting	Data Source	Measure	Value(s)	Linked Measures
Completed Suicide/Death by Suicide	Deaths in the Community	VA VISN 2 Center of Excellence in Suicide Prevention CoE State-level death certificate files (in development) or Ann Arbor, MI VA SMITREC files	Medical Record Cause of Death		
	VA Inpatient Deaths	Inpatient EMR	Suicide Indicator	SUICIDEB = 2 (Suicide)	
	Deaths in the Emergency Room	Outpatient EMR OR Medicare Claims AND Vital Statistics	Suicidal behavior ICD-9 code and matching date of death	See ICD-9 table (below)	Vital Statistics Master File Date of Death
Suicide Attempt	In VA hospitals	Inpatient EMR	Indicator	SUICIDEB = 1 (Attempt)	
	In the Community	In development	Indicator		
	Community/VA	Inpatient EMR OR Outpatient EMR OR Medicare Claims	Suicide Attempt ICD-9	See ICD-9 table (below)	Missing date of death in Vital Statistics
Suicidal Ideation	VA Community	Inpatient EMR OR Outpatient EMR OR Medicare Claims	Suicidal Ideation ICD-9 Admission for any psychoses	V62.84	Missing date of death in Vital Statistics
VA Inpatient Self-Inflicted Injury	Inpatient VA	Inpatient EMR	Suicide Indicator	SUICIDEB = 3 (Self-inflicted injury)	Missing date of death in Vital Statistics
Non-specific Suicidal Behavior or Thoughts	VA	Inpatient OR Outpatient EMR	EMR "Suicide Flag" – 2 weeks on then re-evaluate Suicide Note Clinical text field	Non-missing text	Missing date of death in Vital Statistics

Outcome	Setting	Data Source	Measure	Value(s)	Linked Measures
Undetermined Intent – Fatal Poisoning	VA Community	Inpatient EMR OR Outpatient EMR OR Medicare Claims	Undetermined Intent – Poisoning ICD-9	E980 – E98.2	Matching Date of death, Vital Statistics
Undetermined Intent – Non-Fatal Poisoning	VA Community	Inpatient EMR OR Outpatient EMR OR Medicare Claims	Undetermined Intent – Poisoning ICD-9	E980 – E98.2	Missing Date of death, Vital Statistics
All-Cause Mortality	VA Community	Vital Statistics Master File	Date of Death	NA	NA

Table C2. ICD-9 Codes for Suicidal Behavior and Thoughts (VA and Medicare Data)

ICD-9-CM Diagnoses	Codes
Ideation	V62.84
"Tendencies" or "Risk"	300.9
Attempt/Completed by Trauma	959.9
Attempt/Completed by Poisoning	E950-E952
by anti-depressant	E950.3
by Ibuprofen	E950.0
by carbon monoxide	E952.1
Undetermined Intent - Poisoning	E980-E982
By anti-depressant	E980.3
By ibuprofen	E950.0
By carbon monoxide	E952.1

Table C3. Examples of VA Data Fields for Mediators and Moderators of Suicidal Ideation and Behavior

Mediator/Moderator	Variable and Value
Male	SEX = 1
Married	MARITAL = M
Number of Dependent Children	NODEPS
Number of Dependent Children	NODEPS
Divorced	MARITAL = D
Widowed	MARITAL = W
Catholic	RELIG = 0

REFERENCES

[1]   Ilgen M, Bohnert ASB, Ignacio RV, McCarthy JF, Valenstein MM, Kim M, et al. *Psychiatric diagnoses and risk of suicide in veterans.* Arch Gen Psychiatry. 2010;67(11):1152-8.

[2]   Baldessarinin RG, et al. *Suicide in bi-polar disorder: Risks and management.* CNS Spectr. 20011(6)465-471.

[3]   Nivoli AMA, Colom F, Murru A, Pacchiarotti I, Castro-Loli P, Gonzalez-Pinto A, et al. *New treatment guidelines for acute bipolar depression: A systematic review.* J Affective Disord 129 (2011) 14–26.

[4]   Lavigne JE, Au T, Wu Y, Yi R, Cunningham F, Good JC. *Utilization of Prescription Drugs with warnings of suicidal thoughts and behaviors in the US Department of Veterans Affairs, 2009.* JPHSR. In press.

[5]   US Department of Veterans Affairs/Department of Defense. *Management of Bipolar Disorder (BD) in Adults (2010).* Last accessed 12/22/2011 at: http://www .healthquality.va.gov/Management_of_Bi.asp

[6]   Meltzer HY, Alphs L, Green AI, et al. *International Suicide Prevention Trial Study Group. Clozapine treatment for suicidality in schizophrenia: International Suicide Prevention Trial.* Arch Gen Psychiatry. 2003;60(1):82-91.

[7]   Post RM, Altshuler LL, Frye MA, Suppes T, Keck PE Jr, McElroy SL, Leverich GS, Luckenbaugh DA, Rowe M, Pizzarello S, Kupka RW, Grunze H, Nolen WA. *Complexity of pharmacological treatment required for sustained improvement in outpatients with bipolar disorder.* J Clin Psychiatry. 2010 Sep;7171(9):1176-86.

[8]   Sachs GS, Ice KS, Chappell PB, Schwartz JH, Gurtovaya O, Vanderburg DG, Kasuba B. *Efficacy and safety of adjunctive oral ziprasidone for acute treatment of depression in patients with bipolar I disorder: a randomized, double-blind, placebo-controlled trial.* J Clin Psychiatry. 2011 Oct;72(10):1413-22. Epub 2011 May 3.

[9]   Gibbons RD, Kwan H, Brown CH, Mann JJ. *Relationship between anti-epileptic drugs and suicide attempts in patients with bi-polar disorder.* Arch G Psychiatry. 2009;66 (12):1354-1360.

[10]   Schneeweiss S, Patrick AR, Solomon DH, Mehta J, Dromuth C, Miller M, Less JC, Wang PS. *Variation in the risk of suicide attempts and completed suicides by antidepressant agent in adults: A propensity score-adjusted analysis of 9 years' data.* Arch G Psychiatry. 2010;67(5):497-506.

[11]   Ghaemi SN, Ostacher MM, El-Mallakh RS, Borrelli D, Baldassano CF, Kelley ME, Filkowski MM, Hennen J, Sachs GS, Goodwin FK, Baldassarini RJ. *Antidepressant discontinuation in bipolar depression: a Systematic Treatment Enhancement Program for Bipolar Disorder (STEP-BD) randomized clinical trial of long-term effectiveness and safety.* J Clin Psychiatry. 2010 Apr;71(4):372-80.

[12]   Perlis RH, Ostacher MJ, Miklowitz DJ, Hay A, Nierenberg AA, Thase ME, Sachs GS. *Clinical features associated with poor pharmacologic adherence in bipolar disorder: results from the STEP-BD study.* J Clin Psychiatry. 2010 Mar;71(3):296-303.

[13]   Perlis RH, Ostacher MJ, Miklowitz DJ, Smoller JW, Dennehy EB, Cowperthwait C, Nierenberg AA, Thase ME, Sachs GS. *Benzodiazepine use and risk of recurrence in bipolar disorder: a STEP-BD report.* J Clin Psychiatry. 2010 Feb;71(2):194-200.

[14]   Solomon DH, Rassen JA, Glynn RJ, Lee J, Levin R, Schneeweiss S. *The comparative safety of analgesics in older adults with arthritis.* Arch Intern Med. 2010 Dec 13;170(22):1968-76, (Quote on p. 1968).

[15]   Ray WA, Stein CM. *The aprotinin story--is BART the final chapter?* N Engl J Med. 2008 May 29;358(22):2398-400. Epub 2008 May 14.

[16]   Solomon DH, Rassen JA, Glynn RJ, Garneau K, Levin R, Lee J, Schneeweiss S. *The comparative safety of opioids for nonmalignant pain in older adults.* Arch Intern Med. 2010 Dec 13;170(22):1979-86.

[17]   McCarthy JF, Valenstein M, Kim HM, Ilgen M, Zivin K, Blow FC. *Suicide mortality among patients receiving care in the veterans health administration health system.* Am J Epidemiol. 2009 Apr 15;169(8):1033-8. Epub 2009 Feb 27.

[18]   Kaplan MS, Huguet N, McFarland BH, Newsom JT. *Suicide among male veterans: a prospective population-based study.* J Epidemiol Community Health. 2007 Jul;61(7):619-24.

[19]   Guyatt GH, Oxman AD, Vist G, Kunz R, Falck-Ytter Y, Alonso-Coello P, Schünemann HJ, for the GRADE Working Group. *Rating quality of evidence and strength of recommendations GRADE: an emerging consensus on rating quality of evidence and strength of recommendations.* BMJ 2008;336:924-926.

[20]   Guyatt GH, Oxman AD, Kunz R, Vist GE, Falck-Ytter Y, Schünemann HJ; GRADE Working Group. *Rating quality of evidence and strength of recommendations: What is "quality of evidence" and why is it important to clinicians?* BMJ. 2008 May 3;336(7651):995-8.

[21]   Schünemann HJ, Oxman AD, Brozek J, Glasziou P, Jaeschke R, Vist GE, Williams JW Jr, Kunz R, Craig J, Montori VM, Bossuyt P, Guyatt GH; GRADE Working Group. *Grading quality of evidence and strength of recommendations for diagnostic tests and strategies.* BMJ. 2008 May 17;336(7653):1106-10.

[22]   Guyatt GH, Oxman AD, Kunz R, Jaeschke R, Helfand M, Liberati A, Vist GE, Schünemann HJ; GRADE working group. *Rating quality of evidence and strength of recommendations: Incorporating considerations of resources use into grading recommendations.* BMJ. 2008 May 24;336(7654):1170-3.

[23]   Guyatt GH, Oxman AD, Kunz R, Falck-Ytter Y, Vist GE, Liberati A, Schünemann HJ; GRADE Working Group. *Rating quality of evidence and strength of recommendations: Going from evidence to recommendations.* BMJ. 2008 May 10;336(7652):1049-51.

[24]   Jaeschke R, Guyatt GH, Dellinger P, Schünemann H, Levy MM, Kunz R, Norris S, Bion J; GRADE working group. *Use of GRADE grid to reach decisions on clinical practice guidelines when consensus is elusive.* BMJ. 2008 Jul 31;337:a744.

[25]   Rassen JA, Solomon DH, Glynn RJ, Schneeweiss S. *Simultaneously assessing intended and unintended treatment effects of multiple treatment options: a pragmatic "matrix design".* Pharmacoepidemiol Drug Saf. 2011 Jul;20(7):675-83. doi: 10.1002/pds.2121. Epub 2011 May 30.

[26]   US Department of Veterans Affairs. *Self-Directed Violence Classification System. Self-Directed Violence Toolkit.* Last accessed on 12/29/2011 at: http://www.mirecc.va.gov/visn19/education/nomenclature.asp.

[27] Food and Drug Administration. *U.S. Department of Health and Human Services.
      Center for Drug Evaluation and Research (CDER). (September 2010) Guidance for
      Industry: Suicidality: Prospective Assessment of Occurrence in Clinical Trials.* Last
      accessed on 12/29/2011 at: http://www.fda.gov/downloads/drugs/guidancecompliance
      regulatoryinformation/guidances/ucm225130.pdf

[28] Strom B. (Ed.) *Pharmacoepidemiology.* Wiley, New York (2005).

[29] American Psychiatric Association. (2004) DSM-IV-TR® *Diagnostic and Statistical
      Manual of Mental Disorders.* Last accessed on-line on 12/29/2011 at: http://
      dsm.psychiatryonline.org/book.aspx?bookid=22.

[30] Meyer RE, Salzman C, Youngstrom EA, Clayton PJ, Goodwin FK, Mann JJ, et al.
      *Suicidality and risk of suicide: Definition, Drug Safety Concerns, and a Necessary
      Target for Drug Development.*: A Consensus Statement. J Clin Psychiatry. 2010;71:8
      p. e10.

In: Frontiers in Suicide Risk
Editor: Jill E. Lavigne

ISBN 978-1-62081-373-7
©2012 Nova Science Publishers, Inc.

Chapter 4

BLISTER PACKAGING MEDICATION TO INCREASE TREATMENT ADHERENCE AND CLINICAL RESPONSE: IMPACT ON SUICIDE-RELATED MORBIDITY AND MORTALITY

Peter M. Gutierrez, Lisa A. Brenner, Hal Wortzel, Jeri E. F. Harwood, Rebecca Leitner, Jeffrey Rings and Stephen Bartlett
US Department of Veterans Affairs, Washington, DC, US

ABSTRACT

Medication overdoses account for substantial numbers of cases of self-directed violence (SDV) in several segments of the United States (US) population. The purpose of the study described in this chapter is to determine if medication administration via blister packaging is associated with an increase in treatment adherence and a decrease in intentional overdoses among a high risk population of patients either discharged from psychiatric inpatient units or receiving care in outpatient mental health or substance abuse clinics. As such the research aims are as follows: 1) To explore whether blister packaging medication decreases overall symptom distress; 2) To investigate whether blister packaging medication reduces negative medical and psychiatric outcomes (e.g., emergency department admissions, psychiatric hospitalizations); and 3) To determinewhether blister packaging reduces health care utilization (e.g., clinic visits). If hypotheses are supported, findings from this study will provide evidence that this means of dispensing prescription medications decreases suicide risk through two mechanisms. Specifically, it is expected that increasing adherence will result in a decrease in symptoms reported as well as overall psychological distress. This alone would be expected to decrease an individual's suicide risk. Also, creating appropriate means restriction should result in reduced morbidity and mortality resulting from intentional and accidental overdoses. The theoretical and empirical background, rationale, methods, and measures described in this chapter should help clinicians to appreciate the potential utility of blister packaging medications for their high-risk patients and provide researchers with a promising line of study in the realm of suicide means restriction.

INTRODUCTION

In order to appreciate the rationale behind the study described in this chapter a range of issues related to treatment adherence are reviewed and a summary of what is known about blister packaging and adherence is provided. An overview of the overall prevalence of intentional self-poisoning provides context for the need to study methods to decrease the chances of overdose. Next a summary of the means restriction literature is provided along with a discussion of the interplay of means restriction and adherence, followed by support for blister packaging as means restriction. The introduction concludes with data on the groups at greatest risk of suicide to set the stage for why the specific patient populations were selected for the described study.

First, a clarification of terms is in order. The field of suicidology has been plagued by a lack of consistent terminology, complicating the process of accurate description of behaviors and comparison of results across studies. Two recent efforts (Crosby, Ortega, and Melanson, 2011; Silverman, Berman, Sanddal, O'Carroll, and Joiner, 2007) have sought to address this problem with the development of a single nomenclature for the entire range of behaviors of interest. In this chapter, *self-directed violence (SDV)* is defined as any behavior in which a person engages on purpose which leads to an injury or potential injury (Crosby, Ortega, and Melanson, 2011. A *suicide attempt* is defined as any self-directed behavior with the intention of causing death, with or without injury. *Suicide* is defined as death resulting from intentional self-directed violence. These terms will be used in describing the theory and rationale behind the blister packaging intervention study. When referring to the results of previously published research, the terms used by the authors of those studies will be used.

Definition and Importance of Adherence

Nonadherence, defined as "not having a prescription filled, not taking enough medication, taking too much medication, not observing the correct interval between doses, not observing the correct duration of treatment and taking additional non-prescribed medication" (Bosworth, Oddone, and Weinberger, 2005, p. 149), is a significant issue for those with psychiatric illness. Studies suggest that psychiatric symptoms interfere with adherence and that partial adherence is associated with poorer psychiatric outcomes, including suicide. Specifically, those who are nonadherent are at four to seven times greater risk of death (Llorca, 2008). Among patients with schizophrenia, poor medication adherence has been linked to increases in psychotic symptoms, risk of relapse and rehospitalization, and possibly suicide (Llorca, 2008). Ascher-Svanum and colleagues (2006) examined the relationship between medication adherence and long-term functional outcomes in 1,906 patients with schizophrenia.Nonadherence was associated with greater risks of psychiatric hospitalizations, increased use of emergency psychiatric services, arrests, violence, victimizations, worsening mental health functioning, poorer life satisfaction, an increase in substance use, and an increase in alcohol-related problems. Patients with psychotic disorders struggle equally with adherence to both antipsychotic and nonpsychotropic medications, including antihypertensives, antihyperlipidemics, and antidiabetics (Dolder, Lacro, and Jeste, 2003), suggesting that the medical consequences of nonadherence extend well beyond exacerbation of mental illness. Moreover, poor medication adherence is recognized as a substantial obstacle to optimal treatment across a broad range of medical diagnoses including cardiovascular disease (Wetzels et al., 2006), cancer pain (Miaskowski et al., 2001), chronic obstructive pulmonary disease (Restrepo et al., 2008), and diabetes (Aikens and Piette, 2008). As such, interventions aimed at increasing medication adherence have the potential to positively affect a wide range of patient outcomes.

Blister packaging, a structured means of dispensing medications (Bosworth et al., 2005) is expected to increase medication adherence(and decrease poor outcomes due to nonadherence) in the high risk population of psychiatric inpatients and outpatients in general mental health or specialty clinics. Furthermore, this relatively simple intervention can be accomplished in any treatment setting and does not require any specialized training for pharmacy staff.

Blister Packs and Adherence

Despite well-established problems with medication adherence across a broad range of diagnoses, and the diverse complications that may result, there remains a very limited body of research on interventions aimed at improving treatment adherence. However, several studies addressing the utility of blister packaging suggest that it can be a useful adherence strategy. Connor, Rafter, and Rodgers (2004) performed a systematic review of the literature on improved adherence with fixed-dose combination pills or unit-dose (unit-of-use) packaging (i.e., blister packs and other similar means of dispensing medications). The authors noted that patients responded more positively to simple means of acquiring the correct dose of medication.

As there are no available studies in the psychiatric literature to support the effects of blister packing medication on treatment adherence, data from the broader medical literature is used. Blister packs are a good way to simplify the regimen by making it more clear how much of which medications to take at a time. A study examining the benefit of pre-packaging of a three-day malaria course of medication in Ghana reported significant improvement in treatment adherence compared to standard dispensing (82% adherence in the intervention group versus 60.5% in the control group). Additionally, 50% reductions in both the costs of treatment and clinic waiting time were reported (Yeboah-Antwi et al., 2001). Binstock and Franklin (1988) examined the effects of four adherence strategies on the control of high blood pressure. Their findings included a statistically significant change in both systolic and diastolic blood pressure for those receiving medication in blister packs. Wong and Norman (1987) conducted a prospective, controlled, crossover study of adherence in 22 elderly patients from a geriatric clinic. The authors reported a significant decrease in nonadherence with the blister packs. An eight-month randomized controlled study among 68 diabetic patients with poor glucose control found significant improvement across measures for the blister pack condition relative to controls (Simmons Upjohn, and Gamble, 2000). As noted by Simmons and colleagues (2000, p. 938), "The paucity of reliable evidence about effective strategies for improving adherence is extraordinary." Further consideration of strategies such as blister packaging that could improve adherence, enhance safety, and facilitate better clinical outcomes is needed.

Furthermore, research suggests that both patients and clinicians drastically overestimate the rate of medication adherence (Byerly et al., 2007), suggesting that poor prescription adherence is under recognized as a source of morbidity and mortality. Approximately 20% of changes in adherence are associated with clinically significant differences in outcomes such as symptom report and re-hospitalization (Llorca, 2008).

Prevalence of Intentional Self-Poisoning

Beyond adherence to medication regimens, another unfortunate issue for many patients is taking more medication than they should. Medication overdoses account for a substantial percentage of self-directed violence behaviors in several segments of the US population, including the US military. For example, data from a study of psychiatric admissions in a sample of Veterans Affairs (VA) patients with traumatic brain injury (TBI) indicated that the majority of suicide attempts made by these patients were by overdose on prescribed medications (Gutierrez, Brenner, and Huggins, 2008). Specifically, half of the suicide attempts in this sample were by overdose and of those 57% used one or more of prescription medications. Intentional overdoses have also been identified as a significant problem in Department of Defense Warrior Transition Units (Jelinek, 2008).

Worldwide, intentional self-poisoning is responsible for 90% of suicide-related hospital admissions annually (Beautrais, 2007) and 5 to7% of acute medical admissions (Chan, Critchley, Chan, and Yu, 1994). Chan et al. (1994) reviewed records of all patients admitted to one-half of the general medical wards at a major teaching hospital in Hong Kong over a three-year period. They found that 96% of admissions were due to self-poisoning, with hypnotics/sedatives accounting for 33% of overdoses. In Finland, over a review of more than 7000 emergency department visits to a district hospital over a six-month period determined that 2.3% of visits were drug-related (Juntti-Patinen, Kuitunen, Pere, and Neuvonen, 2006). Of those, 39% were intentional overdoses. The vast majority (60%) of drugs ingested during overdoses were psychotropics, with anti-anxiety, anti-psychotic, and anti-depressants constituting the medications of choice.

A patient history of intentional overdose is associated with a striking mortality rate. In Norway researchers followed 952 patients (1125 total admissions) discharged after medical treatment for overdose (intentional and unintentional) and found that 37.5% had died within 20 years (Bjornaas, Jacobsen, Haldorsen, and Ekeberg, 2009).. Risk of death by suicide was highest in the first year after discharge when the standardized mortality ratio (SMR) was 36.5, followed by an SMR of 36.1 in the first five years after discharge, and 26.65 for the entire 20-year period. Of the patients who died by suicide during the study period, 57% died by intentional overdose suggesting that a persistent major risk of prescription medication overdose. The authors also found that among patients expressing suicide intent upon initial admission following an overdose, risk of death by suicide in the follow-up period was 3.1 times higher than for those not endorsing intent. Overall, the authors concluded that treatment for overdose is a significant risk factor for early death, most strikingly by suicide, and that better management of these patients is warranted. This study also highlights the potential benefits of preventing a first overdose and the concomitant risk associated with it. The question that arises is how to prevent individuals from engaging in intentional overdoses and other forms of self-directed violence.

Means Restriction

The most well-known and widespread limiting of access to means took place in the United Kingdom (UK) when domestic gas for heating and cooking was switched from coal gas containing high concentrations of carbon monoxide to less lethal North Sea natural gas (Hawton, 2007). Prior to this switch, carbon monoxide poisoning was the most frequent cause of suicide deaths in the UK. The change was followed by a sizable decrease in the number of suicides due to carbon monoxide poisoning, with no significant increase in suicides by other methods.

Evidence supporting blister packaging medications is based on the means restriction literature (Beautrais, 2007; Hawton, 2007; Lin and Lu, 2006; Nordentoft, 2007). Hawton (2007) noted that method availability can have a large impact on the survivability of self-directed violence, as most impulsive acts use whatever means is most readily available. Therefore, dispensing prescription medications in blister packs can serve as a method of means restriction.

In addition, Hawton went on to state that for most individuals considering self-directed violence, their strongest impulses may only last a few minutes, suggesting that the additional time required to extract medications out of a blister pack could be enough to prevent a potentially lethal episode of self-directed violence. Even more importantly, after extensively reviewing the suicide prevention literature, Hawton concluded that the vast majority of individuals who engage in self-directed violence (even those surviving near lethal self-directed violence) do not go on to die by suicide or even engage in subsequent self-directed violence using another method. His conclusion further supports the hypothesis that restricting access to means through blister packaging medications could have a generalizable effect on patient suicide rates.

These conclusions are not limited to medication overdoses. An ingenious study in Taiwan (Lin and Lu, 2006) found a strong association between easy access to methods and method-specific suicide rates. In rural areas where highly toxic pesticides are readily available, the majority of suicides result from ingestion of these substances, whereas most people living in urban areas with tall buildings who die by suicide do so by jumping from a height. There were no significant differences noted between rural and urban areas in the proportion of people selecting what the authors termed "equal access methods" (e.g., hanging) after means restriction was implemented. This study provides further evidence that individuals often select the most readily available means of suicide, and that efforts aimed at reducing access should result in lower morbidity and mortality.

Means Restriction and Adherence

Increased adherence via means restriction is expected to decrease overdoses and subsequent suicides. There is evidence from the UK and Australia that legislation requiring changes in medication packaging has led to reductions in the total number of tablets taken in overdose, and subsequent decreased morbidity and mortality (Buckley, Newby, Dawson, and Whyte, 1995; Hawton, 2002; Hawton et al., 2004; Hawton et al., 2001; Prince, Thomas, James, and Hudson, 2000; Robinson, Smith, and Johnston, 2000; Turvill, Burroughs, and Moore, 2000).

Research regarding adults in the UK who attempted suicide by overdose on paracetamol (known as acetaminophen (Tylenol) in the United States) indicated that most acts were impulsive and dependent upon packages of the drug available in the home at the time of overdose (Hawton, 2002). It was therefore hypothesized that the legislation changes in the UK would have a suicide prevention effect.

As expected, altering means of provision from paracetamol in bottles to blister packs resulted in beneficial outcomes. Turvill, Burroughs, and Moore (2000) noted a 21% decrease in all overdoses, including a 64% decrease in what the authors termed "serious overdoses." The authors also looked at rates of overdose on benzodiazepines, the second leading drug on which individuals in the UK intentionally overdose, and found no notable changes.

This finding provides preliminary evidence that means substitution did not happen after restricting access to the primary drug of choice for overdose. Prince, Thomas, James, and Hudson (2000) focused on serious paracetamol overdoses by comparing numbers of patients admitted to a major liver transplant unit and the UK liver transplant register before and after the legislation change. (Liver damage is commonly associated with paracetamol (acetaminophen) overdose.) Significant decreases in admissions and referrals for transplant were noted and attributed to the legislation change.

Robinson, Smith, and Johnston (2000) reported similar decreases in the total number of intentional paracetamol overdoses in the Belfast area as well as in the amount of drug taken in single overdoses. Hawton et al. (2001) undertook a prospective study examining the effects of the legislation change on a variety of outcomes related to paracetamol overdose. The number of pills ingested significantly decreased, there was a 30% decrease in admissions to liver units, and there was a 66% decrease in the number of liver transplants performed.

In a follow-up study, Hawton et al. (2004) examined national data on deaths due to paracetamol overdoses, admissions to liver units, and number of liver transplants, as well as non-fatal self-poisonings over an eight-year period. In the three years following the legislation, 118 fewer individuals in the UK died as a result of paracetamol overdose. Fewer admissions to liver units and subsequent transplants were observed.

Whereas UK studies have focused on the impact of over the counter preparations, an Australian project (Buckley, Newby, Dawson, and White, 1995) focused on prescription carbamazepine, an anticonvulsant used primarily to treat nerve pain or seizures. Based on knowledge that many adult overdoses are relatively impulsive, Australia passed legislation mandating that carbamazepine be dispensed in blister packs. Buckley et al. compared data on carbamazepine self-poisonings at a large regional hospital serving a population of approximately 300,000 before and after the packaging change.

An exclusionary period was utilized to account for those who had supplies of the drug still in bottles.After the mandated switch to blister packaging, the number of patients presenting for emergent care following an intentional overdose feel by 30 percent. In addition, after the legislation, overdoses involved fewer pills (a mean of 7 compared to 20 prior to the change) and smaller doses (a mean of 3,000mg before and 1,400mg after).

Blister Packaging as Means Restriction

Some of the impact of blister packaging on reducing self-directed violence morbidity and mortality may be due to slowing down the process of intentional overdose. As previously stated, acute crises are typically of short duration. Hawton, Cole, O'Grady, and Osborn (1982) reported that one-half of the adolescent suicide attempters (by overdose) in their study had thought about the act for 15 minutes or less and that 60% of them regretted the attempt upon recovery. They compared their results to previous research with adults and found adolescent and adult motivational factors to be quite similar. Therefore, actions designed to delay the person in the midst of a crisis can decrease intent. This effect has been cited as one reason that suicide crisis lines are effective (Kalafat, Gould, Munfakh, and Kleinman, 2007). By requiring extra effort, blister packaging essentially restricts access to means (Chan, 2000; Friedman, 1996; Gunnell et al., 1997). There is also evidence that the increase in time required to gain access to pills in blister packs may be enough to dissuade someone from taking a lethal overdose (Chan, 1997; Hawton et al., 1996). The Hawton study was conducted prior to the UK legislation changes in paracetamol packaging, but examined differences in 80 adult suicide attempts where the paracetamol used was in bottles versus blister packs. Those who had access to bottles of pills were three times more likely to ingest 25 or more pills than those who only had access to blister packs. Interestingly, there were no significant differences in degree of planning or suicide intent between the two groups. Chan's (2000) review of means restriction studies concluded that packaging all medications known to be potentially lethal in overdose in blister packs, smaller quantities, or both is a reasonable suicide prevention approach. Friedman (1996) presented preliminary data on suicide attempts resulting from the ingestion of 50 or more paracetamol tablets, and found that in only one such overdose (out of 14 total) were the tablets from a blister pack rather than a bottle.

Groups at Greatest Risk of Suicide

Taking the above information on treatment adherence and means restriction into consideration, the research team selected a patient population most likely to benefit from a blister packaging intervention and for whom decreasing risk of self-directed violence is highly salient. Psychiatric patients whose disorders are serious enough to require inpatient hospitalization are at increased risk of a range of self-directed violence behaviors. For example, Skeem, Silver, Aippelbaum, and Tiemann (2006) followed over 950 patients for one year post-discharge and found that almost 18% of them had made a suicide attempt. Self-poisoning was the most frequent (39.1%) means of suicide attempt. Those diagnosed with major depression or personality disorders were most likely to make an attempt following discharge. It is also well established that a significant number of suicides occur following discharge from a psychiatric inpatient unit (McKenzie and Wurr, 2001). Meehan et al. (2006) reviewed all registered suicide deaths in England and Wales over a four-year period and found that 23% died within three months of discharge from a psychiatric inpatient unit. Of those who died following hospitalization, 32% were within two weeks of discharge, and the largest number of those deaths was on the first day. Self-poisoning was a frequent cause of suicide in those who died post-discharge. A history of poor treatment adherence was common in these individuals; the treating clinicians believed that as many as 30% of these deaths might have been prevented by better medication adherence. Most recently, Valenstein et al. (2009) reported that among Veterans being treated for depression, suicide rates were highest in the first 12 weeks following discharge from a psychiatric inpatient unit. This finding is notable as the authors based their analyses on data from over 880,000 individuals, constituting the entire population of VA patients treated for depression during the study period. Therefore, their conclusion that suicide prevention resources should be targeted at those recently discharged from a psychiatric inpatient unit following treatment for depression carries significant weight.

Individuals suffering from major mental illnesses are at elevated risk of engaging in self-directed violence behaviors (Maris, Berman, and Silverman, 2000), and are also the group of mental health patients most in need of medications. A recent study examining data from over 39,000 Swedish patients admitted for suicide attempts determined that risk of death by suicide was greatest in the year following discharge (Tidemalm, Waern, Stefansson, Elofsson, and Runeson, 2008). Major affective disorders, substance abuse disorders, and personality disorders are among the forms of psychopathology most strongly associated with suicide risk (Appleby, 1992; Mościcki, 1999). Individuals with personality disorders are also at elevated risk of death by suicide (Maris et al., 2000). Another group of individuals at elevated risk of suicide are those with substance use disorders (Conner, Beautrais, and Conwell, 2003; Modesto-Lowe, Brooks, and Ghani, 2006; Suominen, Isometsä, Haukka, and Lönnqvist, 2004). In one study (Suominen et al., 2004), alcohol-dependent men died by suicide at a rate over three times higher than those in the general population. Patients diagnosed with schizophrenia died by suicide at a rate 8.5 times that of the general population (Montross, Zisook, and Kasckow, 2005), making suicide the leading cause of death for this group of patients. In fact, the vast majority of people who die by suicide in the US each year have one or more diagnosable mental health disorders (Goldsmith, Pellmar, Kleinman, and Bunney, 2002).

What follows is a summary of the methods employed in a study currently being conducted at a large urban VA medical center, testing the impact of blister packaging medications on treatment adherence. It is expected that, in addition to improving treatment adherence, participants receiving prescription medications dispensed in blister packs will have overall better clinical outcomes and will engage in less self-directed violence by means of medication overdose.

METHODS

Participants and Procedures

Participant Recruitment. This study is currently underway. Patients discharged from the psychiatric inpatient unit of the medical center or receiving care in the outpatient mental health or substance abuse clinics are invited to participate in this study based on the criteria articulated below. A total of 414 patients will participate in the study over a 24-month period, resulting in 207 per condition. Review of drop-out rates in other clinical trials, all of which had more complex protocols for patients to follow than the current study, indicate attrition of between 23% and 48% (Claassen et al., 2009; Keith, 2001).

Because a study of this kind has not yet been conducted, procedures developed for providing participants their medications in blister packs have not been assessed for feasibility. Therefore, in addition to the 414 participants needed to test the study hypotheses, 25 initial participants are recruited solely for the purpose of feasibility assessment. These recruits are all assigned to the blister pack condition and provided with a two-week supply of medication followed by one two-week refill. In addition to completing all study measures they are surveyed by phone at the end of the first and third weeks regarding their experiences with receiving medications in blister packs. Pharmacy procedures are also audited to ensure complete compliance with the dispensing protocol (see below). Their responses are then used to make adjustments to study procedures deemed necessary to maintain patient safety and procedural efficacy.

Participant retention. A rigorous methodology is being used to decrease patient attrition and increase compliance with follow-up assessments (Claassen et al., 2009). Specifically, the study relies on telephone-based follow-up which has been shown to reduce attrition and missing data for participants who stayed enrolled in clinical trials. A training manual was developed and used for training research staff and ongoing study management. During the process of securing patient informed consent, potential participants are provided with a detailed explanation of the study via a Participant Roles/Responsibilities document which explains their responsibilities as participants and provides them with contact information for reaching the study team. They are given ample opportunity to ask questions. In order to ensure further patient understanding of the study, only English-speaking participants are being recruited. In consultation with providers, arrangements are made to conduct the baseline assessment either prior to the participant being discharged from the inpatient unit or while they are in the medical center for another appointment. This approach decreases the inconvenience of participation for patients. As often as possible, the same study coordinator maintains contact with the participant throughout the course of the study in order to establish and maintain rapport. Additionally, the study coordinator maintains notes on each follow-up interaction which supports personal, but professional contact. Coordinators may give pre-paid phone cards to participants who would otherwise need to pay for a long distance phone call to reach the study team. Use of this methodology by Claassen et al. in a large multi-site study of treatment of depression in community mental health centers successfully limited missing data for the primary outcome measure to 3.2% and contained attrition at 37.5% over a one year period. The methodology employed in the current study is also consistent with principles of quality improvement utilized in the STAR*D multicenter trial of depression treatment (Warden et al., 2005).

Patients meeting the following criteria are eligible to participate:

- Age 18 or older
- Diagnosed with one of the following (or any combination of these diagnoses):
  o   Major affective disorder,
  o   Bipolar affective disorder,
  o   Posttraumatic stress disorder, or
  o   Schizophrenia
- Currently prescribed and receiving medications from the hospital pharmacy
- Deemed capable of managing their own medications
- Not currently serving on active duty in any branch of the military
- Able to correctly answer questions verifying understanding of the consent form (see below)

- Receiving treatment from the inpatient unit, outpatient mental health or substance-abuse treatment programs
- Not enrolled in any other investigational studies
- English-speaking

The diagnostic groups were selected due to the increased risk of suicide associated with each disorder (Desai, Dausey, and Rosenheck, 2008). At a time deemed appropriate by his or her provider, the study is briefly introduced to the patient by a member of the study staff. If the potential subject is interested, then the clinician pages a member of the research team who comes to provide the potential subject with information about the study and obtain informed consent. Patients are provided a copy of the study consent form, have the opportunity to ask questions about the study, and are assured that regardless of their decision regarding participation, they will continue to receive the same care at the medical center. Due to the potential that complete confidentiality cannot be guaranteed for active duty personnel (because information bearing on a Soldier's health may be required to be reported to appropriate medical or command authorities), such personnel are excluded from participation in the study.

To assess subjects' ability to provide consent to participate, a series of questions adapted from Janofsky, McCarthy, and Folstein (1992) is posed. If subjects are not able to adequately respond to these questions, they are excluded from participation. The questions are as follows: 1) What are you being asked to do? 2) Finish this sentence - The purpose of this study is to find out...3) True or False - After beginning this study, you can decide not to continue at any time, without penalty. 4) What should you do if you have questions about this study? and, 5) Who should you call if you feel you have been harmed in the study? Additionally, participants recruited from the inpatient unit who were on mental health holds must complete a competency measure prior to the baseline assessment to further ensure that they are capable of participating in the study. Prior to the baseline and all follow-up assessments, participants are asked if they have any questions or concerns about the study. They are also asked to affirm their continued consent to participate.

Randomization to Condition. Consenting patients are randomly assigned in a 1:1 ratio to either receive their medications in blister packs or via traditional methods used by the medical center's pharmacy. A randomization schedule was created in advance by utilizing specialized computer software specifically designed for this purpose (nQuery Advisor 7.0 [www.statistical-solutions-software.com]). The randomization is stratified according to inpatient or outpatient recruitment location. The condition the participant is assigned remains blinded to the study staff administering the study assessments. The participants are advised not to disclose the type of medication packaging they receive to any study staff. Dedicated pharmacy staff members are responsible for randomization, dispensing medications in the appropriate packaging (i.e., blister packs vs. pill bottles), counseling participants on the use of their assigned packaging, and all related record keeping.

Pharmacy Procedures. Patients enrolled in this study receive all their medications as usually prescribed. The only difference is that half of the patients receive their oral medications in traditional prescription vials and the other half of participants receives their oral medications in blister packs. Once the study pharmacist verifies that the patient has consented to be in the study via the VA electronic medical record system, they then refer to the randomization list and determine if the patient is to receive medications via regular packaging or blister packs. If regular packaging, then the filled prescriptions are picked up by the patient in the main pharmacy. If randomized to blister packaging, then the study pharmacist repackages each medication as described in the following section. Notations are entered in the pharmacy tracking system to ensure that refill requests are also routed to the study pharmacist for correct packaging. All participants are instructed in how to safely dispose of any old medications they have on hand. Those in the blister pack condition are instructed not to remove medications from the packs until it is time to take a dose. At the conclusion of study participation, pharmacy records are updated to ensure that all patients revert to receiving their prescriptions in standard pill bottles as usual.

Blister Packs. There are a wide variety of blister packs available on the market. These range from packs that hold single daily doses for up to a one-month supply to packs that hold up to four doses per day for a one-week period. In this study, only two types of packs are being used. For drugs that require more than once daily dosing, a pack containing up to four doses per day for a seven day period is used. Each day has a blister designated for a morning, noon, evening and bedtime dose. The medication is placed in the blisters that are appropriate for the dosing of the medication. For medications with a single daily dose and as needed (PRN) medications, a one-month supply pack is used. Limiting the number of possible pack configurations minimizes the potential for patient confusion and repackaging errors. Each medication is packaged in separate blister packs regardless of medication schedule. That is, medications with the same schedule are not packaged in the same blister pack. For each month of medication each patient receives one blister pack for daily and/or PRN medications and four blister packs for greater-than-once daily medications. The blister packs used in the study are cold-sealed.. This has the advantage of quicker and easier packaging and eliminating any concern about medication degradation from heat-seal process.

Assessment Schedule. Baseline testing occurs prior to discharge from the inpatient unit or at a time convenient for outpatients (e.g., prior to a regularly scheduled appointment in the medical center). After baseline testing (Table 1), all patients are assessed on a monthly basis, by telephone, for adherence with their medication regimen, overall psychiatric symptom distress, and self-directed violence. This means of follow-up is convenient for patinets in both urban and rural settings, and has been shown to produce comparable data to in-person assessments without the many logistical challenges associated with decreased participation rates (Claassen et al., 2009). Patients are compensated $25 for the baseline assessment and for each subsequent telephone assessment. This amount has been found to be sufficient for maintaining participation in studies with similar follow-up demands (Claassen et al.). Checks are mailed after each completed follow-up assessment, unless it is easier for the participant to pick up the payment in person, in which case alternative arrangements are made. Secondary data is extracted from participants' VA electronic medical records including timing of medication refills (i.e., early versus late), total number of clinic visits, emergency department and intensive care unit admissions for overdose, and psychiatric inpatient admissions. Information regarding services sought outside the VA also is gathered via a questionnaire administered at each follow-up assessment. Patients are followed for a period of 12 months from study enrollment. After the final follow-up assessment, participants are sent a thank-you letter which acknowledges the importance of their participation in the study and informs them that they will be reverting to their pre-study form of receiving medications.

This follow-up schedule was selected to maximize data points for detecting the outcomes of interest without placing an undue assessment burden on participants.

Measures

The majority of data collected from participants is in the form of self-reports. While there are limitations to this approach, a significant literature base exists supporting its use, particularly in studies of psychological disorders and suicide. Kaplan et al. (1994) reported that, just like the clinical interview, self-report instruments are useful in assessing a wide range of suicide risk factors, including frequency of ideation, previous attempts, and threats of future attempts. In addition, self-report instruments have the advantage of obtaining reliable information about recent suicidal ideation and risk factors that the individual otherwise may not openly communicate. Self-report measures also allow for simple and direct evaluation of symptom severity, especially when the chosen instruments have well-established norms and cut-off scores, and can be administered at multiple points in time (Kendall, Cantwell, and Kazdin, 1989). When the variables of interest are primarily internal affective states and cognitions, one must rely on the individuals' subjective evaluations of these states. Although there are reasons to question self-report data, there are few viable alternatives. Benefits of self-report measures include standardized administration, wording, and ordering of questions. In most cases, self-report questionnaires are preferable to interviews in that they are faster to administer and are more efficient (Eyman and Eyman, 1990). For example, a group of outpatients with a history of prior ideation, past suicide attempts, or current suicidal ideation completed the Harkavy-Asnis Suicide Survey (Harkavy-Friedman and Asnis, 1989) and were interviewed face-to-face regarding suicidal thoughts and behaviors (Kaplan et al., 1994). The authors calculated the Kappa coefficients between the two data sources for a variety of suicide-related behaviors. Kappas ranged from 0.63 for suicidal thoughts in the past week to 1.0 for family history of suicide deaths. Twice as many participants endorsed current ideation on the self-report measure than they had during the interview. The authors concluded that self-report measures of suicide-related behavior are valuable in clinical settings where clients may be more comfortable with the response format.

A summary of the study outcomes, informant type, data source, and timing of data gathering is provided in Table 1.

Demographics. A demographic form is used to summarize information on variables deemed to be important for describing the sample and examining potential sub-group differences. Information is collected from the patients and their medical records on age, gender, ethnicity, and marital status. Patients are asked to indicate their highest level of education attained, highest military rank achieved, VA service connection percentage, drug and alcohol abuse/dependence diagnoses, history of traumatic brain injury, and any problems with the legal system.

The Mini-International Neuropsychiatric Interview-Version 5.0.0 (MINI 5.0.0; Sheehan et al., 2005), a validated psychiatric interview for both the DSM-IV TR and ICD-10, is used to assess for PTSD (current), hypo/manic episode (current/past), major depressive episode (current/recurrent), dysthymia (current), panic disorder (current/lifetime), agoraphobia (current), social anxiety disorder (current), obsessive compulsive disorder (current), alcohol/substance abuse and dependence (past 12 months), generalized anxiety disorder (current), and psychotic disorders, including mood disorder with psychotic features (current/lifetime). Mental health diagnosis is defined as meeting criteria for any current diagnosis on the MINI and it provides confirmation of diagnosis in patients' medical records for purposes of evaluating inclusion criteria.

Brief Adherence Rating Scale (BARS; Byerly, Nakonezny, and Rush, 2008) is a useful measure of medication adherence validated against electronic pill bottle monitoring.

Table 1. Summary of the study outcomes, informant type, data source, and timing of data gathering

Measurement Matrix			
Outcome	Informant	Data Source	Timing (months)
Clinical Diagnosis	Structured interview	MINI	baseline
Treatment Adherence	Self-report	BARS	2-12
	Self-report	BARS-PRN	2-12
Suicide-related Behaviors	Structured interview	SHBQ-Follow-Up	baseline
	Structured interview	SHBQ-R-Follow-Up	2-12
Symptom Distress	Self-report	OQ-45	1-12
Health Status (covariate)	Self-report	SF-36	1-12
ED Visits due to OD	Structured interview	SHBQ-R-Follow-Up	2-12
-VA and non-VA	Records	VA Medical	2-12
ICU Admits due to OD	Structured interview	SHBQ-R-Follow-Up	2-12
-VA and non-VA	Records	VA Medical	2-12
Psychiatric Admissions	Structured interview	SHBQ-R-Follow-Up	2-12
-VA and non-VA	Records	VA Medical	2-12
Health Care Utilization	Records	VA Medical	2-12
-for all clinic visits	Self-report	UQ	2-12

Note: Timing refers to participant month in the study, not overall month of the project. MINI = The Mini-International Neuropsychiatric Interview; BARS = Brief Adherence Rating Scale; BARS-PRN = Brief Adherence Rating Scale for PRN medications; SHBQ = Self-Harm Behavior Questionnaire; SHBQ-R = Revised Self-Harm Behavior Questionnaire with timeframe of "since we last spoke", rather than lifetime; OQ-45 = Outcome Questionnaire 45-item version; SF-36 = Medical Outcomes Study Short Form-36; UQ = Utilization Questionnaire.

The BARS is based upon three questions which Byerly et al. adapted from a more extensive adherence questionnaire developed by McEvoy (2003) and utilized in the CATIE trial. The three questions are: 1) Number of prescribed doses per day; 2) Number of days, over the past month, the patient did not take the prescribed doses; and 3) Number of days, over the past month, the patient took less than the prescribed doses. The responses to these three inquiries are then utilized by the clinician to rate adherence on an overall visual analog rating scale that assesses the proportion of doses taken by the patient over the past month. This rating is the primary outcome measure of medication adherence. A separate BARS is completed for each prescription medication the patient is taking. The BARS demonstrated good sensitivity (73%) and specificity (74%) for detecting patient non-adherence as defined as < 70% mean electronic monitoring adherence, a frequent means of monitoring medication adherence (e.g., Byerly et al., 2007; Diaz et al., 2001). Additionally, greater mean BARS adherence was associated with lower scores on the Positive and Negative Syndrome Scale. Byerly et al. (2008) offer the BARS as a valid, reliable, sensitive and specific tool for approximating medication adherence. The brief nature of the BARS makes it ideal for repeated use in follow-up administrations by phone where one goal is to keep the time burden on participants to a minimum.

Modified BARS (BARS-PRN). In order to assess adherence with PRN medications, minor modifications were made to the standard BARS questions to assess adherence with these medications. No valid and reliable measure specifically for assessing PRN medication adherence was identified in the literature, so this minor modification was deemed acceptable. Reliability and validity of the BARS-PRN is being assessed based on collection of preliminary data, and modifications will be made if deemed necessary after those analyses. Because these are medications to be taken "as needed", adherence was defined as not using up a monthly supply in less than a month. Therefore, the third question was changed to "Over the month since your last visit with me, how many days did you TAKE MORE THAN the prescribed number of pills of your _____ (name of medication)". A separate BARS-PRN is completed for each prescription medication the patient is taking. This rating is the primary outcome of adherence for PRN medications.

Self-Harm Behavior Questionnaire (SHBQ; Gutierrez, Osman, Barrios, and Kopper, 2001). The SHBQ was designed as a self-report measure composed of four sections, each assessing different facets of suicidality (Gutierrez and Osman, 2008). However, it is being administered as an interview, so that follow-up questions can be asked by a member of the research team to ensure accurate data recording. It should be noted that during initial development of this instrument it was used as an interview (Gutierrez, 2001). It provides the necessary data to determine history of suicide attempts prior to study enrollment. The section on non-suicidal self-injury captures information about unintentional overdoses, as it provides prompts related to injury/harm resulting from means other than suicide attempts. Reliability analyses suggest high Cronbach alpha estimates for scores on all SHBQ subscales (Gutierrez and Osman, 2008) and Fliege et al. (2006) reported strong test-retest reliability estimates for each subscale over intervals of 7 to 150 days for adult psychiatric inpatients. Correlations between scores on the SHBQ and a number of validated self-report measures provide adequate evidence for the concurrent-convergent validity of this instrument (Gutierrez and Osman, 2008). In addition to its strong psychometric properties, this measure was chosen because of the research team's familiarity with its scoring and interpretation as it is a primary assessment tool used by their Suicide Consultation Service (Gutierrez et al., 2009). Administering it as an interview rather than a self-administered instrument should not markedly alter its psychometric properties as self-report items are not being altered. Rather, all follow-up questions will be read to every participant.

SHBQ Follow-up. In order to assess history of suicidality during the study period, the SHBQ has been revised so that participants are cued to provide information regarding events occurring over the past month. For example, "Have you ever hurt yourself on purpose?" and "In the past month have you hurt yourself on purpose?". As with the modifications to the BARS described above, this minor change is not assumed to affect the psychometrics of the

SHBQ. To confirm this belief, reliability and validity are being assessed as preliminary data are collected, and modifications made as necessary based on the results of those analyses.

Outcome Questionnaire-45 The OQ-45(Lambert et al., 1996a) is a 45-item questionnairedesigned to measure key areas of mental health functioning (symptoms, interpersonal problems and social role functioning). As such, it is a widely-accepted tool for identifying, tracking, and measuring behavioral health treatment outcomes (Maruish, 2001).The total score is the measure of symptom distress utilized in study analyses. Items were selected due to their common occurrence across a wide variety of disorders, and according to Lambert and Finch (1999) assess personally and socially relevant characteristics that impact quality of life. Moreover, this tool has a history of being used in suicide research (Lambert and Fowler, 1997; Jobes Wong, Conrad, Drozd, and Neal-Walden, 2005). Clinical cut off scores are available for the total and each subscale to aid in interpretation (Lambert and Finch 1999). Reliable Change Indexes (RCI) can also be used to monitor patient status over time (Lambert et al., 1996b). The measure possesses good psychometric properties when used with adult psychiatric patients (Lambert et al., 1996a; Lambert et al., 1996b; Umphress, Lambert, Smart, Barlow, and Clouse, 1997). Acceptable internal consistency and test-retest reliabilities have been reported (Maruish, 2001). Finally, Umphress et al. (1997) analyzed the concurrent and construct validity of the measure, and findings were generally supportive.

Medical Outcomes Study Short Form-36 (SF-36; Ware, Kosinski, and Gandek, 2000) The SF-36 is a quality of life outcome-assessment instrument that is being used as a summary health status measure. The SF-36 contains 36 items and yields a physical and mental health summary score, as well as eight individual scales (United States Department of Veterans Affairs, 2006). The physical health summary score is used as a covariate. In various populations, internal consistency for the scales has been shown to be at least 0.70 (Ware et al., 2000). Convergent and discriminant validity studies have been conducted and are outlined in the SF-36 user's manual (Ware et al., 2000). Of note, Gulf War Veterans who reported current physical or mental health disorders had significantly lower scores on the SF-36 than those without such conditions (Voelker et al., 2002). This measure has been widely used in Veteran populations (USDVA, 2006).

Utilization Questionnaire. A brief questionnaire was developed to inquire about treatment utilization outside of the VA Health Care System. Patients are asked if they have been treated at emergency departments and inpatient facilities (non-psychiatric), and the reason for the treatment. Combined with information drawn from their VA medical records, this provides a comprehensive assessment of their treatment utilization patterns for testing study hypotheses.

CONCLUSION

While few empirical studies of suicide means restriction have been conducted, there is ample evidence that means restriction is a viable suicide prevention strategy. There is also strong evidence that blister packaging increases patients' adherence with prescription drug treatment. The project described in this chapter is the first wide-scale effort to determine if blister packaging of psychiatric patients' medications increases their adherence with treatment, improves clinical outcomes, and decreases self-directed violence by medication overdose. This approach is theoretically-based and feasible (e.g., blister packaging can be easily implemented by any pharmacy). Until final data analyses are complete, clinicians are cautiously encouraged to consider ordering blister packaging of prescription medications for patients who may be at highest risk for suicide. There are no known increased risks to patients of blister packs, and potentially significant benefits. Researchers interested in studying means restriction are welcome to employ the methods described in this chapter in their work. Additionally, replication of this methodology to independently study the impact of blister packaging medications in other settings is encouraged. Despite recognition of the magnitude of suicide as a public health problem in the US, and indeed throughout the world, and significant widespread efforts to prevent suicide, suicide rates in the US have remained essentially unchanged for decades (Crosby et al., 2011). All reasonable interventions with the potential to alter this reality should be considered and rigorously tested.

AUTHOR'S NOTE

This work was supported in part by Department of Defense grant W81XWH-09-1-0723 awarded to the first author. Additional resources and facilities provided by the VA VISN 19 MIRECC at the Denver VA Medical Center, Denver, Colorado. The contents do not represent the views of the Department of Defense, Department of Veterans Affairs or the United States Government.

REFERENCES

Appleby, L. (1992). Suicide in psychiatric patients: Risk and prevention. *British Journal of Psychiatry, 161*, 749–758. doi:10.1192/bjp.161.6.749doi: 10.1192/bjp.161.6.749 doi: 10.1192/bjp.161.6.749 doi: 10.1192/bjp.161.6.749.

Aikens, J. E., and Piette, J. D. (2008). Diabetes patients' medication underuse, illness outcomes, and beliefs about antihyperglycemic and antihypertensive treatments. *Diabetes Care, 32*, 19–24. doi:10.2337/dc08-1533

Ascher-Svanum, H., Faries, D. E., Zhu, B., Ernst, F. R., Swartz, M. S., and Swanson, J. W. (2006). Medication adherence and long-term functional outcomes in the treatment of schizophrenia in usual care. *Journal of Clinical Psychiatry, 67*, 453–460. doi:10.4088/ JCP.v67n0317.

Beautrais, A. (2007). The contribution to suicide prevention of restricting access to methods and sites. *Crisis, 28(Suppl. 1)*, 1–3. doi:10.1027/0227-5910.28.S1.1.

Binstock, M. L., and Franklin, K. L. (1988). A comparison of compliance techniques on the control of high blood pressure. *American Journal of Hypertension, 1*, 192S–194S. Retrieved from http://www.nature.com/ajh/index.html.

Bjornaas, M. A., Jacobsen, D., Haldorsen, T., and Ekeberg, O. (2009). Mortality and causes of death after hospital-treated self-poisoning in Oslo: A 20-year follow-up. *Clinical Toxicology, 47*, 116–123. doi:10.1080/15563650701771981.

Bosworth, H. B., Oddone, E. Z., and Weinberger, M. (2005). *Patient Treatment Adherence: Concepts, interventions, and measurement.* New York: Routledge.

Buckley N. A., Newby, D. A., Dawson, A. H., and Whyte, I. M. (1995). The effect of the introduction of safety packaging for carbamazepine on toxicity in overdose in adults. *Pharmacoepidemiology and Drug Safety, 4,* 351–354. doi:10.1002/pds.2630040606.

Byerly, M. J., Nakonezny, P. A., and Rush, A. J. (2008). The Brief Adherence Rating Scale (BARS) validated against electronic monitoring in assessing the antipsychotic medication adherence of outpatients with schizophrenia and schizoaffective disorder. *Schizophrenia Research, 100,* 60–69. doi:10.1016/j.schres.2007.12.470.

Byerly, M. J., Thompson, A., Carmody, T., Bugno, R., Erwin, T., Kashner, M., and Rush, A. J. (2007). Validity of electronically monitored medication adherence and conventional adherence measures in schizophrenia. *Psychiatric Services, 58,* 844–847. doi:10.1176/appi.ps.58.6.844.

Chan, T. Y. K. (2000). Improvements in the packaging of drugs and chemicals may reduce the likelihood of severe intentional poisonings in adults. *Human and Experimental Toxicology, 19,* 387–391. doi:10.1191/096032700678816142.

Chan, T. Y. K. (1997). Packaging of drugs and the risk of severe toxicity in adult self-poisonings. *Journal of Clinical Pharmacy and Therapeutics, 22,* 157–158. doi:10.1046/j. 1365-2710.1997.8675086.x.

Chan, T. Y. K., Critchley, J. A. J. H., Chan, M. T. V., and Yu, C. M. (1994). Drug overdosage and other poisoning in Hong Kong – The Prince of Wales Hospital (Shatin) experience. *Human and Experimental Toxicology, 13,* 512–515. doi:10.1177/0960327194 01300711.

Claassen, C., Kurian, B., Trivedi, M. H., Grannemann, B. D., Tuli, E., Pipes, R., Preston, A. M., ... Flood, A. (2009). Telephone-based assessments to minimize missing data in longitudinal depression trials: A project IMPACTS study report. *Contemporary Clinical Trials, 30,* 13–19. doi:10.1016/j.cct.2008.08.001.

Conner, K. R., Beautrais, A. L., and Conwell, Y. (2003). Risk factors for suicide and medically serious suicide attempts among alcoholics: Analyses of Canterbury Suicide Project Data. *Quarterly Journal of Studies on Alcohol, 64,* 551–554. Retrieved from http://www.jsad. com/sad/static/about.html.

Connor, J., Rafter, N., and Rodgers, A. (2004). Do fixed-dose combination pills or unit-of-use packaging improve adherence? A systematic review. *Bulletin of the World Health Organization, 82,* 935–939. Retrieved from http://www.who.int/bulletin/en/.

Crosby, A. E., Ortega, L., and Melanson, C. (2011). *Self-directed violence surveillance: Uniform definitions and recommended data elements, Version 1.0.* Atlanta, GA: Centers for Disease Control and Prevention, National Center for Injury Prevention and Control.

Desai, R. A., Dausey, D., and Rosenheck, R. A. (2008). Suicide among discharged psychiatric inpatients in the Department of Veterans Affairs. *Military Medicine, 173,* 721–728. doi:10.1007/s11414-007-9092-0.

Diaz, E., Levine, H. B., Sullivan, M. C., Sernyak, M. J., Hawkins, K. A., Cramer, J. A., and Woods, S. W. (2001). Use of the Medication Event Monitoring System to estimate medication compliance in patients with schizophrenia. *Journal of Psychiatry and Neuroscience, 26,* 325. Retrieved from http://www.cma.ca/index.php/ ci_id/12267/ la_id/1.htm.

Dolder, C. R., Lacro, J. P., and Jeste, D. V. (2003). Adherence to antipsychotic and nonpsychiatric medications in middle-aged and older patients with psychotic disorders. *Psychosomatic Medicine, 65,* 156–162. doi:10.1097/01.PSY.0000040951.22044.59.

Eyman, J. R., and Eyman, S. K. (1990). Suicide risk and assessment instruments. In P. Cimbolic and D. A. Jobes (Eds.), *Youth suicide: Issues, assessment, and intervention.* (pp. 9–32). Springfield, IL: Charles C. Thomas.

Fliege, H., Kocalevent, R., Walter, O. B., Beck, S., Gratz, K. L., Gutierrez, P. M., and Klapp, B. F. (2006). Three assessment tools for deliberate self-harm and suicide behavior: Evaluation and psychopathological correlates. *Journal of Psychosomatic Research, 61,* 113–121. doi:10.1016/j.jpsychores.2005.10.006.

Friedman, T. (1996). Paracetamol overdose. *British Journal of Psychiatry, 168,* 519. doi:10.1192 /bjp.168.4.519b.

Goldsmith, S. K., Pellmar, T. C., Kleinman, A. M., and Bunney, W. E. (Eds.) 2002. *Reducing suicide: A national imperative.* Washington, DC: The National Acadamies Press.

Gunnell, D., Hawton, K., Murray, V., Garnier, R., Bismuth, C., Fagg, J., and Simkins, S. (1997). Use of paracetamol for suicide and nonfatal poisoning in the UK and France: Are restrictions on availability justified? *Journal of Epidemiology and Community Health, 51,* 175–179. doi:10.1136/jech.51.2.175.

Gutierrez, P. M., Brenner, L. A., and Huggins, J. A. (2008). A preliminary investigation of suicidality in psychiatrically hospitalized veterans with traumatic brain injury. *Archives of Suicide Research, 12,* 336–343. doi:10.1080/13811110802324961.

Gutierrez, P. M., Brenner, L. A., Olson-Madden, J. H., Breshears, R., Homaifar, B. Y., Betthauser, L. M., Staves, P., Adler, L. E. (2009). Consultation as a means of Veteran suicide prevention. *Professional Psychology: Research and Practice, 40,* 586–592. doi:10 .1037/a0016497.

Gutierrez, P. M., Osman, A., Barrios, F. X., and Kopper, B. A. (2001). Development and initial validation of the Self-Harm Behavior Questionnaire. *Journal of Personality Assessment, 77,* 475–490. doi:10.1207/S15327752JPA7703_08.

Gutierrez, P. M., and Osman, A. (2008). *Adolescent suicide: An integrated approach to assessment of risk and protective factors.* DeKalb, IL: Northern Illinois University Press.

Harkavy-Friedman, J. M., and Asnis, G. M. (1989). Assessment of suicidal behavior: A new instrument. *Psychiatric Annals, 19,* 382–387. Retrieved from http://www. psychiatricann alsonline.com.

Hawton, K. (2002). United Kingdom legislation on pack sizes of analgesics: Background, rationale, and effects of suicide and deliberate self-harm. *Suicide and Life-Threatening Behavior, 32,* 223–229. doi:10.1521/suli.32.3.223.22169.

Hawton, K. (2007). Restricting access to methods of suicide: Rationale and evaluation of this approach to suicide prevention. *Crisis, 28(Suppl. 1),* 4–9. doi:10.1027/0227-5910.28.S1.4.

Hawton, K., Cole, D., O'Grady, J., and Osborn, M. (1982). Motivational aspects of deliberate self-poisoning in adolescents. *British Journal of Psychiatry, 141,* 286–291. doi:10.1192/bjp. 141.3.286.

Hawton, K., Simkin, S., Deeks, J., Cooper, J., Johnston, A., Waters, K., and Simpson, K. (2004). UK legislation on analgesic packs: Before and after study of long term effect on poisonings. *British Medical Journal, 329,* 1076–1080. doi: 0.1136/bmj.38253. 572581.7C.

Hawton, K., Townsend, E., Deeks, J., Appleby, L., Gunnell, D., Bennewith, O., and Cooper, J. (2001). Effects of legislation restricting pack sizes of paracetamol and salicylate on self poisoning in the United Kingdom: Before and after study. *British Medical Journal, 322,* 1203–1207. doi: 10.1136/bmj.322.7296.1203.

Hawton, K., Ware, C., Mistry, H., Hewitt, J., Kingsbury, S., Roberts, D., and Weitzel, H. (1996). Paracetamol self-poisoning: Characteristics, prevention, and harm reduction. *British Journal of Psychiatry, 168,* 43–48. doi:10.1192/bjp.168.1.43.

Janofsky, J. S., McCarthy, R. A., and Folstein, M. F. (1992). The Hopkins Competency Assessment Test: A brief method for evaluating patients' capacity to give informed consent. *Hospital and Community Psychiatry, 43,* 132–136. Retrieved from http://www. psych.org/.

Jelinek, P. (2008, February 11). Drug deaths among wounded troops investigated. *Army Times.* Retrieved from http://www.armytimes.com/news/2008/02/ap_drugdeaths _080208w/.

Jobes, D. A., Wong, S. A., Conrad, A., Drozd, J. F., and Neal-Walden, T. (2005). The collaborative assessment of and management of suicidality vs. treatment as usual: A retrospective study with suicidal outpatients. *Suicide and Life-Threatening Behavior, 35,* 483–497. doi:10.1521/suli.2005.35.5.483.

Juntti-Patinen, L., Kuitunen, T., Pere, P., and Neuvonen, P. J. (2006). Drug-related visits to a distric hospital emergency room. *Basic and Clinical Pharmacology and Toxicology, 98,* 212–217. doi:10.1111/j.1742-7843.2006.pto_264.x.

Kalafat, J., Gould, M. S., Munfakh, J. L. H., and Kleinman, M. (2007). An evaluation of crisis hotline outcomes part 1: Nonsuicidal crisis callers. *Suicide and Life-Threatening Behavior, 37,* 322–337. doi:10.1521/suli.2007.37.3.322.

Kaplan, M. L., Asnis, G. M., Sanderson, W. C., Keswani, L., DeLecuona, J. M., and Joseph, S. (1994). Suicide assessment: Clinical interview vs. self-report. *Journal of Clinical Psychology, 50,* 294–298. doi:10.1002/1097-4679(199403)50:2<294::AID-JCLP2270 500224>3.0.CO;2-R.

Keith, S. J. (2001). Evaluating characteristics of patient selection and dropout rates. *Journal of Clinical Psychiatry, 62(Suppl 9),* 11–14. Retrieved from http://www.ascpp.org/pages. aspx?PanelID=0andPageName=Journal_of_Clinical_Psychiatry.

Kendall, P. C., Cantwell, D. P., and Kazdin, A. E. (1989). Depression in children and adolescents: Assessment issues and recommendations. *Cognitive Therapy and Research, 13,* 109–146. doi:10.1007/BF01173268.

Lambert, M. J., Burlingame, G., Umphress, V., Hansen, N., Vermeersch, D., Clouse, G., and Yanchar, S. C. (1996a). The reliability and validity of the Outcome Questionnaire. *Clinical Psychology and Psychotherapy, 3,* 249–258. doi:10.1002/(SICI)1099-0879(199612)3:4<249::AID-CPP106>3.3.CO;2-J.

Lambert, M. J., and Finch, A. E., (1999). Outcome Questionnaire. In M. E. Maruish (Ed.), *The use of psychological testing for treatment planning and outcome assessment,* (2nd ed.). Mahwah, NJ: Lawrence Erlbaum Associates.

Lambert, M. T., and Fowler, D. R. (1997). Suicide risk factors among veterans: Risk management in the changing culture of the Department of Veterans Affairs. *Journal of Mental Health Administration, 24*, 350–358. doi:10.1007/BF02832668.

Lambert, M. J., Hansen, N. B, Umphress, V., Lunnen, K., Okiishi, J., Burlingame, G. M., and Reisinger, C. W. (1996b). *Administration and scoring manual for the Outcome Questionnaire (OQ 45.2)*. Wilmington, DE: American Professional Credentialing Services.

Lin, J.-J., and Lu, T.-H. (2006). Association between the accessibility to lethal methods and method-specific suicide rates: An ecological study in Taiwan. *Journal of Clinical Psychiatry, 67*, 1074–1079. doi:10.4088/JCP.v67n0709.

Llorca, P. M. (2008). Partial compliance in schizophrenia and the impact on patient outcomes. *Psychiatry Research, 161*, 235–247. doi:10.1016/j.psychres.2007.07.012.

Maris, R. W., Berman, A. L., and Silverman, M. M. (2000). *Comprehensive textbook of suicidology*. New York: The Guilford Press.

Maruish, M. E. (2001). *Psychological testing in the age of managed behavioral healthcare*. Mahwah, NJ: Lawrence Erlbaum Associates. doi:10.4088/JCP.v67n0709.

McEvoy, J. P. (2003). *CATIE Adherence Questionarre*. Unpublished manuscript.

McKenzie, I., and Wurr, C. (2001). Early suicide following discharge from a psychiatric hospital. *Suicide and Life-Threatening Behavior, 31*, 358–363. doi:10.1521/suli.31.3.358.24244.

Meehan, J., Kapur, N., Hunt, I. M., Turnbull, P., Robinson, J., Bickley, H.,Appleby, L. (2006). Suicide in mental health in-patients and within 3 months of discharge. *British Journal of Psychiatry, 188*, 129–134. doi: 10.1192/bjp.188.2.129.

Miaskowski, C., Dodd, M. J., West, C., Paul, S. M., Tripathy, D., Koo, P., and Schumacher, K. (2001). Lack of adherence with the analgesic regimen: A significant barrier to effective cancer pain management. *Journal of Clinical Oncology, 19*, 4275–4279. Retrieved from http://jco.ascopubs.org/content/by/year .

Modesto-Lowe, V., Brooks, D., and Ghani, M. (2006). Alcohol dependence and suicidal behavior: From research to clinical challenges. *Harvard Review of Psychiatry,14*, 241–248. doi:10. 1080/10673220600975089.

Montross, L. P., Zisook, S., and Kasckow, J. (2005). Suicide among patients with schizophrenia: A consideration of risk and protective factors. *Annals of Clinical Psychiatry, 17*, 173–182. doi:10.1080/10401230591002156.

Mościcki, E. K. (1999). Epidemiology of suicide. In D. G. Jacobs (Ed.), *The Harvard Medical School guides to suicide assessment and intervention* (40-51). San Francisco: Jossey-Bass Publishers.

Nordentoft, M. (2007). Restrictions in availability of drugs used for suicide. *Crisis, 28(Suppl. 1)*, 44–49. doi:10.1027/0227-5910.28.S1.44.

Prince, M. I., Thomas, S. H. L., James, O. F. W., and Hudson, M. (2000). Reduction in incidence of severe paracetamol poisoning. *The Lancet, 355*, 2047–2048. doi:10.1016/S0140-6736 (00)02354-0.

Restrepo, R. D., Alvarez, M. T., Wittnebel, L. D., Sorenson, H., Wettstein, R., Vines, D. L.,Wilkins, R. L. (2008). Medication adherence issues in patients treated for COPD. *International Journal of Chronic Obstructive Pulmonary Disease, 3*, 371–384. Retrieved from http://www.dovepress.com/international-journal-of-chronic-obstructive-pulmonary-disease-journal.

Robinson, D., Smith, A. M. J., and Johnston, G. D. (2000). Severity of overdose after restriction of paracetamol availability: Retrospective study. *British Medical Journal, 321,* 926–927. doi :10.1136/bmj.321.7266.926.

Sheehan, D., Janavs, J., Baker, K., Harnett-Sheehan, K., Knapp, E., and Sheehan, M. (2005). *Mini International Neuropsychiatric Interview*: English Version 5.0.0. Tampa, FL: University of South Florida.

Silverman, M. M., Berman, A. L., Sanddal, N. D., O'Carroll, P., and Joiner, T. E. Jr. (2007). Rebuilding the Tower of Babel: A revised nomenclature for the study of suicide and suicidal behaviors. *Suicide and Life-Threatening Behavior, 37,* 248-277. doi:10.1521 /suli.2007.37.3.264.

Simmons, D., Upjohn, M., and Gamble, G. D. (2000). Can medication packaging improve glycemic control and blood pressure in type 2 diabetes? Results from a randomized controlled trial. *Diabetes Care, 23,* 153–156. doi:10.2337/diacare.23.2.153.

Skeem, J. L., Silver, E., Aippelbaum, P. S., and Tiemann, J. (2006). Suicide-related behavior after psychiatric hospital discharge: Implications for risk assessment and management. *Behavioral Sciences and the Law, 24,* 731–746. doi:10.1002/bsl.726.

Suominen, K., Isometsä, E., Haukka, J., and Lönnqvist, J. (2004). Substance use and male gender as risk factors for deaths and suicide: A 5-year follow-up study after deliberate self-harm. *Social Psychiatry and Psychiatric Epidemiology, 39,* 720–724. doi:10.1007/s00127-004-0796-7.

Tidemalm, D., Waern, M., Stefansson, C. G., Elofsson, S., and Runeson, B. (2008). Excess mortality in persons with severe mental disorder in Sweden: A cohort study of 12,103 individuals with and without contact with psychiatric services. *Clinical Practice and Epidemiology in Mental Health, 4,* 23. Retrieved from http://www.cpemen talhealth.com/.

Turvill, J. L., Burroughs, A. K., and Moore, K .P. (2000). Change in occurrence of para-cetamol overdose in UK after introduction of blister packs. *The Lancet, 355,* 2048–2049. doi:10. 1016/S0140-6736(00)02355-2.

Umphress, V. J., Lambert, M. J., Smart, D. W., Barlow, S. H., and Clouse, G. (1997). Concurrent and construct validity of the Outcome Questionnaire. *Journal of Psycho educational Assessment, 15,* 40–55. doi:10.1177/073428299701500104.

United States Department of Veterans Affairs Health Services Research and Development. (2006, June). Medical Outcomes Study 36-Item Short-Form Health Survey (SF-36). Retrieved from *http://www.hsrd.research.va.gov/for_researchers/measurement/ instrument/instrument_rev iews2.cfm?detail=54.*

Valenstein, M., Kim, H. M., Ganoczy, D., McCarthy, J. F., Zivin, K., Austin, K. L.,Olfson, M. (2009). Higher-risk periods for suicide among VA patients receiving depression treatment: Prioritizing suicide prevention efforts. *Journal of Affective Disorders, 112*(1-3), 50–58. doi: 10.1016/j.jad.2008.08.020.

Voelker, M. D., Saag, K. G., Schwartz, D. A., Chrischilles, E., Clarke, W. R., Woolson, R. F., and Doebbeling, B. N. (2002). Health-related quality of life in Gulf War era military personnel. *American Journal of Epidemiology, 155,* 899–907. doi:10.1093/ aje/ 155.10.899.

Warden, D., Rush, A. J., Trivedi, M., Ritz, L., Stegman, D., and Wisniewski, S. R. (2005). Quality improvement methods as applied to a multicenter effectiveness trial – STAR*D. *Contemporary Clinical Trials, 26,* 95–112. doi:10.1016/j.cct.2004.11.011.

Ware, J. E., Kosinski, M., and Gandek, B. (2000). *SF-36 Health Survey: Manual and interpretation guide*. Lincoln, RI: QualityMetric Incorporated. doi:10.1097/00007632-200012150-00008.

Wetzels, G., Nelemans, P., van Wijk, B., Broers, N., Schouten, J, and Prins, M. (2006). Determinants of poor adherence in hypertensive patients: Development and validation of the "Maastricht Utrecht Adherence in Hypertension (MUAH)-questionnaire". *Patient Education and Counseling, 64,* 151–158. doi:10.1016/j.pec.2005.12.010.

Wong, B. S., and Norman, D. C. (1987). Evaluation of a novel medication aid, the calendar blister-pak, and its effect on drug compliance in a geriatric outpatient clinic. *Journal of the American Geriatric Society, 35,* 21–26. Retrieved from http://www.wiley.com/bw/journal.asp?ref=0002-8614.

Yeboah-Antwi, K., Gyapong, J. O., Asare, I. K., Barnish, G., Evans, D. B., and Adjei, S. (2001). Impact of prepackaging antimalarial drugs on cost to patients and compliance with treatment. *Bulletin of the World Health Organization, 79,* 394–399. Retrieved from http:// www.who.int/bulletin/en/.

CLINICAL SUICIDE RISK ASSESSMENT AND MANAGEMENT

In: Frontiers in Suicide Risk
Editor: Jill E. Lavigne

ISBN 978-1-62081-373-7
©2012 Nova Science Publishers, Inc.

Chapter 5

ADVANCES IN MOTIVATIONAL INTERVIEWING TO ADDRESS SUICIDAL IDEATION (MI-SI)

Peter C. Britton

Clinical Psychologist, US Department of Veterans Affairs,
Center of Excellence for Suicide Prevention,
Canandaigua Medical Center, New York, US

ABSTRACT

Motivational Interviewing (MI) is a client-centered, directive method for helping people explore and resolve their ambivalence about changing. After providing support for its efficacy through clinical trials, investigators began to examine the underlying mechanisms by which MI works, leading to advances in the theory of MI. This chapter describes Motivational Interviewing to Address Suicidal Ideation (MI-SI), an adaptation developed to help suicidal clients explore and resolve their ambivalence about living. We build on MI-SI by applying recent advances in the theory of MI to better understand how MI-SI might be used to resolve suicidal crises.

INTRODUCTION

Motivational Interviewing (MI) is a brief, one or two session intervention that was developed as a person-centered alternative to the traditional twelve-step and behavioral approaches to treating problem drinking (W. R. Miller and Rollnick, 2002). The efficacy of the intervention led researchers to apply it to a variety of problems including suicide prevention (Britton, Patrick, and Williams, 2011; Britton, Williams, and Conner, 2008). Although MI was based on a specific set of principles and techniques, it was born of clinical experience and refined through a series of studies with unanticipated findings and therefore lacked an underlying theory. A growing literature of MI process and outcome research has contributed to the development of a theory of MI (Miller and Rose, 2009). This chapter is devoted to describing MI and its underlying theory, applying the theory to suicide prevention, and exploring the nuances of using an MI-based approach with clients who are in a suicidal crisis.

Motivational Interviewing

MI is "a client-centered, directive method for enhancing intrinsic motivation to change by exploring and resolving ambivalence" (Miller and Rollnick, 2002). Among the insights that led to its development was the recognition that individuals with substance use disorders are often ambivalent about their use. They have reasons to change such as medical, legal, and relational problems, but also have reasons to continue. Change usually requires effort such as the development of new coping skills and comes at a cost including the loss of relationships with other users. MI was developed to help clients align with their reasons for changing hazardous substance use, and to increase the likelihood that they will. Although originally developed for individuals with alcohol-related problems, MI has been found to be efficacious across a number of health-related behaviors, such as diet, exercise, medication compliance, and treatment engagement (Hettema, Steele, and Miller, 2005).

The Theory of MI

As MI became established as an efficacious intervention (i.e., Bien, Miller, and Boroughs, 1993; Brown and Miller, 1993), researchers became increasingly interested in how it works and developed rating systems that could be used by independent observers to code in-session behavior. The Motivational Interviewing Skills Code (MISC) (Miller, Moyers, Ernst, and Amrhein, 2003; Moyers, Martin, Catley, Harris, and Ahluwalia, 2003) is a valid and reliable measure of clinician characteristics, and clinician and client behaviors during sessions. Likert scales with detailed anchors are used to rate clinicians'global MI skills, and clinician and client behavior counts are used to assess specific MI-related verbalizations. However, researchers also wanted the ability to study clinician and client verbal exchanges, and their association with treatment outcome. This led to the development of the Motivational Interviewing Sequential Code for Observing Process Exchanges (MI-SCOPE) (Martin, Moyers, Houck, Christopher, and Miller, 2005), an advanced coding system that allows researchers to sequentially code clinician and client behaviors to better understand the treatment process and its impact on outcome. Research using these tools has led to the development of the theory of MI and suggests that MI works through both interpersonal and technical pathways (Miller and Rollnick, 2002).

MI Spirit

The interpersonal pathway is based on Carl Rogers' critical components of change (Rogers, 1957), which emphasized creating an interpersonal environment that supports individuals' inherent capacity for growth. MI clinicians are trained to be empathic and to have the ability to understand their clients and communicate their understanding with them. They also embody the "spirit" of MI and are *evocative, collaborative, autonomy supportive,* and yet *directive* (Miller and Rollnick, 2002). MI clinicians believe that the necessary elements for change are within clients, and their job is to *evoke* and strengthen them. Clients are experts on themselves and clinicians need to *collaborate* with clients to find out what they want to change, and how change can be achieved. Clinicians' are explicitly *autonomy supportive* because any decision to change must originate in clients, as people are more motivated when they make their own decisions and clients need to maintain their motivation after they leave the therapy room. However, contrary to Roger's person-centered approach, MI clinicians are also *directive* and work towards a desired outcome that is associated with healthier and more adaptive living.

Process research using the MISC rating scales has indicated that both empathy and the spirit of MI contribute to good treatment outcome. Both clinician empathy and the MI spirit have been found to be associated with a strong therapeutic alliance and increased client in-session involvement (Boardman, Catley, Grobe, Little, and Ahluwalia, 2006). The spirit of MI has been shown to increase client cooperation, disclosure, expression of affect, and in-session talk about making changes (Catley et al., 2006; Moyers, Miller, and Hendrickson, 2005), and clinician empathy has been found to be positively associated with treatment outcome (Gaume, Gmel, and Daeppen, 2008). Combined, these findings indicate that empathy and the MI spirit may improve the therapeutic relationship and client engagement, which increases post-treatment behavior change.

MI Techniques

The technical pathway focuses directly on clinician and client communication. The central technique in MI is *reflective listening,* which also formed the basis for Roger's person-centered therapy (Rogers, 1957). Reflective listening requires clinicians to listen to clients and share their understanding to ensure that clients feel heard. Other techniques that are used in MI include *open questions*, *affirmations*, and *summaries*. MI clinicians use open questions to elicit their clients' perspective, affirmations to reinforce desired verbalizations, and summaries to help integrate events, thoughts, and feelings into a coherent narrative. Different from person-centered therapists, MI clinicians are directive and selectively use these techniques to promote "change talk" or talk suggesting movement towards change, and reduce "resistance" or "sustain talk" or talk concerning maintaining the maladaptive behavior (Miller and Rollnick, 2002). Increased change talk and decreased sustain talk are hypothesized to be in-session predictors of post-session behavior change. The use of MI techniques (i.e., reflections, open questions, affirmations, and summaries) is therefore expected to increase change talk and decrease sustain talk, which are expected to improve treatment outcome.

The association between clinician and client verbalizations has been examined in several studies using the sequential measure, the MI-SCOPE. Findings have shown that the use of reflections, open questions, affirmations, and summaries were likely to be followed by change talk (Gaume, Gmel, Faouzi, and Daeppen, 2008; Moyers and Martin, 2006; Moyers et al., 2007; Vader, Walters, Prabhu, Houck, and Field, 2010), but unlikely to be followed by sustain talk (Moyers and Martin, 2006; Moyers et al., 2007). Conversely, MI inconsistent techniques such as confrontation, denial, and warning were likely to be followed by sustain talk (Moyers and Martin, 2006; Moyers et al., 2007), but unlikely to be followed by change talk (Gaume et al., 2008). These associations may be bi-directional as client change talk encourages the use of MI techniques (Moyers and Martin, 2006). Together, these findings support the use of MI techniques to increase change talk and decrease sustain talk, and caution against the use of MI inconsistent techniques such as confrontation, denial, and warning, which may increase sustain talk and decrease change talk. Interestingly, the use of MI inconsistent techniques such as confrontation may improve outcome *if* the clinician is high in MI spirit (Moyers et al., 2005), indicating that confrontation can be helpful in the context of a strong therapeutic relationship.

Although early studies did not find an association between the frequency of change talk and treatment outcome (Miller, Yahne, and Tonigan, 2003; Miller, Benefield, and Tonigan, 1993), later studies using the MISC supported the association. Turning to the linguistic literature, researchers organized change talk into different categories, *preparatory talk* that emphasizes the desire, ability, reasons, and need to change, and *commitment talk* that indicates that the client has decided to change, and examined the association between the strength (rather than frequency) of these categories and treatment outcome (Amrhein, Miller, Yahne, Palmer, and Fulcher, 2003).

Analyses indicated that preparatory talk increased the likelihood of commitment talk, which predicted good treatment outcome. Importantly, commitment talk had a stronger association with change at the end of the session than across the session. Subsequent research has been supportive of the importance of change and sustain talk, with some qualifications. In some studies, both preparatory and commitment talk have been found to be associated with a good outcome (Martin, Christopher, Houck, and Moyers, 2011; Vader et al., 2010). In others, only ability talk or commitment talk were associated with a positive outcome (Gaume et al., 2008; Hodgins, Ching, and McEwen, 2009). As expected, sustain talk was associated with poorer outcomes (W. R. Miller et al., 1993; Vader et al., 2010), but it was related to positive outcomes when it transitioned to change talk during the session (Bertholet, Faouzi, Gmel, Gaume, and Daeppen, 2010).

These associations may also impact the outcome of non-MI psychotherapies. In a study examining the associations in cognitive-behavioral therapy, overall commitment strength was associated with positive treatment outcome, while commitment strength at the end of the session was associated with treatment retention (Aharonovich, Amrhein, Bisaga, Nunes, and Hasin, 2008).

These studies supported the hypothesized associations, but did not test the full causal model. When tested, the use of MI techniques predicted client change talk which predicted positive treatment outcome, as expected (Moyers, Martin, Houck, Christopher, and Tonigan, 2009). Helpful for understanding how MI works, the model has also been used to explain why MI is sometimes ineffective. In a randomized controlled trial of MI for drug abuse, MI did not significantly impact post-treatment drug use (Miller et al., 2003).

When researchers examined the poor outcome group, they found that the clients' commitment language increased during the session, but decreased during the last ten minutes (Miller and Rose, 2009). They noted that the treatment manual required clients to develop a change plan regardless of whether they were ready or not, which may have undermined the motivation of clients who were not ready to do so. This interpretation was supported by a meta-analysis that showed that MI was more effective in studies that did not use a manual, indicating that listening to clients is more important than following the manual (Hettema et al., 2005). It was also supported by a study suggesting that MI techniques and client change talk were associated with the decision to complete a change plan but sustain talk was associated with the decision not to complete a plan (Magill, Apodaca, Barnett, and Monti, 2010).

AMBIVALENCE AND SUICIDALITY

Clinical experience with substance abusing clients who were thinking about suicide led to the application of MI to suicide prevention. Like individuals with substance abuse disorders, people who think about suicide are often ambivalent. They see suicide as means of escaping severe emotional and/or physical pain (Shneidman, 1996), but fear death and injury, feel responsible for loved ones, fear what others might think, or believe that suicide is morally wrong (Jobes and Mann, 1999; Linehan, Goodstein, Nielsen, and Chiles, 1983), and sometimes remember that they once looked forward to special events such as vacations and trips abroad and even more mundane activities such as putting a roof on a house, watching an interesting television show, and eating a favorite meal. Understanding this ambivalence may be critical to treating suicidal clients. Kovacs and Beck wrote that the "overt suicidal act is viewed as the outcome of the internal subjective struggle between the wish to live and the wish to die, rather than the consequence of a single unidirectional motivation (Kovacs and Beck, 1977)." Research testing this hypothesis shows that outpatients who wanted to die more than they wanted to live made more severe attempts (Kovacs and Beck, 1977), and were more likely to die by suicide (Brown, Steer, Henriques, and Beck, 2005). This, however, may work both ways as individuals who want to live as much or more than they want to die may be less likely to attempt and die by suicide (Britton et al., 2008).

Enhancing and resolving suicidal individuals' ambivalence provides an opportunity for intervention. However, working with people who have intensely conflicting feelings is challenging, as they often have to consider both sides of their ambivalence before they know where they stand. If clinicians take one side, clients may want the clinicians to understand the complexity of the decision and will describe the other side. Consequently, clinicians who try to convince suicidal clients to continue living may unintentionally pressure their clients into defending their suicidality. Cognitive-Dissonance Theory (Festinger, 1957) and Self-Perception Theory (Bem, 1967) suggest that this may be problematic. Cognitive-Dissonance Theory posits that people who are experiencing dissonance because their behavior contradicts their beliefs find it easier to change their beliefs. Self-Perception Theory argues that ambivalent individuals decide what they believe by listening to themselves speak. Both theories suggest that clients who are defending their suicidality may convince themselves that suicide is indeed an option. Clinicians must therefore learn how to help clients explore their ambivalence about suicide in a way that increases their desire to live, without reinforcing their suicidality. Motivational Interviewing to Address Suicidal Ideation (MI-SI) may provide one means of doing so.

MOTIVATIONAL INTERVIEWING TO ADDRESS SUICIDAL IDEATION (MI-SI)

MI-SI was developed as a method for addressing ambivalence about living by enhancing the motivation to live and engage in life-enhancing activities (Britton et al., 2008). The overarching goal of MI-SI is to shift motivation away from suicide and towards living and recovery. It is a one to two session intervention that consists of three phases: 1) exploring the presenting problem, 2) building the motivation to live, and 3) strengthening the commitment to living. In *phase 1*, clinicians meet suicidal clients where they are by exploring the presenting problem and how it is contributing to their suicidal thoughts. In *phase 2*, clinicians help clients explore why they are still alive and explore their core beliefs and values to enhance their motivation to live. At the end of this phase, clients often say that they want to live, but that life remains too painful. In *phase 3*, clinicians instill hope and strengthen clients' confidence so that they can establish a life worth living by helping them develop a concrete plan.

THE THEORY OF MOTIVATIONAL INTERVIEWING AND SUICIDE PREVENTION

The application of the theory of MI to suicide prevention proposes a model for how MI-SI works (see Figure 1). It posits an interpersonal pathway through which empathy, evocation, collaboration, and autonomy support increases treatment engagement, thereby increasing its effectiveness. These characteristics may also reduce risk by increasing *living talk*, or talk that indicates that the individual is thinking about living or making life worth living, and decreasing *suicide talk*, or talk that indicates that the individual is thinking about suicide, which may be associated with reduced risk. It also proposes a technical pathway through which clinicians use MI techniques including open questions, reflections, affirmations, and summaries to increase the motivation to live and reduce risk. The strategic use of these techniques may also increase living talk and decrease suicide talk, further reducing clients' risk. Seemingly simple and straightforward, a more detailed discussion is needed to explain how these processes can be applied to suicidal clients.

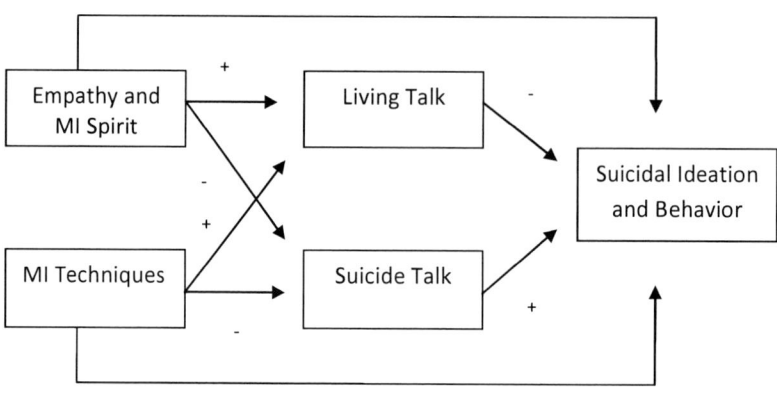

Figure 1. Interpersonal and Technical Mechanisms of MI-SI.

Empathy, MI Spirit, and Suicide Prevention

The theory of MI suggests that clinician empathy, evocation, collaboration, and autonomy support may enable clinicians to develop a positive therapeutic relationship with suicidal clients and allow them to direct the session towards a positive outcome. The therapeutic alliance is a known predictor of treatment outcome (Horvath and Symonds, 1991; Martin, Garske, and Davis, 2000; Zuroff and Blatt, 2006), and suicidologists recommend that therapists who work with suicidal patients should be empathic (Orbach, 2001), validating (Linehan, 1993), and collaborative (D. A. Jobes, 2010).

A strong therapeutic relationship may be particularly important for suicidal clients as it may help them overcome the stigma associated with suicide, the fear of involuntary hospitalization, and the sense of isolation that often accompanies suicidality (Joiner, 2006). Although there is little alliance research with suicidal clients, studies are generally supportive. In a study of suicide hotline calls, a person-centered approach was associated with reduced depression over the course of the call (Mishara and Daigle, 1997). A follow-up study found that empathy and respect, support and good contact, and collaborative problem-solving were also associated with improved call outcomes (Mishara et al., 2007). Overall, these findings indicate that empathy, evocation, collaboration, autonomy support, and direction may enhance the therapeutic process with suicidal clients, thereby improving treatment outcome.

Supporting the autonomy of individuals who are suicidal is more complicated than supporting the autonomy of individuals with substance use disorders. In alcohol treatment, relapses are common, rarely fatal, and often result in additional treatment episodes (Anglin, Hser, and Grella, 1997; Miller, Walters, and Bennett, 2001). If clients continue to abuse alcohol, they often experience additional consequences which may increase their motivation to change.

Change can therefore be viewed as a process, albeit with hills and valleys, through which clinicians can support clients' autonomy while reinforcing their motivation to change. In treatment with suicidal clients, the potential consequences of continued suicidality are serious injury or death. There is also institutional pressure to minimize the risk of litigation and legal responsibility to protect clients from themselves, which rightly limits clinicians' ability to support the autonomy of suicidal clients.

To truly support clients' autonomy, clinicians must acknowledge their limitations and inform clients of the rules of engagement, including the need to break confidentiality and take protective action if the client is deemed to be a danger to self or others. The description of autonomy supportive counselors in the MISC provides further insight, as it is conceptualized as a dimensional construct indicating that there are degrees of autonomy support. It is described thusly:

> "Autonomy supportive counselors accept that clients can choose not to change. They may be invested in specific behavior changes, but do not push for an immediate commitment at the expense of "taking the long view" about the option of change in the future. They emphasize the client's freedom of choice, and convey an understanding that the critical variables for change are within the client and cannot be imposed by others (W. R. Miller et al., 2003, pp. 5.)"

Ultimately, clinicians have little control over suicidal clients as no-harm contracts and hospitalization are often ineffective (Appleby et al., 1999; Goldacre, Seagroatt, and Hawton, 1993; Meehan et al., 2006; Qin and Nordentoft, 2005; Rudd, Mandrusiak, and Joiner, 2006). Understanding that suicidal clients are truly autonomous might actually be critical as loss of autonomy and autonomy-related power struggles may tip the balance towards or away from suicidal behavior (Filiberti et al., 2001; Hendin, Haas, Maltsberger, Koestner, and Szanto, 2006; Jobes, 2011). The proposed model suggests that clinicians should avoid pushing "for an immediate commitment" at the beginning of the session as it may backfire and increase the amount and intensity of suicide talk, which could increase risk.

Clinical Note 1. Although MI is easy is easy to describe, some people learn MI more easily than others (Martino, Canning-Ball, Carroll, and Rounsaville, 2011), and multisite trials often show site effects (Ball et al., 2007; Carroll et al., 2006), indicating that come clinicians are better at MI than others. To illustrate an MI consistent approach to communicating with suicidal clients, it is often helpful to describe behaviors that are consistent with the principles of MI and compare them to behaviors that are not. The list of examples below provides a concrete example of how an MI approach to communicating with suicidal patients might differ from a non-MI approach

MI-Inconsistent	MI-Consistent
Empathy	
-Show little interest in understanding what clients are saying.	-Listen to patients and try to understand what they are saying. -Share understanding with client.
Example: You really need to live for your children.	Example: I hear you saying that you feel like a burden on your children, and wish you were a better father.
Evocation	
-Provide clients with reasons for living without asking for their reasons. -Tell patients what would make life worth living without asking for their thoughts. Example: If you stopped drinking so much you wouldn't feel so bad about yourself and wouldn't be thinking about suicide.	-Ask about and explore clients' reasons for living. -Ask about and explore their thoughts about what will make life worth living. Example: What would make life worth living?
Collaboration	
-Take the expert role and try to solve patients' problems without getting their input. -Tell patients what to do. Example: The only thing that is going to work for you is inpatient treatment.	-Let clients' ideas significantly impact the direction of the session. -Explore patients' options. Example: You have a couple of options, you can try inpatient and stay in the hospital for a few weeks, day treatment where you go to treatment each weekday, or outpatient treatment where you would come in once a week. What do you think would work best for you?
Autonomy	
-Withhold the limits of confidentiality and autonomy from clients, or only tell them after they talk about suicide. -Minimize patients' perception of choice and control. Example: I'm going to hospitalize you until you are safe.	-Explain the limits of confidentiality and autonomy before clients talk about suicide. -Acknowledge and support clients' sense of choice and control, without supporting suicide. Example: You're right, we can't hospitalize you forever. What I'd like to do is keep you safe for a few days and try to help you figure out what needs to change to make life worth living.

Clinicians should also acknowledge that "the critical variables for change are within the client and cannot be imposed" by telling clients that only they can decide to live, which is true and does not reinforce suicidal behavior. Moreover, when clients say they can kill themselves if they want to, clinicians should acknowledge their "freedom of choice", as arguing about it could be construed as a threat to their autonomy with potentially dire results. There are, however, limits to autonomy support and clinicians should avoid supporting their clients' "right" to suicide, as it can be misconstrued as supporting the behavior itself. MI clinicians provide autonomy support, but do not directly support clients' "right" to engage in suicidal behavior, which does not compromise their ethical, institutional, or legal responsibilities. For some clients, the support of their autonomy and freedom of choice may provide them with a sense of agency that helps them resolve their crisis (Faris, Cavell, Fishburne, and Britton, 2009).

MI Techniques and Suicide Prevention

The theory of MI also suggests that clinician behavior may impact clients' risk to engage in suicidal behavior and identifies specific techniques that they should use to elicit and reinforce *living talk,* or talk that indicates that the individual is thinking about living or making life worth living, and decreasing *suicide talk.*

According to the theory, open questions can be used to elicit clients' perspectives on living and dying, reflective listening to help clients feel understood, affirmations to reinforce living talk, and summaries to integrate thoughts and feelings about living and dying into narratives that are designed to elicit more living talk. The importance of living talk is clear as any clinician would prefer it over suicide talk and reasons for living reduce risk for suicidal ideation and behavior (Linehan et al., 1983; Malone et al., 2000). However, it may also be important to attend to the different types of living talk. Preparatory talk such as the ability, need, desire, and reasons to live may increases the strength of commitment talk, which may reduce risk for suicide-related behavior. Additionally, even the well-meaning use of MI inconsistent techniques such as confrontation, denial, and warning may unintentionally increase risk by increasing suicide talk and reducing living talk.

The importance of reducing suicide talk should not be overlooked. Suicide-related thoughts and behavior are among the most robust predictors of suicide (Brown, Beck, Steer, and Grisham, 2000; Harris and Barraclough, 1997; Posner et al., in press), and client estimated risk has a stronger association with actual risk than clinician estimates (Joiner, Rudd, and Rajab, 1999). It is quite possible that suicide talk will have a stronger association with suicide-related behavior than living talk as negative emotions and ideas are often more influential than positive ones (Baumeister, Bratslavsky, Finkenauer, and Vohs, 2001). This raises the question of how to most effectively address suicide-related issues in session. Research strongly encourages directly discussing suicide with clients as asking about suicide risk does not increase distress or suicidality in adolescents (Gould et al., 2005), or adults (Crawford et al., 2011; Reynolds, Lindenboim, Comtois, Murray, and Linehan, 2006), and clinical interventions that focus on suicide-related behavior are likely to be more efficacious than those that focus on other symptoms such as depression or distress (Tarrier, Taylor, and Gooding, 2008).

Clinical Note 2. The discussion examined multiple aspects of living and suicide talk, and it may be difficult for clinicians to identify the important points. A few simple guidelines can be used the summarize information that may be helpful to clinicians

Clients should talk more about living than suicide.
Talk about suicide should occur at the beginning of the session.
Clinicians should reinforce living talk using reflections, affirmations, summaries, and use open questions to encourage elaboration.
Preparatory talk is good (i.e., desire, ability, reasons, and need to live), but commitment talk (e.g., I will not kill myself) may have a stronger association with reduced risk.
Clients should engage in commitment talk at the end of the session.

Reflecting clients' pain, hopelessness, and suicidal thoughts may help them feel understood and free them to talk about their ambivalence about living, which may be protective. Talk about suicide should occur at the beginning of the session rather than at the end as suicide talk that transitions into living talk may be predictive of a good outcome. The amount of time clinicians spend exploring the client's suicidality depends upon its severity, with more severe suicidality being associated with a greater need to talk about it. With clients who want to die more than they want to live, MI-SI clinicians structure the session so that it begins with an exploration of the client's suicidality but ends with the client talking about living and the changes needed to make life worth living. For clients who are already ambivalent, time may be better spent reinforcing the motivation to live and developing a plan to ensure that life is worth living.

CONCLUSION

The purpose of this chapter was to describe MI, explain the supporting theory, and consider the implications of for suicide prevention. The theory of MI suggests that the relationships that clinicians establish with clients, techniques clinicians use, and clinicians' skill in using them can have a significant impact on the outcome of therapy with clients who are thinking about suicide. According to the model, clinicians working with suicidal clients should adopt an approach that is empathic, evocative, collaborative, as autonomy supportive as possible, and yet directs the individual towards talking about living and engaging in life sustaining and enhancing behavior. Clinicians are directive through the selective use of open questions, reflections, affirmations, and summaries to increase living talk, while decreasing talk about suicide and death. An ideal MI-SI session ends with the client making a strong commitment to live and engage in life sustaining and enhancing behavior. However, this is not always realistic as clients can be deeply entrenched in their suicidality. Sometimes, a successful session will end with a client who was previously committed to suicide rediscovering his reasons for living and becoming ambivalent. Although the application of the theory of MI to suicide prevention is intriguing, the efficacy and effectiveness of MI-SI needs to be established using Randomized Controlled Trial methodology. Conducting these trials will also provide data for studying the process of MI-SI, which may provide critical insights into how clinicians can effectively address suicidality in session.

REFERENCES

Aharonovich, E., Amrhein, P. C., Bisaga, A., Nunes, E. V., and Hasin, D. S. (2008). Cognition, commitment language, and behavioral change among cocaine-dependent patients. *Psychology of Addictive Behaviors, 22*(4), 557-562.

Amrhein, P. C., Miller, W. R., Yahne, C. E., Palmer, M., and Fulcher, L. (2003). Client commitment language during motivational interviewing predicts drug use outcomes. *Journal of Consulting and Clinical Psychology, 71*(5), 862-878.

Anglin, M. D., Hser, Y., and Grella, C. E. (1997). Drug addiction and treatment careers among clients in the drug abuse treatment outcome study (DATOS). *Psychology of Addictive Behaviors, 11*(4), 308-323.

Appleby, L., Shaw, J., Amos, T., McDonnell, R., Harris, C., McCann, K., Parsons, R. (1999). Suicide within 12 months of contact with mental health services: National Clinical Survey. *BMJ (Clinical Research Ed.), 318*(7193), 1235-1239.

Ball, S. A., Martino, S., Nich, C., Frankforter, T. L., Van Horn, D., Crits-Christoph, P., National Institute on Drug Abuse Clinical Trials Network. (2007). Site matters: Multisite randomized trial of motivational enhancement therapy in community drug abuse clinics. *Journal of Consulting and Clinical Psychology, 75*(4), 556-567.

Baumeister, R. F., Bratslavsky, E., Finkenauer, C., and Vohs, K. D. (2001). Bad is stronger than good. *Review of General Psychology, 5*(4), 323-370.

Bem, D. J. (1967). Self-perception: An alternative interpretation of cognitive dissonance phenomena. *Psychological Review, 74*(3), 183-200.

Bertholet, N., Faouzi, M., Gmel, G., Gaume, J., and Daeppen, J. B. (2010). Change talk sequence during brief motivational intervention, towards or away from drinking. *Addiction, 105*(12), 2106-2112.

Bien, T. H., Miller, W. R., and Boroughs, J. M. (1993). Motivational interviewing with alcohol outpatients. *Behavioural and Cognitive Psychotherapy, 21*(4), 347-356.

Boardman, T., Catley, D., Grobe, J. E., Little, T. D., and Ahluwalia, J. S. (2006). Using motivational interviewing with smokers: Do therapist behaviors relate to engagement and therapeutic alliance? *Journal of Substance Abuse Treatment, 31*(4), 329-339.

Britton, P. C., Patrick, H., and Williams, G. C. (2011). Motivational interviewing, self-determination theory, and cognitive behavioral therapy to prevent suicidal behavior. *Journal of Cognitive Behavioral Practice, 18*(1), 16-27.

Britton, P. C., Williams, G. C., and Conner, K. R. (2008). Self-determination theory, motivational interviewing, and the treatment of clients with acute suicidal ideation. *Journal of Clinical Psychology, 64*(1), 52-66.

Brown, G. K., Steer, R. A., Henriques, G. R., and Beck, A. T. (2005). The internal struggle between the wish to die and the wish to live: A risk factor for suicide. *The American Journal of Psychiatry, 162*(10), 1977-1979.

Brown, G. K., Beck, A. T., Steer, R. A., and Grisham, J. R. (2000). Risk factors for suicide in psychiatric outpatients: A 20-year prospective study. *Journal of Consulting and Clinical Psychology, 68*(3), 371-377.

Brown, J. M., and Miller, W. R. (1993). Impact of motivational interviewing on participation and outcome in residential alcoholism treatment. *Psychology of Addictive Behaviors, 7*(4), 211-218.

Carroll, K. M., Ball, S. A., Nich, C., Martino, S., Frankforter, T. L., Farentinos, C., National Institute on Drug Abuse Clinical Trials,Network. (2006). Motivational interviewing to improve treatment engagement and outcome in individuals seeking treatment for substance abuse: A multisite effectiveness study. *Drug and Alcohol Dependence, 81*(3), 301-312.

Catley, D., Harris, K. J., Mayo, M. S., Hall, S., Okuyemi, K. S., Boardman, T., and Ahluwalia, J. S. (2006). Adherence to principles of motivational interviewing and client within-session behavior. *Behavioural and Cognitive Psychotherapy, 34*(1), 43-56.

Crawford, M. J., Thana, L., Methuen, C., Ghosh, P., Stanley, S. V., Ross, J., Bajaj, P. (2011). Impact of screening for risk of suicide: Randomised controlled trial. *The British Journal of Psychiatry, 198*, 379-384.

Faris, A. S., Cavell, T. A., Fishburne, J. W., and Britton, P. C. (2009). Examining motivational interviewing from a client agency perspective. *Journal of Clinical Psychology, 65*(9), 955-970.

Festinger, L. (1957). *A theory of cognitive dissonance.* Stanford, CA: Stanford University Press.

Filiberti, A., Ripamonti, C., Totis, A., Ventafridda, V., Conno, F., Contiero, P., and Tamburini, M. (2001). Characteristics of terminal cancer patients who committed suicide during a home palliative care program. *Journal of Pain and Symptom Management, 22*(1), 544-553.

Gaume, J., Gmel, G., and Daeppen, J. (2008). Brief alcohol interventions: Do counsellors' and patients' communication characteristics predict change? *Alcohol and Alcoholism, 43*(1), 62-69.

Gaume, J., Gmel, G., Faouzi, M., and Daeppen, J. B. (2008). Counsellor behaviours and patient language during brief motivational interventions: A sequential analysis of speech. *Addiction, 103*(11), 1793-1800.

Goldacre, M., Seagroatt, V., and Hawton, K. (1993). Suicide after discharge from psychiatric inpatient care. *Lancet, 342*(8866), 283-286.

Gould, M. S., Marrocco, F. A., Kleinman, M., Thomas, J. G., Mostkoff, K., Cote, J., and Davies, M. (2005). Evaluating iatrogenic risk of youth suicide screening programs: A randomized controlled trial. *JAMA: Journal of the American Medical Association, 293*(13), 1635-1643.

Harris, E. C., and Barraclough, B. (1997). Suicide as an outcome for mental disorders: A meta-analysis. *British Journal of Psychiatry, 170*(3), 205-228.

Hendin, H., Haas, A. P., Maltsberger, J. T., Koestner, B., and Szanto, K. (2006). Problems in psychotherapy with suicidal patients. *American Journal of Psychiatry, 163*(1), 67-72.

Hettema, J., Steele, J., and Miller, W. R. (2005). Motivational interviewing. *Annual Review of Clinical Psychology, 1*(1), 91-111.

Hodgins, D. C., Ching, L. E., and McEwen, J. (2009). Strength of commitment language in motivational interviewing and gambling outcomes. *Psychology of Addictive Behaviors, 23*(1), 122-130.

Horvath, A. O., and Symonds, B. D. (1991). Relation between working alliance and outcome in psychotherapy: A meta-analysis. *Journal of Counseling Psychology, 38*(2), 139-149.

Jobes, D. A. (2011). Suicidal blackmail: Ethical and risk management issues in contemporary clinical care. In W. B. Johnson, and G. P. Koocher (Eds.), *Casebook on ethically challenging work settings in mental health and the behavioral sciences.* New York, NY: Oxford University Press.

Jobes, D. A. (2010). Managing suicidal risk: A collaborative approach. New York, NY: Guilford Press.

Jobes, D. A., and Mann, R. E. (1999). Reasons for living versus reasons for dying: Examining the internal debate of suicide. *Suicide and Life-Threatening Behavior, 29*(2), 97-104.

Joiner, T. E. J. (2006). *Why people die by suicide.* Cambridge, MA: Harvard University Press.

Joiner, T. E. J., Rudd, M. D., and Rajab, M. H. (1999). Agreement between self- and clinician-rated suicidal symptoms in a clinical sample of young adults: Explaining discrepancies. *Journal of Consulting and Clinical Psychology, 67*(2), 171-176.

Kovacs, M., and Beck, A. T. (1977). The wish to die and the wish to live in attempted suicides. *Journal of Clinical Psychology, 33*(2), 361-365.

Linehan, M. M. (1993). *Cognitive-behavioral treatment of borderline personality disorder.* New York, NY: Guilford Press.

Linehan, M. M., Goodstein, J. L., Nielsen, S. L., and Chiles, J. A. (1983). Reasons for staying alive when you are thinking of killing yourself: The reasons for living inventory. *Journal of Consulting and Clinical Psychology, 51*(2), 276-286.

Magill, M., Apodaca, T. R., Barnett, N. P., and Monti, P. M. (2010). The route to change: Within-session predictors of change plan completion in a motivational interview. *Journal of Substance Abuse Treatment, 38*(3), 299-305.

Malone, K. M., Oquendo, M. A., Haas, G. L., Ellis, S. P., Li, S., and Mann, J. J. (2000). Protective factors against suicidal acts in major depression: Reasons for living. *American Journal of Psychiatry, 157*(7), 1084-1088.

Martin, T., Moyers, T. B., Houck, J. M., Christopher, P. J. and Miller, W. R. (2005). *Motivational interviewing sequential code for observing process exchanges (MI-SCOPE) coder's manual.* Retrieved May/20, 2010, from http://casaa.unm.edu/download/scope.pdf

Martin, D. J., Garske, J. P., and Davis, M. K. (2000). Relation of the therapeutic alliance with outcome and other variables: A meta-analytic review. *Journal of Consulting and Clinical Psychology, 68*(3), 438-450.

Martin, T., Christopher, P. J., Houck, J. M., and Moyers, T. B. (2011). The structure of client language and drinking outcomes in project match. *Psychology of Addictive Behaviors, 25*(3), 439-45.

Martino, S., Canning-Ball, M., Carroll, K. M., and Rounsaville, B. J. (2011). A criterion-based stepwise approach for training counselors in motivational interviewing. *Journal of Substance Abuse Treatment, 40*(4), 357-365.

Meehan, J., Kapur, N., Hunt, I. M., Turnbull, P., Robinson, J., Bickley, H., Appleby, L. (2006). Suicide in mental health in-patients and within 3 months of discharge. National Clinical Survey. *British Journal of Psychiatry, 188*, 129-134.

Miller, W. R., Moyers, T. B., Ernst, D. and Amrhein, P. (2003). *Manual for the motivational interviewing skill code (MISC): Version 2.0*. Retrieved November 14, 2010, 2010, from http://motivationalinterview.org/training/MISC2.pdf

Miller, W. R., Walters, S. T., and Bennett, M. E. (2001). How effective is alcoholism treatment in the United States? *Journal of Studies on Alcohol, 62*(2), 211-220.

Miller, W. R., Yahne, C. E., and Tonigan, J. S. (2003). Motivational interviewing in drug abuse services: A randomized trial. *Journal of Consulting and Clinical Psychology, 71*(4), 754-763.

Miller, W. R., Benefield, R. G., and Tonigan, J. S. (1993). Enhancing motivation for change in problem drinking: A controlled comparison of two therapist styles. *Journal of Consulting and Clinical Psychology, 61*(3), 455-461.

Miller, W. R., and Rollnick, S. (2002). *Motivational interviewing: Preparing people for change (2nd ed.)*. New York, NY: Guilford Press.

Miller, W. R., and Rose, G. S. (2009). Toward a theory of motivational interviewing. *American Psychologist, 64*(6), 527-537.

Mishara, B. L., Chagnon, F., Daigle, M., Balan, B., Raymond, S., Marcoux, I., Berman, A. (2007). Which helper behaviors and intervention styles are related to better short-term outcomes in telephone crisis intervention? Results from a silent monitoring study of calls to the U.S. 1-800-SUICIDE network. *Suicide and Life-Threatening Behavior, 37*(3), 308-321.

Mishara, B. L., and Daigle, M. S. (1997). Effects of different telephone intervention styles with suicidal callers at two suicide prevention centers: An empirical investigation. *American Journal of Community Psychology, 25*(6), 861-885.

Moyers, T. B., and Martin, T. (2006). Therapist influence on client language during motivational interviewing sessions. *Journal of Substance Abuse Treatment, 30*(3), 245-251.

Moyers, T. B., Martin, T., Houck, J. M., Christopher, P. J., and Tonigan, J. S. (2009). From in-session behaviors to drinking outcomes: A causal chain for motivational interviewing. *Journal of Consulting and Clinical Psychology, 77*(6), 1113-1124.

Moyers, T. B., Martin, T., Christopher, P. J., Houck, J. M., Tonigan, J. S., and Amrhein, P. C. (2007). Client language as a mediator of motivational interviewing efficacy: Where is the evidence? *Alcoholism: Clinical and Experimental Research, 31*(Suppl 3), 40S-47S.

Moyers, T. B., Miller, W. R., and Hendrickson, S. M. L. (2005). How does motivational interviewing work? Therapist interpersonal skill predicts client involvement within motivational interviewing sessions. *Journal of Consulting and Clinical Psychology, 73*(4), 590-598.

Moyers, T., Martin, T., Catley, D., Harris, K. J., and Ahluwalia, J. S. (2003). Assessing the integrity of motivational interviewing interventions: Reliability of the motivational interviewing skills code. *Behavioural and Cognitive Psychotherapy, 31*(2), 177-184.

Orbach, I. (2001). Therapeutic empathy with the suicidal wish: Principles of therapy with suicidal individuals. *American Journal of Psychotherapy, 55*(2), 166-184.

Posner, K., Brown, G. K., Stanley, B., Brent, D. A., Yershova, K. V., Oquendo, M. A., Mann, J. J. (2011). The Columbia–Suicide severity rating scale: Initial validity and internal consistency findings from three multisite studies with adolescents and adults. *American Journal of Psychiatry, 168*(12), 1266-1277.

Qin, P., and Nordentoft, M. (2005). Suicide risk in relation to psychiatric hospitalization: Evidence based on longitudinal registers. *Archives of General Psychiatry, 62*(4), 427-432.

Reynolds, S. K., Lindenboim. N., Comtois, K. A., Murray, A., and Linehan, M. M. (2006). Risky assessments: Participant suicidality and distress associated with research assessments in a treatment study of suicidal behavior. *Suicide and Life Threatening Behavior, 36*(1), 19-34.

Rogers, C. R. (1957). The necessary and sufficient conditions of therapeutic personality change. *Journal of Consulting Psychology, 21*(2), 95-103.

Rudd, M. D., Mandrusiak, M., and Joiner, T. E. J. (2006). The case against no-suicide contracts: The commitment to treatment statement as a practice alternative. *Journal of Clinical Psychology, 62*(2), 243-251.

Shneidman, E. S. (1996). *The suicidal mind.* New York, NY: Oxford University Press.

Tarrier, N., Taylor, K., and Gooding, P. (2008). Cognitive-behavioral interventions to reduce suicide behavior: A systematic review and meta-analysis. *Behavior Modification, 32*(1), 77-108.

Vader, A. M., Walters, S. T., Prabhu, G. C., Houck, J. M., and Field, C. A. (2010). The language of motivational interviewing and feedback: Counselor language, client language, and client drinking outcomes. *Psychology of Addictive Behaviors, 24*(2), 190-197.

Zuroff, D. C., and Blatt, S. J. (2006). The therapeutic relationship in the brief treatment of depression: Contributions to clinical improvement and enhanced adaptive capacities. *Journal of Consulting and Clinical Psychology, 74*(1), 130-140.

In: Frontiers in Suicide Risk
Editor: Jill E. Lavigne

ISBN 978-1-62081-373-7
©2012 Nova Science Publishers, Inc.

Chapter 6

TRAUMATIC BRAIN INJURY AND SUICIDE: CONTRIBUTING FACTORS, RISK ASSESSMENT AND SAFETY PLANNING

Gina M. Signoracci,[+*] *Bridget B. Matarazzo*[*] *and Nazanin H. Bahraini*[*]

Veteran Integrated Service Network (VISN) 19 Mental Illness Research, Education, and Clinical Center (MIRECC)
University of Colorado School of Medicine, Department of Psychiatry, Colorado, US

INTRODUCTION

The relationship between *Traumatic Brain Injury* (TBI) and suicide is gaining attention, due in part to increased rates of physical injury being sustained by Operation Enduring Freedom (OEF)/Operation Iraqi Freedom (OIF) military personnel and the growing concern regarding suicidal behavior among this group of service members [1]. The increased interest in this topic has contributed to a growing body of research clearly showing that among members of the general population, individuals with TBI are at higher risk for suicidal ideation [2], suicide attempts [3], and suicide completions [4]. Similarly, increased rates of suicidal behavior in Veterans with a history of TBI have been demonstrated. A recent study by Brenner et al. [5] showed that among Veterans seeking services within the Veterans Health Administration (VHA), those with a history of TBI were 1.55 times more likely to die by suicide than those without a history of TBI. The authors were also able to establish that this increased risk was not solely due to the presence of psychiatric disorders or demographic factors, providing further evidence that history of TBI is an independent risk factor for suicide. Due to the growing understanding of the relationship between TBI and suicide,

---

[+] Correspondence concerning this chapter should be sent to Gina Signoracci, VISN 19 MIRECC, 1055 Clermont St., Denver, Colorado 80220, E-mail: Gina.Signoracci@va.gov

[*] Disclaimer: The views expressed in this chapter are those of the authors and do not necessarily represent the official policy or position of the Department of Veterans Affairs or the United States Government.

clinical researchers are poised to further inform clinical practice to assist mental health providers working with patients in crisis, including those who may be in danger of engaging in self-directed violence.

The purpose of this chapter is to provide an overview of the relationship between TBI and suicide, to review risk factors associated with elevated suicide risk in those with TBI, and to provide treatment providers with general guidelines for suicide risk assessment and safety planning when working with individuals who have a history of TBI.

TRAUMATIC BRAIN INJURY

In 2011, The Centers for Disease Control and Prevention (CDC) [6] reported that, on average, approximately 1.7 million people sustain a TBI each year. TBI is caused by a "blow or jolt to the head or a penetrating head injury that disrupts the normal functioning of the brain" [6]. As seen in Table 1, TBI severity can range from *mild* (e.g., a brief alteration in consciousness) to *severe* (e.g., a prolonged period of unconsciousness) [7]. Criteria based upon brain functioning following TBI (e.g., length of loss of consciousness) and imaging results are often used to assess injury severity. Individuals who sustain moderate to severe injuries generally seek medical attention with positive physiologic markers determined through medical evaluation to assist with the diagnostic process (e.g., imaging, prolonged loss of consciousness). Therefore, assessment and diagnosis of more severe injuries is less complicated. Further, tracking incidence, prevalence, and recovery from severe injuries is facilitated by availability of medical data. This is generally not the case for mild injuries for which individuals often do not seek medical care.

The majority of military and civilian TBIs sustained, approximately 80%, are mild in nature [8,9]. The American Congress of Rehabilitation Medicine [10] definition for *Mild Traumatic Brain Injury (mTBI)* includes presence of at least one of the following: 1) any period of *Loss of Consciousness* (LOC); 2) any loss of memory for events immediately before or after the event; 3) any *Alteration of Consciousness* (AOC) at the time of the event (e.g., feeling dazed, disoriented, or confused); and 4) focal neurological deficit(s) that may or may not be transient, but where severity of the injury does not exceed the following: loss of consciousness of approximately 30 minutes; a *Glasgow Coma Sale* (GCS) of 13-15 after 30 minutes; and *Post Traumatic Amnesia* (PTA) of 24 hours [10].

Table 1. Severity Grades of TBI [7]

Mild	Moderate	Severe
Altered or LOC<30 minutes with normal CT and/or MRI	LOC<6 hours with abnormal CT and/or MRI	LOC>6 hours with abnormal CT and/or MRI
GCS 13-15	GCS 9-12	GCS<9
PTA<24 hours	PTA<7 days	PTA>7days

The CDC [6] reported that TBI in the civilian population most commonly occurs secondary to falls, motor vehicle/traffic events, being struck by/against objects, and assaults, respectively. It has also been reported that among the civilian population, children aged 0 to 4 years; adolescents aged 15 to 19 years; and adults aged 65 and older are most likely to sustain TBI [6]. Finally, males are more likely to sustain TBI than females in all age groups with males aged 0 to 4 having the highest rates of TBI-related emergency department visits, hospitalization, and deaths [6].

Regarding military personnel, those serving in Iraq and Afghanistan are reportedly sustaining TBIs of all severity levels [11-13]. Belanger et al. [14] reported that an estimated 78% of OEF/OIF combat injuries are secondary to explosive munitions or blasts. Explosive munitions include artillery, rocket and mortar shells, mines, and bombs including improvised explosive devises (IEDs) and rocket propelled grenades (RPGs). Okie [15] and Warden [16] estimated that more than 60 percent of blast injuries result in TBI, which has become known as the signature wound of the current conflicts [15].

Finally, supporting existing literature regarding prevalence of mTBI, Belanger et al. [14] reported that concussion or mTBI is the most common form of combat-related injury, which is often missed by health professionals, particularly in patients with polytrauma in which other wounds are easily seen.

TBI SEQUELAE

For those with mTBI, associated post-concussive (PC) symptoms often include headaches, fatigue, poor memory and concentration, and dizziness. Although most individuals who have sustained mTBI recover within three months post injury [17], it has been suggested that between 7% and 33% of those who sustain an mTBI have PC symptoms that persist beyond three months [18].

PC symptoms secondary to mTBI may complicate the diagnostic and treatment picture as symptoms are associated with a number of conditions, including depression and Posttraumatic Stress Disorder (PTSD) [19-21].

As those with moderate to severe injury typically seek medical attention, short-term symptoms are often addressed in acute medical and rehabilitation settings. Cognitive impairment secondary to moderate to severe TBI may include deficits in attention, memory, executive functioning, language and communication, visual spatial skills, and processing speed [22,23].

Furthermore, individuals with moderate to severe TBI may have perceptual deficits (e.g., decreased visual field, diplopia or double vision, loss of sensation in extremities, decreased hearing) and motor deficits (e.g., paralysis) [22,24-27].

Long-term impairments of all levels of injury can include cognitive (e.g., executive dysfunction) and behavioral (e.g., aggression) symptoms [22,28]. Approximately 80,000 to 90,000 individuals per year in the U.S. experience long-term disability as a result of TBI sequelae [9] including cognitive, physical, and emotional sequelae, all of which can impact occupational, social and psychological functioning [22,23,29].

The significance of this impact can be such that it serves as a risk factor for suicide. The following section details how TBI sequelae, in addition to conditions that are associated with TBI, relate to increased suicide risk.

RISK FACTORS FOR SUICIDE AMONG TBI PATIENTS

Psychiatric Risk Factors

The relationship between TBI and psychiatric illness has been well established[29-31], and should be considered when assessing suicide risk. A study by Silver[3] showed a higher prevalence of psychiatric diagnoses in those with a TBI history compared to those with no TBI history and that individuals with a TBI history were significantly more likely to have had a lifetime history of a suicide attempt. Mainio et al. [32] conducted a study to evaluate the prevalence of psychiatric disorders in individuals with TBI who had attempted suicide. Authors not only reported presence of psychiatric diagnoses including alcohol related disorders and depression pre-existing TBI, but also showed increases in psychiatric diagnoses following TBI. Finally, Olson-Madden et al.[33] conducted a study to better understand the occurrence of psychiatric diagnoses in Veterans with TBI seeking substance abuse treatment, and found that Veterans in this sample had an average of 2.9 psychiatric diagnoses per person. The most common non–substance abuse-related psychiatric diagnoses were depression-related disorders (i.e., Dysthymia, Depressive Disorder NOS, and Major Depressive Disorder) followed by PTSD, Bipolar Mood Disorder, anxiety-related disorders, Adjustment Disorder, and Schizoaffective Disorder [33].

Mood disturbances appear to be the most commonly reported post injury psychiatric sequelae [31,33]. In fact, a number of studies have shown that Major Depressive Disorder (MDD) in particular may be the most salient psychiatric condition in individuals with TBI [29,34-36]. In another study, Jorge et al. [35] showed that MDD was significantly more frequent among patients with TBI compared to those without TBI, and that 33% of TBI patients experienced MDD at least once in the first year after their injury. Similarly, Bombardier et al.[34] revealed that 53% of patients hospitalized for complicated mild, moderate or severe TBI met the criteria for MDD within a year after sustaining their injury. Furthermore, a number of studies have shown that higher rates of suicidal ideation and suicidal behaviors following TBI may in part be due to increased rates of depression in this population [37].

Evidence has also suggested that increased prevalence of depression is observed at multiple time points after injury [4,34]. Because the risk of depression after TBI remains high over an extended period, early and continued screening over time may be warranted. Moreover, severity of TBI has not been established as an accurate predictor of depression, suggesting the need for awareness across all severities of TBI [34,38].

In addition to mood disorders, presence of psychosis following TBI has also been documented. Ahmed and Fujii [30] and Fann et al.[38] found that TBI is linked to an increased risk of psychosis and that individuals with TBI history have a two to five-fold greater risk of developing symptoms of psychosis post injury. Arciniegas et al.[39] reported that albeit relatively infrequent, psychosis following TBI exceeds incidence of that in the general population [40-42] and that because onset of psychotic symptoms may occur following significant delay post injury, differentiation from symptoms related to Schizophrenia may be difficult and complicated [43]. In an effort to facilitate accurate diagnosis of post injury psychosis, Arciniegas et al. [39] outlined the importance of comprehensive evaluation including assessment of pre injury factors (i.e., neurodevelopment,

neurological disorders, and history of psychiatric illness); injury specific factors "
(i.e., neuroanatomical location of injury and neuroimaging abnormalities); and post injury
factors (i.e., electroencephalographic [EEG] abnormalities, epilepsy, cognitive impairment,
and psychiatric sequelae).

Another psychiatric disorder that is found to be co-morbid with a history of TBI is PTSD.
Although estimates regarding co-occurring TBI and PTSD have not been reported for the
general population, reported estimates regarding military personnel with mTBI that have been
diagnosed with co-occurring PTSD range from 11% to 23% [11,20,21,44,45]. It is recommended that clinicians give attention to the complex relationship between TBI and PTSD by
assessing the impact of symptoms on overall functioning and quality of life as symptoms can
be "mutually exacerbating" when both diagnoses are present [46, p.3] and may significantly
contribute to distress.

Substance Abuse

A major contributor to an increased constellation of interacting suicide risk factors for
persons with a history of TBI is substance abuse. Evidence has suggested that individuals
with TBI history are also likely to have a history of alcohol abuse [33,47].

Corrigan [48] found that one-third to one-half of individuals hospitalized secondary to
TBI were either intoxicated at the time of injury or had a history of alcohol abuse. Studies
have also shown that individuals with TBI often return to and/or increase level of pre injury
use after 1 year and that continued increases persist with time post injury [49, 50]. Regarding
illicit drug use among those with TBI history, Kreutzer et al.[49] reported the prevalence of
the following in descending order of frequency: marijuana, cocaine, and other illicit drugs
such as LSD and amphetamines.

Teasdale and Engberg[4] found that patients with a history of TBI and substance misuse
were four times more likely than individuals with TBI and no history of substance misuse and
seven times more likely than members of the general population to die by suicide. Also, work
by Simpson and Tate [51] found that individuals with a post injury history of
psychiatric/emotional disturbance and substance abuse were 21 times more likely than the
general population to have attempted suicide post TBI.

Psychiatric disorders associated with TBI are concerning from a suicide risk perspective.
A vast majority of suicides in the general population are associated with psychiatric disorders
[52] and most of these disorders are unmanaged at time of death.

Some have proposed that the higher rate of psychiatric disorders in TBI could be due to
the effects of the injury on brain functioning, the psychological impact of the event or the
psychosocial effects of disabilities resulting from the TBI [3]. There is also some evidence for
psychiatric disorders as a predisposing risk factor for TBI [29].

Based on these findings, targeting patients with a pre-morbid history of psychiatric illness
coupled with early post injury assessment and psychiatric intervention may enhance suicide
prevention efforts and improve treatment of individuals with TBI who are at risk for suicidal
behavior.

Executive Functioning

Executive functioning describes a complex set of cognitive processes involved in the planning, initiation, and self-regulation of goal-directed behavior [22,27]. Cognitive flexibility (i.e., the ability to switch between tasks and ideas) is also a key component of executive functioning [27]. Injuries involving the frontal lobes and related sub-cortical structures often result in *executive dysfunction* [53]. Therefore, individuals with TBI involving the frontal lobes may evidence difficulties with these tasks as well as decreased decision-making ability and increased impulsivity and aggression [54-57]. Several studies investigating suicidality in those with and without TBI have identified executive dysfunction as a contributing factor (e.g., Jollant et al.[58]; Keilp et al.[59]; Oquendo et al.[28]).

Jollant et al. [58] explored the role of impaired decision-making in individuals who have attempted suicide. Using a standard neuropsychological measure, they found that those who had attempted suicide scored lower in the area of decision-making than a group without suicidal ideation or attempts. Mann et al.[60] found that lifetime, externally-directed aggression and impulsivity distinguished past suicide attempters from non-attempters. Further, Dumais et al.[61] conducted a psychological autopsy study and found that after controlling for gender, age, substance use, and major psychopathology, lifetime aggression and impulsivity were associated with violent suicide deaths (e.g., hanging, firearms, jumping from height). Oquendo et al.[28] conducted a study highlighting the complicated and important relationships between TBI history, aggression, and suicidal behavior. Specifically, the authors found that increased aggression was a risk factor for both suicidal behavior and history of TBI. They also found that those with TBI endorsed higher levels of aggression post injury, suggesting that the increased risk of suicide was at least in part related to TBI history.

Psychosocial Risk Factors

Increased effort has been made to better understand psychosocial risk factors for suicide in those with TBI. For example, Gould et al.[62] found that unemployment, pain, unproductive coping style, and poor quality of life were associated with psychiatric disorders following TBI. Authors went on to say that clinicians designing interventions aimed at reducing maladaptive coping styles in persons with TBI should consider the relationship between coping and executive dysfunction. Brenner et al. [63] conducted qualitative interviews with Veterans with a history of TBI and found that common precipitating factors for suicidality included feelings of loss due to role changes, difficulties interacting with others, difficulties in cognitive functioning, and recently developed emotional and psychiatric difficulties [63]. Authors provided several examples of these factors including challenges related to the transition between having an identity and sense of purpose while in the military to decrease in status and purpose after discharge from the military; being unemployed and unable to provide financial support for a child's college education; and not being able to function as desired secondary to cognitive and/or emotional difficulties [63]. Protective factors included returning to school, reconnecting with family members, taking on new hobbies, and engagement in mental health care [63].

SUICIDE RISK ASSESSMENT IN THE TBI POPULATION

As described above, individuals with a history of TBI are at increased risk for suicide. Because there is a lack of strong evidence for a specific timeframe of suicide risk post injury[4], clinical risk assessment should be a component of routine and ongoing care for this population [64]. Although no evidence-based suicide risk assessment and intervention practices currently exist for this population, Simpson and Tate [37] recommended that clinicians adhere to existing practice guidelines for the assessment and management of risk, while conducting best practice treatment of TBI-related psychiatric sequelae. Dennis et al. [64] also suggested that clinicians familiarize themselves with factors found to be related to suicide in the larger population to facilitate risk assessment in the TBI population. Additionally, if clinicians are working with individuals with a history of TBI, it behooves them to assess whether or not psychiatric symptoms are well-managed and to assess suicide risk [65]. While the literature on suicide risk assessment is extensive and beyond the scope of this chapter, what follows are some general recommendations regarding suicide risk assessment with this population. These recommendations are based on research findings in the field of suicidology and Joiner's [66] interpersonal-psychological theory of suicide, which is applied to the TBI population.

Assessment of Risk and Protective Factors

Traditional means of suicide risk assessment have often focused on the identification of risk and protective factors while paying special attention to those that are acute and modifiable [67]. The systematic gathering of these factors contributes to an evaluation of an individual's level of risk and lends itself to treatment and the management of one's suicidality. Risk factors tend to be empirically derived, relatively stable, distal factors that have been found to correlate with suicide [68]. Examples of risk factors include demographics (e.g., white, male, older age), history (e.g., of suicide attempts, family history of attempts, trauma), and psychiatric diagnoses [69, 70]. After obtaining information about an individual's risk factors, the clinician should determine if they are non-modifiable (e.g., family history, demographics) or modifiable (e.g., psychiatric symptoms, social support, access to lethal means) and incorporate this information into the risk assessment. Risk factors for suicide that are of particular relevance to the TBI population include co-morbid psychiatric conditions (e.g., MDD and substance use disorders) and executive dysfunction (e.g., impaired decision-making capability and increased impulsivity). Additionally, Simpson and Tate[2] identified hopelessness, suicidal ideation, history of suicide attempts and emotional/psychiatric disturbance as critical indicators of risk in individuals with a history of TBI. Feeling a loss of self, changes in role and status, and relationship difficulties have also been shown to serve as precipitating events to suicidal thoughts or behavior in those with TBI [63].

Compared to the distal nature of suicide risk factors, warning signs are precipitating emotions, thoughts, or behaviors, that have a more proximal relationship to suicidal behavior and imply imminent rather than long-term risk [68]. Rudd et al. [68, p.258] defined a warning sign as "the earliest detectable sign that indicates heightened risk for suicide in the near-term (i.e., within minutes, hours, or days)". Examples of warning signs include hopelessness, anger, feeling trapped, anxiety, and having no reason for living [68]. In addition to risk factors and warning signs, clinicians should assess protective factors. Protective factors can serve the function of counterbalancing risk factors [70] and thus, are an important component of risk assessment. Examples include social support, self-control, and problem-solving ability [71]. Research is still needed to identify warning signs and protective factors that are of particular relevance to the TBI population [1,37]. With respect to protective factors, preliminary work in this area suggests that social support, having hope for the future and a sense of purpose, religion or spirituality, and being engaged in mental health treatment may mitigate suicide risk for Veterans with a history of TBI [63]. Clinicians are urged to identify protective factors, risk factors and warning signs as described above and understand these within the context of TBI sequelae when conducting a thorough suicide risk assessment with this population.

Information regarding an individual's risk and protective factors, as well as warning signs, should be obtained from multiple sources [64], including collateral information, thorough chart review, clinical interview, and suicide assessment scales. It is important for clinicians to be aware that none of these sources of information should be used in isolation. Rather, a thorough risk assessment involves the integration of all available clinical information [72]. Of note, this process is used to identify one's level of risk. This information does not enable clinicians to make a prediction as to whether or not one will die by suicide. Clinicians can utilize decision trees, such as that set forth by Joiner et al.[71], in which the clinician answers questions to help determine what category of risk an individual falls into (e.g., mild, moderate, severe).

When assessing and treating symptoms of TBI, the interplay of physical, psychiatric, and psychosocial deficits may serve as risk factors for suicide. As such, it is important that clinicians understand the complicated constellation and interaction of risk factors. For example, cognitive deficits associated with PC symptoms may impact one's ability to effectively manage PTSD symptoms (e.g., affect regulation). Additionally, while the deficits (e.g., memory) one may have are likely to exist in multiple contexts (i.e., work, home, school) their impact on suicide risk may vary. For example, not being able to remember things at school may be more distressing than when this occurs at home. Therefore, it is important to gather information related to an individual's perception of these experiences and how they may relate to suicide risk.

Assessment of Executive Functioning

Executive functioning includes abilities pertaining to judgment; reasoning; abstraction; initiation; organizing, planning, and carrying out tasks; mental flexibility, and impulse control [22,27]. Deficits in executive functioning, or executive dysfunction, can influence other cognitive processes [22] and cause impairment in adaptive functioning [73] and one's ability to participate in *Activities of Daily Living* (ADLs) and *Instrumental Activities of Daily Living* (IADLs). ADLs, which are sometimes referred to as Personal Activities of Daily Living (PADLs) [74] or Basic Activities of Daily Living (BADLs) [75] describe fundamental activities that are necessary for daily functioning and include hygiene practices, dressing and undressing, eating, transfers (from sit to stand, on and off of the toilet, etc.), ambulation or transport using an assistive device, and bowel and bladder management. IADLs refer to higher order tasks that facilitate independent living [74,76] and include caretaking; using the telephone, computer or other devices; transportation within the community; financial management; health management (including taking medications, managing appointments, etc.); meal preparation; and ability to engage in safety procedures. Due to the nature of executive deficits, individuals are vulnerable to quickly finding themselves in challenging situations in which they can become overwhelmed and unable to problem solve or self-regulate effectively. Such difficulties, may interfere with effective engagement in daily living tasks. For example, an individual may experience distress related to difficulties preparing a meal as desired and go without food. Another example is feeling hopeless when unable to access a resource (e.g., medication, social support, medical provider, financial support [paycheck or social security check], transportation) and not seeking appropriate alternatives such as calling helpful contacts to meet needs. Finally, for individuals with difficulties regulating emotions and behavior, having a fight with a another person may lead to acting out toward that person or others. Executive functions, including mental flexibility (i.e., switching between tasks and ideas), inhibition (i.e., regard for or ability to adhere to rules), impulse control, and managing emotions, are needed not only to carry out basic and instrumental ADLS, but also to employ strategies to appropriately cope with suicide-related crises and manage suicidal impulses and urges. For example, Elbogen et al. [77] noted that among individuals with TBI, difficulty managing anger and hostility in particular, increase risk for suicide. In clinical practice, neuropsychological testing is often utilized to formally assess different aspects of executive functioning. However, basic assessment of executive functions can be incorporated into routine clinical practice without the need for formal neuro-psychological measures or other time-consuming procedures [78]. For example, observation of the individual as they engage in a variety of settings can also provide rich, in vivo, data that can be helpful to inform the diagnostic picture and may allow clinicians to best understand and design interventions geared to address situations that are most likely to lead to crisis and increase risk for suicide. Observing individuals as they engage in ADLs or IADLs will likely provide information regarding an individual's abilities as they relate to executive functioning. It is recommended that clinicians also observe individuals with TBI performing additional activities that include pathfinding (following directions to get from one location to another); social interactions with others; writing checks and other financial management tasks; making a list of items needed at the store and shopping for those items using the list; and coordination of transportation to and from appointments may also prove useful.

In summary, assessment of executive functioning in individuals with TBI is paramount to understanding the extent of an individual's deficits and how dysfunction may impact suicide risk factors, such as hopelessness. This assessment may in turn, help the clinician design individualized and meaningful interventions to reduce the impact of impairments on functioning and mitigate suicide risk.

JOINER'S INTERPERSONAL-PSYCHOLOGICAL THEORY OF SUICIDE

A risk assessment based on warning signs, risk factors and protective factors can be enhanced by using Joiner's [66] interpersonal-psychological theory of suicide. This theory maintains that there are three elements that characterize lethally suicidal individuals, as depicted in Figure 1. First, *perceived burdensomeness* refers to when individuals view themselves as an unbearable burden on their family, friends and/or larger community. Second, these individuals experience a sense of *failed belongingness*, or a feeling that their efforts at establishing and maintaining social connectedness have repeatedly been thwarted or have failed. Finally, *acquired capability* is used to describe the process through which suicidal individuals habituate to the pain and fear associated with self-injurythereby increasing their capacity to engage in suicidal behavior. This is accomplished through a multitude of experiences (i.e., repeated exposure to pain). Joiner [66] contends that when these three elements (perceived burdensomeness, failed belongingness, and acquired capability) co-exist, lethal suicidal behavior is likely and imminent. Thus, suicide risk assessment should include the assessment of these elements[79].

The interpersonal-psychological theory of suicide [66] can be applied to risk assessment in individuals with TBI. This application is facilitated by the World Health Organization's[80] concept of disability [81] such that assessment should include information regarding the three components of disability (i.e., impairment in bodily function, activity limitation or participation restriction). An important component of both the assessment of disability and suicide risk entails at least a basic assessment of any cognitive impairment as described above that may influence an individual's self-observation and self-report. It is recommended that clinicians consider all findings regarding risk within the context of one's disability when conducting a comprehensive suicide risk assessment. For example, following TBI, someone might have great difficulty organizing, planning and making decisions, such that they can no longer work. This disability (e.g., activity limitation and participation restriction) can lead to feelings of burdensomeness and hopelessness. As a result of TBI sequelae, the person might have difficulty generating ideas regarding how to cope with these feelings and suicidal thinking might emerge in response.

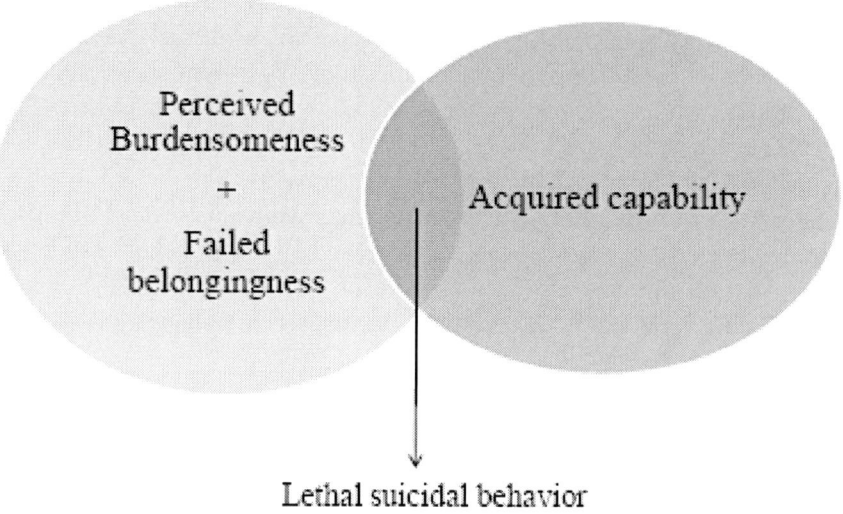

Figure 1. Interpersonal-Psychological Theory of Suicide Risk. Adapted from T.E. Joiner [66, p.138].

Drawing from Joiner's [66] theory, clinicians should assess an individual's desire for death, feelings of perceived burdensomeness, failed belongingness, and habituation to pain. These factors should be considered in light of both one's potential enduring TBI sequelae and overall emotional functioning. Regarding perceived burdensomeness, the clinician should assess if the individual with a history of TBI feels like a burden to his or her family, friends or society. For example, one might report feeling like a burden because they can no longer drive or work. In order to assess failed belongingness, clinicians should ask about attempts to create and maintain interpersonal relationships. This may include one's difficulty maintaining desired interaction with social supports (e.g., friends, family and community) post injury, which may lead to a sense of failed belongingness. With respect to habituation, clinicians should ask questions related to individuals' exposure to physical and emotional pain. Specifically, clinicians should ask about increased pain tolerance over their lifetime. In order to accomplish this, Brenner and Homaifar [81] suggested using an approach similar to a timeline. If a history of habituation to pain exists in the context of a desire for death, one is expected to be at increased risk for suicide. Evaluation of all of these factors will result in a thorough risk assessment that is grounded in an empirically-supported theory[82] of suicide and is applicable to the TBI population.

SAFETY PLANNING AND THE TBI POPULATION

While there are no evidence-based treatments for suicide in those with TBI, *safety planning* is one intervention that may be particularly useful for managing suicide risk in this population. Safety planning should not be used in isolation to manage an individual's suicidality, but it can be a crucial component of treatment that enables the individual to have more control over their suicidal thoughts and behaviors. Safety planning is a brief clinical intervention that was developed for this purpose. The safety plan is intended to be used preceding or during a suicidal crisis and is comprised of coping strategies and sources of support [83]. Although it was developed for Department of Veteran Affairs mental health clinicians, it can be modified for a variety of populations, including individuals with TBI sequelae. As described above, individuals with a history of TBI may have enduring sequelae including executive dysfunction. Factors such as impaired decision-making and impulsivity can impact how one copes with a suicidal crisis. The safety plan enables an individual to have a well thought-out, personalized plan written down before a suicidal crisis emerges.

A safety plan is distinct from a no-suicide contract. One disadvantage of no-suicide contracts is that they can provide clinicians with a false sense of security because of the legal connotation of using the term "contract" [84]. It has also been suggested that they limit communication between patients and clinicians because patients may believe that genuinely discussing their suicidal thoughts and behaviors may be in violation of the contract [84].

No-suicide contracts also tell patients what *not to do*, but do not guide them in what *to do* during a suicidal crisis. Further, no-suicide contracts do not provide clinicians with the opportunity to identify important information regarding warning signs, which are crucial to risk assessment, as described above. In contrast to no-suicide contracts, safety plans can also be used to guide treatment planning. For example, a patient might have difficulty identifying social support and in this process, the clinician becomes aware of an important treatment need of the patient. Jobes [85] proposed that most suicidal people do not actually want to die; rather, they want to end their suffering and because of a lack of coping methods, they think suicide is the only way to accomplish this goal. The safety plan provides patients with other options for coping that they have had difficulty thinking of and/or enacting thus far. Safety plan development should be a collaborative process between the patient and the clinician that yields empowerment, hope and individual potential [83]. Table 2 lists the six steps of the safety planning process, as described by Stanley and Brown [83]. For details regarding each of these steps refer to, *Safety Plan Treatment Manual to Reduce Suicide Risk: Veteran Version* [83].

Table 2. The Six Steps of Safety Planning

Step Number	Name
1	Recognizing warning signs
2	Using internal coping strategies
3	Utilizing social contacts that can serve as a distraction from suicidal thoughts and who may offer support
4	Contacting family members or friends who may offer help to resolve the crisis
5	Contacting professionals and agencies
6	Reducing the potential for use of lethal methods

A crucial component of the safety plan development process includes assessing barriers to implementation of the safety plan [83]. A common barrier identified by patients is that they do not know how they will remember to use their safety plan. Techniques such as encouraging the patient to review their plan each day, keeping it in a visible location, and creating a pocket-size version can improve the likelihood that one will utilize the plan. Educating and involving an individual's social support into the employment of the safety plan can also assist with implementation and problem-solving around barriers. Family members, for example, can help remind patients of their safety plan and help them go through the steps of the plan when they are feeling acutely distressed. These strategies, along with those listed in Table 3 below may help individuals with enduring TBI sequelae.

Also, clinicians can collaboratively modify the safety plan using information gained in their assessment regarding sequelae and other barriers to implementation. As described above, individuals with a history of TBI can experience wide-ranging deficits. Specifically related to executive dysfunction, individuals may demonstrate difficulty effectively creating and carrying out plans to solve problems and completing tasks listed in a safety plan. Those with executive dysfunction may also have difficulty thinking of and considering short and long-term consequences of their behavior as well as considering both gains and losses so as to make the best decisions. Difficulties with problem solving may be expressed by engaging in activities that place one at risk for imminent harm to self (e.g., abrupt discontinuation of medications; substance use; or disconnection from social support). Finally, when engaging in risk assessment and safety planning with individuals with executive dysfunction, it may be helpful to consider their abilities to effectively switch between tasks and/or ideas. Thus, the strategies listed in Table 3 are recommended when collaborating with an individual with TBI sequelae on the development of a safety plan to help manage their suicide risk.

Table 3. Inclusive Strategies to Facilitate Effective Safety Planning with TBI Patients

Strategy	Function	Example(s)
Slow pace of conversation	Facilitate learning and memory for individuals who may become overwhelmed with auditory information	N/A
Use patient's language	Reduce miscommunication while facilitating establishment of rapport	Clinician uses same language as an individual who refers to a difficult experience with a particular term or phrase (e.g., "the accident", "when I got hurt", etc)
Take short breaks	Prevent cognitive overload Increase opportunities for consolidation of information	Input from individual will be helpful to determine length of breaks needed and when breaks should be implemented
Write things down/draw things out collaboratively with the patient	Facilitate organization Facilitate learning and memory for individuals who may become overwhelmed by auditory information Facilitate understanding of circumstances and events that may precede suicidal ideation and/or engagement in self-directed violence	Write down key points/information/examples when in session Draw timelines to capture sequence of events that may have preceded crisis
Utilize visual cues	Create environmental prompts to engage in coping strategies	Posting safety plans, pictures representing protective factors, inspirational quotes in easy to see/highly used areas
Incorporate supports proactively	Consistently engage social supports to reduce isolation and increase active engagement in coping strategies. Educate social supports about the plan and incorporating them in a proactive and meaningful way may increase likelihood of successful implementation of the safety plan	Regularly scheduled check-ins with social supports Appointments (medical, mental health, social support groups, community activities) Sharing the safety plan with social supports identified in the plan
Ask the patient to provide summaries	Provide opportunity for individuals to consolidate and articulate their understanding of information	Individual provides a summary of self-assessment (e.g., When I am by myself for long periods of time, I am more likely to hurt myself) Individual provides a summary of planning strategies (e.g., After I have been by myself for more than 3 hours, I will call someone listed on my safety plan and make arrangements to spend time together)
Role-play	Practice engaging in coping strategies with support and opportunities for modification to reduce challenges/barriers and increase problem solving	Practice engaging in coping strategies Practice using the safety plan (calling supports, engaging in self-care activities, etc)
Utilize patient identified coping strategies and work collaboratively to design implementation	Increase likelihood of implementation of safety plan by planning engagement in meaningful activities that facilitate coping	Provider facilitates planning for meaningful activities as identified by the patient (e.g., working out, calling a support, spending time with favorite pet)

CONCLUSION

Individuals with a history of TBI are at increased risk for engaging in suicidal behavior. Moreover, the increased risk of suicide among those with TBI does not appear to be fully explained by symptoms associated with co-occurring mental health conditions (e.g., depression). As such, comprehensive evaluation and close monitoring of suicide risk factors should be considered a part of routine clinical care for members of this population.

Based upon information presented in this chapter, suicide risk assessment practices for those with a history of TBI should focus on the identification of psychiatric, psychosocial and cognitive risk factors for suicide. For example, assessment of post injury psychiatric symptoms, degree of impairment or disability secondary to injury, substance abuse, and executive dysfunction are all important components of suicide risk assessment and treatment planning in this population. Clinicians should also keep in mind that although theory and resources provide useful information, person-specific factors may be complex and must be considered when conceptualizing individual risk [5]. As such, identification of person-specific warning signs is also highly recommended [68].While most of the suicide warning signs that have been identified for the general population are also relevant to those with TBI, future research aimed at identifying warning signs that are unique to those with TBI is needed to further inform clinical practice and suicide prevention efforts for this population.

Despite the growing body of research, which has suggested that individuals with a history of TBI are at increased risk for suicide, there continues to be a lack of evidence-based suicide prevention treatments for those with TBI [1]. While future efforts should be aimed at identifying evidence based assessment and treatment practices for managing suicidality in those with TBI, a number of current suicide management practices may be adapted to treat individuals with TBI who are at risk for suicidal behavior. One promising intervention for managing suicidal behavior in those with TBI is safety planning. Safety planning is a brief stand alone intervention that can be modified for a variety of populations, including individuals with TBI. The safety plan provides the individual with a written, well thought-out, personalized plan to be used before or during a suicidal crisis. For individuals with TBI, some of whom may have enduring sequelae that may impact problem solving and other executive functions, the safety plan can be particularly useful in providing other options for coping that can be easily accessed and utilized during a crisis.

Finally, research has shown that training clinicians who are likely to come in contact with individuals at risk for suicide contributes not only to better identification of suicidal risk, but can also facilitate increased management of suicidal behavior [86]. As such, education on suicide assessment and suicide prevention practices should be aimed towards rehabilitation providers as well as other professionals (e.g., mental health clinicians, primary care physicians) who deliver care to patients with TBI [87].

FURTHER READINGS

Brenner LA, Homaifar BY, Wolfman JH, Kemp J, Adler LE. Suicidality and veterans with a history of traumatic brain injury: precipitating events, protective factors, and prevention strategies. *Rehabil Psychol.* 2009;54:390–397.

Dennis P, Ghahramanlou-Holloway M, Cox DW, Brown GK. A guide for the assessment and treatment of suicidal patients with traumatic brain injuries. *J Head Trauma Rehabil.* 2011;26(4):244-256.

Joiner TE. *Why People Die by Suicide*. Cambridge, MA: Harvard University Press; 2005.

Simpson G, Brenner L. Perspectives on suicide and traumatic brain injury. *J Head Trauma Rehabil.* 2011;26(4):241-243.

Simpson G, Tate R. Clinical features of suicide attempts after traumatic brain injury. *J Nervous Ment Dis.* 2005;193:680-685.

Stanley B, Brown GK with Karlin B, Kemp JE, VonBergen HA. *Safety Plan Treatment Manual to Reduce Suicide Risk: Veteran Version*. Unpublished manuscript; 2008.

Teasdale TW, Engberg AW. Suicide after traumatic brain injury: a population study. *J Neurol, Neurosurg Psychiatry.* 2001;71:436-440.

REFERENCES

[1] Simpson G, Brenner L. Perspectives on suicide and traumatic brain injury. *J Head Trauma Rehabil.* 2011;26(4):241-243.

[2] Simpson G, Tate R. Suicidality after traumatic brain injury: demographic, injury and clinical correlates. *Psychol Med.* 2002;32:687-697.

[3] Silver JM, Kramer R, Greenwald S, Wiessman M. The association between head injuries and psychiatric disorders: findings from the New Haven NIMH Epidemiologic Catchment Area Study. *Brain Inj.* 2001;15:935-945.

[4] Teasdale TW, Engberg AW. Suicide after traumatic brain injury: a population study. *J Neurol, Neurosurg Psychiatry.* 2001;71:436-440.

[5] Brenner L, Gutierrez P, Huggins J, Olson-Madden J. Traumatic brain injury and suicide. In: Berman AL, Pompili M, eds. *Medical Conditions Associated with Suicide Risk*. Washington, DC: American Association of Suicidology; 2011:299-307.

[6] Center for Disease Control and Prevention. Traumatic Brain Injury. Center for Disease Control Web site. *http://www.cdc.gov/traumaticbraininjury. Published 2011. Accessed August 1, 2011.*

[7] Department of Veterans Affairs. *Trauma Brain Inj.* Department of Veterans Affairs Employee Education System; 2004.

[8] Ivins BJ, Schwab KA, Warden D, Harvey LT, Hoilien MA, Powell CO, Johnson CS, Salazar AM. Traumatic brain injury in US Army paratroopers: Prevalence and character. *J Trauma.* 2003;55:617-621.

[9] Langlois JA, Rutland-Brown W, Thomas KE. Traumatic brain injury in the United States: emergency department visits, hospitalizations, and deaths. *http://www.cdc.gov/ncipc/pubres/tbi_in_us_04/tbi%20in%20the%20us_jan_2006.pdf. Published 2006. Accessed August 1, 2011.*

[10] Kay T, Harrington DE, Adams R, et al. Definition of mild traumatic brain injury. *J Head Trauma Rehabil.* 1993;8(3):86-87.

[11] Terrio H, Brenner LA, Ivins BJ, et al. Traumatic brain injury screening: preliminary findings regarding prevalence and sequelae in a US army brigade combat team. *J Head Trauma Rehabil.* 2009;24(1):14-23.

[12] Lew HL, Cifu DX, Sigford B, Scott S, Sayer N, Jaffee MS. Team approach to diagnosis and management of traumatic brain injury and its comorbidities. *J Rehabil Research and Dev.* 2007;44(7):vii-xi.

[13] Warden D. Military TBI during the Iraq and Afghanistan wars. *J Head Trauma Rehabil.* 2006;21:398–402.

[14] Belanger HG, Uomoto JM, Vanderploeg RD. The veterans health administration system of care for mild traumatic brain injury: costs, benefits, and controversies. *J Head Trauma Rehabil.* 2009;24(1):4-13.

[15] Okie S. Traumatic brain injury in the war zone. *N Engl J Med.* 2005;352:2043-2047.

[16] Warden DL, Ryan LM, Helmick KM, et al. War neurotrauma: the Defense and Veterans Brain Injury Center (DVBIC) experience at Walter Reed Army Medical Center (WRAMC) .*Journal of Neurotrauma.* 2005;22:1178.

[17] Alexander M. Mild traumatic brain injury: pathophysiology, natural history, and clinical management. *Neurology.* 1995;45(7):1253-1260.

[18] Belanger HG, Curtiss G, Demery JA, Lebowitz BK, Vanderploeg RD. Factors moderating neuropsychological outcomes following mild traumatic brain injury: a meta-analysis. *J Int Neuropsychol Soc.* 2005;11:215–227.

[19] Hoge CW, Terhakopian A, Castro CA, Messer SC, Engel CC. Association of posttraumatic stress disorder with somatic symptoms, health care visits, and absenteeism among Iraq war veterans. *Amer J Psychiatry.* 2007;164(1):150-153.

[20] Hoge CW, McGurk D, Thomas JL, Cox AL, Engel CC, Castro CA. Mild traumatic brain injury in U.S. Soldiers returning from Iraq. *N Engl J Med.* 2008;358(5):453-463.

[21] Schneiderman AI, Braver ER, Kang HK. Understanding sequelae of injury mechanisms and mild traumatic brain injury incurred during the conflicts in Iraq and Afghanistan: persistent postconcussive symptoms and posttraumatic stress disorder. *Amer Journal Epidemiol.* 2008;167(12):1446-1452.

[22] Lezak MD, Howieson DB, Loring DW. *Neuropsychological Assessment.* 4th ed. New York, NY: Oxford University Press, Inc.; 2004.

[23] National Institutes of Health. *Rehabilitation of persons with traumatic brain injury: NIH Consensus Statement.* 1998 Oct 26-28;16(1):1-41.

[24] Arlinghaus, KA, Shoaib, AM, Price TR. Neuropsychiatric assessment. In: Silver JM, McAllister TW, Yudofsky SC, eds. *Textbook of Traumatic Brain Injury.* Washington, DC: American Psychiatric Publishing, Inc.; 2005:59-78.

[25] DiBiase P, Arriaga MA. Post traumatic hydrops. *Otolaryngology Clinics of NorthAmerica.* 1997;30:1117–1122.

[26] Hawley CA. Return to driving after head injury. *J Neurol, Neurosurg, Psychiatry.* 2001;70:761–766.

[27] McCullagh S, Feinstein A. Cognitive changes. In: Silver JM, McAllister TW, Yudofsky SC, eds. *Textbook of traumatic brain injury.* Washington, DC: American Psychiatric Publishing, Inc.; 2005: 321-335.

[28] Oquendo MA, Friedman JH, Grunebaum MF, Burke A, Silver JM, Mann JJ. Suicidal behavior and mild traumatic brain injury in major depression. *J Nervous Ment Dis.* 2004;192:430-434.

[29] Hibbard MR, Uysal S, Kepler K, Bogdany J, Silver J. Axis I psychopathology in individuals with traumatic brain injury. *J Head Trauma Rehabil,* 1998; 13(4):24-39.

[30] Ahmed I, Fujii D. Posttraumatic psychosis. *Semin Clin Neuropsychiatry.* 1998;3:23–33.

[31] Anstey KJ, Butterworth P, Jorm AF, Christensen H, Rodgers B, Windsor T. A population survey found an association between self-reports of traumatic brain injury and increased psychiatric symptoms. *J Clin Epidemiol.* 2004;57:1202–1209.

[32] Mainio A, Kyllönen T, Viilo K, Hakko H, Särkioja T, Räsänen P. Traumatic brain injury, psychiatric disorders and suicide: a population-based study of suicide victims during the years 1988-2004 in Northern Finland. *Brain Inj.* 2007;21(8):851-855.

[33] Olson-Madden JH, Brenner L, Harwood JEF, Emrick CD, Corrigan JD, Thompson C. Traumatic brain injury and psychiatric diagnoses in veterans seeking outpatient substance abuse treatment. *J Head Trauma Rehabil.* 2010;25(6):470-479.

[34] Bombardier CH, Fann JR, Temkin NR, Esselman PC, Barber J, Dikmen SS. Rates of Major Depressive Disorder and clinical outcomes following traumatic brain injury. *JAMA.* 2010;303(19):1938-1945.

[35] Jorge RE, Robinson RG, Moser D, Tateno A, Crespo-Facorro B, Arndt S. Major depression following traumatic brain injury. *Arch Gen Psychiatry.* 2004;61(1):42-50.

[36] Robinson RG, Jorge RE. Mood disorders. In: Silver JM, McAllister TW, Yudofsky SC, eds. *Textbook of traumatic brain injury.* Washington, DC: American Psychiatric Publishing, Inc.; 2005:201-212.

[37] Simpson G, Tate R. Suicidality in people surviving a traumatic brain injury: prevalence, risk factors and implications for clinical management. *Brain Inj.* 2007;21(13-14):1335-11351.

[38] Fann JR, Burington B, Leonetti A, Jaffe K, Katon W, Thompson RS. Psychiatric illness following traumatic brain injury in an adult health maintenance organization population. *Arch Gen Psychiatry.* 2004;61:53–61.

[39] Arciniegas DB, Harris SN, Brousseau, KM. Psychosis following traumatic brain injury. *Int Rev Psychiatry.* 2003;15:328-340.

[40] Davison K, Bagley CR. Schizophrenia-like psychoses associated with organic disorders of the central nervous system: a review of the literature. In: Herrington RN, ed. *Current Problems in Neuropsychiatry: Schizophrenia, Epilepsy, the Temporal Lobe.* London: Headley; 1969:113-184.

[41] Achte K, Hillbom E, Aalberg V. Psychoses following war brain injuries. *Acta Psychiatrica Scandinavica.* 1969;45:1-18.

[42] Achte K, Jarho L, Kyykka T, Vesterinen E. Paranoid disorders following war brain damage. Preliminary report. *Psychopathology.* 1991;60:231-236.

[43] Sachdev P, Smith JS, Cathcart S. Schizophrenia-like psychosis following traumatic brain injury: a chart-based descriptive and case-control study. *Psychological Medicine.* 2001;31:231-239.

[44] Tanielian T, Jaycox L, eds. *Invisible Wounds of War: Psychological and Cognitive Injuries, their Consequences, and Services to Assist Recovery.* Santa Monica, CA: RAND Corporation; 2008.

[45] Schwab KA, Ivins B, Cramer G, et al. Screening for traumatic brain injury in troops returning from deployment in Afghanistan and Iraq: initial investigation of the usefulness of a short screening tool for traumatic brain injury. *J Head Trauma Rehabil.* 2007;22(6):377-389.

[46] King NS. PTSD and traumatic brain injury: Folklore and fact? *Brain Inj.* 2008;22(1): 1-5.

[47] Corrigan JD, Bogner, JA, Mysiw, WJ, Clinchot D, Fugate, L. Life satisfaction after traumatic brain injury. *J Head Trauma Rehabil.* 2001; 16: 543-555.

[48] Corrigan, J.D. Substance abuse as a mediating factor in outcome from traumatic brain injury. *Arch Phy Med Rehabil.* 1995;83:1765-1773.

[49] Kreutzer JS, Witol AD, Harris-Marwitz JH. Alcohol and drug use among young persons with traumatic brain injury. *J Learning Disabilities.* 1996;29(6):643- 651.

[50] Bombardier CH, Temkin NR, Machamer J, Kimen SS. The natural history of drinking and alcohol-related problems after traumatic brain injury. *Arch Phys Med Rehabil.* 2003;84:185-191.

[51] Simpson G, Tate R. Clinical features of suicide attempts after traumatic brain injury. *J Nervous Ment Dis.* 2005;193:680-685.

[52] Bertolote JM, Fleischmann A. Suicide and psychiatric diagnosis: a worldwide perspective. *World Psychiatry.* 2002;1(3):181-185.

[53] McDonald BC, Flashman LA, Saykin AJ. Executive dysfunction following traumatic brain injury: neural substrates and treatment strategies. *Neuro Rehabil.* 2002;17: 333-344.

[54] Dyer KF, Bell R, McCann J, Rauch R. Aggression after traumatic brain injury: analyzing socially desirable responses and the nature of aggressive traits. *Brain Inj.* 2006;20:1163–1173.

[55] Kim E. Agitation, aggression, and disinhibition syndromes after traumatic brain injury. *Neuro Rehabil.* 2002;17:297-310.

[56] Marson DC, Dreer LE, Krzywanski S, Huthwaite JS, Devivo MJ, Novack TA. Impairment and partial recovery of medical decision-making capacity in traumatic brain injury: a 6-month longitudinal study. *Arch Phys Med Rehabil.* 2005;86:889-895.

[57] Salmond CH, Sahakian BJ. Cognitive outcome in traumatic brain injury survivors. *Current Opinion Critical Care.* 2005;11:111-116.

[58] Jollant F, Bellivier F, Leboyer M, et al. Impaired decision making in suicide attempters. *Amer J Psychiatry.* 2005;162:304-310.

[59] Keilp JG, Sackeim HA, Brodsky BS, Oquendo MA, Malone KM, Mann JJ. Neuropsychological dysfunction in depressed suicide attempters. *Amer J Psychiatry.* 2001;158:735-741.

[60] Mann JJ, Waternaux C, Haas GL, Malone KM. Toward a clinical model of suicidal behavior in psychiatric patients. *Amer J Psychiatry.* 1999;156:181-189.

[61] Dumais A, Lesage AD, Lalovic A, et al. Is violent method of suicide a behavioral marker of lifetime aggression? *Amer Journal Psychiatry.* 2005;162:1375–1378.

[62] Gould KR, Ponsford JL, Johnston L, Schonberger M. Predictive and associated factors of psychiatric disorders after traumatic brain injury: a prospective study. *J Neurotrauma.* 2011;28:1155-1163.

[63] Brenner LA, Homaifar BY, Wolfman JH, Kemp J, Adler LE. Suicidality and veterans with a history of traumatic brain injury: precipitating events, protective factors, and prevention strategies. *Rehabil Psychol.* 2009;54:390–397.

[64] Dennis P, Ghahramanlou-Holloway M, Cox DW, Brown GK. A guide for the assessment and treatment of suicidal patients with traumatic brain injuries. *J Head Trauma Rehabil.* 2011;26(4):244-256.

[65] Brenner L. Application of a novel therapeutic model to suicide risk assessment after traumatic brain injury. *Brain Inj Professional.* 2008;5:26-28.

[66] Joiner TE. *Why People Die by Suicide*. Cambridge, MA: Harvard University Press; 2005.

[67] Simon RI. *Suicide Risk: Assessing the Unpredictable. Textbook of Suicide Assessment and Management*. Washington, DC: The American Psychiatric Publishing; 2006.

[68] Rudd MD, Berman AL, Joiner TE, et al. Warning signs for suicide: theory, research and clinical applications. *Suicide Life Threatening Beh*. 2006;36(3):255-262.

[69] Risk Factors for Suicide and Suicidal Behaviors. American Association of Suicidology Web site. *http://www.suicidology.org/web/guest/stats-and-tools/fact-sheets. Published 2010. Retrieved August 19, 2011.*

[70] Maris RW, Berman AL, Silverman MM. *Comprehensive Textbook of Suicidology*. New York, NY: The Guilford Press; 2000.

[71] Joiner TE, Walker RL, Rudd MD, Jobes DA. Scientizing and routinizing the assessment of suicidality in outpatient practice. *Professional Psycho: Res Pract*. 1999;30(5):447-453.

[72] American Psychiatric Association. Practice guidelines for the assessment and treatment of patients with suicidal behaviors *http://www.psychiatryonline.com/pracGuide/prac GuideChapToc_14.aspx. Published 2003. Accessed August 1, 2011.*

[73] Silver JM, McAllister TW, Yudofsky SC, eds. *Textbook of Traumatic Brain Injury*. Washington, DC: American Psychiatric Publishing, Inc.; 2005

[74] Frank RG, Rosenthal M, Caplan B, eds. *Handbook of Rehabilitation Psychology*. Washington, DC: American Psychological Association; 2010:147-164.

[75] Mioshi E, Kipps CM, Dawson K, Mitchell J, Graham A, Hodges JR. Activities of daily living in frontotemporal dementia and Alzheimer disease. *Neurol*. 2007;68:2077-2084.

[76] Marshall GA, Rentz DM, Frey MT, Locascio JL, Johnson KA, Sperling RA, and the Alzheimer's Disease Neuroimaging Initiative. Executive function and instrumental activities of daily living in mild cognitive impairment and Alzheimer's disease. *Alzheimer's Dementia*. 2011;7;300-308.

[77] Elbogen EB, Wagner HR, Fuller SR, Calhoun PS, Kinneer PM, Mid-Atlantic Mental Illness Research, Education, and Clinical Center Workgroup, Beckham JC. Correlates of anger and hostility in Iraq and Afghanistan war veterans. *Amer J Psychiatry*. 2010;167(9):1051-1058.

[78] Homaifar BY, Bahraini NH, Silverman MM, Brenner LA. Executive functioning and suicide risk assessment: strategies for incorporating standard clinical information. *Journal of Mental Health Counseling.*2012;34(2):110-120.

[79] Wingate LR, Joiner TE, Rudd MD, Jobes DA. Empirically informed approaches to topics in suicide risk assessment. *Behav Sci Law*. 2004;22:651-665.

[80] World Health Organization. *International Classification of Functioning, Disability and Health*. Geneva, Switzerland: World Health Organization; 2001.

[81] Brenner L, Homaifar B. Deployment-acquired TBI and suicidality: risk and assessment. In Sher L, Vilens A, eds. *War and Suicide*. New York, NY: Nova Science Publishers; 2009:189-202.

[82] Van Order KA, Witte TL, Gordon KH, Bender TW, Joiner TE. Suicidal desire and the capability of suicide: test of the interpersonal-psychological theory of suicidal behavior among adults. *J Counseling Clin Psychol*. 2008;76(1):72-83.

[83] Stanley B, Brown GK with Karlin B, Kemp JE, VonBergen HA. *Safety Plan Treatment Manual to Reduce Suicide Risk: Veteran Version*. Unpublished manuscript; 2008.

[84] Miller MC. Suicide-prevention contracts. In: Jacobs DG, ed. *The Harvard Medical School Guide to Suicide Assessment and Intervention*. San Francisco, CA: Jossey-Bass; 1999.

[85] Jobes DA. *Managing Suicide Risk: A Collaborative Approach*. New York, NY: The Guilford Press; 2006.

[86] Mann JJ, Apter A, Bertolote J, et al. Suicide prevention strategies: A systematic review. *JAMA*. 2005;*294(16):2064-2074.*

[87] Wasserman L, Shaw T, Vu M, Ko C, Bollegala D, Bhalerao S. An overview of traumatic brain injury. *Brain Inj*. 2008;22(11):811-819.

In: Frontiers in Suicide Risk
Editor: Jill E. Lavigne

ISBN 978-1-62081-373-7
©2012 Nova Science Publishers, Inc.

Chapter 7

INTERVENTIONS TO ADDRESS SUICIDAL BEHAVIOR IN ADULTS WITH SUBSTANCE USE DISORDERS

Kenneth R. Conner

VISN 2 Center of Excellence for Suicide Prevention,
Canandaigua VA Medical Center, Canandaigua, NY. Department of Psychiatry,
University of Rochester Medical Center, Rochester, NY US

ABSTRACT

Data are reviewed to show that patients in treatment for substance use disorders (SUD) are at elevated risk for attempted suicide and suicide, necessitating a focus on SUD treatment venues in prevention efforts. For the remainder of the chapter, intervention and training relevant to suicide risk in SUD treatment settings is reviewed. Cognitive therapy and cognitive-behavioral therapy (CBT) and dialectical behavior therapy (DBT) are discussed because they have well-established efficacy with high-risk patients including those with SUDs. A limitation of CBT for suicide prevention and DBT is that that they are complex and intensive therapies that may be difficult to implement in routine SUD treatment. Other newer treatments for SUD patients and trainings for SUD providers with potentially greater ease of implementation in SUD programs are also discussed including Treatment Improvement Protocol Number 50 (TIP 50), Safety Planning, and Preventing Addiction Related Suicide (PARS). These novel treatments require further study.

INTRODUCTION

1. Link between Substance Use Disorders and Suicidal Behavior

Much of the research on risk for suicide in individuals with substance use disorders (SUDs) is focused on alcohol use disorders including alcohol abuse and dependence. These data show that alcohol use disorders confer increased risk for suicide (Wilcox, Conner, and Caine, 2004) and are the second most prevalent category of mental disorder among suicide decedents, behind only mood disorders (Cavanagh, Carson, Sharpe, and Lawrie, 2003). With rare exception (Phillips et al., 2002), postmortem psychological autopsy studies show that alcohol use disorders confer risk for suicide after adjusting for other risk factors (Cheng, 1995; Kolves, Varnik, Tooding, and Wasserman, 2006; Lesage et al., 1994). Alcohol use disorders also confer risk for suicide attempts (Kessler, Borges, and Walters, 1999). Individuals who present for alcoholism treatment, a more severe population compared to those who go untreated, have high lifetime rates of suicide attempt (Roy and Janal, 2007; Wojnar et al., 2009) and are at high risk for eventual suicide (Wilcox et al., 2004).

There are fewer data on risk for suicidal behavior associated with specific non-alcohol drug use disorders although available data consistently links stimulants (cocaine and amphetamines) and opiates (both licit and illicit) to suicide (Degenhardt, Roxburgh, and Barker, 2005; Karch, Barker, and Strine, 2006; Wilcox et al., 2004).

Drug use disorders broadly also confer elevated risk for suicide attempts (Kessler et al., 1999). Individuals obtaining treatment for drug use disorders including cocaine dependence (Roy, 2001), opiate dependence (Darke, Ross, Lynskey, and Teesson, 2004), and a mixture of drug use disorders (K. R. Conner, Pinquart, and Gamble, 2009; Ilgen, Harris, Moos, and Tiet, 2007; Wines, Saitz, Horton, Lloyd-Travaglini, and Samet, 2004) have high lifetime prevalence rates of attempt.

2. Cognitive Behavior Therapy (CBT) and Dialectical Behavior Therapy (DBT)

Data from rigorous randomized clinical trials (RCTs) show that cognitive therapy or cognitive-behavioral therapy (CBT) and dialectical behavior therapy (DBT) are efficacious in reducing risk for suicide reattempt in high-risk clinical samples (Brown et al., 2005; Linehan et al., 2006). The evidence base includes an exemplary study of CBT conducted with an urban sample of suicide attempters that showed that participants assigned to CBT were at decreased risk for re-attempt over 18-month follow-up (Brown et al., 2005) and a rigorous study of DBT with high-risk patients with borderline personality disorder that showed decreased risk for reattempt over 24-month follow-up (Linehan et al., 2006).

Importantly, 68% of the participants in the CBT study had a SUD and 73% of those in the DBT study had a history of SUD, suggesting that these treatments are efficacious in reducing risk for suicide attempts in patients with SUD. Moreover, the efficacy of CBT to reduce substance use is well-established (Magill and Ray, 2009) and emerging data support the efficacy of DBT as a treatment for substance use (Harned et al., 2008; Linehan et al., 1999). Limitations include that CBT for suicidal behavior and DBT are complex and intensive treatments, factors that create a challenge for widespread implementation with reasonable fidelity in SUD treatment venues and other clinical settings. Also, the potential impact of CBT and DBT in preventing suicide deaths has yet to be determined.

3. Treatment Improvement Protocol Number 50 (Tip 50)

SUD treatment providers carry large caseloads, have a primary focus on substance use, and clinical practice guidelines indicate that independent management of suicide risk is beyond the scope of practice of many SUD treatment providers. Therefore, few frontline SUD treatment providers are in a position to deliver multi-session CBT or DBT protocols to patients deemed to be at risk for suicidal behavior. Typically such intensive interventions will be delivered by other members of a multidisciplinary treatment team with specialized training and and/or provided externally by mental health clinicians working in coordination with SUD treatment programs. Nonetheless, it is essential that all SUD treatment providers have practical, tailored training in suicide risk management and receive adequate supervision and administrative support to perform these duties as needed during the routine course of SUD treatment. In recognition of this need, the Center for Substance Abuse Treatment (CSAT) at the Substance Abuse and Mental Health Services Administration (SAMHSA) produced a Treatment Improvement Protocol (TIP 50) (Center for Substance Abuse Treatment, 2009). TIP 50 provides a practical manual for front-line substance abuse counselors, supervisors, and program administrators to manage suicide risk. The centerpiece is an overarching framework referred to as GATE: Gather Information, Access Supervision, Take Appropriate Action, Extend the Action (beyond the immediate situation).

Subsequently, the Veterans Administration (VA) produced a TIP 50 training video designed to introduce TIP 50 (*Addressing suicidal thoughts and behaviors in substance abuse treatment.* 2010). The 1¼ hour video features a panel of VA clinicians who explain GATE and other key points in TIP 50. GATE is further illustrated through a series of dramatic vignettes of the case of Antonio, a 25-year old Veteran of the Iraq War who becomes suicidal during the course of outpatient SUD treatment. Although the case is fictitious, it is based on common features of suicide risk in Veterans with SUD and is generalizable to civilian SUD treatment settings. A 2-hour curriculum was developed that consisted of showing the TIP 50 training video, discussing the video briefly, and passing out the TIP 50 manuals and encouraging their use. This training was delivered to 273 treatment providers who primarily worked in Veterans Health Administration (VHA). The training was evaluated based on within subject comparisons of self-report questionnaires administered at pre-training, post-training, and 2-month follow-up. Results showed statistically significant changes in knowledge, self-efficacy, and suicide prevention practice behaviors (Conner, Wood, Pisani, and Kemp, in press). The brevity of the training (2 hours or less), its simplicity (show video, pass out manual), and ease of dissemination (TIP 50 video and TIP 50 manuals are free and accessible) underscore the potential for widespread implementation. Limitations include that the evaluation documented within participant changes (no control group), data were based on self-report, follow-up was limited to 2 months with significant attrition, and impact of the training on SUD patients was not assessed. Accordingly, the TIP 50 materials (manual, video) show promise yet require further evaluation.

4. Safety Plan

The "safety plan" is a CBT-based intervention designed to be delivered in one session (Stanley and Brown, 2012). It is done collaboratively with at-risk patients in order to produce a written 6-step hierarchical strategy for managing suicidal crises. At each progressive step a more intensive action is taken to manage risk, beginning with low intensity interventions that can be done alone (e.g., taking a shower to distract oneself) to high intensity actions that require outside intervention (e.g., presenting to an emergency department). If a given step in the hierarchy proves inadequate, patients are instructed to move up a step until the crisis is resolved. Training materials were created to introduce safety planning to Veterans Health Administration (VHA) treatment providers (*Safety planning for suicide prevention.* 2008; Stanley and Brown, 2008), along with a standard template for conducting a safety plan and documenting it in the VHA clinical record. Subsequently, safety planning has been widely implemented in VHA and is now considered a standard practice for patients with indications of acute risk. Currently there is an ongoing, multi-site evaluation of safety planning in VHA emergency departments for patients at intermediate risk for suicidal behavior, "SAFE VET", as well as an ongoing study of active military, "SAFE MIL." Assuming these studies show favorable results, a next logical step would be to examine the use of safety planning in SUD treatment venues because the brevity and relative simplicity of the intervention suggests the potential for adoption by SUD programs.

5. Preventing Addiction Related Suicide (PARS)

All of the interventions discussed thus far (CBT, DBT, GATE, Safety Plan) are *indicated* prevention strategies, in other words they are designed only for patients who are deemed to be at elevated risk. In contrast, Preventing Addiction Related Suicide (PARS) is an educational curriculum designed to be delivered as a routine part of treatment to all SUD patients attending intensive outpatient treatment groups (Ries, 2010), with a rationale that such education should be provided as a standard part of treatment because a high percentage of adults in SUD treatment have experienced suicidal thoughts or behaviors (Conner et al., 2009; Darke et al., 2004; Ilgen et al., 2007; Roy, 2001; Roy and Janal, 2007; Wines et al., 2004; Wojnar et al., 2009). PARS was developed through a bottom-up process that included focus groups and trial runs with SUD patients and frontline treatment providers (Ries, 2010), along with experience gained researching SUD patients admitted for suicide risk (Ries, Yuodelis-Flores, Comtois, Roy-Byrne, and Russo, 2008). The result is a one-session training curriculum delivered using Powerpoint slides or handouts (depending on counselor preference) in an interactive format. The PARS curriculum reviews that SUD patients are at increased risk for suicidal behavior compared to non substance abusers, discusses reasons for the connection between addiction and suicidal behavior, goes over risk factors and warning signs – emphasizing factors most applicable to substance abusers (e.g., role of relapse), and reviews actions to take when risk factors and warning signs occur or intensify. Pilot research on the impact of the PARS curriculum on patient knowledge about suicide, willingness for help seeking pertaining to suicide, and actual help seeking at 1-month follow-up is ongoing, with future plans to expand the focus to examine impact on suicidal thoughts or behaviors in SUD patients. Accordingly, PARS is a promising intervention at an early stage of evaluation.

CONCLUSION

Alcohol use disorders are prevalent among suicide decedents and are a potent risk factor for suicide and suicide attempt. Some major classes of drug use disorders also confer substantial risk. Individuals in treatment for SUD(s), representing a severe subpopulation, are especially vulnerable. These data demand that suicide prevention efforts focus on SUD treatment populations.

CBT and DBT are efficacious treatments for the prevention of suicide reattempts in high-risk patients, and individuals with SUD have been well-represented in these studies. Additional support for using CBT and DBT to prevent suicidal behavior in SUD patients comes from the demonstrated efficacy of these treatments in reducing substance use. Further research on implementation of these treatments and the impact on suicide deaths are needed.

Promising interventions in the early stages of evaluation include TIP50 and PARS. In the future, safety planning in SUD treatment venues would prove a natural advance if current evaluation efforts show a positive effect of efforts in these settings.

REFERENCES

Brown, G. K., Have, T. T., Henriques, G. R., Xie, S. X., Hollander, J. E., and Beck, A. T. (2005). Cognitive therapy for the prevention of suicide attempts: A randomized controlled trial. *JAMA, 294*, 563-570.

Cavanagh, J. T. O., Carson, A. J., Sharpe, M., and Lawrie, S. M. (2003). Psychological autopsy studies of suicide: A systematic review. *Psychological Medicine, 33*, 395-405.

Center for Substance Abuse Treatment. (2009). *Addressing suicidal thoughts and behaviors in substance abuse treatment.* HHS No. (SMA) 09-4381.). Rockville, MD: Substance Abuse and Mental Health Services Administration.

Cheng, A. T. A. (1995). Mental illness and suicide. *British Journal of Psychiatry, 170*, 441-446.

Conner, K. R., Wood, J., and Pisani, A.R., and Kemp, J. (in press). Evaluation of a suicide prevention training curriculum for substance abuse treatment providers based on treatment improvement protocol number 50 (TIP 50). *Journal of Substance Abuse Treatment.*

Conner, K. R., Pinquart, M., and Gamble, S. A. (2009). Meta-analysis of depression and substance use among individuals with alcohol use disorders. *Journal of Substance Abuse Treatment, 37*, 127-137.

Darke, S., Ross, J., Lynskey, M., and Teesson, M. (2004). Attempted suicide among entrants to three treatment modalities for heroin dependence in the australian treatment outcome study (ATOS): Prevalence and risk factors. *Drug and Alcohol Dependence, 73*(1), 1-10.

Degenhardt, L., Roxburgh, A., and Barker, B. (2005). Underlying causes of cocaine, amphetamine and opioid related deaths in australia. *Journal of Clinical Forensic Medicine, 12*(4), 187-195. doi:10.1016/j.jcfm.2004.11.003

Harned, M. S., Chapman, A. L., Dexter-Mazza, E. T., Murray, A., Comtois, K. A., and Linehan, M. M. (2008). Treating co-occurring axis I disorders in recurrently suicidal women with borderline personality disorder: A 2-year randomized trial of dialectical behavior therapy versus community treatment by experts. *Journal of Consulting and Clinical Psychology, 76*, 1068-1075.

Ilgen, M. A., Harris, A. H., Moos, R. H., and Tiet, Q. Q. (2007). Predictors of a suicide attempt one year after entry into substance use disorder treatment. *Alcoholism: Clinical and Experimental Research, 31*, 635-642.

Karch, D. L., Barker, L., and Strine, T. W. (2006). Race/ethnicity, substance abuse, and mental illness among suicide victims in 13 US states: 2004 data from the national violent death reporting system. *Injury Prevention, 12 (suppl)*, ii22-ii27.

Kessler, R. C., Borges, G., and Walters, E. E. (1999). Prevalence of and risk factors for lifetime suicide attempts in the national comorbidity survey. *Archives of General Psychiatry, 56*, 617-625.

Kolves, K., Varnik, A., Tooding, L. M., and Wasserman, D. (2006). The role of alcohol in suicide: A case-control psychological autopsy study. *Psychological Medicine, 36*, 923-930.

Lesage, A. D., Boyer, R., Grunberg, F., Vanier, C., Morisette, R., Ménard-Buteau, C., and Loyer, M. (1994). Suicide and mental disorders: A case-control study of young men. *American Journal of Psychiatry, 151*(7), 1063-1068.

Linehan, M. M., Comtois, K. A., Murray, A. M., Brown, M. Z., Gallop, R. J., and Heard, H. L. (2006). Two-year randomized controlled trial and follow-up of dialectical behavior therapy vs therapy by experts for suicidal behaviors and borderline personality disorders. *Archives of General Psychiatry, 63*, 757-766.

Linehan, M. M., Schmidt, H. I., Dimeff, L. A., Craft, C. J., Kanter, J., and Comtois, K. A. (1999). Dialectical behavior therapy for patients with borderline personality disorder and drug-dependence. *American Journal on Addictions, 8*, 279-292.

Magill, M., and Ray, L. A. (2009). Cognitive-behavioral treatment with adult alcohol and illicit drug users: A meta-analysis of randomized controlled trials. *Journal of Studies on Alcohol and Drugs, 70*(4), 516-527.

Phillips, M. R., Yang, G., Zhang, Y., Wang, L., Ji, H., and Zhou, M. (2002). Risk factors for suicide in china: A national case-control psychological autopsy study. *The Lancet, 360*, 1728-1736.

Ries, R. K. (2010). *Preventing addiction related suicide (PARS)*. U.S. NIH Grant 5R21DA026494-02.

Ries, R. K., Yuodelis-Flores, C., Comtois, K. A., Roy-Byrne, P., and Russo, J. E. (2008). Substance-induced suicidal admissions to an acute psychiatric service: Characteristics and outcomes. *Journal of Substance Abuse Treatment, 34*, 72-79.

Roy, A. (2001). Characteristics of cocaine-dependent patients who attempt suicide. *American Journal of Psychiatry, 158*, 1215-1219.

Roy, A., and Janal, M. N. (2007). Risk factors for suicide attempts among alcohol dependent patients. *Archives of Suicide Research, 11*, 211-217.

Stanley, B., and Brown, G. K. (2012). Safety planning intervention: A brief intervention to mitigate suicide risk. *Cognitive and Behavioral Practice, 19, 256-264.*

Stanley, B., and Brown, G. K. (2008). *The safety plan treatment manual to reduce suicide risk: Veteran version.* Washington, D.C.: United States Department of Veterans Affairs.

VA Employee Education System (Producer)(2008). *Safety planning for suicide prevention.* [Video/DVD] Washington, DC:

VA Employee Education System (Producer) (2010). *Addressing suicidal thoughts and behaviors in substance abuse treatment.* [Video/DVD] Washington, DC.

Wilcox, H. C., Conner, K. R., and Caine, E. D. (2004). Association of alcohol and drug use disorders and completed suicide: An empirical review of cohort studies. *Drug and Alcohol Dependence, 76 (Suppl),* S11-S19.

Wines, J. D., Saitz, R., Horton, N. J., Lloyd-Travaglini, C., and Samet, J. H. (2004). Suicidal behavior, drug use and depressive symptoms after detoxification: A 2-year prospective study. *Drug and Alcohol Dependence, 76(Suppl 7),* S21-S29.

Wojnar, M., Ilgen, M. A., Czyz, E., Strobbe, S., Klimkiewicz, A., Jakubczyk, A. Brower, K. (2009). Impulsive and non-impulsive suicide attempts in patients treated for alcohol dependence. *Journal of Affective Disorders, 115,* 131-139.

In: Frontiers in Suicide Risk
Editor: Jill E. Lavigne

ISBN 978-1-62081-373-7
©2012 Nova Science Publishers, Inc.

Chapter 8

OLDER MEN AND SUICIDE RISK: CLINICAL AND RESEARCH IMPLICATIONS[*]

Alisa A. O'Riley and Phillip N. Smith

[1]Department of Psychiatry,
University of Rochester School of Medicine and Dentistry,
Rochester, New York, US
[2]Department of Psychology, University of South Alabama,
Mobile, Alabama, US

ABSTRACT

Older white men have disproportionately high rates of suicide in the United States and in many other countries around the world. This chapter will provide a brief overview of what is known about suicide risk in older men. We will begin with an examination of the epidemiology of suicide and known risk factors for suicide in late life. We will then discuss two theoretical explanations for why older men are at increased risk for death by suicide. Lastly, we will discuss research and clinical implications for increased risk for suicide among older men.

INTRODUCTION

Older adults are at disproportionately high risk for death by suicide in the United States (U.S.) and many countries around the world (World Health Organization; WHO, 2011). Further, there exist significant gender and racial/ethnic disparities in suicide rates (Center for Disease Control; CDC, 2007). Figure 1 depicts rates of death by suicide in the U.S. by age, sex, and race/ethnicity. As is evident in this figure, older white males have the highest rates of suicide. In 2007, older white men had a rate of death by suicide of 31.13 (CDC, 2007). In contrast, the rate of death by suicide in the general population was 11.47 (CDC, 2007). Thus, in many ways, the problem of suicide in the U.S. is centered on older white men.

[*] This work was supported in part by Grant No. T32MH20061 from the National Institute of Mental Health.

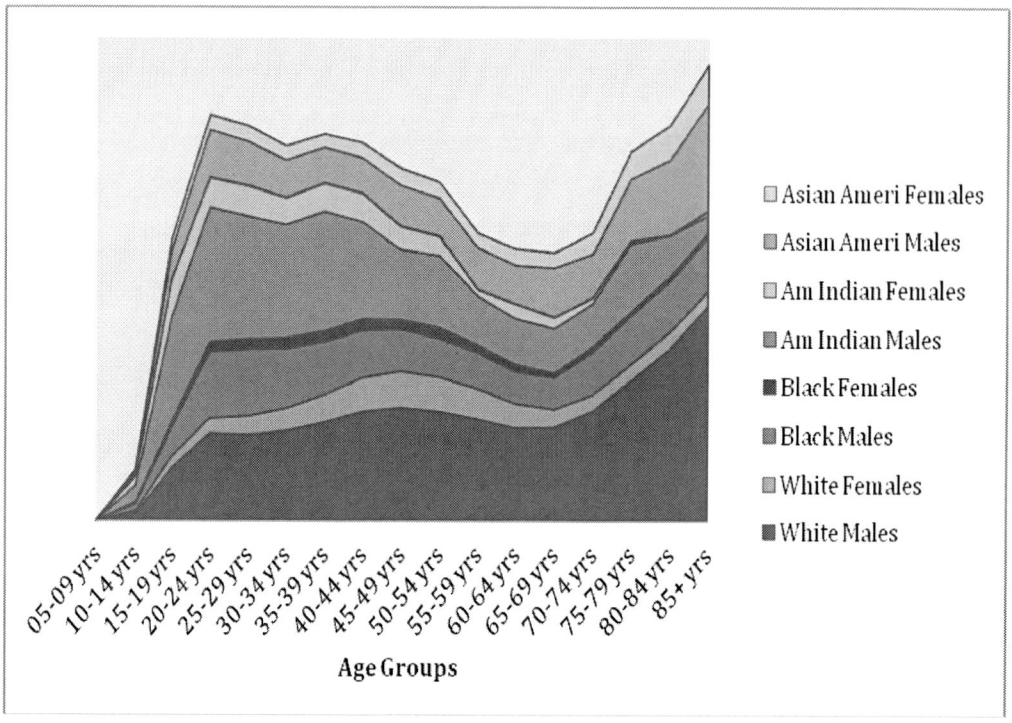

Figure 1. Area graph depicting suicide rates by age, race/ethnicity, and gender in the U.S. from 2000-2007 (CDC, 2007).

We would argue that, given the high concentration of suicide rates in this particular demographic group, efforts to reduce overall suicide rates must address the specific needs of suicidal older men.

Given this goal, the focus of this chapter will be on examining suicidal behavior in older men. Suicide in older men makes intuitive sense to people living in Western cultures where late life, especially for men, is seen as a time of loss (Heckhausen, Dixon, and Baltes, 1989). There is an assumption that men are not equipped to cope effectively with losses commonly experienced by older adults (e.g. loss of loved ones, loss of physical health, loss of function, loss of employment, and loss of cognitive ability; Canetto, 2008). However, the fact that older men experience significant losses in numerous domains does not, in and of itself, explain suicidal behavior in late life.

When we examine data on psychological functioning in older adults we find that, in actuality, the majority of older adults, men and women alike, cope very well with stressors common in older adulthood. Longitudinal research has demonstrated that negative affect decreases in late life and positive affect remains stable (Carstensen et al., 2011).

Rates of Major Depressive Disorder are also lower in older adults than in younger adults (Fiske, Wetherall, and Gatz, 2009). These data indicate that the majority of older men are capable of coping with the losses associated with aging, and the very small group of older men who die by suicide likely differ from the average older man in significant ways. This chapter explores what is currently known about older men and suicidal behavior.

The chapter will discuss risk factors for suicide among older adults and gender differences in these risk factors, potential theoretical explanations for the gender differences in suicide, and research and clinical implications for these gender differences.

RISK FACTORS FOR SUICIDE IN OLDER MEN

In order to develop effective programs to prevent and treat suicidal behavior in late life, we must begin by identifying factors that put certain men at increased risk for developing suicidal behavior (O'Riley et al., in press). Knowledge of risk factors allows us to appropriately target both individuals at high risk for suicide and potential points of intervention to prevent suicidal behavior (Caine and Conwell, 2001). Risk factors for suicidal behavior can be described as varying across two dimensions (Caine and Conwell). These dimensions contrast in regards to their relative proximity in time to suicide (distal versus proximal) and their degree of modifiability (static versus dynamic or changeable; Caine and Conwell; Jobes, Rudd, Overhosler, and Joiner, 2008). For the purposes of this chapter, we will focus on risk factors that are potentially modifiable.

Research has been conducted examining risk factors for suicide in late life using a variety of methods (Conwell and Thompson, 2008; O'Riley et al., in press). One of the most common methods for examining risk factors for death by suicide is the psychological autopsy (PA) study (O'Riley et al.). PA studies involve data collected retrospectively about individuals who died by suicide (O'Riley et al.). This post-mortem data is collected from a variety of sources, including: medical and legal records, informant interviews, and proxy questionnaires, among others. Unfortunately, although extensive research has been done examining risk factors for suicide in late life, less is known about risk factors for suicidal behavior in older men in particular. We have included information on gender differences whenever possible; however, when gender differences have not been examined we refer to data on older adults more generally.

In the general population of older adults, one of the most prominent dynamic risk factors for death by suicide is a diagnosis of Major Depressive Disorder (MDD; Conwell et al., 1996; Conwell and Thompson, 2008; O'Riley et al., in press). Evidence suggests that more than 80% of older adults who die by suicide have symptoms of depression at the time of their deaths (O'Riley et al., in press). Additionally, depression appears to be a more important risk factor for suicide in older adults compared to substance abuse and personality disorder diagnosis, which are important in younger individuals (Conwell et al., 1996; Dumais et al., 2005). Research has also demonstrated that suicidal behavior in late life is associated with other personality traits (Duberstein et al., 2000). Specifically, older adults who die by suicide are more likely to score high on measures of neuroticism (a trait strongly associated with negative affect) and low on measures of openness to experience (a trait associated with flexibility). Little research has been done examining gender differences in these personality risk factors for suicide. Finally, although traits such as impulsivity are risk factors for suicide across the lifespan, some research has shown that older men who die by suicide were less likely to have engaged in impulsive or aggressive behaviors prior to their deaths than younger suicide decedents (Dumais et al., 2005). We will address the role of impulsivity further when we discuss aspects of male gender that contribute to suicide risk.

In addition to psychiatric disorders and behavioral risk factors for suicide, research has also demonstrated that, in the general population of older adults, physical illness and functional disability are significant risk factors for suicide (Conwell and Thompson, 2008; O'Riley et al., in press). One case-controlled PA study found that physical illness was a significant risk factor for suicide for older men (OR = 4.2; Waern et al., 2002) but not for women. At the current time, little is known about gender differences in the risk for suicide related to functional impairment. One important empirical question centers on whether physical illness and functional impairment are dynamic risk factors for suicide (Fiske, O'Riley, and Widoe, 2008). Some evidence suggests that modifiable aspects of illness confer risk (e.g. pain); while other studies have suggested that non-modifiable changes associated with physical illness (e.g. neurological changes) confer increased risk (Fiske et al., 2008).

Finally, in addition to health status and individual characteristics, research has shown that a variety of variables related to social isolation and disconnection are associated with death by suicide in older adults (Conwell and Thompson, 2008; O'Riley et al., in press). We are not aware of any studies that examine gender differences in suicide risk associated with these variables.

THEORETICAL CONSIDERATIONS

Although knowledge of variability in suicide rates by sex and race/ethnicity as well as risk factors for suicide in these specific demographic groups can help direct efforts for prevention, a better theoretical understanding of these differences will inform points of intervention to direct such efforts.

In this section, we will discuss some recent theoretical explanations of why men, and older men in particular, are at increased risk for suicide in the U.S.

Gender Norms and Suicidal Behavior. One possible explanation for gender differences in suicidal behavior centers on the notion that men are at increased risk for suicide in the U.S. and other Western countries because suicide is in keeping with gender norms in these cultures (Canetto, 2008; Stice and Canetto, 2008). The conclusion that suicide is consistent with male gender norms is based, in part, on examinations of media reporting on prominent suicide deaths in the U.S. (Canetto, 2008). Newspaper reports of deaths by suicides were found to possess some common themes. First, newspaper stories often noted that older white men who died by suicide had debilitating illnesses that prevented them from engaging in typical masculine activities (Canetto, 2008). Second, these reports often noted that older white males who died by suicide had difficulties adjusting to getting older (Canetto, 2008). Finally, Canetto judged the tone of these reports to suggest that suicide is a rational choice for older white men. However, if the older white man was known to have mental illness, the articles did not have a positive tone.

Based on these findings, Canetto (2008) concluded that, in Western cultures, dying by suicide is viewed as a masculine act and an appropriate choice for older men, especially when a man has some sort of illness or disability. Additionally, Canetto noted that suicide stands in stark contrast to slowly wasting away from an illness, which is viewed as a passive, feminine action. This view was supported in studies in which participants judged more positively the suicide of older men as compared to older women and younger decedents in fictitious vignettes (Dahlen and Canetto, 2002; Stice and Canetto, 2008).

The Capability for Suicide. In addition to the possibility that suicide is consistent with a male gender role (Canetto 2008), we argue that men are more likely than women to experience a specific condition that is vital for death by suicide. This condition is called the acquired capability for suicide and is a major component of the Interpersonal Theory of

Suicide (hereafter referred to as the Interpersonal Theory; (Joiner, 2005; Van Orden et al., 2010). Compared to previous models that conceptualize suicide risk according to the presence and severity of specific risk factors, such as hopelessness (Beck, Brown, and Steer, 1989; McMillan, Gilbody, Beresford, and Neilly, 2007), the Interpersonal Theory holds as its main assumption that the desire for suicide is distinct from the capability for suicide (Ribeiro and Joiner, 2009). The theory states that only when someone who desires suicide has also developed the capability for suicide will he or she be at risk for death by suicide. This acquired capability is a limiting factor that explains why many who desire suicide, as indicated by severe suicidal ideation, never engage in any form of suicidal behavior and even fewer die by suicide (Selby et al., 2010; Smith, Cukrowicz, Poindexter, Hobson, and Cohen, 2010; Van Orden, et al., 2010).

The acquired capability for suicide is described as a reduced sense of fear and pain sensitivity that develops in response to repeated exposure to psychologically provocative or fear inducing and physically painful events (Van Orden, et al., 2010). Smith and Cukrowicz (2010) described the process by which acquired capability is developed as involving separate but related processes of habituation to fear and physical pain. These processes are separate in that they advance at different rates, but related in that many events that facilitate habituation will involve elements of both fear and pain (Smith and Cukrowicz, 2010). Van Orden et al. (2010) has further suggested that the two components of acquired capability may operate at different points along the trajectory to suicide. Specifically, a lowered fear of death allows for the development of suicidal intent while the degree to which one has an increased tolerance for physical pain will determine whether this intent will translate into lethal action.

The importance of the acquired capability in the developmental trajectory leading to suicide is supported by a growing body of evidence. Factor analyses of suicide assessments (e.g., the Modified Scale for Suicide Ideation; (Miller, Norman, Bishop, and Dow, 1986) support the distinction between the desire and capability for suicide (Joiner, Rudd, and Rajab, 1997; Joiner et al., 2003; Witte et al., 2006). Self-reported acquired capability, as measured by the Acquired Capability for Suicide Scale (Van Orden et al., 2008), and highly related constructs (e.g., fear of suicide) were associated with a history of suicide attempts, particularly multiple attempts, in clinical and military samples (Bryan, Cukrowicz, West, and Morrow, 2010; Bryan, Morrow, Anestis, and Joiner, 2010; Linehan, Goodstein, Nielsen, and Chiles, 1983; Malone et al., 2000; Smith, et al., 2010; Van Orden, Witte, Gordon, Bender, and Joiner, 2008). Suicide attempters also evidence greater subjective and objective pain thresholds and tolerance compared to non-attempters in laboratory pain administration tasks (e.g., cold presser, thermal sensory analyzer; (Orbach, Mikulincer, King, Cohen, and Stein, 1997; Orbach, Palgi, et al., 1996; Orbach, Stein, et al., 1996) .

There is currently preliminary support that men are higher in acquired capability compared to women. When examining gender disparities in suicidal behavior, older men are more likely than other groups to use highly lethal means for suicide, such as firearms (see Figure 2; CDC, 2007). In fact, the gender disparity in suicide rates is often ascribed heavily to variability in the lethality of suicide methods used by men versus women (Dombrovski et al., 2008). We argue that the reason men are able to use more lethal means is due to higher levels of acquired capability in men. Further, many of the studies supporting the role of acquired capability referenced above have found that men endorse greater levels of self-reported acquired capability as well as higher subjective and objective evaluations of pain tolerance

(Berkley, 1997; Berkley, Zalcman, and Simon, 2006; Bryan, Cukrowicz, et al., 2010; Linehan, et al., 1983; Orbach, et al., 1997; Witte, Gordon, Smith, and Van Orden, 2011).

Men are socialized to engage in the behaviors that facilitate acquired capability. Men are, on average, more likely to engage in risky and impulsive behaviors, such as early substance use, sexual promiscuity, gambling, reckless driving, among others (Cross, Copping, and Campbell, 2011; Levant, Wimer, Williams, Smalley, and Noronha, 2009; Martins, Tavares, da Silva Lobo, Galetti, and Gentil, 2004). As to what aspects of male gender socialization are important for the development of acquired capability, there is some support that impulsivity, emotional stoicism, and sensation seeking, all features of male gender socialization (Cross, et al., 2011; Mahalik et al., 2003; O'Neil and et al., 1986), may be important in the development of acquired capability. Bender et al. (2010) demonstrated that impulsivity was associated with suicidal behavior by its influence on the likelihood of exposure to painful and provocative experiences and acquired capability. This is contrasted against the notion of an "impulsive suicide attempt" wherein an individual may act without prior consideration of suicide. Previously referenced data suggesting that older men who die by suicide may be less impulsive than their younger counterparts supports the idea that impulsivity is more distally related to suicide by fostering one's ability to develop plans and preparations for suicide (Dumais et al., 2005). Consistent with this interpretation, more highly impulsive adolescent suicide attempters were shown to have exhibited more prior planning of suicide compared to low impulsive adolescents (Witte et al., 2008).

Recent findings from the second author's research team found additional support for the role of male gender norms as important in the development of acquired capability. Specifically, in two geographically distinct samples of undergraduate students, sensation seeking and emotional stoicism were found to mediate the relationship between gender and acquired capability.

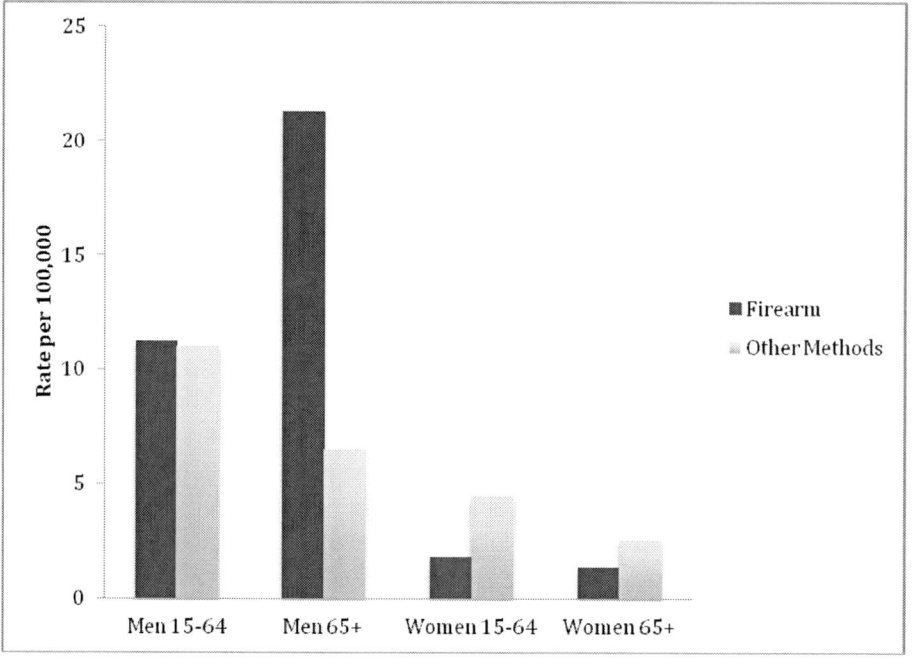

Figure 2. Method of death by suicide by age and sex in the U.S. from 2000-2007 (CDC, 2007).

These norms operated differently on the two components of acquired capability. Emotional stoicism mediated the influence of gender on pain insensitivity whereas sensation seeking mediated the effect of gender on fearlessness of death. Taken together, these data support the notion that male gender socialization prescribes behaviors that place men at greater risk for suicide compared to women due to higher levels of acquired capability stemming from greater exposure to painful and provocative life events.

Considering these findings on gender differences in acquired capability with data supporting the role of acquired capability in suicidal behaviors (Smith, et al., 2010; Van Orden, et al., 2008) there is preliminary support for the notion that gender differences in acquired capability are, at least in part, responsible for the gender discrepancy in suicide rates. In regards to the influence of age, older adults by virtue of having lived longer are afforded more time in which to have experienced sufficient exposure to painful and provocative life events and experience the habituation process involved in acquired capability. Additionally, older adults are more exposed to the notion of death, either by the loss of friends and family members or by thinking about coming closer to death, which may further facilitate acquired capability (O'Riley et al., in press).

RESEARCH IMPLICATIONS

Although the aforementioned explanations of the higher rate of suicide in older men are both compelling and supported by evidence, there are critical questions yet to be addressed. Most importantly, the notion of suicide as a component of male gender norms has not been tested amongst individuals to whom such norms are most important (i.e., suicidal older men). Although the finding that male suicide is rated as more acceptable under conditions of physical impairment by non-suicidal participants (i.e., undergraduate students and community-dwelling older adults) is interesting, this does not necessarily mean that this view is held by individuals at risk. Furthermore, gender norms are fluid. Longitudinal research on the evolution of social norms regarding death and suicide is needed.

Despite the growing support for the role of the acquired capability for suicide, research on this construct is still very recent and no studies have examined this construct in older adults. Furthermore, this construct remains poorly specified and defined. More conceptual clarity on the nature of fearlessness and the experience of pain is needed. For example, although research has used behavioral pain administration tasks, it is unclear whether an individual's objective pain experience or his/her subjective evaluation of his/her ability to tolerate pain (another construct we argue is heavily tied to male gender norms) is critical for the capability for suicide. Furthermore, research on the acquired capability for suicide has used a single, as yet unvalidated self-report measure of the construct. Factor analytic, reliability, and validity data on the Acquired Capability for Suicide Scale (Van Orden et al, 2008) are clearly required. Lastly, little research has been conducted on the specific events that are believed to facilitate acquired capability. Although "painful and provocative events", as measured by the Impulsive Behaviors Scale and the Painful and Provocative Life Events Scale, are correlated with higher acquired capability (Bender, Gordon, Bresin, and Joiner, 2010; Smith, et al., 2010) more research is needed. This need for greater understanding of critical life events is particularly true given the over reliance on individuals' suicide attempt status as a marker of suicide risk (Joiner, Van Orden, Witte, and Rudd, 2009; Rudd, Joiner, and Rajab, 1996), given that the majority of older adult suicide decedents die on their first attempt (Conwell and Thompson, 2008; O'Riley et al., in press). Despite these limitations, however, these explanations provide important implications for the assessment and management of suicide risk in older men.

CLINICAL IMPLICATIONS

Assessing and managing suicide risk is a difficult undertaking in the best of circumstances (Jobes et al., 2008); however, assessing and managing suicide risk in older men may be particularly complex for a variety of reasons. In the next section, we will discuss the clinical assessment and management/treatment of suicide risk in older men. Our discussion will focus on highlighting some of the complexities of risk assessment in older men.

Assessment. One of the more challenging realities in understanding the high rates of suicide in men versus women is the higher prevalence of depressive disorders among women. Depressive disorders, as previously discussed, constitute the highest psychiatric risk factor for suicide (Conwell et al., 1996). Yet, men experience Major Depression almost half as frequently compared to women (Kessler, McGonagle, Zhao, Nelson, and et al., 1994). Some have argued that this disparity in depression rates is actually caused by our poor conceptualization and definition of depression in men (Rabinowitz and Cochran, 2008). Although there is much debate about whether this confusion is a result of variant manifestations of the same disease process or represents a separate condition, what is generally agreed upon is that depression in men is likely to go undetected (Addis, 2008; Cochran and Rabinowitz, 2003; Moller-Leimkuhler, Bottlender, Strauss, and Rutz, 2004; Scheibe, Preuschhof, Cristi, and Bagby, 2003). As such, it is important that depression assessments be tailored to the specific needs of men. Specifically, evaluating depression and suicide in men must go beyond assessing sadness and depressed affect. Men often present with increased anger and substance use (Addis, 2008; Rabinowitz and Cochran, 2008). Depression assessments in men should also explore somatic symptoms, which men may endorse more readily than negative affect.

Research has also demonstrated age differences in depressive symptoms (Fiske et al., 2009). Specifically, older adults are less likely to meet full criteria for Major Depressive Disorder (Fiske et al.). Research has demonstrated, however, that subsyndromal depression in older adults is associated with numerous negative physical and mental health outcomes (Lyness et al., 2007). In addition to this difference in degree of symptoms, other age differences in the presentation of depressive symptoms exist. First, older adults are more likely to report symptoms of anhedonia and less likely to report symptoms of dysphoria than younger adults (Fiske et al., 2009). Older adults are also more likely to report somatic symptoms of depression (Fiske et al., 2009). This finding is complicated in that clinicians are faced with the task of differentially diagnosing somatic symptoms due to physical illness and somatic symptoms due to depression. Some researchers and clinicians have attempted to circumvent this difficulty by using instruments that do not include somatic items; however, given the high prevalence of somatic symptoms of depression in older adults, this tactic likely results in poor sensitivity (Fiske and O'Riley, 2008).

In addition to the possible difficulties in detecting depression in older men due to a mismatch in how depression is defined and experienced or expressed, older men are also less likely to disclose depressive symptoms and suicidal ideation compared to younger adults (Addis and Mahalik, 2003; Moller-Leimkuhler, 2002; Moller-Leimkuhler, Heller, and Paulus, 2007; Schomerus and Angermeyer, 2008; O'Riley et al., in press). The lack of disclosure of mental health issues may be due, in part, to the influence of restricted emotionality, but also may stem from the desire for men to conform to the masculine gender role and mask potentially non-masculine experiences of behaviors (Addis and Mahalik, 2003). Older adults who die by suicide are also less likely to have a previous history of suicide attempts than younger adults who die by suicide (Conwell and Thompson, 2008; O'Riley et al.). Therefore, the lack of a history of prior suicidal behavior should not be interpreted as an indication that older men are not at risk for suicide. The stigma associated with disclosure of such issues can be a strong deterrent against receiving help. These findings suggest that suicide risk may be more difficult to detect in older adults. Some experts in the field of late life suicide prevention have suggested that clinicians ask older adults about death ideation (i.e., more general thoughts of death and dying) and meaning in life to facilitate discussions of thoughts of self-harm (O'Riley et al.).

One consequence of lower disclosure in depressed, suicidal older men is that they do not tend to present in mental health care settings. In fact, research has found, that only about one third of older adults who die by suicide received care in mental health settings (Conwell, 2009; Louma, Martin, and Pearson, 2002). In comparison, an estimated 75% of older adults who died by suicide were seen by a primary medical provider within the 12 months prior to their death. This finding suggests that it may be more effective to screen for depression and suicide risk in primary care settings. Additional data from PA studies also highlight the role of diminished physical capacity and increased need for intensive medical care (Conwell et al., 2010), suggesting that depression and suicide risk be assessed in medical and long-term settings as well (Conwell, 2009; Conwell and Thompson, 2008). The utility of such assessment practices and subsequent engagement in treatment is encouraging (Alexopoulos et al., 2009).

Treatment and risk management. Management of risk for suicide in older adults is complicated by several factors. First, as was mentioned earlier, older adults are less likely to disclose thoughts of suicide or seek mental health care (Conwell, 2009). This finding suggests the need for screening in alternative settings (e.g. community agencies, primary care offices, long term care facilities). Second, older adults who die by suicide are more likely to live alone than older adults who do not die by suicide (Conwell and Thompson, 2008; O'Riley et al., in press). In addition to presenting a risk factor for suicide, in terms of loneliness and social disconnection, this finding also presents a difficulty in monitoring the safety of older adults at risk for suicide. Clinicians may need to develop creative plans of ensuring the older adult at risk's safety (e.g. using telephone check-ins, asking neighbors for help). Finally, it may be difficult to limit access to means for older adults at risk for suicide. Certainly, clinicians must work to eliminate all access to firearms for older adults at risk for suicide, because older adults with access to firearms are much more likely to die from a suicide attempt (Conwell et al., 2002). However, older adults often have access to other lethal means, such as potentially-lethal medications. Medications may be especially lethal if the older adult at risk is also physically frail (O'Riley et al.). Again, clinicians may need to develop creative methods to limit access to means such as medications (e.g. having a loved one dispense all medications, having medications delivered weekly in order to limit supply).

Because depression is such a strong risk factor for death by suicide among older adults, most older adults at risk for suicide require treatment for depression. Evidence suggests that depression is highly treatable in older adults (Scogin, Welsh, Hanson, Stump, and Coates, 2005) through either medication or evidence-based psychotherapy. Recent research has demonstrated that treating late life depression in primary care settings may be a particularly effective way of reducing suicide risk in older adults (Alexopoulos et al., 2009). In addition to treatment of depression, some experts in the field of late life suicide prevention have also suggested that reducing social isolation among older adults may effectively reduce suicide risk for some individuals (O'Riley et al., in press). Research is underway examining this possibility.

CONCLUSION

More work needs to be done examining gender disparities in late life suicidal behavior. Evidence suggests that older white men, who carry disproportionately high levels of suicide risk in many countries around the world, may carry different risk factors for suicide than other groups. Addressing suicide risk in older men also presents unique clinical challenges, which will require much more empirical investigation. Developing a better understanding of suicide risk in older men will ultimately lead to less lives lost to suicide.

REFERENCES

Addis, M. E. (2008). Gender and depression in men. *Clinical Psychology: Science and Practice*, 15, 153-168.

Addis, M. E., and Mahalik, J. R. (2003). Men, masculinity, and the contexts of help seeking. *American Psychologist*, 58, 5-14.

Alexopoulos, G. S., Reynolds, C. F., III, Bruce, M. L., Katz, I. R., Raue, P. J., Mulsant, B. H., Ten Have, T. (2009). Reducing suicidal ideation and depression in older primary care patients: 24-month outcomes of the PROSPECT Study. *The American Journal of Psychiatry*, 166, 882-890.

Beck, A. T., Brown, G., and Steer, R. A. (1989). Prediction of eventual suicide in psychiatric inpatients by clinical ratings of hopelessness. *Journal of Consulting and Clinical Psychology*, 57, 309-310.

Bender, T. W., Gordon, K. H., Bresin, K., and Joiner, T. E., Jr. (2010). Impulsivity and suicidality: The mediating role of painful and provocative experiences. *Journal of Affective Disorders*. 129(1-3), 301-307.

Berkley, K. J. (1997). Sex differences in pain. *The Behavioral and brain sciences*, 20, 371-380; discussion 435-513.

Berkley, K. J., Zalcman, S. S., and Simon, V. R. (2006). Sex and gender differences in pain and inflammation: a rapidly maturing field. *American journal of physiology. Regulatory, integrative and comparative physiology*, 291, R241-244.

Bryan, C. J., Cukrowicz, K. C., West, C. L., and Morrow, C. E. (2010). Combat experience and the acquired capability for suicide. *Journal of Clinical Psychology in Medical Settings*, 66, 1044-1056.

Bryan, C. J., Morrow, C. E., Anestis, M. D., and Joiner, T. E. (2010). A preliminary test of the interpersonal-psychological theory of suicidal behavior in a military sample. *Personality and Individual Differences*, 48, 347-350.

Caine, E. D., and Conwell, Y. (2001). Suicide in the elderly. *International Clinical Psychopharmacology*, 16(Suppl2), S25-S30.

Canetto, S. S. (2008, April). *Gender and suicide.* Paper presented at the meeting of the American Association of Suicidology Boston, MA.

Carstensen L.L., Turan, B., Scheibe, S., Ram, N., Ersner-Hershfield, H., Samanez-Larkin, G. R., Nesselroade, J. R. (2011). Emotional experience improves with age: Evidence based on over 10 years of experience sampling. *Psychology and Aging*, 26, 21-33.

Center for Disease Control (CDC). (2007). Web-based injury statistics query and reporting system (WISQARS). *National Center for Injury Prevention and Control*. Retrieved August 10, 2011, from http://www.cdc.gov/injury/wisqars/index.html.

Cochran, S. V., and Rabinowitz, F. E. (2003). Gender-sensitive recommendations for assessment and treatment of depression in men. *Professional Psychology-Research and Practice*, 34, 132-140.

Conwell, Y. (2009). Suicide prevention in later life: A glass half full, or half empty?. *The American Journal of Psychiatry*, 166, 845-848.

Conwell, Y., Duberstein, P. R., Connor, K., Eberly, S., Cox, C., and Caine, E. D. (2002). Acces to firearms and risk for suicide in middle-aged and older adults. *American Journal of Geriatric Psychiatry, 10(4),* 407-416.

Conwell, Y., Duberstein, P. R., Cox, C., Herrmann, J. H., Forbes, N. T., and Caine, E. D. (1996). Relationships of age and axis I diagnoses in victims of completed suicide: a psychological autopsy study. *The American Journal of Psychiatry*, 153, 1001-1008.

Conwell, Y., Duberstein, P. R., Hirsch, J. K., Conner, K. R., Eberly, S., and Caine, E. D. (2010). Health status and suicide in the second half of life. *International Journal of Geriatric Psychiatry*, 25, 371-379.

Conwell, Y., and Thompson, C. (2008). Suicidal behavior in elders. *The Psychiatric Clinics of North America*, 31, 333-356.

Cross, C. P., Copping, L. T., and Campbell, A. (2011). Sex Differences in Impulsivity: A Meta-Analysis. *Psychological Bulletin*, 137, 97-130.

Dahlen, E. R., and Canetto, S. S. (2002). The role of gender and suicide precipitant in attitudes toward nonfatal suicidal behavior. *Death Studies*, 26, 99-116.

Dombrovski, A. Y., Szanto, K., Duberstein, P., Conner, K. R., Houck, P. R., and Conwell, Y. (2008). Sex differences in correlates of suicide attempt lethality in late life. *The American Journal of Geriatric Psychiatry*, 16, 905-913.

Duberstein, P., Conwell, Y., Seidlitz, L., Denning, D. G., Cox, C., and Caine, E. D. (2000). Personality traits and suicidal behavior and ideation in depressed inpatients 50 years of age and older. *Journal of Gerontology: Psychological Sciences*, 55B, 18-26.

Dumais, A., Lesage, A. D., Phil, M., Alda, M., Rouleau, G., Dumont, M.,…Turecki, G. (2005). Risk factors for suicide completion in major depression: A case-control study of impulsive and aggressive men. *American Journal of Psychiatry, 162,* 2116-2124.

Fiske, A., Wetherell, J. L., and Gatz, M. (2009). Depression in older adults. *Annual Review of Clinical Psychology*, 5, 363-389.

Fiske, A., and O'Riley, A. A. (2008). Assessment of depression in later life. In J. D. Hunsley, and E. S. Mash (Eds.), *A guide to assessments that work* (pp. 138-157). Oxford, UK: Oxford University Press.

Fiske, A., O'Riley, A.A., and Widoe, R. K. (2008). Physical health and suicide in late life: An evaluative review. *Clinical Gerontologist*, 31, 31-50.

Heckhausen, J., Dixon, R.A., and Baltes, P.B. (1989). Gains and losses in development throughout adulthood as perceived by different adult age groups. *Developmental Psychology*, 25, 109-121.

Jobes, D. A., Rudd, M. D., Overhosler, J. C., and Joiner, T. E.J. (2008). Ethical and competent care of suicidal patients: Contemporary challenges, new developments, and considerations for clinical practice. *Professional Psychology: Research and Practice*, 39, 405-413.

Joiner, T. (2005). *Why people die by suicide*. Cambridge, MA, US: Harvard University Press.

Joiner, T. E., Jr., Rudd, M. D., and Rajab, M. H. (1997). The Modified Scale for Suicidal Ideation: factors of suicidality and their relation to clinical and diagnostic variables. *Journal of Abnormal Psychology*, 106, 260-265.

Joiner, T. E., Jr., Van Orden, K. A., Witte, T. K., and Rudd, M. D. (2009). *The interpersonal theory of suicide: Guidance for working with suicidal clients*. Washington, DC: American Psychological Association.

Joiner, T. E., Steer, R. A., Brown, G., Beck, A. T., Pettit, J. W., and Rudd, M. D. (2003). Worst-point suicidal plans: a dimension of suicidality predictive of past suicide attempts and eventual death by suicide. *Behaviour Research and Therapy*, 41, 1469-1480.

Kessler, R. C., McGonagle, K. A., Zhao, S., Nelson, C. B., and et al. (1994). Lifetime and 12-month prevalence of DSM-III--R psychiatric disorders in the United States: Results from the National Comorbidity Study. *Archives of General Psychiatry*, 51, 8-19.

Levant, R. F., Wimer, D. J., Williams, C. M., Smalley, K., and Noronha, D. (2009). The relationships between masculinity variables, health risk behaviors and attitudes toward seeking psychological help. *International Journal of Men's Health*, 8, 3-21.

Linehan, M. M., Goodstein, J. L., Nielsen, S. L., and Chiles, J. A. (1983). Reasons for staying alive when you are thinking of killing yourself - the reasons for living inventory. *Journal of Consulting and Clinical Psychology*, 51, 276-286.

Louma, J. B., Martin, C. E., and Pearson, J. L. (2002). Contact with mental health and primary care providers before suicide: A review of the evidence. *American Journal of Psychiatry*, 159, 909-916.

Lyness, J. M., Kim, J., Tang, W., Tu, X., Conwell, Y., King, D. A., and Caine, E. D. (2007). The clinical significance of subsyndromal depression in older primary care patients. *American Journal of Geriatric Psychiatry*, 15, 214-223.

Mahalik, J. R., Locke, B. D., Ludlow, L. H., Diemer, M. A., Scott, R. P., Gottfried, M., and Freitas, G. (2003). Development of the Conformity to Masculine Norms Inventory. *Psychology of Men and Masculinity*, 4, 3-25.

Malone, K. M., Oquendo, M. A., Haas, G. L., Ellis, S. P., Li, S. H., and Mann, J. J. (2000). Protective factors against suicidal acts in major depression: Reasons for living. *American Journal of Psychiatry*, 157, 1084-1088.

Martins, S. S., Tavares, H., da Silva Lobo, D. S., Galetti, A. M., and Gentil, V. (2004). Pathological gambling, gender, and risk-taking behaviors. *Addictive Behaviors*, 29, 1231-1235.

McMillan, D., Gilbody, S., Beresford, E., and Neilly, L. (2007). Can we predict suicide and non-fatal self-harm with the Beek Hopelessness Scale? A meta-analysis. *Psychological Medicine*, 37, 769-778.

Miller, I. W., Norman, W. H., Bishop, S. B., and Dow, M. G. (1986). The Modified Scale for Suicidal Ideation: Reliability and validity. *Journal of Consulting and Clinical Psychology*, 54, 724-725.

Moller-Leimkuhler, A. M. (2002). Barriers to help-seeking by men: A review of sociocultural and clinical literature with particular reference to depression. *Journal of Affective Disorders*, 71(1-3), 1-9.

Moller-Leimkuhler, A. M., Bottlender, R., Strauss, A., and Rutz, W. (2004). Is there evidence for a male depressive syndrome in inpatients with major depression? *Journal of Affective Disorders*, 80, 87-93.

Moller-Leimkuhler, A. M., Heller, J., and Paulus, N.-C. (2007). Gender-Role Orientation, Risk of Male Depression and Help-seeking of Male Adolescents. *Psychiatrische Praxis*, 34(Suppl1), S173-S175.

O'Neil, J. M., and et al. (1986). Gender-Role Conflict Scale: College men's fear of femininity. *Sex Roles*, 14(5-6), 335-350.

Orbach, I., Mikulincer, M., King, R., Cohen, D., and Stein, D. (1997). Thresholds and tolerance of physical pain in suicidal and nonsuicidal adolescents. *Journal of Consulting and Clinical Psychology*, 65, 646-652.

Orbach, I., Palgi, Y., Stein, D., HarEven, D., LotemPeleg, M., Asherov, J., and Elizur, A. (1996). Tolerance for physical pain in suicidal subjects. *Death Studies*, 20, 327-341.

Orbach, I., Stein, D., Palgi, Y., Asherov, J., HarEven, D., and Elizur, A. (1996). Perception of physical pain in accident and suicide attempt patients: Self-preservation vs self-destruction. *Journal of Psychiatric Research*, 30, 307-320.

O'Riley, A. A., Van Orden, K., and Conwell, C. (in press). Suicide in late life: Risk and protective factors. In M. van Dulmen, M. Swahn and R. Bossarte (Eds.), *Developmental and public health perspectives on suicide prevention: An integrated approach*. Kent, OH: Kent State University Press.

Rabinowitz, F. E., and Cochran, S. V. (2008). Men and therapy: A case of masked male depression. *Clinical Case Studies*, 7, 575-591.

Ribeiro, J. D., and Joiner, T. E. (2009). The interpersonal-psychological theory of suicidal behavior: Current status and future directions. *Journal of Clinical Psychology*, 65, 1291-1299.

Rudd, M. D., Joiner, T., and Rajab, M. H. (1996). Relationships among suicide ideators, attempters, and multiple attempters in a young-adult sample. *Journal of Abnormal Psychology*, 105, 541-550.

Scheibe, S., Preuschhof, C., Cristi, C., and Bagby, R. M. (2003). Are there gender differences in major depression and its response to antidepressants? *Journal of Affective Disorders*, 75, 223-235.

Schomerus, G., and Angermeyer, M. C. (2008). Stigma and its impact on help-seeking for mental disorders: what do we know? *Epidemiologia E Psichiatria Sociale-an International Journal for Epidemiology and Psychiatric Sciences*, 17, 31-37.

Scogin, F., Welsh, D., Hanson, A., Stump, J., and Coates, A. (2005). Evidence-based psychotherapies for depression in older adults. *Clinical Psychology: Science and Practice*, 12, 222-237.

Selby, E. A., Anestis, M. D., Bender, T. W., Ribeiro, J. D., Nock, M. K., Rudd, M. D., . . . Joiner, T. E. (2010). Overcoming the fear of lethal injury: Evaluating suicidal behavior in the military through the lens of the Interpersonal-Psychological Theory of Suicide. *Clinical Psychology Review*, 30, 298-307.

Smith, P. N., and Cukrowicz, K. C. (2010). Capable of suicide: A functional model of the acquired capability component of the interpersonal-psychological theory of suicide. *Suicide and Life-Threatening Behavior*, 40, 266-275.

Smith, P. N., Cukrowicz, K. C., Poindexter, E. K., Hobson, V., and Cohen, L. M. (2010). The acquired capability for suicide: A comparison of suicide attempters, suicide ideators, and non-suicidal controls. *Depression and Anxiety*, 27, 871–877.

Stice, B. D., and Canetto, S. S. (2008). Older adult suicide: Perceptions of precipitants and protective factors. *Clinical Gerontologist: The Journal of Aging and Mental Health*, 31, 4-30.

Van Orden, K. A., Witte, T., Cukrowicz, K. C., Braithwaite, S. R., Selby, E. A., and Joiner, T. (2010). The interpersonal theory of suicide. *Psychological Review*, 117, 575-600.

Van Orden, K. A., Witte, T. K., Gordon, K. H., Bender, T. W., and Joiner, T. E., Jr. (2008). Suicidal desire and the capability for suicide: Tests of the interpersonal-psychological theory of suicidal behavior among adults. *Journal of Consulting and Clinical Psychology*, 76, 72-83.

Waern, M., Rubenowitz, E., Runeson, B., Skoog, I., Wilhelmson, K., and Allebeck, P. (2002). Burden of illness and suicide in elderly people: Case-control study. *British Medical Journal*, 324(1355), 1359.

Witte, T., Gordon, K. H., Smith, P. N., and Van Orden, K. A. (2011). *Stoicism and sensation seeking: male vulnerabilities for the acquired capability for suicide*. Manuscript in preparation.

Witte, T. K., Joiner, T. E., Brown, G. K., Beck, A. T., Beckman, A., Duberstein, P., and Conwell, Y. (2006). Factors of suicide ideation and their relation to clinical and other indicators in older adults. *Journal of Affective Disorders*, 94(1-3), 165-172.

Witte, T. K., Merrill, K. A., Stellrecht, N. E., Bernert, R. A., Hollar, D. L., Schatschneider, C., and Joiner, T. E., Jr. (2008). "Impulsive" youth suicide attempters are not necessarily all that impulsive. *Journal of Affective Disorders*, 107(1-3), 107-116.

World Health Organization (WHO). *Suicide prevention (SUPRE)*. Retrieved August 10, 2011, http://www.who.int/mental_health/prevention/suicide/suicideprevent/en/.

STATISTICAL METHODS AND ISSUES
IN THE STUDY OF SUICIDE

In: Frontiers in Suicide Risk
Editor: Jill E. Lavigne

ISBN 978-1-62081-373-7
©2012 Nova Science Publishers, Inc.

Chapter 9

STATISTICAL METHODS AND ISSUES IN THE STUDY OF SUICIDE

Y. Xia[1,3], N. Lu[1,3], H. Zhang[4], D. Gunzler[5], G. S. Zubenko[6] and X. M. Tu[1,2,3]

[1]Department of Biostatistics and Computational Biology,
University of Rochester, Rochester, New York, US
[2]Department of Psychiatry, University of Rochester, Rochester, New York, US
[3]Center of Excellence for Suicide Prevention,
Canandaigua VA Medical Center, Canandaigua, New York, US
[4]Department of Biostatistics, St. Jude Children's Research Hospital,
Memphis, Tennesse, US
[5]Center for Health Care Research and Policy,
Case Western Reserve University at MetroHealth Medical Center, US
[6]Department of Psychiatry, University of Pittsburgh,
Pittsburgh, Pennsylvania, US

ABSTRACT

Suicide is a major public health problem that both reflects and creates considerable human suffering. Suicide and suicide attempts are leading causes of death and morbidity worldwide at all ages. In the United States, suicide is the 11th leading cause of death, accounting for over 30,000 deaths per year. An even greater number of people attempt suicide. Because suicide is a very complex, multicausal human behavior with many "causes" involving biological as well as psychosocial and cultural components, coupled with extremely low base-rate of suicide behavior in the general population, it is quite a challenging task to model the multiple risk and protective factors and their interactions in an integrated pathway to suicide and suicide attempt. This challenge is further compounded by the limited analytic tools that have been used in the extant literature.

In this chapter, we first provide a brief review of conceptually sound as well as accepted models for suicide and suicide attempt and discuss the limitations of statistical methods currently used for studies in this field. We then introduce the structural equation model as a way to integrate multi-faceted and -dimensional outcomes to provide a powerful framework for the complex pathways of suicide and suicide attempt. We illustrate this methodology by applying it to a simulated study sample with the underlying pathway from depression to suicide ideation derived based on the popular diathesis-stress model for pathways of suicide.

INTRODUCTION

Suicide, a self-directed act characterized by at least some intent to die (Mann et al., 2009; Posner et al., 2007), is a major public health problem that both reflects and creates considerable human suffering. According to data from the World Health Organization (WHO), suicide and suicide attempts are leading causes of death and morbidity worldwide at all ages. In the United States, suicide is the 11th leading cause of death; it accounts for over 30,000 deaths per year (Centers for Disease Control and Prevention, 2007). An even greater number of people attempt suicide. Although uncertain due to lack of national statistics, the number of attempted suicides (non-fatal) is estimated to be ten to 20 times higher than those of completed suicides (Bertolote and Fleischmann,2005; World Health Organization, 2009).

Based on data from community surveys, approximately 5% of adults have made a serious suicide attempt (Kessler et al., 1999). In the United States, suicide is the 4th most common cause of death among 10-14 year old, and the 3rd most common cause of death among 15-24 year old (Anderson and Smith, 2003). Suicide attempts are the primary reason for referrals to child and adolescent psychiatric emergency services (Peterson et al., 1996). The incidence rates of suicide attempts among older adolescents range from 7% to 9% (CDC, 2004). Prospective findings show that: [1] adolescents who attempt suicide are at risk of future non-lethal suicide attempts, and the risk increases with multiple suicide attempts (Goldston et al., 1999; Wingate et al., 2004); [2] adolescents who died by suicide have histories of suicidal ideation (Beck et al., 1999) and non-lethal suicide attempts (Shaffer et al., 1996); and [3] the period from 6 to 12 months following discharge from psychiatric hospitalization is marked by a heightened risk for suicide attempts (Goldston et al., 1999).

Suicide behavior is often related to mental disorders, such as severe affective disorder, schizophrenia, substance use disorder or borderline personality disorder. Mental health problems are some of the best-known and well-studied risk factors linked to suicidal ideation, suicide attempts, and suicide mortality. Approximately 90% of all individuals who completed suicide met criteria for one or more diagnosable psychiatric conditions. Mental health conditions most strongly associated with fatal and non-fatal suicide attempts include depression, bipolar disorder, schizophrenia, posttraumatic stress disorder, and alcohol and/or drug use disorders (Kessler et al., 1999; Harris and Barraclough, 1997; Cavanagh et al., 2003). Although suicide behavior is often related to mental health problems, the majority of psychiatric patients, however, never attempted suicide.

The studies of familial clustering of suicidal acts have shown that suicidal behavior runs in families and to some extent independently from the familial aggregation of psychiatric disorders (Brent and Mann, 2005). These risk factors are of various types, including a history of self-injurious behavior, social isolation, marital problem, work problems, poor physical health, alcohol or substance intake, physical or sexual abuse during childhood, feelings of hopelessness, and aggressive-impulsive traits. Different risk factors seem to interact with each other (Hawton and Heeringen, 2009; Mann, 2002; Waern et al., 2002).

Suicide is a very complex, multicausal human behavior with many "causes" and several biological as well as psychosocial and cultural components (Rihmer, 2007). Thus, causation of suicide behavior is multi-factorial with interactions of factors, but the mechanisms of interactions are largely unknown. Due to this limited knowledge of causality and the extremely low base-rate of suicide behavior in the general population, sensitive and specific risk assessment is a challenging task (Mann, 2002). Besides mental disorders, impulsive-aggressive behaviors in families could also contribute to the familial transmission of suicidal behavior (Brent and Mann, 2006; McGirr and Turecki, 2007; Turecki, 2001). Family, adoption, twin, molecular genetic, geographic, and migrant studies have shown that familial clustering of suicidal behavior has both genetic and environmental causes (Baldessarini and Henne, 2004; Brent and Mann, 2005; Turechi, 2001; Wasserman et al., 2007; Voracek and Loibl, 2007, 2008). Therefore, other risk factors must often be involved in the suicide process.

OVERVIEW OF THE MODELS USED IN SUICIDE STUDY

As summarized above, causation of suicide behavior is multi-factorial with interactions among the factors. To explore the mechanisms underlying suicide behavior, various approaches have been proposed in the suicide study literature, including register, family, genetic, and psychological autopsy studies. Different approaches have their respective strengths and limitations (Leenaars et al., 1997). When viewed from different perspectives, each approach has its own focuses and aims, all attempting to find the reasons or mechanisms leading to suicide and thus to improve suicide prevention, i.e., why there is suicide behavior?, What risk factors lead to suicide behavior? and when suicide strikes an individual person? Thus, studies in the literature all focus on these three primary questions: [1] causality, [2] risk and protective factors, and [3] individual suicidal process.

From the causality perspective, that is, to describe and explain how suicidal behavior actually comes about, there are several models in the literature. Among them, the diathesis-stress model is particularly popular. The model is based on the theory in psychology that explains behavior as a result of both biological and genetic vulnerability and attributes stress to life experiences. The term diathesis is used to refer to a genetic predisposition toward an abnormal or diseased condition. According to this diathesis-stress model, this predisposition, when interacted with certain kinds of environmental stress, results in abnormal behavior. This same theory is also often applied to mental disorder such as schizophrenia, depression, and anxiety.

The diathesis concept has a long history in the medical nomenclature. The word diathesis derives from the ancient Greek idea of disposition, but the term "diathesis-stress" was coined by psychologists Manfred Bleuler and David Rosenthal in the 1960s in their development of new theories about schizophrenia. Their model posits that the onset of a certain disorder results from a combination of one's biological disposition towards the given disorder and stressful events that bring about the onset to such disorder. Mann and colleague (1999) first applied the diathesis-stress model to the study of suicide. They outlined the theoretical interlocking relationships between stress, risk factors, and diathesis as their diathesis- stress model for suicide. In their model, impulsivity is the proximal factor leading to suicidal behaviors, but other factors can also contribute to suicidal behaviors by modifying the level of impulsivity to increase the risk of suicidal behaviors (Brent and Mann, 2003; Mann, 2003). In Mann's original model of suicidal behavior, poor impulse control mediates the relationship between suicidal planning and suicide attempt. Impulsivity can be modified primarily through psychiatric state and life events or serotonin function and substance use. Suicidal behaviors generally occur through two types of diathesis or vulnerabilities: [1] major psychopathology (most commonly depression); and [2] impulsive-aggression and its neurobiological correlates (impaired executive function, and serotonin dysregulation in the ventral prefrontal cortex) (Brent and Mann, 2003; Mann et al., 1999).

In order to provide a plausible mechanism to explain how, when, and to what extent interactions among these risk factors occurs in adolescents, the same diathesis-stress model has been applied in family studies to illustrate familial processes leading to suicidal behavior in adolescents (Brent and Mann, 2006). Familial factors, such as parental mood disorders, parental impulsive-aggressive traits and parental suicide attempts, produce altered serotonin function and deficits in executive functioning. Although diathesis-stress model applied in family studies generally provides strong evidence for familial aggregation or transmission of suicidal behavior, family studies alone cannot disentangle the relative impacts of genes and environment, and must be complemented by gene-environment interaction studies in order to tease out the interactions between the factors (Brezo et al., 2010; Brent and Mann, 2006).

From the perspective of risk and protective factors, Maris (2002) depicted a two-dimensional model to explain the risk and protective factors of suicidal behavior. One dimension includes factors leading to or protecting from suicidal behavior with corresponding primary, secondary, and tertiary prevention, while the second pertains to individual and social areas of relevance. The interaction between the two dimensions provides various cells of risk or prevention conditions.

The third popular model is the diathesis-stress plus model, in which the diathesis-stress perspective, risk and protective factors, and the development of the suicide process in the individual are considered. The two adverse processes are focused in this model: how the suicidal process completed and how it faded away due to treatment or coping. Various risk factors including stress and acute triggers for suicidal behavior lead to suicidal process completed in the individual, while various protective factors including cognitive style and personality, and family and social support help the individual thwart suicide attempts (Wasserman, 2001).

ISSUES AND LIMITATIONS OF STATISTICAL METHODS

Numerous methodological difficulties have been identified with respect to research on suicidal behavior (Smith and Maris, 1986; McIntosh, 2002). According to the McIntosh (2002), a number of authors over time have questioned the use or validity of official statistics on suicide. The primary argument focuses on nonrandom and systematic biases in the data. Biases may arise from cultural beliefs and attitudes towards suicide, and thus intentional misclassfication of suicide cases.

In addition, many other factors also affect the official suicide data (McIntosh, 2002). Among them are errors of entry of some other cause of death, concealed evidence, circumstances that make suicide death difficult to be recognized, and changing classification schemes used for deaths.

The latter data issues also arise from and are relevant to the field in general, since as mentioned earlier, all approaches in the extant literature on suicide, such as register, family, genetic and psychological autopsy studies, rely on good quality of data. However, we focus on limitations of statistical models for suicide risk and behavior in this chapter.

Regression Models

More than a century has passed since Emile Durkheim published his classic study of suicide (Durkheim's (2006 [1897]) On Suicide), in which he pioneered a stunning application of macro-sociological analysis although it is primitive. Durkheim sought to show that each society had a collective inclination towards suicide more or less distinct from the individual roots of suicidal behavior. But in the 1890s he lacked the necessary statistical tools to confirm his hypotheses about the contextual analysis.

Karl Pearson and his colleague and student George Udny Yule are credited for applying correlation and regression analysis to social science, medicine and other fields (Jones, 1995; Selvin, 1965; Hepple, 2001). For example, Yule found that the high positive correlation between yearly number of suicides and membership in the Church of England due not to cause, but to other variables that also varied over time (Aldrich, 1995). This finding enabled Yule to explain high correlations between unrelated quantities, which had puzzled him over a course of time. Correlational and regression analyses denominated various research fields several decades, particularly in the research on suicide.

Bivariate analyses, such as the chi-square and Fisher's exact tests for binary outcomes and the Mann-Whitney U Statistics test for continuous variables, have been popular analytic strategies for research on suicide. These tools are suitable, when suicide or suicidal behavior is characterized by dichotomous or continuous variables, such as attempt vs. non attempt, or number of suicide attempts.

Investigation of more complex relationships are facilitated by employing regression models such as logistical, linear and Cox regression models, depending on the types of analysis (standard vs. survival analysis) and the response, or dependent variable (e.g., continuous vs. binary). For example, if we treat suicide variable as a dichotomous variable, that is, completed vs. non-completed, or attempted vs. non-attempted, then logistical regression can be used to estimate the relative risk of such a suicide outcome and how it is associated with a change in a predictor (Breslow et al., 1981; Leon et al., 1990). If we code suicidal behavior as a continuous outcome, such as lethality of attempt (e.g., a scale outcome), we can use multiple regression to estimate association of the outcome with a range of predictors such as stressful life events (Leon et al., 1990).

Survival analysis has been underutilized in suicide studies; prior to 1990, only one study of suicide modeled the "time until suicidal behavior" using survival methodology (Leon et al., 1990; Barner-Rasmussen, 1986; Barner-Rasmussen,et al., 1986). However, things have been changed and survival analysis seems to have been increasingly used in more recent studies, especially in the study of suicidal behavior such as suicide attempt, an event of higher prevalence than complete suicide (Leon et al., 1990).

Limitations of Regression Methods

As elaborated in Section 2, risk for suicide or suicide attempt (SA) is a complex behavior involving the host of biological and environmental factors. For example, the popular diathesis-stressor model indicates that SA is not merely determined by psychiatric illness (stressor) but by genetic and familial factors (diathesis) as well, as depicted by a path diagram based on this conceptual model of Mann et al. (1999) in Figure 1. By integrating biological trait factors with social and psychiatric illness and associated comorbid conditions and risk factors (e.g., alcohol and substance use), this model overcomes the limitations of most earlier studies on suicide that are restricted to one domain of risk factors such as familial and psychiatric variables, since any single factor alone is generally a necessary but insufficient condition for SA. Although recent studies have tried to examine the multiple risk factors in unison, they all have failed to acknowledge the interactions, and more importantly the varying roles played by the different variables.

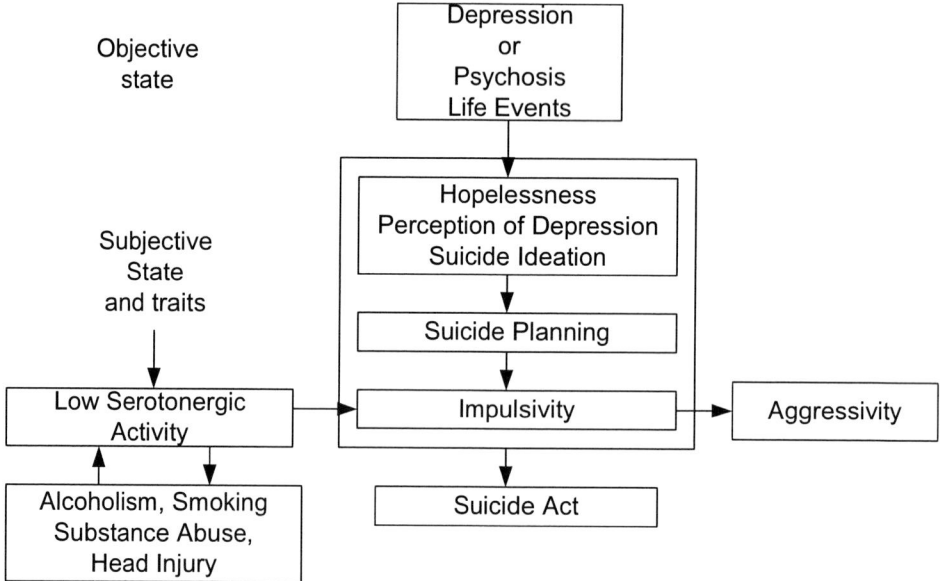

Figure 1. A diathesis-stress model for pathways of suicide (Mann et al., 1999).

For example, SA may be both an effect-receiving and effect-imparting variable; an earlier event of SA is not only the result of severe psychiatric illness in its most extreme form (effect-receiving), but may also be predictive of subsequent events of SA (effect-imparting). The popular regression paradigm including correlation analysis is ill-suited for modeling such a complex and dynamic system of cause-effect relationships, since an outcome such as SA is not allowed to play the dual role of an effect-receiving and -imparting variable (Kowalski and Tu, 2007).

A new integrative approach, not only combining all risk factors, but accommodating the different roles each one plays in the cause-effect chain, is needed to validate and extend this and other related conceptual model for suicide.

TOWARD AN INTEGRATED FRAMEWORK

Since suicidal behavior is influenced by multiple factors, such as genetic, biochemical, physiological, cognitive, and environmental variables, developmental assessments of suicidal behavior require the use of integrated, multilevel bio-psycho-social models (Cicchetti, 1993; Hinshaw, 2002; Windle and Wiesner, 2004; Windle and Davies, 1999; Zucker et al., 1995). The study of the effects of collective or group characteristics on individual-level outcomes has been termed contextual (Blalock and Wilken, 1979; Blalock, 1984; Diez-Roux, 1998; Iversen, 1991; Scheuch, 1969) or multilevel analysis (Von Korff et al., 1992; Hermalin, 1986; Hox and Kreft, 1994). Empirically, contextual analysis involves the incorporation of group-level variables into individual-level models, appropriate for the study of persons as the unit of analysis. Such contextual or multilevel models acknowledge that the lives of individuals are affected not only by their personal characteristics but by characteristics of the social groups to which they belong. The underlying idea is that social groups are legitimate units of analysis, that group properties are distinct from those of individual members, and that these macro-level variables may affect outcomes independently of individual characteristics or modify how individual characteristics are related to outcomes of suicide (Diez-Roux, 1998; Blalock and Wilken, 1979; Hox and Kreft, 1994).

Under this integrated framework, assessments of the influences of the different types of variables are conducted concurrently to better understand suicidal behavior. This developmental approach includes the principles of reciprocal causation. For example, in studying adolescent suicide, an adolescent's behavioral characteristics elicit particular behavioral responses from parents and peers, which at the same time influences the adolescent's behavior and induce interactions between the individual and his/her environment (e.g.,gene-environment interactions and correlations). The goal of this approach is to examine patterns of interpersonal interactions and associated behavioral outcomes (e.g., Caspi and Moffit, 1995; Caspi et al., 2003; Hinshaw, 2002).

In summary, the etiology of suicide or suicide attempt is quite a complex process, involving multiple factors and their interactions. A new modeling paradigm for integrating the multitude of biological and environmental factors is needed to understand the complex mechanisms underlying suicidal behavior and effectively predict how, when and to what extent the putative risk and protective factors influence suicidal behavior. As a result, we cannot examine and test the validity of models for such relationships using correlation (or association) and/or regression analysis. Although conceptually sound models have been developed for integrating genetic, biophysilogical and environmental variables such as the diathesis-stress model, and relevant variables have been collected in many recent studies, an integrated approach is woefully lacking to take such multifaceted and -dimensional data to validate and even extend the conceptual models.

Structural Equation Models

The structural equation model (SEM), a system of regression-type models linked together to capture the relationships among a web of variables, is the most popular paradigm for modeling cause-effect pathways. Although similar in appearance, SEM is fundamentally different from regression. For example, applications of regression mandate a clear distinction between dependent (effect-receiving) and independent (effect-imparting) variables, but such concepts only apply in relative terms in SEM, since a dependent variable in one model equation can become an independent variable in other components of the SEM system (Bollen, 1989;. Kowalski and Tu, 2007). It is precisely this type of reciprocal role a variable plays that enables SEM to infer causal relationships.

To enable infer causal relationship, variables in SEM are classified into endogenous and exogenous. An endogenous variable is an effect-receiving, or dependent variable, in at least one of the equations, while an exogenous variable always plays the role of effect-impart, akin to an independent variable in regression. The causal relationship is then represented by the path diagram, which consists of nodes representing the variables, and arrows showing relations between them. In a path diagram, latent variables (e.g., construct of mental disorder) are distinguished from their observed counterparts (e.g., diagnosis of a particular mood disorder) by using a circle or ellipse rather than the rectangular or square box, designated for the observed counterparts. Arrows are used to represent relationships among the variables; a single straight arrow indicates a causal relation from the base to the head of the arrow, while two straight single-headed arrows in opposing directions connecting two variables indicate a reciprocal relationship.

Structural equation models (SEM) provide a perfect framework for testing and validating conceptually sound models for suicide behavior such as the well-accepted diathesis-stress model by permitting SA to play the dual roles of both an effect-receiving variable for suicide ideation, planning and impulsivity, but an effect-imparting variable for subsequent SA's as well. Below, we focus on an important class of applications of SEM, the mediation analysis, and illustrate how such analyses can be used to validate some important pathways to suicide as depicted by the diathesis-stress model.

Mediation Models for Suicide Behavior

A popular application of SEM is mediation analysis, particularly for investigating mechanisms of action of a causal agent in psychosocial research (Conner et al., 2011;.Kowalski and Tu, 2007; Cole and Maxwell, 2003; MacKinnon and Fairchild, 2009). With mediation analysis, we gain insight and acquire deep understanding about the mechanism of action of pharmacological and psychotherapeutic treatments. Such information provides an added dimension to understand the etiology of disease and pathways of therapeutic effects so more efficacious and cost efficient alternative therapies may be developed.

For example, in treatment studies, it is often of great interest to identify and study mechanisms by which an intervention achieves its effect. Consider a tobacco prevention program may teach participants how to stop taking smoking breaks at work, thereby changing the social norms for tobacco use. As a result, this change in social norms reduces cigarette smoking (MacKinnon and Fairchild, 2009).

Shown in Figure 2 is the path diagram for the causal relationship between the three variables in the smoking prevention example discussed earlier. The three variables, prevention intervention (x_{i1}), social norm (z_{i2}), and amount of smoking (y_{i3}), are measured at three assessment points in chronological order starting at baseline within a longitudinal setting. Also, all effect-receiving variables such as the social normal and amount of smoking in this example are called endogenous variables, and effect-imparting variables such as the prevention intervention are known as exogenous variables in the nomenclature of SEM. By investigating such a mediational process through which the treatment affects study outcomes, not only can we further our understanding of the pathology of the disease and treatment, but may also provide alternative intervention strategies for the disease with efficient use of resources.

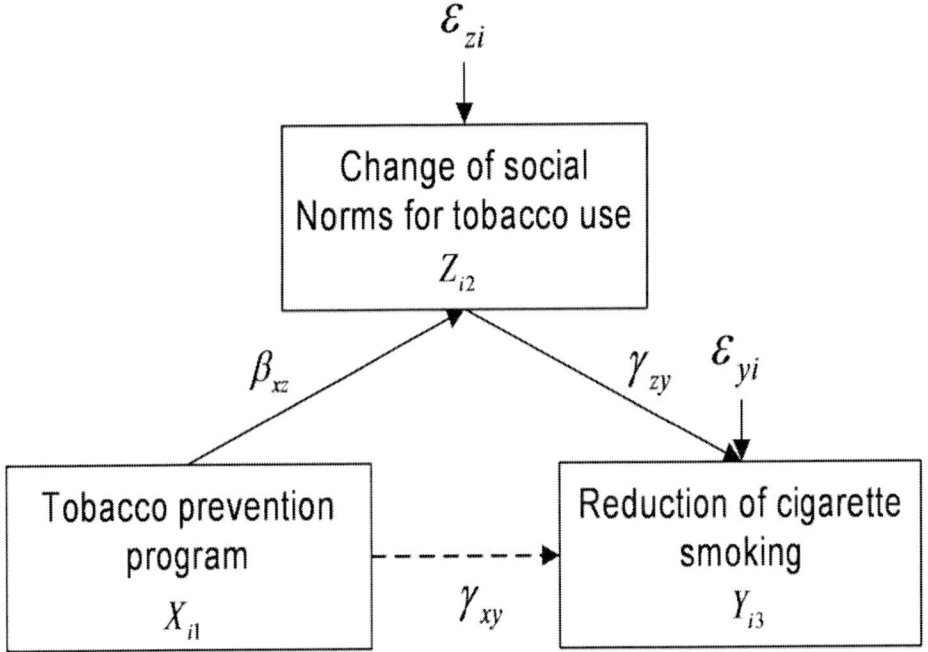

Figure 2. A hypothetical mediation model involving one mediator for mediating the effect of a tobacco prevention program on the reduction of smoking.

The SEM for testing the causal relationship depicted in Figure 2 has the following form:

$$Z_{i2} = \beta_0 + \beta_{xz}X_{i1} + \varepsilon_{zi}, \quad Y_{i3} = \gamma_0 + \gamma_{xy}X_{i1} + \gamma_{zy}Z_{i2} + \varepsilon_{yi},$$

$$\left(\varepsilon_{yi}, \varepsilon_{zi}\right)^{\mathrm{T}} \sim N\left(\mathbf{0}, \Psi\right), \quad \Psi = \begin{pmatrix} \sigma_{\varepsilon y}^2 & \sigma_{\varepsilon yz}^2 \\ & \sigma_{\varepsilon z}^2 \end{pmatrix}, \quad X_{i1} \perp \varepsilon_{zi}, \quad X_{i1}, Z_{i2} \perp \varepsilon_{yi}, \tag{1}$$

where $N(\mathbf{\mu}, \Psi)$ denotes a multivariate normal distribution with mean $\mathbf{\mu}$ and variance σ^2, ? denotes stochastic independence, and ε_{yi} and ε_{zi} are the error terms for the respective equations. In the above, X_{i1} is an exogenous variable, while Z_{i2} and Y_{i3} are both endogenous. Let $\mathbf{\theta} = \left(\gamma_0, \gamma_{zy}, \gamma_{xy}, \beta_0, \beta_{xz}, \sigma^2_{\varepsilon y}, \sigma_{\varepsilon yz}, \sigma^2_{\varepsilon z} \right)^T$ be the vector of parameters of the SEM in Equation [1].

The direct effect is the pathway from the exogenous variable X_{i1} to the outcome Y_{i3}, while controlling for the mediator Z_{i2}. Therefore, γ_{xy} is the direct effect for the mediation model in Figure 2. The indirect effect describes the pathway from the exogenous variable to the outcome through the mediator. This path is represented through the product of β_{xz} and γ_{zy}. Finally, the total effect is the sum of the direct and indirect effects of the exogenous variable on the outcome, $\gamma_{xy} + \beta_{xz}\gamma_{zy}$.

For mediation analysis, the primary interest is the hypothesis of full mediation $H_0 : \gamma_{xy} = 0$. Under this null, the direct path from X_{i1} to Y_{i3} is broken, with the effect of X_{i1} on Y_{i3} fully mediated through the change in Z_{i2}, and the total effect equal to the indirect effect $\beta_{xz}\gamma_{zy}$.

Stochastic independence is not taken for granted, as it is particularly important for causal inference. To facilitate validation, the usual independence is replaced by zero correlation, which can be empirically checked. Such an assumption is known as *pseudo-isolation* in SEM. For example, to assess the causal effect of X_{i1} and Z_{i2} in Equation [1], it is critical that X_{i1} be uncorrelated with ε_{yi} in the first and both X_{i1} and Z_{i2} be uncorrelated with ε_{yi} in the second equation of the SEM. It is then readily checked that

$$Cov\left(\varepsilon_{zi}, \varepsilon_{yi}\right) = Cov\left(\varepsilon_{yi}, Z_{i2}\right) = 0. \tag{2}$$

In other words, ε_{zi} and ε_{yi} are uncorrelated as well, i.e., $\sigma_{\varepsilon_y \varepsilon_z} = 0$, for this particular SEM, and thus $\mathbf{\theta}$ reduces to $\mathbf{\theta} = \left(\gamma_0, \gamma_{zy}, \gamma_{xy}, \beta_0, \beta_{xz}, \sigma^2_{\varepsilon z}, \sigma^2_{\varepsilon y} \right)^T$.

Figure 2 depicts a relatively simple mediation model involving only one mediator. Mediation processes defined by multiple mediators also often arise in practice. For example, shown in Figure 3 is the path diagram for a pathway to suicide ideation, derived based on the diathesis-stress model, involving three mediators, Z_{i1t}, Z_{i2t} and Z_{i3t}, representing three risk factors for suicide ideation, alcohol, tobacco and drug use, respectively. We can readily revise the SEM in [1] to accommodate the additional mediators by adding the extra equations pertaining to these added mediators:

$$Z_{i12} = \beta_{01} + \beta_{xz1}X_{i1} + \varepsilon_{zi1},$$
$$Z_{i22} = \beta_{02} + \beta_{xz2}X_{i1} + \varepsilon_{zi2},$$
$$Z_{i32} = \beta_{03} + \beta_{xz3}X_{i1} + \varepsilon_{zi3},$$
$$Y_{i3} = \gamma_0 + \gamma_{xy}X_{i1} + \gamma_{zy1}Z_{i12} + \gamma_{zy2}Z_{i22} + \gamma_{zy3}Z_{i32} + \varepsilon_{yi},$$

$$\boldsymbol{\varepsilon}_i = \left(\varepsilon_{yi}, \varepsilon_{zi1}, \varepsilon_{zi2}, \varepsilon_{zi3}\right)^{\mathrm{T}} \sim N\left(\mathbf{0}, \Psi\right), \quad \Psi = \begin{pmatrix} \sigma_{\varepsilon y}^2 & \sigma_{\varepsilon yz1}^2 & \sigma_{\varepsilon yz2}^2 & \sigma_{\varepsilon yz3}^2 \\ & \sigma_{\varepsilon z1}^2 & \sigma_{\varepsilon z12}^2 & \sigma_{\varepsilon z13}^2 \\ & & \sigma_{\varepsilon z2}^2 & \sigma_{\varepsilon z23}^2 \\ & & & \sigma_{\varepsilon z3}^2 \end{pmatrix},$$

$$X_{i1}, Z_{i12}, Z_{i22}, Z_{i32} \perp \varepsilon_{yi}, \quad X_{i1} \perp \varepsilon_{zik}, \quad 1 \le k \le 3,$$

(3)

In the above SEM, γ_{xy} is the parameter linking depression (X_{i1}) to SA (Y_{i3}), γ_{zyk} associates each of the mediators with suicide ideation, while β_{zyk} relates X_{i1} to each of the three mediators Z_{ik2} $\left(1 \le k \le 3\right)$. As in the SEM in Equation [1], ε_{zik} and ε_{yi} represent the error terms in the equations for the respective variables. Finally, the assumption of pseudo-isolation for the simpler SEM in [2] is readily adapted to the context of the more general SEM in [3] (Kowalski and Tu, 2007).

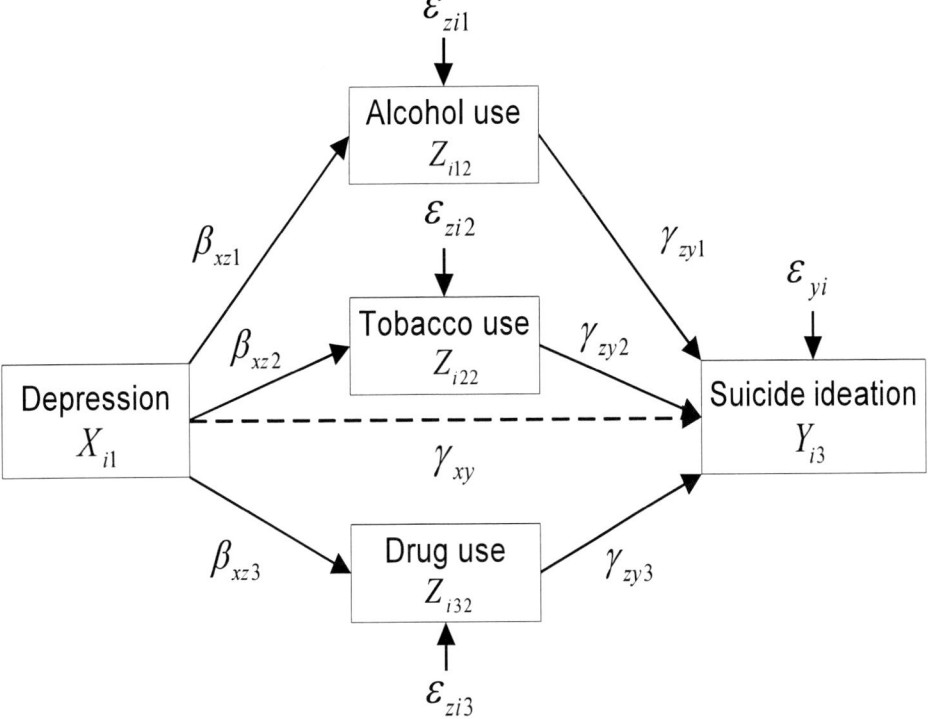

Figure 3. A three-mediator model for the relationship between depression and suicide ideation derived from the diathesis-stress model.

Note that for illustration purposes, we assumed interval-scaled, or continuous variables for all the outcomes, X_{i1}, Z_{ik2} and Y_{i3} so that the relationships among them can be modeled by linear regression $(1 \leq k \leq 3)$. These continuous variables can represent severity of depression, amount of alcohol, tobacco and dug use, and suicide ideation, respectively. However, the linear SEM in Equation [3] is readily generalized to accommodate non-continuous outcomes. For example, if Y_{i3} is binary represents suicide attempt, then we can replace the linear regression relating Y_{i3} to X_{i1} and Z_{ik2} by a logistic regression model with Y_{i3} serving as the response, and X_{i1} and Z_{ik2} as explanatory variables.

With the SEM in Equation [3], we can readily test mediation effects on the relationship between depression and suicide attempt by the three substance use variables. We first test the total effect, $\gamma_{xy} + \beta_{xz1}\gamma_{zy1} + \beta_{xz2}\gamma_{zy2} + \beta_{xz3}\gamma_{zy3}$, since this is often of primary interest in mediation analysis. A mediation effect may exist, regardless of whether there is a statistically significant effect of the independent (depression within our context) on the outcome (suicide in our setting), especially in multiple mediator models like the one in Equation [3]. The reason is that multiple mediators may be negatively related to the outcome, reducing the effect of the independent variable on the outcome.

Like the one-mediator model in Equation [3], the primary interest is the hypothesis of full mediation by the three mediators, i.e., $H_0 : \gamma_{xy} = 0$. Under this null, the direct path from X_{i1} to Y_{i3} is completely broken, with the effect of X_{i1} on Y_{i3} fully mediated through the changes in the Z_{ik2}'s $(1 \leq k \leq 3)$, and the total effect equals to the indirect effect $\beta_{xz1}\gamma_{zy1} + \beta_{xz2}\gamma_{zy2} + \beta_{xz3}\gamma_{zy3}$. Direct, indirect and total effects for the three mediator model, which are readily evaluated by extending the formulas for the simpler model in Equation [1], can be obtained from popular packages for SEM such as SAS, SPSS, LISREL and Mplus. Mplus provides both total indirect effects involving all mediators, $\beta_{xz1}\gamma_{zy1} + \beta_{xz2}\gamma_{zy2} + \beta_{xz3}\gamma_{zy3}$ within the current context of the three-mediator model, and specific indirect effects pertaining to each particular mediator, $\beta_{xzk}\gamma_{zyk}$ $(1 \leq k \leq 3)$.

Since a path diagram can become quite complex, it is important to assess model fit when modeling such a pathway, especially if the model is premised on a conceptual basis. For example, the mediation relationship depicted in Figure 3 may be incorrect, and the true pathway is actually described by the diagram shown in Figure 4.

Model selection criteria provide an objective means to confirm the validity of a hypothesized pathway as well as to guide us in choosing an optimal model among a set of competing alternatives. Popular criteria for assessing model fit for SEM include Comparative Fit Index (CFI), Tucker-Lewis Index (TLI) and Root Mean Square Error of Approximation (RMSEA). TLI is a goodness of fit measure adjusted for model complexity, thereby providing a measure of goodness of fit for the model of interest in relation to a baseline model. CFI is directly based on the non-centrality measure, but confined to a range between 0 and 1 since it is set to 1 (0) if the non-centrality measure yields a value greater (less) than one (zero).

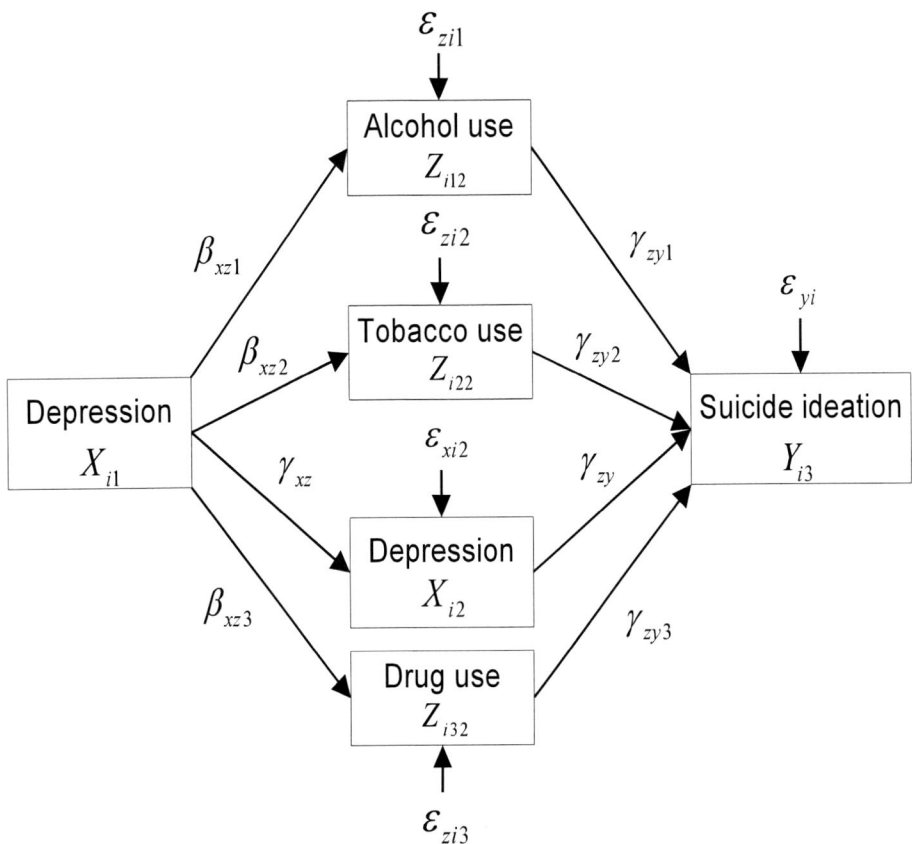

Figure 4. An alternative pathway from depression to to suicide attempt bsaed on the diathesis-stress concept.

If CFI is less than one, then the CFI is always greater than TLI. CFI pays a penalty of one for every parameter estimated. CFI/TLI greater than 0.9 indicates a good mode fit. RMSEA is another popular model fit index, and it takes into account the population error of approximation and the number of degrees of freedom in the model. If the approximation is good, RMSEA should be small. MacCallum, Browne and Sugawara (1996) have used 0.01, 0.05, and 0.08 to indicate excellent, good, and mediocre fit respectively. In practice, a value of approximately 0.05 or less indicates a good fit of the model.

A SIMULATED STUDY EXAMPLE

We illustrate an application of the three-mediator model discussed in the preceding section with data from a simulated study. We set the sample size $n = 200$ and level of statistical significance at alpha = 0.05. We performed the analysis using Mplus, which is one of the most popular packages for fitting SEM models (Muthén and Muthén, 1998-2010).

For the simulation study, we set:

$$\gamma_0 = \gamma_{zyk} = 1, \quad \beta_{0k} = \beta_{xzk} = 1, \quad \gamma_{xy} = 0,$$

$$\sigma_x^2 = \sigma_{\varepsilon y}^2 = \sigma_{\varepsilon zk}^2 = 0.2, \quad \sigma_{\varepsilon yzk}^2 = 0, \quad 1 \le k \le 3,$$

$$\theta = \left(\gamma^T, \beta^T, \varphi^T\right)^T, \quad \beta = \left(\beta_{01}, \beta_{02}, \beta_{03}, \beta_{xz1}, \beta_{xz2}, \beta_{xz3}\right)^T, \tag{4}$$

$$\gamma = \left(\gamma_0, \gamma_{xy}, \gamma_{zy1}, \gamma_{zy2}, \gamma_{zy3}\right)^T, \theta = \left(\sigma_{\varepsilon y}^2, \sigma_{\varepsilon z1}^2, \sigma_{\varepsilon z2}^2, \sigma_{\varepsilon z3}^2\right)^T.$$

Thus, the data was simulated from a full mediation model with $\gamma_{xy} = 0$. With the values of the parameters set in Equation [4], we first simulated X_{i1} from a normal $N(1,1)$, followed by simulating ε_{yi} and ε_{zik} $(1 \le k \le 3)$ from $N(0,0.2)$. The variables Y_{i3} and Z_{ik2} $(1 \le k \le 3)$ were then constructed from the SEM in (3) based on the values of γ and β in Equation [4].

Shown in Table 1 are the estimated γ and β along with their respective standard errors. All estimated coefficients were quite close 1, the true value of the parameters. To see if the effect of depression severity X_{i1} on suicide ideation is fully mediated by the three variables Z_{ik2}, we tested the null hypothesis: $H_0 : \gamma_{xy} = 0$. Shown in the Table 1 are the statistics and p-value for testing this null. The estimate (standard error) of the direct effect from X_{i1} to Y_{i3} is -0.086 (0.076), yielding a p-value of 0.259, which is not statistically significant. The null hypothesis $H_0 : \gamma_{xy} = 0$ is therefore not rejected, as expected because of the way the data was generated. Thus, the results show full mediation by the three mediators, consistent with the posited model in Equation (4).

Table 1. Estimates of parameters and standard errors, along with statistics and p-values for testing the null of full mediation for the three-mediator model based on a simulated sample

Estimates, standard errors and p-value based on normally distributed X_{i1} and error terms, with sample size n = 200											
	γ_0	γ_{xy}	γ_{zy1}	γ_{zy3}	γ_0	β_{01}	β_{02}	β_{03}	β_{xz1}	β_{xz2}	β_{xz3}
Estimate	0.91	−0.08	0.991	1.05	1.04	0.997	0.999	0.994	0.998	1.003	0.995
Std. error	0.07	0.076	0.043	0.046	0.04	0.005	0.004	0.004	0.005	0.004	0.004
Full mediation hypothesis $H_0 : \gamma_{xy} = 0$											
Estimate (Std. error) of $\gamma_{xy} = -0.086(0.076)$, p-value $= 0.259$											
Goodness of fit statistics											
CFI = 1		TLI = 1	RMSEA = 0								

As discussed at the end of Section 4.2, it is important to assess the fit of a SEM model, because of the multitude of different relationships that may be constructed among the variables. Goodness of fit criteria enable us to objectively valid a theory-driven model so that it can withstand the test of time.

Shown in Table 1 are the popular model fit criteria for SEM discussed in Section 4.2 when applied to the simulated data. We can see all the fit indices show a good fit of the model. Both the CFI and TLI were 1, exceeding the cut-off of 0.9 for good fit. The RMSEA was 0, less than 0.05, the threshold for good fit.

Based on the suggested guidelines by MacCallum et al. (1996), the fit was indeed excellent, which was expected because the data was generated by exactly the same model fit to it. Thus, all three indices consistently show a good model fit here.

CONCLUSION

In this chapter, we have provided a brief review of conceptually sound as well as accepted models for suicide and suicide attempt, discussed limitations of statistical methods currently used for studies in this field, and introduced and illustrated the structural equation model (SEM) as a way to integrate multi-faceted and -dimensional outcomes to provide a powerful framework for the complex pathways of suicide and suicide attempt.

Our review shows, on the one side, significant progress achieved in the field by developing sound conceptual models for the complex pathway towards suicide and suicide attempt such as the well-accepted diathesis-stress model and the approach of contextual (multilevel) analysis, and on the other side, several limitations of currently employed statistical methods in testing and validating such models, thereby hampering the efforts to develop effective prevention interventions.

A fundamental limitation with the popular regression paradigm is the clear distinction between dependent, or effect-receiving, and independent, or effect-imparting, variables, which does not fit well with causal inference theories where such a differentiation is not permitted since an outcome can play both roles of effect-receiving and -imparting. Although researchers have begun to adopt structural equation models in one form or another in their respective fields of research, especially in recent years, this class of models still has not found its way to the study of suicide.

We have demonstrated an important of class of applications of SEM by testing a mediation process for the pathway from depression to suicide ideation based on data from a simulated study. The mediation hypothesis is developed based on the well-accepted diathesis-stress model, albeit simplified to fit the purpose of exposition. This approach overcomes the limitations of standard regression to allow us to model a complex and dynamic system of cause-effect pathway from depression to alcohol or drug or tobacco use to suicide ideation by integrating all respective outcomes under a single unified modeling framework.

The classic SEM discussed in this chapter is parametric, in the sense that analytic distributions such as normality are assumed for inference. Computation of estimates is quite a complex task for such parametric models. However, significant advances have been made over the past few decades in the theory and applications as well as software development for fitting SEM models. For example, in addition to specialized packages such as LISREL

(Jöreskog and Sörbom, 1974) and Mplus (Muthén and Muthén, 1998-2010), procedures for fitting SEM are also available from general-purposes statistical packages such as R and SAS. These packages provide inference based on maximum likelihood (ML), generalized least squares (GLS), and weighted least squares (WLS). While ML assumes a multivariate normal for the joint distribution of all variables (exogenous plus endogenous variables), GLS and WLS do not, thereby providing more robust estimates, at least in theory.

Another drawback of the classic SEM is that biased estimates may arise if data do not support the assumed distribution models, which is too often the case because most variables in real studies do not fit the confine of a few available well-shaped mathematical models such as the normal distribution.

In recent years, many software packages have implemented robust variance estimates to improve the validity of inference in the presence of departures from assumed parametric models. For example, such approaches for standard longitudinal models have demonstrated quite robust estimates under departures from the assumed normal distribution (Maas and Hox, 2004; Van der Leeden et al., 1997).

In a recent study, we have also showed that estimates from the classic SEM, including all three types of ML, GLS and WLS, are highly biased when data deviate from the assumed parametric distributions (Lu et al., 2009). Thus, to improve the performance and reliability of SEM and make it truly a useful analytic tool to facilitate suicide research, it is important that we address such limitations.

REFERENCES

Aldrich, J. (1995). Correlations Genuine and Spurious in Pearson and Yule. *Statistical Science*, Vol. 10, No. 4, 364-376.

Anderson, R.N. and Smith, B.L. (2003). Deaths: Leading causes for 2001. *Natl. Vital Stat.Rep.*, 52:1-85.

Baldessarini, R.J. and Henne,J. (2004). Gnetics of suicide: an overview. *Harv Rev Psychiatry*,12,1-13.

Barner-Rasmussen, P. (1986). Suicide in psychiatric patients in Denmark, 1971-1981. *Acta Psychiatrica Scandinavia*, 73:449-455.

Barner-Rasmussen, P., DuPont, A., and Bille, H. (1986). Suicide in psychiatric patients in Denmark, I97 I -I 98 I. *Acta Psychiatrica Scandinavia*, 73:44 I-448.

Beck,A.T., Brown,G.K.,Steer, R.A., Dahlsgaard,K.K., and Grisham, J.R. (1999). Suicide Ideation at Its Worst Point: A Predictor of Eventual Suicide in Psychiatric Outpatients. *Suicide and Life-Threatening Behavior*, Vol. 29(1): 1-9.

Bertolote, J.M. and Fleischmann, A. (2005). Suicidal Behavior Prevention:WHO Perspectives on Research. *American Journal of Medical Genetics Part C (Semin. Med. Genet.)* 133C:8--12.

Beskow, J. (1979).Suicide and mental disorder in Swedish men. *Acta Psychiatrica Scandinavica*, Vol Suppl 277, 138.

Blalock, H.M. (1984). Contextual-effects models: theoretical and methodological issues. *Annu Rev Sociol.* 10:353-372.

Blalock, H.M., Wilken, P.H. (1979). Intergroup Processes: A Micro-Macro Perspective. New York, NY: Free Press.

Bollen, K. A. (1989). *Structural Equations with Latent Variables*. Wiley Series in Probability and Mathematical Statistics. New York: Wiley.

Brezo,J. Bureau, A., Mérette, C., Jomphe, V. , Barker, E.D., Vitaro, F.,Hébert, M., Carbonneau, R.,Tremblay, R.E., and Turecki, G. (2010). Differences and similarities in the serotonergic diathesis for suicide attempts and mood disorders: a 22-year longitudinal gene--environment study. *Molecular Psychiatry*, 15, 831--843.

Brent, D.A. and Mann, J.J. (2003). Familial factors in adolescent suicidal behavior. In: King, R.A., Apter, A., eds. S*uicide in children and adolescents*. Cambridge, UK: Cambridge University Press. 86-117.

Brent, D.A. and Mann, J.J. (2005). Family Genetic Studies, Suicide, and Suicidal Behavior. *American Journal of Medical Genetics Part* C (Semin. Med. Genet.) 133C:13--24.

Brent, D. A., and Mann, J.J. (2006). Familial Pathways to Suicidal Behavior ---Understanding and Preventing Suicide among Adolescents. *N Engl J Med* 355, 2719-21.

Breslow, N.E. and Day, N.E. (1981). Statistical Methods in Cancer Research: Volume 1 - The analysis of case-control studies. Geneva: World Halth Organization.

Caspi, A. and Moffitt, T.E. (1995). The continuity of maladaptive behavior: From description to understanding in the study of antisocial behavior. In: Cicchetti, D, Cohen, D, eds. *Developmental Psychopathology*. Vol. 2. New York: Wiley. 472-511.

Caspi, A., Sugden, K., Moffitt, T.E. et al. (2003). Influence of life stress on depression: Moderation by a polymorphism in the 5-HTT gene. *Science*, 18:386-389.

Cavanagh, J.T., Carson, A.J., Sharpe, M., Lawrie, S.M. (2003). Psychological autopsy studies of suicide: a systematic review [published correction appears in Psychol Med. 2003;33:947]. *Psychol Med*, 33:395-405.

Centers for Disease Control and Prevention. National Center for Injury Prevention and Control: Data and Statistics (WISQARS™); 2007. http://www.cdc.gov/injury. Accessed September 23, 2011.

Centers for Disease Control and Prevention, National Center for Injury Prevention and Control. Web-based Injury Statistics Query and Reporting System (WISQARS): www.cdc.gov/ncipc/wisqars.

Cicchetti, D. (1993). Developmental psychopathology: Reactions, reflections, projections. *Dev.Review*, 13:471-502.

Cole, D. A. and Maxwell, S. E. (2003). Testing mediational models with longitudinal data: Questions and tips in the use of Structural Equation Modeling. *Journal of Abnormal Psychology*, 4, 558-577.

Conner, K.R., Gunzler, D., Tang, W., Tu, X.M., and Maisto, S.A. (2011). Test of a clinical model of drinking and suicidal risk. Alcoholism: *Clinical and Experimental Research,* 35: 60-68.

Conner, K, Bossarte, R, Kaukeinen, K, Tu, X.M, Houston, R, Wyman, P, Lu, N, Chan, G, Goldston, D, Schuckit, M, Bucholz, K, Hesselbrock, M, Kramer, J, Kuperman, S. and Hesselbrock, V. (2011). Suicide Attempts in Adolescence and Emerging Adulthood: Analysis of COGA Data. Poster presentation at the 34th Annual Research Society on Alcoholism Scientific Meeting. Atlanta, Georgia.

Durkheim, E. (1952 [1897]), *Suicide: A Study in Sociology*, London, Routledge and Kegan Paul (translated by J.A. Spaulding and G. Simpson).

Durkheim E. (2006 [1897]). *On Suicide*. London: Penguin Classics.

Diez-Roux, A.V., (1998). Bringing context back into epidemiology: variables and fallacies in multilvel analysis. *Am J Public Health*, 88:216-222.

DIGS 3.0, 03-Nov-1999: http://www-grb.nimh.nih.gov/gi.html.

Durkheim, E. (1952 [1897]), *Suicide: A Study in Sociology*, London, Routledge and Kegan Paul (translated by J.A. Spaulding and G. Simpson).

Durkheim E. (2006 [1897]). *On Suicide*. London: Penguin Classics.

Goldston, D.B., Daniel, S.S., Reboussin, D.M., Reboussin, B. A., Frazier, P. H., and Kelley, A. E. (1999). Suicide attempts among formerly hospitalized adolescents: A prospective naturalistic study of risk during the fi rst fi ve years following discharge. *J. Am.Acad. Child Adolesc.* Psychiatry, 38:660--71.

Harris, E.C., and Barraclough, B.(1997). Suicide as an outcome for mental disorders. A meta-analysis. *Br J Psychiatry*, 170:205-228.

Hawton K, van Heeringen, K. (2009). Suicide. *Lancet* 373:1372--1381.

Hepple, L. W. (2001). Multiple regression and spatial policy analysis: George Udny Yule and the origins of statistical social science. *Environment and Planning D: Society and Space* 19(4) 385 -- 407.

Hermalin, A.l. (1986).The multilevel approach: theory and concepts. In: The Methodology for Measuring the Impact of Family Planning Programmes on Fertility. New York, NY: United Nations; 15-31. Population Studies 66. Addendum Manual IX.

Hinshaw, S.P. (2002). Process, mechanism, and explanation related to externalizing behavior in developmental psychopathology. *J. Abnorm. Child Psychol.*, 30:431-46.

Hox, J, and Kreft, I. (1994). Multilevel analysis methods. *Sociol Methods Res*, 22:283-299.

Iversen, G. (1991). Contextual Analysis. Newbury Park, Calif: Sage Publications.

Jones, F.L. (1995). Micro-macro linkages in sociological analysis: theory, method and substance, *Journal of Sociology*, 31; 74.

Kessler, R.C., Borges, G., Walters, E.E. (1999). Prevalence of and risk factors for lifetime suicide attempts in the National Comorbidity Survey. *Arch Gen Psychiatry*, 56: 617-626.

Kowalski, J., Tu, X. M. (2007). *Modern Applied U Statistics*, Wiley, New York.

Leenaars, A.A, Leo, D.D., Diekstra, R.F.W., Goldney, R.D., and Kelleher, M.J. (1997). Consultations for research in suicidology. *Archives of Suicide Research* 3: 139--151.

Leon, A.C., Richard, A. Friedman, R.A., Sweeney, J.A., Brown, R.P., and Mann, J.J.(1990). Statistical issues in the identification of risk factors for suicidal behavior: *Psychiatry Research*.31, 99-108.

Levinson, D.F., Zubenko, G.S., Crowe, R.R. et al. (2003). Genetics of Recurrent Early-Onset Depression (GenRED): Design and Preliminary Clinical Characteristics of a Repository Sample for Genetic Linkage Studies. *American Journal of Medical Genetics*, 119B:118.130.

Lu, N., Tang, W., He, H., Yu, Q., Crits-Christoph, P., Zhang, H. and Tu, X.M. (2009). On the Impact of Parametric Assumptions and Robust Alternatives for Longitudinal Data Analysis, *Biometrical Journal*, 51: 627-643.

Maas, C.J. and Hox, J.J. (2004). Robustness issues in multilevel regression. *Statistica Neerlandica.*, 58: 127--137.

MacCallum, R. C., Browne, M. W., and Sugawara, H. M. (1996). Power analysis and determination of sample size for covariance structure modeling. Psychological Methods, 1, 130-149.

MacKinnon, D., Fairchild, A. (2009). Current Directions in Mediation Analysis, *Current Directions in Psychological Science*, 18,16-20.

Mann, J.J. (2002). A Current Perspective of Suicide and Attempted Suicide. *Ann Intern Med.* 136:302-311.

Mann, J.J. (2003). Neurobiology of suicidal behavior. *Nat Rev Neurosci* 4, 819-28.

Mann,J.J., Arango,V.A., Avenevoli, S., Brent, D.A., Champagne,F.A., Clayton, P., Currier,D., Dougherty, D.M., Haghighi, F., Hodge,S.E., Kleinman,J., Lehner,T., McMahon, F., Mościcki,E.K., Oquendo,M.A., Pandey, G.N.,Pearson, J., Stanley,B., Terwilliger,J., and Wenzel.A. (2009). Candidate Endophenotypes for Genetic Studies of Suicidal Behavior.*BIOL PSYCHIATRY*. 65:556--563.

Mann, J.J., Waternaux, C., Haas, G.L. et al. (1999). Toward a clinical model of suicidal behavior in psychiatric patients. *Am. J. Psychiatry*, 156:181-9.

Maris, R. W. (2002). Suicide. *Lancet*, 360, 319-326.

McGirr, A. and Turecki, G. (2007). The relationship of impulsive aggressiveness to suicidality and other depression-linked behaviors. *Current Psychiatry Reports*, 9, 460--466.

Mclntosh, J. L.(2002). Quantitative Methods in Suicide Research: Issues Associated with Official Statistics. *Archives of Suicide Research*, 6:41-54.

Muthén, L.K. and Muthén, B.O. (1998-2010). Mplus User's Guide. Sixth Edition. Los Angeles, CA: Muthén and Muthén.

Peterson, B.S., Zhang, H., Santa Lucia, R., King, R. A, and Lewis, M.(1996). Risk factors for presenting problems in child psychiatric emergencies. *J. Am. Acad.Child Adolesc. Psychiatry*, 35:1162--73.

Posner,K., Oquendo,M.A., Gould,M., Stanley, B., Davies, M.(2007). Columbia Classification Algorithm of Suicide Assessment (C-CASA): Classification of Suicidal Events in the FDA's Pediatric Suicidal Risk Analysis of Antidepressants. *Am J Psychiatry*. 164:1035--1043.

Rihmer, Z. (2007). Suicide risk in mood disorders. Current Opinion in Psychiatry.Issue: Volume 20(1), January 2007, 17--22.

Selvin, H.C. (1965), Durkheim's Suicide: Further Thoughts on a Methodological Classic, in R.A. Nisbet (ed.), Emile Durkheim, Makers of Modern Social Science, Englewood Cliffs: Prentice Hall: 113-36.

Scheuch, E.K. (1969). Social context and individual behavior. In: Dogan, M, Rokkam,S., eds. *Social Ecology*. Boston, Mass: MIT Press;133-155.

Smith, K. and Maris, R.(1986). Suggested recommendations for the study of suicide and other life-threatening behaviors. *Suicide and Life-Threatening Behavior*, Vol 16(1), Spr 1986, 67-69.

Turecki, G (2001). Suicidal behavior: is there a genetic predisposition? Bipolar Disord 3: 335--349.

Von Korff, M, Koepsell, T, Curry, S, and Diehr, P. (1992). Multi-level research in epidemiologic research on health behaviors and outcomes. *Am. J. Epidemiol.*, 135: 1077-1082.

Voracek, M, Loibl, L.M. (2007). Genetics of suicide : a systematic review of twin studies. *Wiener Klinische Wochenschrift* 119, 463--475.

Voracek M, Loibl, L.M. (2008). Consistency of immigrant and country-of-birth suicide rates : a meta-analysis. *Acta Psychiatrica Scandinavica* 118, 259--271.

Wasserman, D. A. (2001). stress-vulnerability model and the development of the suicidal process. In: Wasserman D, editor. Suicide -- an unnecessary death. London: Dunitz; 13--27.

Wasserman, D, Geijer, T, Sokolowski, M, Rozanov, V, Wasserman, J (2007). Nature and nurture in suicidal behavior, the role of genetics : some novel findings concerning personality traits and neural conduction. Physiology and Behavior 92, 245--249.

Wasserman, D. (2001). A stress-vulnerability model and the develpment of the suicide process. In Suicide:an unnecessary death (ed. D.Wasserman), 13-27. Unitz: London.

Windle, M. and Davies, P. (1999). Developmental theory and research. In: Leonard KE, Blane HT eds. Psychological Theories of Drinking and Alcoholism. 2nd ed. New York, NY: Guilford Press. 164-202.

Windle, M. and Wiesner, M. (2004). Trajectories of marijuana use from adolescence to young adulthood: Predictors and outcomes. *Dev. Psychopathol.*, 16:1007-27.

Van der Leeden, R. and Busing, F. (1994). First Iteration versus IGLS/RIGLS Estimates in Two-level Models: a Monte Carlo Study with ML3. Department of Psychometrica and research Methodology, Leiden University, Leiden.

Waern,M., Rubenowitz,E., Runeson, B., Skoog, I.,Wilhelmson, K., and Allebeck. P.(2002). Burden of illness and suicide in elderly people: case-control study. BMJ;324:1355.

Wingate, L.R., Joiner, T.E. Jr., Walker, R.L. et al. 2004. Empirically informed approaches to topics in suicide risk assessment. *Behav. Sci.Law.*, 22:651--65.

World Health Organization. (2009). http://www.who.int/topics/suicide/en/.

Yule, G. U. (1926). Why do we sometimes get nonsense correlations between time-series? A study in sampling and the nature of time-series. *J. Roy. Statist. Soc. Ser.* A 89 1-69.

Zucker, R.A., Fitzgerald, H.E. andMoses, H.D. (1995). Emergence of alcohol problems and the several alcoholisms: A developmental perspective on etiologic theory and life course trajectory. In: Cicchetti, D, Cohen ,D, eds. Developmental Psychopathology. Vol 2: Risk, disorder, and adaptation. New York, NY: Wiley. 677-711.

POPULATION-BASED APPROACHES
TO SUICIDE RESEARCH AND PREVENTION

In: Frontiers in Suicide Risk
Editor: Jill E. Lavigne

ISBN 978-1-62081-373-7
©2012 Nova Science Publishers, Inc.

Chapter 10

BUILDING CONNECTIONS: STRATEGIES TO MITIGATE SUICIDE RISK IN CIVILIANS AND MILITARY VETERANS LIVING IN NON-URBAN AND RURAL AREAS WITH A FOCUS ON TELECOMMUNICATION AND INTERNET TECHNOLOGIES

John F. Crilly

US Department of Veterans Affairs, South Central MIRECC
Department of Psychiatry, Tulane University, Louisiana, US

ABSTRACT

Mental disorders are highly correlated with increased risk of suicide. These disorders promote or exacerbate social isolation due both to their nature and the accompanying stigma, which in turn exacerbates suicide symptoms. The geographic isolation experienced by individuals living in rural or remote areas adds additional risk, particularly for Veterans of military service who are predominantly from rural and remote areas. In this chapter we will explore the problems experienced by rural populations and identify strategies to build connections which can be used to decrease isolation, thereby mitigating suicide risk.

Overview of Suicide and Suicide Prevention

Suicide is a major public health problem, and in 2009 was the 10th leading cause of death overall, the 3rd leading cause of death for individuals 15-24, and the 4th leading cause of death for individuals 25-44 (Kochanek et al., 2011). Between 1999 and 2007, suicide was the 4th leading cause of death for individuals aged 18-55, increasing steadily from 20,209 deaths in 1999 to 23,941 deaths in 2007 (see http://webappa.cdc.gov/sasweb/ncipc/ mortrate 10_sy.html). Its movement from 11th place overall where it was in 2007 and 2008 was not because its incidence grew, but because the incidence of other causes of death fell (Kochanek et al., 2011). All leading causes of death are tragic, and while the incidence for suicide is relatively low, it is the extremely damaging effects that it has on the individuals themselves who suffer and those around them – family, friends, and community - that make it important. Suicide behavior is best described as a series of steps the suicidal person experiences to reach the suicide or suicide attempt (Maris, 1990). Although suicidal individuals may feel alone and isolated, they are often not. They have people around – families, relatives, close friends or neighbors – who are concurrently experiencing an entirely different and not inconsequential pain and suffering. For the introductory purposes of this chapter, the struggles caretakers face occur parallel to the suicide symptoms of the individual and can be summarized into 3 categories: 1) Pre-Suicide: the long struggle which lasts between the first occurrence of suicide symptoms and a suicide death, 2) Post-Suicide: the time period, usually lifelong, for survivors after a suicide death, and 3) Chronic Suicidality: prolonged, ongoing suicide behavior and crises which involve varying levels of suicide ideation and many suicide attempts but not a suicide death.

It is difficult to over-emphasize the progressively intensive pain and isolation that suicidal persons and their family members and friends experience over the course of these stages. Most individuals with suicide symptoms do not end their lives by suicide. For those who do die by suicide, the post-suicide category is particularly difficult and isolating for survivors. Prolonged suffering and conflict occur for those who have constant suicide ideation and intermittent suicide attempts but never die by suicide. Family members and friends of such individuals exist in a type of chronic survivor mode, trying to handle the responsibilities of everyday life while simultaneously trying to handle the crushing responsibility of keeping their family member(s) alive. Suicide ideation, the contemplation of suicide, can arrive without warning and become a constant feature of the individual's suffering. The presence of suicide contemplation can cause severe consternation among family members and friends, and can be very disturbing for the individual, especially at first onset. For some, the suicidal contemplation period is a one-time occurrence. For most, it is with them for much of their lives. As the pre-suicide period becomes filled with intermittent or even frequent suicide attempt events, the pressure grows on family members, friends, and the suicidal individual to "prevent" suicide. While an attempt might be stopped if caught in time that once, and although helpful interventions such as motivational interviewing (e.g., Britton et al., 2008) can be given at the time of the attempt, these individuals will likely return to their lives with little changed. For many suicidal individuals, the pain and suffering is so great and so prolonged that even such positive approaches as motivational interviewing have only limited potential for sustained positive outcomes. Therefore, it is the family and friends who must then continue, once again, their suicide prevention efforts to help maintain the individual's safety.

The focus of suicide prevention is, certainly, the prevention of the act which causes death. In this context, the "prevention" aspect may be somewhat of a misnomer because it is difficult to demonstrate that formal suicide prevention efforts actually prevent suicides. Indeed, more suicides occur each subsequent year than the previous year. Interventions may prevent a single instance from escalating towards suicide, but since the impetus and the opportunity always exist, the suicidal person has many chances to complete a suicide if so inclined. Instead, the majority of work referred to as "suicide prevention" focuses primarily on mitigation of suffering throughout long periods of ideation and repeated attempts, with the indirect effect of preventing deaths.

The act of "prevention" itself can be considered by some family caretakers as a double-edged sword. Hidden within the intimate worlds of families dealing with suicidal members day-to-day, acts of their prevention prolong the pain and misery which the suicidal individual is experiencing. Prevention is an extremely hard and lonely road which caregivers travel, and include frequent emergency room (ER) visits, locked medications, lethal means removal, constant vigilance, lack of a normalized living environment, and other issues, often for years and sometimes for life. The long, repetitive process of preventing a family member's suicide may even be seen by those individuals, families, and friends as prolonging the pain. It is hellish to watch this pain occur and can seem unethical to force its prolongation, especially since those who want to help most can often feel helpless. Caregivers or suicide watchers become exhausted and numb. Conversely, as pain subsides, even briefly, families can agree that their heroic efforts to keep their loved one alive "just one more day," day after day, had been worth it, until the cycle starts again.

Compounding these problems and the deep and excruciating accompanying pain is that much of the anguish of suicide ideation, attempts, and death occur in isolation. Because of this, the real day-to-day suicide prevention processes carried out by the individual, family, and friends is hidden from the community and healthcare systems. This is not because these systems do not care or are unattached, but because communities and healthcare systems cannot get as close to the situation as they must to be of actual help – that is to carry out true "suicide prevention."

It is the parent who stops the knife, the spouse that finds a suicide attempt in progress, the sibling who notices the pills just swallowed, the friend who takes away the gun who actually do "suicide prevention." What the rest of us do as healthcare providers is something different. We provide support and encouragement, give expert advice, and provide some tools such as medications or therapy. These actions are more support than prevention. We support those who prevent, and other than a fortunate intervention where healthcare providers by chance happen to be directly involved, we really are not in the position to actually prevent suicide.

One of the key components of providing support is the ability to have a presence and to be available to provide support where and when it is needed. In this chapter we will explore how to best reach out to, connect with, and support isolated individuals dealing with suicide. This will be done in the context of rural communities which are particularly challenging because they are already geographically isolated.

Deep within these communities and families, suicide and suicide behavior remain secretive and taboo topics. This can either be positive (we handle it ourselves around here because we know the community, the family, and the individual) or negative (we need help and don't know what to do – so we struggle on without it). Although the healthcare system encourages people to talk about suicide, this is difficult to achieve in rural areas. Rural people are private people who are resilient and self-sufficient. Such people do not feel drawn to talk with others, even with families and friends, about this type of situation.

Close family members or caretakers may not feel free or comfortable discussing such issues with others, particularly if situations are ongoing (people may get sick of hearing about it, feel uncomfortable because there is little they can do to help anyway, or simply do not want to come across as complaining). Family members may also be forbidden by the suffering individual from disclosing anything about the issues, which greatly increases social isolation of the entire family unit. Self- or family-imposed isolation is a major issue and effectively removes care providers and even healthcare systems from the discussion. Ruralness and culture magnify these issues, making rural areas the most challenging frontline of suicide prevention.

Urban vs. Rural: Definitions and Descriptions

Rural communities and rural families live in a different "universe" from urban communities and families, isolated and often insulated by geography from contact with diverse groups of people. Yet, in another sense, they are neither isolated nor insulated. Families and neighbors can live some distance apart and still know each other's business and be there to help or keep an eye out if needed.

Families who have lived for generations in rural communities may have irregular contact but may know enough about each other to know when something is wrong. Today, sprawling urban areas give way to sprawling suburbs, and in many areas the distinction can be blurred between rural and suburban. It is important to be able to accurately define and describe non-urban and rural areas.

Hart et al. (2005) describe and compare taxonomies designed to delineate urban vs. non-urban and rural areas. Two such taxonomies are commonly used, one from the US Bureau of the Census (Census Bureau) and the other from the US Department of Agriculture (USDA). The distinction of "urban" vs. "rural" is generally described by the Census Bureau across four primary categories: 1) Urbanized Areas are continuously built-up areas with populations of 50,000 or more, with a central core area surrounded by densely populated areas (suburbs), 2) Urban Places Outside of Urbanized Areas consist of incorporated places (i.e., small towns and villages) with populations between 2,500 to 50,000, 3) Rural Places and Territories are incorporated places with fewer than 2,500 people, 4) Extended Cities are incorporated areas that cover large expanses of sparsely populated territory. These are not suburban areas, but large, contiguous, predominantly rural counties (US Census).

The USDA has developed a more specific scheme to classify both urban and rural areas, shaped around a continuum from rural to urban. The two maps in Figure 1 depict the broader definitions as applied by the Census Bureau (on the left, "Nonmetropolitan and metropolitan," available at http://www.census.gov/geo/www/GARM/Ch12GARM.pdf) compared to the more specific delineation by the USDA (on the right, "Rural-Urban Continuum," available at http://www.ers.usda.gov/Briefing/Rurality/RuralUrbCon/).

Perhaps the most robust delineation scheme of rural and urban areas are the Rural Urban Commuting Area (RUCA) Codes, which factor in not only the Census Bureau and USDA definitions but also the amount of time needed to drive from the area of residence to an urban area, and the numbers of individuals who do so regularly (see http://www.ers. usda.gov/ briefing/Rurality/RuralUrbanCommutingAreas/ for a description of the 10 categories and 41 sub-categories of the RUCA codes). Regardless of the method used, it is clear from all of these categorizations that the US has substantially more rural areas than urban.

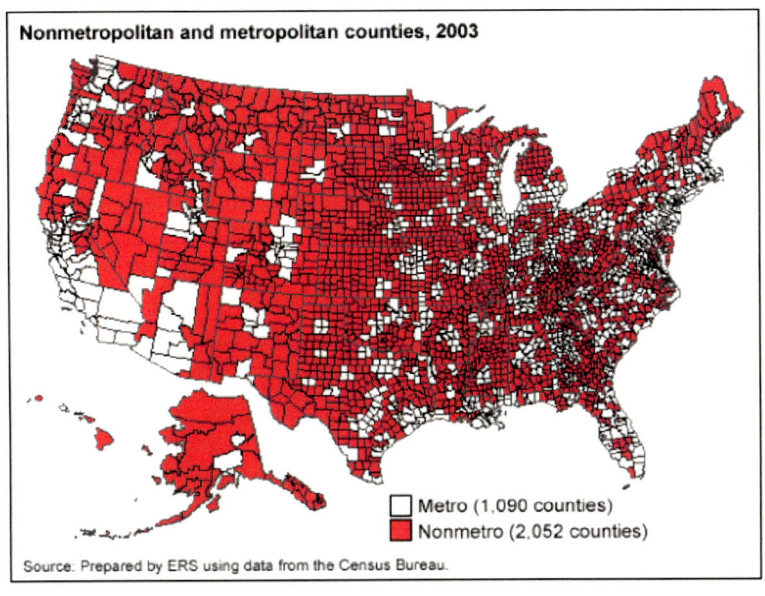

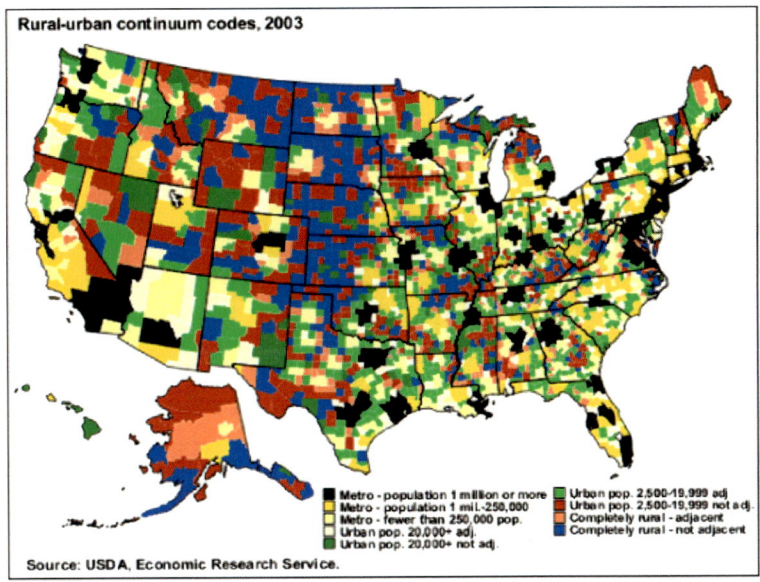

Figure 1. US Census Bureau and USDA Urban/Rural Categories.

Non-Urban Areas and Cultures

Understanding the geographic and demographic data of rural areas is important but only gives a limited description of the area. Perhaps of greater importance is better understanding these areas themselves, the types of individuals who live there, and how each has its own unique culture. "Rural" is often portrayed as farmland, or some kind of small-town or idyllic country setting, such as in the flat Midwest or well-established, long-populated areas along the East Coast. Such settings are indeed rural, but rural settings are much more diverse. The back hills and valleys (or "hollers") of Kentucky and Appalachia are rural but are hidden deep within mountain settings. This Appalachia mountain setting is different from the environment of the Rocky Mountains which has a vastly different terrain and is more similar to living in parts of the Adirondack Mountains in New York State. Agriculture is difficult to sustain in these mountainous areas– climate and terrain provide little nurture.

Farming and agriculture are substantial portions of designated rural areas because of the vast amounts of land required. These areas contain important, specific population factors, less about the farm owners than the farm workers. Migrant laborers, whether legal or not, flow across the country following crops and seasons in large numbers. They follow crops which require hands-on labor such as citrus, grapes, tomatoes, peppers, cherries, and peaches. Corn, wheat, soy, sugar cane and other such crops require only minimal migrant labor because care and harvest is highly mechanized. They also follow animal and fish harvests and can be found on shrimping boats in the Gulf of Mexico, catfish farms in Mississippi, and livestock farms in Kansas and Texas. Migrant workers spend the majority of their lives in rural areas and although transient are counted as part of the rural population. Travel is difficult, living conditions are poor, consistent healthcare does not exist, and injury risk is high among this group. Education is difficult to maintain and migrant workers are susceptible to theft and are victims of racism. The risk factors they face for physical and mental illnesses are further accentuated by language barriers.

Coastal marine fishing communities such as in Maine, Washington, Florida, and Texas are also rural, but in very different ways from mountains or farmland. The communities are less diffuse because they are not dependent on large tracts of land. The close proximity to the water and the nature of fishing creates bonds in these communities, made up of old families with overlapping skills and similar knowledge sets. Competition between families is strong but is generally not a barrier to community cohesion. Coastal marine fishing communities along the Atlantic, Pacific, and Gulf coasts are different from inland fishing communities along the Great Lakes and rivers like the Mississippi. Marine fishing is highly seasonal so there are months during the year when fishers are idle. It is difficult to find steady work in small communities for 6 months out of the year, periods when most of the local population is in the same situation. Inland fishing is less reliant on seasonal shifts, but markets are more variable and narrow. Inland fishers often simultaneously find work around a number of skills (masonry, carpentry, plumbing, and mechanical) or run small businesses (tour boats, fishing guides) which have flexible hours. This way many can stay "employed" by jumping to different job opportunities quickly while still fishing.

Geography matters. States like Texas or Kansas have wide open agricultural or ranching spaces. These areas are easily accessible by car or truck. States like Louisiana or Alaska have environmental features which prevent easy access and navigation. Louisiana's substantial swampland and dangerous wildlife make access hazardous and keeps residents isolated. Alaska's tundra and desolate terrain also prevent easy access to the extent that many areas require airplanes for access. The forbidding terrain of states like Wyoming and the Dakotas earn it a special designation of rural: "remote." Employment opportunities in these areas are fairly constricted, and young people are faced with the choice of following any family business which may exist, joining the military, or relocating away from their family and closer to an urban center.

Rural places are quite diverse yet segregated in ways similar to urban areas, by race and socio-economic status. Native American tribes, both Federally-recognized and not, exist in communities and on reservations across the country in areas which are generally rural. Tribes which are recognized only by States generally do not have designated reservations, but members can live in close proximity by individually owning private lands near other tribe members or the tribe itself can purchase land or arrange for land donations. The use of itinerant farm workers across the US who are from Mexico, South America, and the Caribbean has created pockets of these workers in largely white communities. Rural communities of African-American farmers are predominant across the Deep South. Fishing communities along the Gulf and West Coasts have expanded to include commercial fisherman of Vietnamese, South American, and Mexican heritage.

Health and Mental Health Services in Rural Areas

Geography and lack of economic opportunity affect the distribution of health services. Rural areas face significant challenges in obtaining access to appropriate medical resources (Connor et al., 1995; Scroeder and Beachler, 1995; Rabinowitz et al., 2001). Many individuals living in rural areas lack adequate access to health and mental health service providers (Ziller et al., 2010; Fortney et al., 2010; Hanrahan and Hartley, 2008; Jameson and Blank, 2007; Merwin et al., 2003; Wang et al., 2005; Wagenfeld, 2000). The prevalence of mental illness in rural areas is equal to or greater than in urban populations, with rural residents reporting greater rates of depression and suicide, particularly among men (Eberhart, 2009). Some report difficulties in knowing whether mental health services are needed, whom to see for the services, and how to get to the services and pay for them, placing rural individuals at a significant disadvantage (Smalley et al., 2010; Bird et al., 2001). Among those in geographically isolated areas who are able to access mental health services, some state that they must travel to distant towns and frequently receive care from providers who may not be qualified to meet their mental health needs (Myers, 2000; Smalley et al., 2010). Others must travel longer periods to be seen for mental health treatment (Norris, 2000), receive fewer sessions with qualified mental health professionals, and are often less satisfied with the services they receive than individuals in urban areas (Hodges et al, 2005). In addition, many rural residents report that they would choose to access psychotherapy services rather than take psychiatric medications to treat their presenting issues if psychotherapy were available to them (Ziller et al, 2010; Dwight-Johnson et al, 2000; Brody et al., 1997).

Military Veterans in Rural Areas

A large percentage of military Veterans live in rural areas and as a group is at higher risk for suicide than the general population. Veterans have served in one of the five military branches: Army, Navy, Air Force, Marines, and Coast Guard. There are also two auxiliary branches which serve on demand: National Guard, and Reservists. When active duty military personnel leave the military, they are designated "Veterans" and can receive healthcare services from the US Department of Veterans Affairs (VA). National Guard and Reservists can be deployed to active duty from a civilian status and serve in the military alongside enlisted soldiers. When their deployment is over, they return directly to civilian life. Because of this transition, although they are by definition "Veterans," they are at high risk for losing contact with the US Department of Veterans Affairs (VA) and access to healthcare benefits. Of the 23 million Veterans in this country, roughly 8 million are enrolled with the VA. Approximately 40 percent of these Veterans live in rural and highly rural (remote) areas. This population also has fewer financial resources compared to urban Veterans. One-third of Veterans returning from the Operation Enduring Freedom (OEF), Operation Iraqi Freedom (OIF), and Operation New Dawn (OND) conflicts live in rural or highly rural areas but three-fourths of all rural Veterans are age 55 and older (Skupien, 2010). Rural Veterans face the same healthcare access difficulties as other rural residents: disparate access to higher quality services, shortages in qualified health professionals, and limited transportation options. According to a study by Skupien (2010), on average, rural Veterans travel between 60-120 minutes for inpatient care and 30-90 minutes for primary care.

Recent war veterans are expected to return to their homes in rural areas and many will likely cope with post-traumatic stress disorder (PTSD) and traumatic brain injury (US Dept. of Veterans Affairs). Typically, whether military Veterans or not, younger Americans with identified mental health issues are most likely to either perceive that treatment is not necessary or try to handle the issues on their own (Kessler et al., 2001). Isolation is a significant problem. Studies of OEF/OIF/OND Veterans have not only identified an increased prevalence of mental disorders but also an ambivalence or refusal to engage in receiving mental health services. Hoge et al. (2004) found that although 11%-17% of military service members met screening criteria for mental disorders only 23%-40% of this group sought treatment. A later study (Hoge et al., 2006) examined a much larger group and found similar trends. Returning service members (19.1% for OIF and 11.5% for OEF) indicated mental health problems. Of this group 50% referred for treatment actually followed through to visit a VA facility but only 35% agreed to receive treatment. These patterns are similar to those found in service members from before the OEF/OIF/OND conflicts (Hourani and Yuan, 1999) and recently (Harpaz-Rotem and Rosenheck, 2011), but OEF/OIF/OND service members are more likely to remain in VA treatment longer than their counterparts from the Vietnam War era.

Not all individuals identified with a mental disorder need services (Kessler and Wang, 2008). For Veterans who choose not to be in treatment at any point, it remains important to make it clear that help is there for them when they decide it is needed. Maintaining a healthy, no-pressure connection with Veterans through simple, non-intrusive means could help Veterans more easily seek care and treatment when the needs arise. A prescient example of this is the difficult post-deployment period. OEF/OIF/OND Veterans are at risk for post-deployment stress which carries increased risk of developing PTSD and suicide behavior. Suicide symptoms co-occur with psychiatric disorders and are particularly common with PTSD (Wilcox et al., 2009). Veterans are at high risk for developing PTSD (Hoge et al., 2007) and although have been found overall to have heightened risk for suicide compared to the general population (Kaplan et al., 2007), PTSD and post-deployment stress can disproportionately increase this risk (Kang and Bullman, 2008; Vasterling et al., 2010; Pietrzak et al., 2010a; Pietrzak et al., 2010b). As military Veterans begin to recognize the impact that PTSD is having on their lives and are considering treatment, it is important that the VA or any healthcare system has not been a "stranger" during that time. Developing such connections can have a powerful effect preventing full-blown mental and physical disorders.

The 2009 American Community Survey estimates that 9.5% of the overall US civilian population 18 years and older are military Veterans, over 40% of whom live in rural areas (US Census Bureau, 2009). Geographically, 8.9% of urban and 11.2% of rural populations are Veterans. Results from the latest National Veterans Survey indicate that 36.2% of Veterans are between 18 and 55 years and 11.7% of all Veterans served after September 11, 2001 (US Department of Veterans Affairs, 2010). The three states with the largest Veteran populations (California, Florida, and Texas) had the largest numbers of Veterans 25 years old and younger (between 18,001 and 31,400) (US Department of Veterans Affairs, 2007a). However, the five central South (Texas, Louisiana, Alabama, Arkansas, and Oklahoma) and five central North (Idaho, Montana, Wyoming, North Dakota, South Dakota) states, along with Alaska and West Virginia, are highly rural and contain the highest percentage of Veterans under 25 (1.5-2.2%) (US Department of Veterans Affairs, 2007b).

Rural military veterans are less likely to receive mental healthcare services than non-rural Veterans, and when they do, they have fewer visits than urban military veterans (Cully et al., 2010), despite care being covered under VA benefits (Fortney, 2010). These factors may cause Veterans to forgo needed mental health treatment, thereby increasing the risks of suicidal behavior, higher use of emergency and inpatient services (Gold et al., 2006), poorer health, impaired functioning (Broadhead et al., 1990; Wagner et al., 2000), and an overall lower quality of life. Moreover, the stigma associated with mental health issues is enhanced by the lack of anonymity associated with living and receiving treatment in non-urban/rural areas (Boyd et al., 2006). This singles out rural Veterans as being a high priority target group for suicide prevention efforts.

The wars in Iraq and Afghanistan have had a substantial impact on rural Americans, highlighted by the injury inflicted by Improvised Explosive Device (IED) to produce traumatic brain injury and the high incidence of PTSD. However, some Veterans still may not be diagnosed and may not be aware that they have suffered an injury at all. Unfortunately, many returnees will come home to their rural families and communities and need to travel some distance to reach a healthcare facility which can meet all of their complex needs. In addition, VA benefits are not as accessible to National Guard and Reserve members. This puts increasing pressure on community healthcare systems and providers to reach the high level of expertise and knowledge necessary to successfully treat these individuals. Adequately addressing these issues in rural areas will require new, flexible approaches to develop communication and connections with this broad range of individuals.

Suicide Rates in Rural Areas

Singh and Siahpush (2002) examined mortality, census, and geographical data for suicide trends in urban and rural areas from 1970 to 1997. They found that the rates of suicide in rural areas were significantly higher than in urban areas and growing steadily. At the starting point of 1970, rural and urban rates were relatively similar but eventually separated over time as rural suicide rates increased and urban suicide rates decreased. There are also clear gender differences. Across 5 year periods from 1980 to 1997, the suicide rates for rural men were 21%, 26%, 37%, and 54% (in 1995-1997) higher than their urban counterparts. Women showed the opposite pattern: rural women were significantly *less* likely than urban women to suicide but in declining rates: 52%, 30%, 24%, and 16% to a point where there was no difference. Overall, suicide rates for rural men increased as rates for urban men decreased. Suicide rates for both rural and urban women decreased but at different rates, eventually reaching the same general level. Adjustment for ethnicity and divorce rates actually widened the differentials for rural vs. urban men, but made no difference for women.

The adjacent figure is a map generated from the Center for Disease Control (CDC) data which depicts state rates of suicides during 2000-2006 (http://wisqars.cdc.gov:8080/cdcMapFramework/mapModuleInterface.jsp). It is clear that the generally rural states from up and down the Midwest along with Alaska and West Virginia have the highest rates in the country. Middle states have mid- to lower-range rates while East coast states have the lowest rates. Large states with major metropolitan centers such as New York, Texas, California, Minnesota, Illinois, and Georgia have some of the lowest rates.

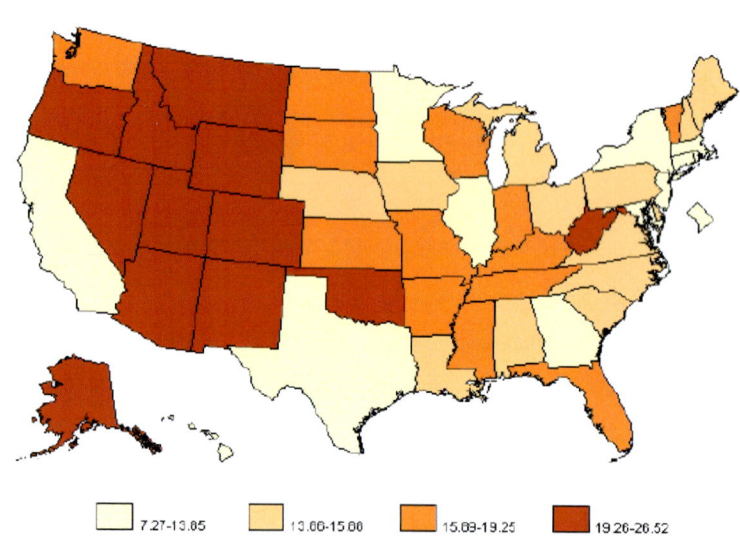

Figure 2. US Suicide Rates by State, 2000-2006.

Strategies to Mitigate Suicide in Rural Areas

Social isolation has consistently been shown to be a significant risk factor for suicide (Trout, 1980; Kposowa et al., 1996; Seeman, 1996). Studies have found that rural individuals who complete suicide are less likely to have close, intimate relationships with others than their urban counterparts (Isometsa et al., 1997; Turvey et al., 2002). Individuals who are isolated are at greater risk for suicide, and those who are also geographically isolated are at greatest risk. These conditions form the basis for conceptualizing strategies to mitigate suicide in rural areas.

Forming connections with caring individuals such as family and friends (MMari et al., 2010) as well as with healthcare providers can be powerful platforms for new approaches to suicide prevention. The development of social bonds is a basic form of human function, and its study spans nearly a century. Recently Chayko (2007) juxtaposed conventional descriptions of social bonds with newer formulations based on the rapidly expanding development of electronic communication technologies. Social bonds are social connections of varying strength and intensity, requiring contact for maintenance and growth. In relation to electronic technologies, Chayko (2007) describes new types of bonds within a technologically-generated social structure. One such bond is described as "sociomental," a social exchange or environment in which people derive a sense of togetherness by being socially oriented towards and engaged with one another through basic forms of electronic communication. Different communities are formed, such as 'support communities,' generally comprised of individuals facing similar difficulties. This concept of "connection" is key to successful suicide prevention.

Before the era of modern-day electronic communications, Veterans faced potential isolation and exacerbation of post-deployment stress issues. Often facing hostile, alienating communities, Veterans had few ways to form their own support connections. King et al. (1998) found in a sample of Vietnam Veterans that the most important postwar mediator of the risks for PTSD and suicide behavior was perceived social support. Koenen et al. (2003) showed that the positive or negative responses of the communities to which Vietnam Veterans returned following deployment had a significant impact on whether, and the extent to which, they developed PTSD and suicide behavior. The VA now supports a number of creative outreach programs. One is "Buddy-to-Buddy" (Greden et al., 2010) which links peer service members to returning members of the Reserve and National Guard to increase their social support systems and ease their transition back to civilian life. In 2007 the VA National Office for Suicide Prevention started the Veterans Crisis Line, a confidential 24/7 telephone service for Veterans in crisis and their families, regardless of VA enrollment. In 2009 it added a one-to-one Chat capability accessible through the Internet to reach individuals who prefer to interact through that medium, the first of its kind in the country. A Veterans Homeless Helpline and Chat were added in 2010. The VA has also made a serious investment to reach out to Veterans online using the latest social media and created the Office of New Media, directed by an experienced OIF Veteran. As of this writing, the VA has 87 Facebook pages with a combined subscribership of nearly 220,000 fans (the main Facebook page has over 100,000 subscribers), one of the largest in the federal government. For Twitter, VA has 51 Twitter feeds with a combined followership of nearly 35,000. The VA also has an active blog called VAntage Point.

In non-Veteran populations methods by healthcare systems to reach out to those at risk for self-harm behavior have shown success. Early studies (Morgan et al., 1993; Evans et al., 1999; Evans et al., 2005) allowed high risk patients the opportunity to directly call their healthcare providers when in crisis. A series of studies during the past decade have shown the positive effect of "caring" contacts, letters, and postcards sent to patients following healthcare contacts related to suicide events. These have shown success in communities in Norway (Dieserud et al., 2000), the United States (Motto and Bostrom, 2001), and Australia (Carter et al., 2005). A recent paper by Fleischmann et al. (2008) reported pilot testing of brief telephone or in-person contacts in five countries which led to significant reductions in suicides and deaths over 18 months. The retention rate of 91% suggests that this type of interaction is acceptable to such high-risk individuals.

This general approach uses brief, supportive contacts through simple, common methods of communication to let individuals know that they are remembered by their healthcare providers. Motto and Bostrom (2001) mailed contact letters which contained expression of concern that the recipient was "getting along all right." The note also invited the recipient to return a response if they wished. Letters were always worded differently, were individually typed, and included responses to comments from the patients if such comments had previously been received. Carter et al. (2005) adapted the Motto and Bostrom approach but used postcards delivered in envelopes. Their message included wording such as: "Dear_____: It has been some time since you were here at the hospital, and we hope things are going well for you. If you wish to drop us a note we would be glad to hear from you." They did not ask for return information but wanted to impart the feeling that the treatment providers remained aware of their existence and maintained positive feelings toward them.

Forming connections through simple, commonly used communication avenues among populations at high risk for suicide is an important prevention approach. The use of postal mail and telephone calls are expensive and now less accepted than newer forms of electronic communication. Markopoulos (2009) and others have characterized these new platforms as "awareness systems," representing all communication systems that help individuals maintain contact with others, but with minimal intrusion to the individual. Building such an awareness system based on electronic communication to help support suicide prevention is particularly relevant to rural areas.

Electronic Media and M-Health

In order to shape current electronic technology to our needs, we need to develop a thorough understanding of what is available for use and, more importantly, its readiness and acceptability. The pioneering electronic technology of recent decades is the Internet. Individuals can use the Internet to interact with their healthcare providers (Daetwyler et al., 2010), access portions of their electronic health records (Crilly et al., submitted), and find a broad array of health and behavioral health-related information (Hale et al., 2010). An increasing number of online mental health treatment services have been made available as the interactive nature of the online environment has come to mirror the interpersonal interactions that are the cornerstone of mental health treatment. A number of studies testing online treatment for various behavioral health diagnoses, including depression (Titov et al., 2009; Kessler et al., 2009), substance abuse (Bickle et al., 2008; Kypri et al., 2009), post-traumatic stress disorder (Litz et al., 2007), panic disorder (Shandley et al., 2008), and bulimia (Crow et al., 2009), have shown that users respond positively to online treatment.

The Internet is an important augmenting tool for healthcare information and services (Crilly and Lewis, 2010), but is not available in every household. Terrain and population density have a substantial impact on whether and which kind of Internet service can be provided to any particular household. Because of this, rural areas lag behind urban areas in the type and distribution of the Internet. The type of access is divided into two main categories, dial-up and broadband, based on the speed of the connection and the amount of material that can be simultaneously handled, or its "bandwidth." Dial-up, the older category, has narrow bandwidth and can handle only low-bandwidth applications such as e-mail or text-based interactions adequately. Broadband has broad bandwidth and can handle up to 50 megabytes per second, enabling users to take much greater advantage of the Web's resources.

Cost and quality are key to Internet access for rural areas. Not all broadband is high speed, and low speed broadband is not much faster than dial-up. If a rural area does have "broadband," it most likely has low-speed. Areas with a single Internet provider (IP) (generally non-urban/rural areas) have greater access costs while costs in areas with three IPs or more (generally urban areas) are substantially lower (Horrigan, 2009). Consequently, urban areas are well saturated with lower-priced high speed broadband capability while non-urban/rural areas are more likely to have dial-up connections or low-speed broadband. Mountainous rural or remote areas are the least likely to have broadband access because of the difficulty laying physical cable and the terrain blocking satellite streams. A 2009 FCC report (Copps, 2009) noted that there is low IP penetration in the West, Midwest, and Alaska; across Appalachia through the Adirondack Mountains in New York; and minimal IP penetration in southern Florida, northern Maine, and various sections along the West coast. Using the 2007 Current Population Survey (CPS) Internet Supplement (the most recent data available) for adults ages 18-65 (Census Bureau, 2007) we found that there are a substantial number of households, from 15% to 32% in the rural south, which do not have access to the Internet. Between 68% and 85% of individuals nationwide access the Internet in some location, the majority (between 80% and 90%) from home. Non-urban/rural areas are nearly twice as likely as urban areas to use dial-up services. The Internet, therefore, is not a dependable communication medium because it is neither available to nor used by a substantial group of individuals across the country, mostly those who live in rural areas.

New Inroads for Connection: M-Health

The concept of "m-health" (the use of mobile communication devices and software to assist healthcare delivery and communication) has the potential to be the most powerful tool for reaching individuals in need and for sharing important information (Mirza et al., 2009). m-Health also has the greatest potential to be successful in rural areas. Perhaps the most visible use of m-Health is through the development of smartphone (e.g., iPhone, Droid, Blackberry) applications ("apps"). These may seem quite widespread and viable but are only available to and used by a small segment of the population. Although the numbers of health-related apps are rapidly increasing, this does not necessarily translate into an increase in use, and most are rarely, if ever, used. A recent survey by Consumer Health Information Corporation (CHIC, 2011) found that 26% of all apps are used only once and 74% are dropped by their 10th use. Only 26% retain longer-term customer loyalty, generally those with practical uses such as tipping calculators and map finders.

Another way to form connections with individuals is through social media such as Facebook, MySpace, and recently Google+. These social media sites promote social networking and provide ways that individuals can communicate with others via several methods (email, instant messaging, interactive video). These are excellent formats to maintain connections, but there are major privacy concerns for their use around sensitive topics such as suicide prevention. For example, families struggling with a suicidal individual may find that they can reach other family members and close friends on Facebook to talk about what is happening, but the goal of these sites is to make it easy to share information but difficult to maintain primacy. Therefore, social networking sites are not yet useful in these important contexts.

The CHIC (2011) survey found that users preferred interactions from healthcare providers to be delivered via text messaging. Text messages are brief text communications between mobile phone users delivered in blocks of up to 160 characters. Of all electronic media available today, only text messaging can provide an environment which fits with what is needed to provide support to rural individuals: it can be used by any cell phone – smart or not, cell phones are ubiquitous in rural areas, text messaging is a familiar and widely used form of communication, it is person-to-person, it can be private as long as the receiving device uses simple privacy features, it can reach people at any time and virtually any place, and it requires only a minimal signal to send and receive messages.

The usefulness of text messaging can be quite expansive (e.g., Cheverst et al., 2007), but must be more contained for use in healthcare settings. Text messaging also has an established track record as an effective m-health tool in health promotion and treatment engagement. It has been used to increase adherence to treatment in a Kenyan AIDS cohort (Lester et al., 2010), improve outpatient clinic attendance (Downer et al., 2006), and as part of "mCare" developed by the US Army to help re-integrate wounded service members into family and society. In the broader public health spectrum, the Center for Disease Control has developed several mobile phone text messaging programs (e.g., for HIV and H1N1 virus) and the Veterans Health Administration and Veterans Benefits Administration utilize text messaging to conduct certain business with Veterans. Because of their mobility cell phones are at risk for loss, theft, or damage. Crankshaw et al. (2010) found that the majority of cell phone users (95%) in their South African AIDS study used pre-paid service. Of that group, 39% reported cell phone turnover (loss, theft, damage) during the previous 3 years.

The practice of "texting" has arisen as the most recognizable use of text messaging. "Texting" refers to casual back-and-forth (two-way) conversational communication between two parties, often including informal word abbreviations and innuendo. The daily practice of texting can make users unaware of how text messaging can conflict with HIPAA policies. It is important that health-related text messages do not contain personal health information, so it is not appropriate for back-and-forth therapy-related conversation between client and provider. The "safest" form for use in healthcare settings is one-way text messaging, where the recipient of health-related text messages cannot reply to the sender. This can be used to send supportive comments or information, and reminders. Two-way text messaging is much more useful as long as four key areas are considered: 1) message delivery: ensure that the receiver is the person for whom the message is intended, 2) message content: ensure that messages do not contain patient identifiable or personal health information, 3) message construction: ensure clear wording with limited use of abbreviations, and 4) message security: ensure the security of the conduit over which text messages are sent and received.

The ability to send and receive text messages, the "awareness system" platform, is the foundation necessary for "sociomental" connections to occur. How can this be useful for suicide prevention in rural areas? We already know that individuals most at risk do not use primary care or attend regular mental health services. Suicide expert Eric Caine, MD has described the suicide or suicide attempt as the "tip of an iceberg" with hosts of issues beneath the surface, but that iceberg must show its tip for the healthcare system to know that an iceberg even exists. That showing of the iceberg tip typically comes in the form of a healthcare system contact such as an ER visit following a suicide attempt or the report of serious suicide ideation. Once in the ER, the patient is typically seen by an ER social worker, part of whose job is to contact family members and establish a safe discharge plan. If that patient is admitted for an inpatient stay, this same procedure is followed there. This is one healthcare system entry point where providers can begin the process of encouraging the addition of a text messaging awareness system into the support system of the patient.

This approach can offer four primary connection plans, and the patient and family can chose one or more: 1) connection between the healthcare system/provider and the family for the purpose of support, 2) connection between the healthcare system and the patient for the purpose of support, 3) helping to establish an internal family connection between family members and the suicidal individual (if one does not yet exist), and 4) providing promotion of a text message dissemination tool and then sustaining the "awareness platform." It is entirely likely that families and the suicidal individuals already have informal support and crisis networks formed and that text messaging is a central part of their communication methods. These likely work very effectively, but what is typically lacking is any connection to a resource which can provide support and expert advice quickly and easily. Rural healthcare systems cannot typically provide this level of availability, but this can be feasibly integrated into the national web of local crisis hotlines of the National Suicide Prevention Lifeline (www.suicidepreventionlifeline.org). Local hotlines have trained staff who can handle both telephone calls and one-to-one online chat calls related to suicide. Having a text messaging capability which can proactively disseminate supportive messages to individuals and families which are linked through the ER/healthcare awareness system or respond to information and support requests from families and individuals would complete this foundation. These local hotlines can develop a series of supportive messages to send to individuals and can serve as a vital link for rural families or suicidal individuals who need to interact with an expert resource. The figure below outlines how this Awareness System can integrate a Text Message (TM) Support Line.

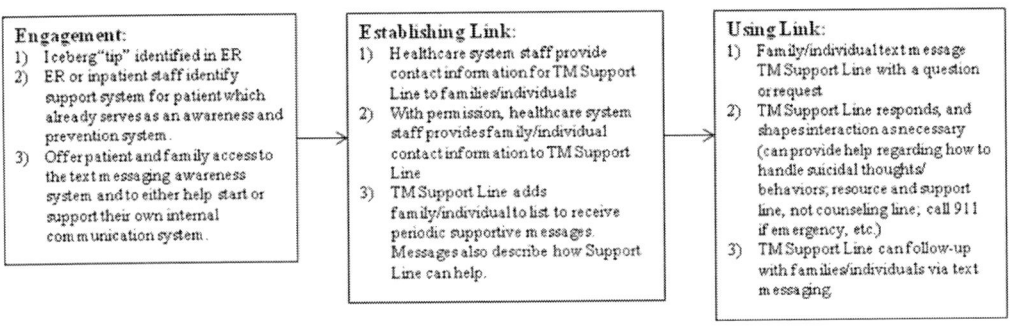

Figure 3. Integrating a Text Message Support Line Into the Family/Individual Awareness System.

The infrastructure for a system such as the TM Support Line exists in every community across the country and within nearly every household in every rural area. Two additional components would be necessary: 1) working with the local healthcare system(s) to develop the Engagement and Linking process with families and individuals, and 2) working with the National Suicide Prevention Lifelines and their local affiliates to implement this capability. As more local lifelines bring the Live Chat capability on board, they will have the capacity to simultaneously provide a TM Support Line. Family/individual cell phone numbers can be entered into the local Lifeline databases. Text messaging services allow both automated and live messages to be sent directly from a computer email system such as Microsoft Outlook to a cell phone. Automated messages can be sent without live interaction, but the Live Chat responders can interact with families/individuals who send text messages in requesting help or input as needed. Since this would not be available to the general public but targeted specifically for individuals who enter healthcare systems, its use and demand can be better predicted and regulated. Rather than starting an entire new system, this approach for addressing suicide prevention in rural areas encourages collaboration between existing systems, honors the privacy of the family/individual while being available to rapidly provide help directly to where it is needed.

DISCUSSION

Evaluation of large systems initiatives have shown that contained groups such as the US Air Force can successfully prevent suicide with high level support and centralized planning and execution teams (Knox et al., 2003), but are unlikely to be replicable in civilian communities and are not feasible in rural areas. However, they can serve as models for innovative uses in other contexts. The core requirements necessary to address suicide prevention in rural areas are those which 1) seek to enable connections among individuals or with healthcare systems and 2) seek to be as supportive as possible to those families and friends of suicidal individuals who perform the actual suicide prevention. The research which comes closest to these requirements for rural suicide prevention are the Caring Letters projects by Carter and others mentioned above and the telephone crisis hotlines (e.g., Kalafat et al., 2007; Gould et al., 2007, Mischara et al., 2007a, 2007b). As of this writing, addressing suicide prevention in rural areas using electronic communication has been slowly gaining recognition in the literature (e.g., Crilly and Lewis, 2010, Luxton et al., 2011; Crilly et al., submitted). These methods can be key to developing better ways to help the family member "suicide preventers" as they struggle during the Pre-Suicide period, deal with the aftermath of a suicide death during the Post-Suicide period, and provide strength to those family members, relatives, and friends who work day-to-day throughout the Chronic Suicidality period.

Some recommendations in the literature around gatekeeping for suicide prevention are only marginally appropriate for rural populations. For example, in a literature review paper, Luoma et al. (2002) summarized findings that some individuals who complete suicide had contact with mental health and primary care providers both within one month and one year of the suicide. They reviewed 40 US and non-US studies, completed between 1965 and 1999, generally using data collected from medical chart reviews and/or survivor reports. The majority of health systems contacts noted across these studies were by individuals 55 and older and the least for individuals 35 and younger, data similar to general population data. Louma et al. (2002) point out that elderly individuals tend to use the healthcare system at higher rates than other groups and therefore are more likely to have seen a healthcare provider at some point relatively close to their suicide. Young people tend to use see their providers only rarely. This study was intended to fortify a recommendation that was published as part of the National Strategy for Suicide Prevention (US Department of Health and Human Services, 2001) calling for increased awareness training for frontline, primary care providers to serve as suicide prevention gatekeepers. This study was also used as a foundation for the Suicide Prevention Toolkit for Rural Areas (McFaul et al., 2009) created as a response to this Strategy. Training primary care providers to screen their elderly patients for suicide symptoms only should be the target. Young adults need an entirely different approach. For rural areas, primary care providers area a scarce resource and would not be an optimal choice to serve as gatekeepers.

In his conclusions to an extensive literature review of rural suicide research (much also non-US data), Hirsch (2006) suggests that there are elements of strengths or assets found in rural areas that can be exploited for suicide prevention. The main vehicles for suicide prevention, he suggests, should be the community resources of clergy and physician gatekeepers. This raises the same concern as the Louma et al. (2002) paper. The use of primary care physicians and the gatekeepers as the main conduit for suicide prevention would be inappropriate in most rural areas. There are few professions more overworked than primary care providers and clergy members in rural areas, and they must cover vast territories. They are simply not available and would be poor choices for such important roles. They are better suited to be supportive of suicide prevention but should not be considered as "gatekeepers," perhaps with the exception of elderly individuals.

It is more useful to draw upon the findings of other studies to serve as models for rural suicide prevention. Perhaps the most successful and best evaluated large-scale suicide prevention program is by the US Air Force. Knox et al. (2010) describe a program which has its base of power and legitimacy at high levels of authority. There is an infrastructure for message delivery from the high levels of military authority to front line commanders who are the ones formally charged with actual suicide prevention. This may include a number of intervention options. Frontline commanders have much influence on whether and how the suicidal soldier seeks help and treatment. Although there is not the strict element of military command in civilian communities this entire structure is analogous to how suicide support and suicide prevention can work in rural areas. The Air Force command is akin to the healthcare or public health systems. They do not participate in the actual suicide prevention but provide the support (in this case, impetus) to the frontline commanders who are akin to the family members and fellow troops who are akin to close friends. It is these individuals who will notice mood shifts or suicide talk, pills taken, or a gun at the ready. These individuals would prevent the suicide, get the individual into treatment, be at the watch and ready for additional suicide attempts, and provide encouragement. What the Air Force structure provided was a no-fail approach to communication, or connection, among all members of this team. Without it, their approach would likely not have shown as much enduring success as it has. Rural areas and communities already have the critical elements of this type of system: healthcare systems, family members/relatives/close friends, and methods to use to interact (cell phones). In the decentralized civilian population and in fragmented rural areas, the healthcare system can perform a vital coordinating and supportive role to link the existing communication systems within families to a supportive and expert resource such as a TM Support Line. This could be achieved with relatively minor expense using the national synergy that already exists with the VA National Office of Suicide Prevention, the National Suicide Prevention Lifeline and their local affiliates, and the Substance Abuse and Mental Health Administration (SAMHSA), which funds the Lifeline initiatives.

CONCLUSION

The concept of connections has been elusive in the past to healthcare systems seeking to impact the prevalence of suicide. It has begun to enter the discussion regarding rural suicide prevention. Today's era of electronic communication technology can provide new formats through which healthcare systems and healthcare providers can maintain contact with suicidal individuals and family member caretakers. One format, text messaging, can be implemented within systems relatively rapidly and at low cost. Now, as in no other time, suicide prevention emanating from healthcare systems can actually have a broader relevance to individuals, families, and friends on the ground. It is important that the suicide prevention field acts quickly to implement this new frontier of prevention as the mainstay of the next generation of suicide prevention tools for reaching rural populations at risk for suicide.

REFERENCES

Bickle, W, Marsch L, Buchhalter A, Badger G (2008). Computerized behavior therapy for opioid-dependent outpatients: a randomized controlled trial. Experimental and Clinical Psychopharmacology, 16(2): 132-43.

Bird, DC, Dempsey P, Hartley D (2001). Addressing mental health workforce needs in underserved rural areas: Accomplishments and challenges. Portland, ME: Maine Rural Health Research Center.

Boyd CP, Aisbett DL, Francis K, Kelly M, Newnham K, Newnham K (2006). Issues in rural adolescent mental health in Australia. Rural and Remote Health, 6(online), 501, http://www.rrh.org.au.

Britton PC, Williams GC, Conner KR (2008). Self-determination theory, motivational interviewing, and the treatment of clients with acute suicidal ideation. Journal of Clinical Psychology, 64(1): 52-66.

Broadhead, WE, Blazer DG, George LK, Tse CK (1990). Depression, disability days, and days lost from work in a prospective epidemiologic survey. Journal of the American Medical Association, 264(19): 2524-28.

Brody DS, Khaliq AA, Thompson TL (1997). Patients' perspectives on the management of emotional distress in primary care settings. Journal of General and Internal Medicine, 12: 403-6.

Carter GL, Clover K, Whyte IM, Dawson AH, D'Este C (2005). Postcards from the EDge project: randomised controlled trial of an intervention using postcards to reduce repetition of hospital treated deliberate self-poisoning. BMJ, doi:10.1136/bmj.38579.455266.E0 (published 23 September 2005).

Chayko M (2007). The portable community: envisioning and examining mobile social connectedness. International Journal of Web-Based Communities, 3(4): 373-85.

Cheverst K, Dix A, Fitton D, Rouncefield M (2007). Exploring awareness-related messaging through two situated-display-based systems. Human-Computer Interactions, 22: 173-220.

Computer and internet use in the United States: October 2007. United States Department of Commerce. Bureau of the Census, United States Department of Labor, Bureau of Labor Statistics. Current Population Survey. ICPSR22781-v1. Ann Arbor, MI: Inter-university Consortium for Political and Social Research [distributor], 2008-07-21. doi:10.3886/ICPSR22781. Available at http://www.census. gov/population/www/ socdemo /computer /2007.html. Accessed August 13, 2011.

Connor R, Hillson S, Krawelski J (1995). Competition, professional synergism, and the geographic distribution of rural physicians. Medical Care. 33: 1067–1078.

Consumers and health information technology: A national survey. Oakland: California HealthCare Foundation. Available at: http://www.chcf.org/ publications /2010/04 /consumers-and-health-information-technology-a-national-survey. Accessed August 13, 2011.

Copps, MJ. Bringing broadband to rural America: Report on a rural broadband strategy, Federal Communications Commission, May 22, 2009. Available at http://hraunfoss. fcc.gov/edocs_public/attachmatch/DOC-291012A1.pdf. Accessed August 13, 2011.

Crankshaw T, Corless IB, Giddy J, Nicholas PK, Eichbaum Q, Butler LM (2010). Exploring the patterns of use and the feasibility of using cellular phones for clinic appointment reminders and adherence messages in an antiretroviral treatment clinic, Durban, South Africa. AIDS Patient Care and STDs, 24(11): 729-34.

Crilly JF, Keefe RH, Volpe F (2011). Use of electronic technologies to promote community and personal health for individuals unconnected to healthcare systems. American Journal of Public Health, 101(7): 1163-7.

Crilly JF, Keefe RH, Volpe F, Taylor M (Submitted). Advancing online behavioral health treatment in non-urban/rural areas.

Crilly J, Lewis J (2010, April). Internet-based psychiatric interventions: Applications for rural veterans at risk for suicide. Proceedings of the International Conference for Society and Information Technology.

Crow SJ, Mitchell JE, Crosby RD, Swanson SA, Wonderlich S, Lancanster K (2009). The cost effectiveness of cognitive behavioral therapy for bulimia nervosa delivered via telemedicine versus face-to-face. Behavior Research and Therapy, 47(2): 451-3.

Cully JA, Jameson JP, Phillips LI, Kunik ME, Fortney JC (2010). Use of psychotherapy by rural and urban veterans. *The Journal of Rural Health*, 26(3): 225-33.

Daetwyler CJ, Cohen DG, Gradely E, Novack DH (2010). eLearning to enhance physician patient communication: A pilot test of "doc.com" and "WebEnounter" in teaching bad news delivery. Medical Teacher, 32, e381-e390. doi: 10.3109/0142159X.2010.495759.

Department of Veterans Affairs, Office of the Actuary, Veteran Population Projection Model (VetPop), (2007a). Available at http://www.va.gov/vetdata/docs/Maps/VetPop_ Percent_Under25.pdf. Accessed August 13, 2011.

Department of Veterans Affairs, Office of the Actuary, Veteran Population Projection Model (VetPop), (2007b). Available at http://www.va.gov/vetdata/docs/Maps/VetPop_ Under25.pdf. Accessed August 13, 2011.

Dieserud G, Loeb M, Ekeberg O (2000). Suicidal behavior in the municipality of Baerum, Norway: a 12-year prospective study of parasuicide and suicide. Suicide and Life Threatening Behavior, 30(1): 61-73.

Downer SR, Meara JG, Da Costa AC, Sethuraman K (2006). SMS text messaging improves outpatient attendance. Australian Health Review, 30(3): 389-96.

Dwight-Johnson M, Sherbourne CD, Liao D, Wells KB (2000). Treatment preferences among depressed primary care patients. *Journal of General Internal Medicine*, 15(8): 527–34.

Screoder S, Beachler M (1995). Physician shortages in rural America. Lancet. 345(8956):1001-2.

Eberhardt MS, Ingram DD, Makuc DM, et al (2001). Urban and Rural Health Chartbook. Health, United States, 2001. Hyattsville, Maryland: National Center for Health Statistics.

Evans J, Evans M, Morgan HG, Hayward A, Gunnell D (2005). Crisis card following self-harm: 12-month follow-up of a randomised controlled trial. *British Journal of Psychiatry*,187(8): 186-7.

Evans MO,Morgan HG, Hayward A, Gunnell D (1999). Crisis telephone consultation for deliberate self harm patients: effects on repetition. *British Journal of Psychiatry*, 175(7): 23-7.

Fleischmann A, Bertolote JM, Wasserman D, DeLeo D, Bolhari J, Botega NJ, De Silva D, Phillips M, Vijayakumar L, Varnik A, Schlebusch L, Tanh HTT (2008). Effectiveness of brief intervention and contact for suicide attempters: a randomized controlled trial in five countries. Bulletin of the World Health Organization, 86(9): 703-9.

Fortney JC (2010). A commentary on rural mental health services research. The Journal of Rural Health, 26: 203-4.

Fortney JC, Harman JS, Xu S, Dong F (2010). The association between rural residence and the use, type, and quality of depression care. *The Journal of Rural Health*, 26(3): 205-13.

Gold PB, Meisler N, Santos AB, Carnemolla MA, Williams OH, Keleher J. (2006). Randomized trial of supported employment integrated with assertive community treatment for rural adults with severe mental illness. Schizophrenia Bulletin, 32(2): 378-95.

Greden JF, Valenstein M, Spinner J, Blow A, Gorman LA, Dalack GW, Marcus S, Kees M (2010). Buddy-to-Buddy: a citizen soldier peer support program to counteract stigma, PTSD, depression, and Suicide. Annals of the New York Academy of Sciences, 1208(1): 90-7.

Hale TM, Cotton SR, Drentea P, Goldner M (2010). Rural-urban differences in general and health-related internet use. American Behavioral Scientist, 53(9): 1344-66.

Hanrahan MP, Hartley D (2008). Employment of advanced-practice psychiatric nurses to stem rural mental health workforce shortages. Psychiatric Services, 59(1): 109-11.

Harpaz-Rotem I, Rosenheck R (2011). Serving those who served: retention of newly returning Veterans from Iraq and Afghanistan in mental health treatment. Psychiatric Services, 62(1): 22-7.

Hart LG, Larson EH, Lishner DM (2005). Rural definitions for health policy and research. *American Journal of Public Health*, 95(7): 1149-55.

Hirsch (2006). A review of the literature on rural suicide: risk and protective factors, incidence, and prevention. Crisis, 27(4): 189-99.

Hodges JQ, Markward M, Yoon DP, Evans CJ (2005). Rural and urban differences among mental health consumers in one Midwestern state: Implications for policy, practice, and research. *Journal of Social Work in Disability and Rehabilitation*, 41(2): 105-20.

Hoge CW, Auchterlonie JL, Milliken CS (2006). Mental health problems, use of mental health services, and attrition from military service after returning from deployment to Iraq or Afghanistan. JAMA 295(9): 1023–32.

Hoge CW, Castro CA, Messer SC, McGurk D, Cotting DI, Koffman RL (2004). Combat duty in Iraq and Afghanistan, mental health problems, and barriers to care. *New England Journal of Medicine*, 351(1): 13–22.

Hoge CW, Terhakopian A, Castro KA, Messer SC, Engel CC (2007). Association of posttraumatic stress disorder with somatic symptoms, health care visits, and absenteeism among Iraq war Veterans. *American Journal of Psychiatry*, 164(1): 150-3.

Horrigan J (2009). Home broadband adoption 2009. Broadband adoption increases but monthly prices do too. Available at http://pewintenet.org/Reports/2009/10-Home-Broadband-Adoption-2009.aspx. Accessed August 13, 2011.

Hourani LL, Yuan H (1999). The mental health status of women in the Navy and Marine Corps: preliminary findings from the Perceptions of Wellness and Readiness Assessment. Military Medicine, 164(3): 174–181.

Isometsa E, Heikkinen M, Henriksson M, Marttunen M, Aro H, Lonnqvist J (1997). Differences between urban and rural suicides. Acta Psychiatrica Scandinavica, 95(4): 297–305.

Jameson JP, Blank MB (2007). The role of clinical psychology in rural mental health services: Defining problems and developing solutions. Clinical Psychology: Science and Practice, 14(3): 283-98.

Kalafat J, Gould MS, Munfakh JLH, Kleinman M (2007). An evaluation of crisis hotline outcomes part 1: nonsuicidal crisis callers. Suicide and Life Threatening Behavior, 37(3): 322-37.

Kang HK, Bullman TA (2009). Risk of suicide among US Veterans returning from the Iraq or Afghanistan war zones. JAMA, 300(6): 652-3.

Kaplan MS, Huguet N, McFarland BH, Newson JT (2007). Suicide among male veterans: a prospective population-based study. *Journal of Epidemiology and Community Health*, 61(7): 619-24.

Kessler RC, Berglund PA, Bruce ML (2001). The prevalence and correlates of untreated serious mental illness. Health Services Research 36(6, Pt. 1): 987–1007.

Kessler, D., Lewis, G., Kaur, S., Wilies, N., King, M., Weich, S., Sharp, D., Araya, R., Hollinghurst, S., and Peters, T. (2009). Therapist-delivered internet psychotherapy for depression in primary care: A randomised controlled trial. The Lancet, 374(9690): 628-34.

Kessler RC, Wang PS (2008). The descriptive epidemiology of commonly occurring mental disorders in the United States. Annual Review of Public Health, 29(1): 115-29.

King LA, King DW, Fairbank JA, Keane TM, Adams GA (1998). Resilience-recovery factors in post-traumatic stress disorder among female and male Vietnam veterans: hardiness, post-war social support, and additional stressful life events. *Journal of Personality and Social Psychology*, 74(2): 420–34.

Knox KL, Litts DA, Talcott GW, Feig JC, Caine ED (2003). Risk of suicide and related adverse outcomes after exposure to a suicide prevention program in the US Air Force: cohort study. BMJ, 327(7428): 1376-80.

Knox KL, Pflanz S, Talcott GW, Campise RL, Lavigne JE, Bajorska A, Tu X, Caine ED (2010). The US Air Force Suicide Prevention Program: implications for public health policy. American *Journal of Public Health*, 100(12): 2457-63.

Kochanek KD, Xu J, Murphy SL, Minino AM, Kung HC (2011). Deaths: Preliminary Data for 2009. National Vital Statistics Report, Center for Disease Control, 59(4). Available at http://www.cdc.gov/nchs/data/nvsr/nvsr59/nvsr59_04.pdf. Accessed August 13, 2011.

Koenen KC, Stellman JM, Stellman SD, Sommer JF Jr. (2003). Risk factors for course of post-traumatic stress disorder among Vietnam veterans: a 14-year follow-up of American Legionnaires. *Journal of Consulting Clinical Psychology*, 71(6): 980–86.

Kposowa AJ, Breault KD, Singh GK (1995). White male suicide in the United States: a multivariate individual level analysis. Social Forces. 1995;74(1): 315–23.

Kypri K, Hallett J, Howat P, McManus A, Maycock B, Bowe S, Horton N (2009). Randomized controlled trial of proactive web-based alcohol screening and brief intervention for university students. Archives of Internal Medicine, 169(16), 1508-14.

Lester RT, Ritvo P, Mills EJ, Kairiri A, Karanja S, Chung MH, Jack W, Habyarimana J, et al. (2010). Effects of mobile phone short message service on antiretroviral treatment adherence in Kenya (WelTel Kenya1): a randomised trial. The Lancet, 376(9755): 1838-45.

Litz B, Engel C, Bryant R, Papa A (2007). A randomized, controlled proof-of-concept trial of an internet-based therapist-assisted self-management treatment for post-traumatic stress disorder. *American Journal of Psychiatry,* 164(11): 1676-83.

Luoma JB, Martin CE, Pearson JL (2002). Contact with mental health and primary care providers before suicide: a review of the evidence. *American Journal of Psychiatry*, 159(6): 909-16.

Luxton DD, June JD, Kinn JT (2011). Technology-based suicide prevention: current applications and future directions. Telemedicine and e-Health, 17(1): 1-5.

Mari K, Bradshow C, Sudhinaraset M, Blum R (2010). Exploring the role of social connectedness among military youth: perceptions from youth, parents, and school personnel. Child and Youth Care Forum, 39(5): 351-66.

Maris RW. The developmental perspective of suicide. In Life Span Perspectives of Suicide: Time-Lines in the Suicide Process, AA Leenaars (Ed.), 1990, Plenum, New York.

Markopoulos P (2009). Awareness systems and the role of social intelligence. Artificial Intelligence and Society, 24(2): 115-22.

McFaul M, Ciarlo J, Demmler J, Smith C, DeHay T (2009). Addressing suicide potential and prevention in rural and frontier areas: suicide prevention toolkit for rural primary care providers. The WICHE Center for Rural Mental Health Research. Summary Report. August. Available at http://wiche.edu/info/publications/McFaulY4Proj1Summary Report.pdf

Merwin E, Hinton I, Dembling B, Stern S (2003). Shortages of rural mental health professionals. Archives of Psychiatric Nursing, 17(1): 42-51.

Mirza F, Norris T, Stockdale R (2008). Mobile technologies and the holistic management of chronic diseases. *Health Informatics Journal*, 14(4): 309-21.

Mishara BL, Chagnon F, Daigle M, Balan B, Raymond S, Marcoux I, Bardon C, Campbell JK, Berman A (2007a). Comparing models of helper behavior to actual practice in telephone crisis intervention: a silent monitoring study of calls to the 1-800-SUICIDE network. Suicide and Life-Threatening Behavior, 37(3): 291-307.

Mishara BL, Chagnon F, Daigle M, Balan B, Raymond S, Marcoux I, Bardon C, Campbell JK, Berman A (2007b). Which helper behaviors and intervention nstyles are related to better short-term outcomes in telephone crisis intervention? Results from a silent monitoring study of calls to the 1-800-SUICIDE network. Suicide and Life-Threatening Behavior, 37(3): 308-21.

Morgan HG, Jones EM, Owen JH (1993). Secondary prevention of non-fatal deliberate self-harm. The green card study. *British Journal of Psychiatry*, 163(1): 111-12.

Motto JA, Bostrom AG (2001). A randomized controlled trial of postcrisis suicide prevention. Psychiatric Services, 52(6): 828-33.

Myers WW (2000). The federal role in rural graduate medical education initiatives. *The Journal of Rural Health*, 16(3): 301-3.

Norris TE (2000). Education for rural practice: A saga of pipelines and plumbers. *The Journal of Rural Health*, 16(3): 208-12.

Pietrzak RH, Goldstein MB, Malley JC, Rivers AJ, Johnson DC, Morgan CA, Southwick SM (2010a). Post-traumatic growth in Veterans of Operations Enduring Freedom and Iraqi Freedom. *Journal of Affective Disorders*, 126(2): 230-5.

Pietrzak RH, Russo AR, Ling Q, Southwick SM (2010b). Suicidal ideation in treatment-seeking Veterans of Operations Enduring Freedom and Iraqi Freedom: The role of coping strategies, resilience, and social support. Journal of Psychiatric Research, Epub ahead of print: December 22. http://dx.doi.org/10.1016/j.jpsychires.2010.11.015.

Rabinowitz H, Diamond J, Markham F, Paynter N (2001). Critical factors for designing programs to increase the supply and retention of rural primary care physicians. JAMA, 286(9): 1041–8.

Seeman TE (1996). Social ties and health: the benefits of social integration. Annals of Epidemiology, 6(5): 442–51.

Shandley K, Austin D, Klein B, Pier C, Schattner P, Pierce D, Wade V (2008). Therapist-assisted, internet-based treatment for panic disorder: Can general practitioners achieve comparable patient outcomes to psychologists? *Journal of Medical Internet Research*, 10(2): e14.

Singh GK, Siahpush M (2002). Increasing rural-urban gradients in US suicide mortality, 1970-1997. American *Journal of Public Health*, 92(1): 1161-7.

Skupian, MB (2010). The health needs of rural Veterans. Forum, 1-2. Available at http://www.hsrd.research.va.gov/publications/internal/forum10_10.pdf. Accessed August 13, 2011.

Smalley KB, Yancey CT, Warren JC, Naufel K, Ryan R, Pugh JL (2010). Rural mental health and psychological treatment: A review for practitioners. *Journal of Clinical Psychology*, 66(5): 479-89.

Titov N, Andrews G, Robinson E, Schwencke G, Johnston L, Solley K, Choi I (2009). Clinician-assisted internet treatment is effective for generalized anxiety disorder: Randomized controlled trail. Australian and New Zealand Journal of Psychiatry, 43(10): 905-12.

Trout DL (1980). The role of social isolation in suicide. Suicide Life Threatening Behaviors, 10(1): 10–23.

Turvey C, Stromquist A, Kelly K, Zwerling C, Merchant J (2002). Financial loss and suicidal ideation in a rural community sample. Acta Psychiatrica Scandinavica, 106(5): 373–80.

US Census Bureau: 2009 American Community Survey, Military Veterans in Rural and Urban Areas. http://www.factfinder.census.gov/servlet/GCTTable?_bm=yand-geo_id= and-ds_name=ACS_2009_1YR_G00_and-_lang=enand-redoLog=trueand-mt_name=ACS_2009_1YR_G00_GCT2101_US37and-format=US-37and-CONTEXT= gct. Accessed August 13, 2011.

US Department of Health and Human Services, Public Health Service (2001). National Strategy for Suicide Prevention: Goals and Objectives for Action. Rockville, Md. Available at http://www.ncbi.nlm.nih.gov/books/NBK44281/. Accessed August 13, 2011.

S Department of Veterans Affairs (2010). National Survey of Veterans, Active Duty Service Members, Demobilized National Guard and Reserve Members, Family Members, and Surviving Spouses. October. Available at http://www.va.gov/ vetdata/docs/Surveys AndStudies /NVSSurveyFinalWeightedReport.pdf. Accessed August 13, 2011.

asterling JJ, Proctor SP, Friedman MJ, Hoge CW, Heeran T, King Lynda A, King DW (2010). PTSD symptom increases in Iraq-deployed soldiers: Comparison with nondeployed soldiers and associations with baseline symptoms, deployment experiences, and postdeployment stress. *Journal of Traumatic Stress*, 23(1): 41-51.

Wagenfeld MO (2000). Delivering mental health services to persistently and seriously mentally ill in frontier areas. *The Journal of Rural Health*, 16(1), 91-96.

Wagner HR, Burns BJ, Broadhead WE, Yarnal, KS, Sigmon A, Gaynes BN (2000). Minor depression in family practice: Functional morbidity, co-morbidity, service utilization and outcomes. Psychological Medicine, 30(6): 1377-90.

Wang PS, Lane M, Olfson J, Pincus HA, Wells KB, Kessler RC (2005). Twelve-month use of mental health services in the United States: Results from the National Comorbidity Survey Replication. Archives of General Psychiatry, 62(6): 629-40.

Wilcox HC, Storr CL, Breslau N (2009). Posttraumatic stress disorder and suicide attempts in a community sample of urban American young adults. *Archives of General Psychiatry,* 66(3): 305-11.

Ziller EC, Anderson NJ, Coburn AF (2010). Access to rural mental health services: service use and out-of-pocket costs. *Journal of Rural Health*, 26(3): 214-24.

In: Frontiers in Suicide Risk
Editor: Jill E. Lavigne

ISBN 978-1-62081-373-7
©2012 Nova Science Publishers, Inc.

Chapter 11

OPERATION S.A.V.E.: SUICIDE PREVENTION TRAINING FOR FRONT-LINE EMPLOYEES IN THE US DEPARTMENT OF VETERANS HEALTH AFFAIRS

Deborah A. King[1,2]*, Heather Von Bergen (In Memoriam),
Kerry L. Knox [1,2], Jane Wood[1], Krista Stephenson[1],
Lynda Chauncey[1], Naji Lu[3], Kimberly Kaukeinen[3]
and Janet E. Kemp[4]

[1]US Department of Veterans Health Affairs,
VISN 2 Center of Excellence for Suicide Prevention
[2]Department of Psychiatry, University of Rochester, NY, US
[3]Department of Biostatistics, University of Rochester, NY US
[4]US Department of Veterans Health Affairs, Office of Mental Health, US

ABSTRACT

Available evidence suggests that Veterans may be at greater risk for suicide than members of the general population. Operation S.A.V.E. was developed as the first Veteran-specific gatekeeper training program for suicide prevention to be used with front-line Department of Veterans Health Affairs (VHA) staff across the nation. To determine if the training influenced participants' attitudes towards suicide prevention or their knowledge of basic suicide facts and myths, we surveyed 7,431 VHA staff who participated in SAVE training before and after the training about their confidence in responding to a suicidal veteran, their acceptance of suicide prevention as part of their job, and their basic suicide knowledge. Respondents also were asked about their satisfaction with the training.

After training, participants reported increased confidence in their ability to respond to suicidal Veterans, increased acceptance of suicide screening as part of their job, and

---

* Correspondence concerning this paper should be addressed to Deborah King, Department of Psychiatry, 300 Crittenden Blvd., Rochester NY 14620. Email: deborah_king@urmc.rochester.edu

enhanced knowledge about suicide. Although originally designed for non-clinicians, exploratory analyses suggested that SAVE training outcomes were similarly positive for VA clinicians as well as non-clinicians. These findings suggest that gatekeeper training may be an effective suicide prevention strategy for a wide variety of frontline VHA staff, although future studies should employ more rigorous sampling methods and assess for changes in observed skills of training participants.

INTRODUCTION

An estimated one million people die each year from suicide, resulting in a global mortality rate of 16 per 100,000 (World Health Organization [WHO], 2009). Over 30,000 Americans commit suicide each year, resulting in a national mortality rate of approximately 13 per 100,000 (Centers for Disease Control and Prevention, 2009). Emerging evidence suggests that suicide rates are higher among Veterans who receive care from the Veterans Health Administration (VHA) than individuals in the general population (Kaplan, Huguet, McFarland, and Newsom, 2007; McCarthy, Valenstein, Kim, Ilgen, Zivin and Blow, 2009). Compared to the US general population, VHA patients are typically older, male, suffer higher prevalence of substance use, mental illness and have ready access to firearms; all factors associated with increased risk for suicide. One study using National Death Index data revealed that VHA patients were 66% more likely to die by suicide than the general population (McCarthy et al., 2009).

The VHA serves a subset of the Veteran population, and a prospective follow-up study of all Veterans (not just those served by the VHA), reported that male Veterans were twice as likely to die by suicide as male non-Veterans (Kaplan et al., 2007). The VHA Mental Health Strategic Plan outlined multiple initiatives to address the problem of suicide among Veterans (U.S. Department of Veterans Affairs Office of the Inspector General, 2007), including the provision of suicide prevention training to all front-line staff and health care professionals. Gatekeeper training is a promising form of suicide prevention that employs a case finding strategy. "Gatekeepers" are those who have primary contact with individuals at risk for suicide and who are trained to to recognize suicide risk factors and warning signs in order to refer affected individuals for assessment and treatment (Centers for Disease Control and Prevention, 1992; Gould and Kramer, 2001).

Gatekeepers have been characterized as "designated" or "emergent," respectively, depending on whether they are performing the function as part of their professional role (e.g., physicians, nurses) or as a result of being in a non-clinical relationship with a suicidal individual (e.g., police, family members) (Isaac et al, 2009; Ramsey, Cooke and Lange, 1990). Gatekeeper training programs vary in content and duration, but typically include education about risk factors and warning signs, methods of asking about suicide, and strategies for effecting a referral. Several gatekeeper training programs are available commercially, including Applied Suicide Intervention Skills Training (ASIST; LivingWorks, 2007); Question, Persuade and Respond (QPR Institute, 1999), and Yellow Ribbon International for Suicide Prevention (Yellow Ribbon International, 2007).

Numerous studies have reported positive effects of gatekeeper programs on participants' knowledge of suicide, confidence in responding to suicidal individuals and/or suicide intervention skills (Capp, Deane and Lambert, 2001; Chagnon, Houle, Marcoux, and Renaud,

2007; Cross, Matthieu, Lezine and Knox, 2010; Kalafat and Elias, 1995; Matthieu, Cross, Batres, Flora and Knox, 2008; Stuart, Waalen, and Haelstromm, 2003; Wyman et al., 2008). As well, some reported actual reductions in suicidal ideation, attempts and/or deaths by suicide (Hegerl et al., 2006; Henriksson and Isacsson, 2006; Knox, Litts, Talcott, Feig and Caine, 2003; Mann et al., 2005; Rutz, von Knorring, and Walinder, 1992; Szanto, Kalmar, Hendin, Rihmer and Mann, 2007).

In terms of programs targeting Veterans or military personnel specifically, Matthieu and colleagues (2008) applied QPR gatekeeper training and brief behavioral rehearsal to clinical and non-clinical staff of Veterans counseling centers (Vet Centers) and reported increased gatekeeper knowledge and self-efficacy after the training. Knox and colleagues (2003) conducted a multipronged, quasi-experimental cohort study of US Air Force personnel that included gatekeeper training and reported a 33% relative risk reduction in the suicide rate. Given the promising evidence regarding the effectiveness of gatekeeper training programs, Operation S.A.V.E. was developed by the Education, Training and Dissemination Core of the VISN2 Center of Excellence for Suicide Prevention as part of the VA's comprehensive approach to suicide prevention (U.S. Department of Veterans Affairs Office of the Inspector General, 2007, Joshua Omvig Veterans Suicide Prevention Act, 2007).

To our knowledge, it was the first gatekeeper training developed specifically for those working with Veterans. We predicted that after the training, participants would report increased confidence in their ability to work with suicidal Veterans, increased acceptance of suicide prevention as part of their job, increased knowledge about basic suicide facts versus myths, and a high degree of satisfaction with the training.

The literature distinguished clinical from non-clinical gatekeepers (Isaac et al., 2009; Matthieu et al., 2008), so we conducted additional exploratory analyses to determine if training outcomes differed accordingly.

METHOD

Operation S.A.V.E. was developed in five modules to allow flexibility in adapting the program to different VHA settings and audiences. The modules were: I. A Brief Overview of Suicide in the Veteran Population, II. Suicide Myths and Misinformation, III. Risk Factors for Suicide, IV. S.A.V.E. Components (Signs of suicide, Asking about suicide, Validating feelings, Encouraging the Veteran to seek help and expediting referral), V. Closing Summary and Evaluation. The S.A.V.E. training package included a PowerPoint presentation and training script; an instructor's guide and toolkit; pre-post evaluation instructions, evaluation forms (questionnaires), tracking sheets and supporting pamphlets.

As part of its comprehensive suicide prevention strategy, the VHA also initiated the hiring of Suicide Prevention Coordinators (SPCs) in all VA Medical Centers (VAMCs) across the country in February of 2007. SPCs were nurses, social workers and psychologists who were hired to coordinate suicide prevention activities at their respective facilities, including administration of the S.A.V.E. program. In preparation for administering the training program, SPCs were required to attend at least one of two conference calls held nationwide to review the training materials and their use.

Participants

The study was approved by the US Department of Veterans Health Affairs VISN 2 Human Subjects Review Board in Syracuse, New York. Participation was required of all non-clinical VHA staff as a condition of their employment as per Public Health law 110-110 (Joshua Omvig Suicide Prevention Act, 2007). Participants were front-line VHA staff, including staff from medical center, outpatient and community-based outpatient clinics. According to the VHA Human Resources listing of clinical and non-clinical positions, participants were primarily non-clinical front-line staff such as ward clerks, housekeepers, security officers and maintenance personnel. However, some SPCs included clinical trainees such as physicians, nurses, dentists or social workers.

Therefore, additional analyses were conducted to determine if clinicians responded to the training differently than non-clinicians. This report is based on a sample of 7,431 training evaluation questionnaires of more than 30,000 completed by VHA employees representing 246 VA medical centers (VAMCs) across the nation. Five VAMCs were already using an established gatekeeper training program such as ASIST or QPR so these five facilities were excluded from the study. Resource constraints prevented data entry and analysis of the more than 35,000 paper questionnaires collected between February 1 and September 30, 2008. Therefore, clerical staff blindly (i.e., without reading content) selected 7,431 questionnaires to send to a data analyst for coding and data entry. The sample includes questionnaires from the entire 8-month period.

Design and Measures

Consistent with other gatekeeper training programs (Isaac, et al, 2009), this study employed a pre- post-training design. The questionnaire was created specifically for this study, although its design was informed by other suicide prevention program evaluation materials (Matthieu et al., 2008; Wyman et al., 2008). The questionnaire elicited participants' age, gender, and job title. It also contained four items assessing participants' confidence in responding to a suicidal Veteran and their beliefs about whether helping a suicidal Veteran was part of their job. Each of item was rated on a 4-point Likert scale ranging from "disagree" to "completely agree."(Table 1). Participants' knowledge of basic suicide facts (versus myths) was assessed using four True/False questions (Table 2). Post-training items re-assessed the items described above and also elicited trainee satisfaction with the training materials, the content of the training information, and the trainer's expertise.

Statistical Analyses

Data were analyzed using SAS 9.1 (SAS Institute Inc., 2003). The generalized estimating equations (GEE) approach with exchangeable working correlation was used to address correlated responses in the data. The GEE approach is utilized widely due to its less stringent distributional assumptions and robustness properties, yielding valid inferences regardless of the data distribution (Liang and Zeger, 1986). The training effect for all outcomes was tested controlling for age and gender. Exploratory analyses tested whether clinical (versus non-clinical) employee status was a moderator of training outcomes by adding an interaction term to the model.

Table 1. Number (Percent) of Total Training Participants, Non-Clinicians, and Clinicians Indicating Confident Response of "Mostly" or "Completely Agree" on Pre- and Post-Training Assessments of Suicide Prevention Confidence and Role Acceptance

Questionnaire Item	Pre-Training	Post-Training	Statistics (n)
"I know enough about suicide"			
All Participants	2056 (31%)	4332 (60%)	Z = 52.2** (N=7352)
Non-Clinicians	1139 (30%)	2205 (62%)	
Clinicians	933 (32%)	1895 (69%)	
"I am prepared to handle a suicidal Veteran"			
All Participants	1864 (28%)	4333 (66%)	Z = 61.4** (N=7342)
Non-Clinicians	899 (24%)	2133 (61%)	
Clinicians	996 (34%)	1995 (73%)	
"I am comfortable talking about suicide"			
All Participants	3915 (59%)	5108 (77%)	Z = 31.8** (N=7348)
Non-Clinicians	2151 (57%)	2617 (74%)	
Clinicians	1838 (63%)	2236 (82%)	
"It is my job to help suicidal Veterans."			
All Participants	4591 (70%)	5636 (86%)	Z = 30.1** (N=7335)
Non-Clinicians	2346 (63%)	2839 (81%)	
Clinicians	2337 (80%)	2531 (92%)	

** p < .0001.

Table 2. Number (Percent) of Total Training Participants, Non-Clinicians, and Clinicians Who Gave Correct Answers to Suicide Questions on Pre- and Post-Training Assessments

Questionnaire Item	Pre-Training	Post-Training	Statistics (n)
"If I ask a Veteran about suicide, they are more likely to commit suicide."			
All Participants	6538(91%)	6422(90%)	Z = -0.14 (N=7354)
Non-Clinicians	3370(90%)	3158(89%)	
Clinicians	2709(92%)	2606(93%)	
"Veterans only talk about suicide when they want attention."			
All Participants	6359(93%)	6494(95%)	Z = -6.73** (N=7346)
Non-Clinicians	3404(91%)	3305(93%)	
Clinicians	2795(95%)	2701(97%)	
"Veterans are two times more likely to commit suicide than other Americans."			
All Participants	5886(82%)	6297(92%)	Z = 18.1** (N=7345)
Non-Clinicians	3305(81%)	3227(91%)	
Clinicians	2489(85%)	2615(94%)	
"If a Veteran has made up their mind about suicide, they cannot be stopped."			
All Participants	6231(90%)	6316(92%)	Z = -3.1* (N=7338)
Non-Clinicians	3380(90%)	3214(91%)	
Clinicians	2700(92%)	2634(95%)	

*p < .001, **p < .0001.

RESULTS

Demographics

Of the 7,431 training participants, 2,619 were male and 4,812 were female. Mean age was 46.3 years (SD = 11.5, range = 18 to 85). 3,853 participants were non-clinical front-line staff; 2,988 were clinical providers.

Suicide Prevention Confidence and Role Acceptance

Frequency counts and percentages of those answering "Completely Agree" or "Mostly Agree" to the four questions before and after training appear in Table 1. Participants were more likely to indicate that they (1) knew enough about suicide ($Z = 52.2$, $p < .0001$), (2) were prepared to handle a suicidal Veteran ($Z = 61.4$, $p < .0001$), and (3) were comfortable talking about suicide ($Z = 31.8$, $p < .0001$) after training. Participants were also more likely to indicate that it was their job to help a suicidal Veteran after training ($Z = 30.1$, $p < .0001$).

Analyses exploring differences in the amount of change between clinicians and non-clinicians after training indicated that non-clinicians were more likely to move toward agreeing that it was their job to help a suicidal Veteran than clinicians ($Z = -2.14$, $p = .033$). However, clinicians were more likely to indicate that they knew enough about suicide ($Z = 2.82$, $p = .005$) and felt comfortable talking about suicide ($Z = 2.43$, $p = .015$) than non-clinicians. There was no significant difference in the amount of change between clinicians and non-clinicians on the item "I am prepared to handle a suicidal Veteran."

Knowledge about Suicidal Veterans

Frequency counts and percentages of those answering "True" or "False" to the four knowledge questions are shown in Table 2. Results indicated significant increases in accurate knowledge regarding suicide after the training for three of the four items: "Veterans only talk about suicide when they want attention." ($Z = -6.73$, $p < 0.0001$), "Veterans are two times more likely to commit suicide than other Americans." ($Z = 18.1$, $p < 0.0001$), and "If a Veteran has made up their mind about suicide they cannot be stopped." ($Z = -3.1$, $p < 0.001$). The item "If I ask a Veteran if s/he is suicidal, they are more likely to commit suicide." was not associated with a statistically significant change in accurate knowledge after training.

Additional analyses exploring change differences between clinicians and non-clinicians before and after training indicated that clinicians were more likely to improve their knowledge on three of the items: "If I ask a Veteran if s/he is suicidal, they are more likely to commit suicide." ($Z = -2.87$, $p = 0.004$) , "If a Veteran has made up their mind about suicide they cannot be stopped." ($Z = -3.79$, $p < 0.0001$) and "Veterans are two times more likely to commit suicide than other Americans." ($Z = 3.16$, $p = 0.0016$).

There was no significant difference between clinicians and non-clinicians in the amount of pre- post-training change on the item: "Veterans only talk about suicide when they want attention."($Z = -1.52$, $p = 0.13$).

Satisfaction with Training

Of the more than 7,431 respondents in our sample, 6,394 (93%) reported being completely or mostly satisfied with the training materials; 6,525 (95%) with the content of training; and 6,638 (96%) with the trainer's expertise. Contrary to expectation, secondary analyses revealed that clinicians felt more satisfied with the training materials (χ^2=13.6, p = 0.0002) and the content of training than non-clinicians (χ^2=12.5, p = 0.0004). There was no difference between the groups in terms satisfaction with the trainer's expertise (χ^2=0.06, p = 0.81).

CONCLUSION

S.A.V.E. participants reported increased confidence in their suicide prevention knowledge and skills, increased acceptance of suicide prevention as part of their job, and increased knowledge of basic suicide facts. Our findings suggest that Operation S.A.V.E. was well-received by VHA employees. Participants reported a high degree of satisfaction with the training and with the expertise of the Suicide Prevention Coordinators who conducted the program.

These findings should be interpreted cautiously, however, due to methodological limitations. First, the sample of training questionnaires studied here was selected blindly for coding by office staff from a larger set of surveys. The sampling was not randomized across time, trainers or geographic regions. Therefore, the sample may not be representative of all respondents, all VHA personnel or all trainers. In addition, the training was mandated and participants may have wished to demonstrate that they had met the requirement by reporting high satisfaction or improved confidence after the training. Yet, the results suggested increased knowledge of basic suicide facts (versus myths) after the training, and therefore a positive training effect.

Exploratory analyses suggested that non-clinical staff showed greater change toward agreeing that it was their job to help a suicidal Veteran. In contrast, clinical staff showed greater change towards comfort and confidence in working with suicidal Veterans. In terms of suicide knowledge, clinicians evidenced more change relative to non-clinicians, even though non-clinicians also demonstrated increased knowledge after training. Although the results of exploratory analyses must be interpreted cautiously, it is possible that clinicians were faster learners and more able to enhance their knowledge base after the relatively brief training sessions. Despite the suggestion of positive training outcomes associated with Operation S.A.V.E., future trainings should include more rigorous sampling methods and assess participants' actual ability to put suicide prevention training into action. For example, observational measures of trainees' skill in asking about suicide and encouraging treatment could be obtained from standardized role-plays conducted before and after training (cf. Cross et al., 2010). As well, it is important to assess other higher level outcomes such as whether or not more Veterans are effectively referred for suicide evaluation and treatment after the initiation of gatekeeper training programs. These investigations are of critical importance if we are to determine the most effective suicide prevention training strategies for VHA staff and others who come in contact with at-risk Veterans.

Acknowledgment

We thank Cynthia Claassen for her thoughtful suggestions regarding this paper and Kimberly Woehr for administrative and clerical assistance with all aspects of the project.

References

Capp, K., Deane, F., and Lambert, G. (2001). Suicide prevention in Aboriginal communities: Application of community gatekeeper training. *Australian and New Zealand Journal of Public Health*, 25, 315-321.

Centers for Disease Control and Prevention. (1992). Youth suicide prevention programs: A resource guide. Atlanta, GA: National Center for Injury Prevention and Control.Centers for Disease Control and Prevention. (2009). National suicide statistics at a glance. Retrieved from http://www.cdc.gov/violenceprevention/suicide/statistics/trends01.html

Chagnon, F., Houle, J., Marcoux, I. and Renaud, J. (2007). *Suicide and Life-Threatening Behavior*, 37, 135-144.

Cross, W., Matthieu, M.M., Levine, D., and Knox, K.L. (2010). Does a brief suicide prevention gatekeeper training program enhance observed skills? *Crisis*, 31, 149-159.

Gould, M. and Kramer, R. (2001). Youth suicide prevention. *Suicide and Life-Threatening Behavior*, 31, 6-31.

Hegerl, U., Althaus, D., Schmidtke, A., and Niklewski, G. (2006). The alliance against depression: 2-year evaluation of a community-based intervention to reduce suicidality. *Psychological Medicine,* 36, 1225-1233.

Henriksson, S. and Isacsson, G. (2006). Increased antidepressant use and fewer suicides in Jamtland county, Sweden, after a primary care educational programme on the treatment of depression. *Acta Psychiatrica Scandinavia*, 114, 159-167.

Implementing VHA's mental health strategic plan initiatives for suicide prevention.VAOIG Report No. 06-03706-126. Retrieved from http://www4.va.gov/oig/54/reports/VAOIG-06-03706-126.pdf

Isaac, M., Elias, B., Katz, L., Belik, S., Deane, F., Enns, M., et al. Gatekeeper training as a preventative intervention for suicide: A Systematic review. *Canadian Journal of Psychiatry*, 54, 260-268.

Joshua Omvig Veteran's Suicide Prevention Act, H.R. 327 (2007). Public law 110-110, 110th Congress. Retrieved from http://frwebgate.access.gpo.gov/cgi-bin/getdoc.cgi?dbname= 110_cong_public_lawsanddocid=f:publ110.110.pdf

Kalafat, J. and Elias, M. (1995). Suicide prevention in an educational context: Broad and narrow foci. *Suicide and Life-Threatening Behavior*, 25, 123-133.

Kaplan, M., Huguet, N., McFarland, B., and Newsom, J. (2007). Suicide among male veterans: A prospective population-based study. *Journal of Epidemiology and Community Health*, 61, 619-624.

Knox, K.L, Litts, D., Talcott, W., Feig, J., and Caine, E. (2003). Risk of suicide and related adverse Outcomes after exposure to a suicide prevention programme in the US Air Force: Cohort study. *British Medical Journal,* 327, 1.5.

Liang, K., and Zeger, S. (1986). Longitudinal data analysis using generalized linear models. *Biometrika*, 73, 13-22.

LivingWorks Education, Inc. (2005). Applied Suicide Intervention Skills Training. Retrieved from http://www/livingworks.net

Mann, J., Apter, A., Bertolote, J., Beautrais, A., Currier, D., Haas, A., et al. (2005). Suicide prevention strategies: A systematic review. *JAMA*, 294, 2064-2074.

Matthieu, M., Cross, W., Batres, A., Flora, C. and Knox, K. (2008). Evaluation of gatekeeper training for suicide prevention in veterans. *Archives of Suicide Research*, 12, 148-154.

McCarthy, J., Valenstein, M., Kim, H., Ilgen, M., Zivin, K., and Blow, F. (2009). Suicide mortality among patients receiving care in the Veterans Health Administration Health System. *American Journal of Epidemiology*, 169, 1033-1038.

QPR Institute (1999). Training options for QPR gatekeeper training for suicide prevention. Retrieved from http://www.qprinstitute.com

Ramsay, R., Cooke, M., and Lang, W. (1990). Alberta's suicide prevention training programs: A retrospective comparison with Rothman's developmental research model. *Suicide and Life-Threatening Behavior*, 20, 7-22.

Randomized trial of a gatekeeper program for suicide prevention: 1-Year impact on secondary school staff. *Journal of Consulting and Clinical Psychology*, 76, 104-115.

Rutz, W., von Knorring, L., and Walinder, J. (1992). Long-term effects of an educational program for general practitionersgiven by the Swedish Commitee for the Prevention and Treatment of Depression. *Acta Psychiatrica Scandinavia*, 85, 83-88.

SAS Statistical Software. SAS 9.1.3 (2003). Cary, NC: SAS Institute Inc.

Stuart, C., Waalen, J. and Haelstromm, E. (2003). Many helping hearts: An evaluation of peer gatekeeper training in suicide risk assessment. *Death Studies*, 27, 321-333.

Szanto, K., Kalmar, D., Hendin, H., Rihmer, Z., and Mann, J. (2007). A suicide prevention program in a region with a very high suicide rate. *Archives of General Psychiatry*, 64, 914-920.

U.S. Department of Veterans Affairs Office of the Inspector General. (2007).

World Health Organization. (2009). Suicide statistics. In Suicide prevention. Retrieved from http://www.who.int/mental_health/prevention/suicide/suicideprevent/en/print.html

Wyman, P., Brown, C., Inman, J., Cross, W., Schmeelk-Cone, K., Guo, J. et al. (2008).

Yellow Ribbon International. (2007). Yellow Ribbon Suicide Prevention Program. Retrieved from http://www.yellowribbon.org

Yellow Ribbon International. (2007). Yellow Ribbon Suicide Prevention Program. Retrieved from http://www.yellowribbon.org

In: Frontiers in Suicide Risk
Editor: Jill E. Lavigne

ISBN 978-1-62081-373-7
©2012 Nova Science Publishers, Inc.

Chapter 12

PHARMACIST AND PHARMACY STAFF KNOWLEDGE, ATTITUDES AND MOTIVATION TO REFER PATIENTS FOR SUICIDE RISK ASSESSMENT: LESSONS FROM OPERATION S.A.V.E.

Jill E. Lavigne[1], Deborah A. King[2,3], Nai Ji Lu[4], Kerry L. Knox[2,3] and Jan E. Kemp[3,5]

[1]Wegmans School of Pharmacy, St. John Fisher College,
Rochester, New York, US
[2]Department of Psychiatry, University of Rochester Medical Center,
Rochester, New York, US
[3]VISN2 Center of Excellence for Suicide Prevention,
Canandaigua, New York, US
[4]Department of Biostatistics, University of Rochester Medical Center,
Rochester, New York, US
[5]Office of the National Suicide Prevention Coordinator,
US Department of Veterans Affairs, Canandaigua, New York, US

ABSTRACT

Objectives: To report the results of a national program to train US Department of Veterans Health Affairs (VA) pharmacy staff and other employees with direct patient contact to serve as suicide preventionguides. Setting: VA Medical Centers nationwide. Subject Description: 7,431 VA employees completed training between February 1 and September 30, 2008, including 290 pharmacy staff members. Practice Innovation: Since 2007, the VA has required all staff with direct patient contact to train as "guides" in suicide prevention. The VA developed and disseminated nationally a classroom-based mandatory program to train gatekeepers to: [1] Identify a veteran who may be at risk of suicide; [2] Ask questions about suicide in an objective and non-threatening way; and [3] Refer a veteran for evaluation and treatment. Main Outcome Measures: Knowledge about suicide and guiding, and attitudes and motivation to perform guiding before and after training. Results: On all measures, training was associated with a statistically significant (p<0.001) increase in the proportion of pharmacy staff with [1] correct responses to knowledge questions about suicide, and [2] positive attitudes towards gatekeeping. Yet, fewer pharmacy staff reported being comfortable talking about suicide or being prepared to handle a suicidal veteran. Conclusions: Pharmacy staff knowledge, attitudes and motivation improved significantly after the mandated training. Yet, compared to all other VA employees, pharmacy staff reported less confidence in dealing with suicidal veterans after training. Future training and prevention efforts may need to target specific needs of pharmacy staff in a wide range of pharmacy practice settings.

INTRODUCTION

Suicide is the 11th leading cause of death in the US, ahead of hypertension, homicide and HIV.1 It is the second leading cause of death among adults ages 25-44 and the third leading cause of death for adults ages 15 to 24.2 Each year, more than 34,000 people kill themselves, and more than 376,000 people are treated in emergency rooms for self-inflicted injuries.3 About 80% of all suicides occur in men,4 and 20% of all suicides occur in veterans.4 Of the veterans who die by suicide, approximately 28% are patients in the US Department of Veterans Affairs, Veterans Health Administration (VA) at the time of their deaths. 4 Although the overall suicide rate has remained stable at about 10.9 per 100,000 people since 2000, military suicide rates have increased over the same period, peaking in the Marines at 24 per 100,000 in 2009.5

Suicide is the most severe behavior on a continuum that includes: [1] thoughts about ending one's life ("suicidal ideation"), [2] plans to die by suicide, [3] non-fatal suicidal behavior ("suicide attempt"), and [4] ending one's life ("suicide"). [6]

In the US, the most common means of suicide are firearms. Yet, fatal overdose by prescription and over the counter medications are common and misuse sometimes occurs in conjunction with firearm injuries and deaths. To prevent the use of prescription medications as a means of suicide, the Centers of Disease Control (CDC) has instituted prescription monitoring and medication packaging as research priorities.2 Similarly, the Department of Defense has funded a VA study of blister packaging for psychiatric medications in an effort to both reduce access to means and increase adherence to pharmacotherapy regimens for conditions associated with suicide [7].

Practice Setting

On November 5, 2007, the Joshua Omvig Veterans Suicide Prevention Act became law. The Law directed the Secretary of Veterans of Affairs to:

> ... develop and carry out a comprehensive program designed to reduce the incidence of suicide among veterans. Requires the program to include: [1] mandatory training for appropriate staff and contractors of the Department of Veterans Affairs (VA) who interact with veterans ...
> --Library of Congress. HR 327 CRS Summary. Bill Summary and Status 110th Congress (2007 - 2008). Last accessed on September 14, 2011 at: http://thomas.loc.gov/cgi-bin/bdquery/z?d110:HR00327:@@@Dandsumm2=mand.

To implement the new training requirement and to meet related needs in suicide prevention, the VA established a new position at every US VA medical center: the Suicide Prevention Coordinator (SPC). SPCs are typically nurses, social workers, and psychologists who manage suicide prevention efforts, including suicide prevention training of staff, on a full-time basis.

To meet this training mandate, the VA Center of Excellence at Canandaigua (Canandaigua, New York) developed a new curriculum, Operation S.A.V.E., as the first training installment to be implemented nationwide.8-9 Operation S.A.V.E. was initially deployed on November 14, 2007. Here we report the training results of pharmacy staff compared to other VA front line staff.

Practice Innovation: Operation S.A.V.E.

Briefly, *Operation S.A.V.E.* includes a PowerPoint presentation, training script, instructors guide and toolkit, pre and post-evaluation instructions, evaluation forms, tracking sheets, and *Operation S.A.V.E.* brochures. This 1 to 2-hour classroom training uses a mix of short lectures and role playing exercises to deliver 4 modules: [1] Brief overview of suicide in Veterans, [2] Suicide myths and misinformation, [3] Risk factors, [4] SAVE model (Signs of suicide, Asking about suicide, Validating feelings, Encouraging help, Expediting treatment). Operation SAVE was developed based on existing "gatekeeper" training programs in suicide prevention. "Gatekeeper" is a term used in managed care for the primary care physician charged with controlling patient access to specialist care. Yet, the VA gatekeeper system was designed to do the opposite: Increase care to Veterans who may be at risk. Therefore, the term "gatekeeper" was replaced with "guide".

After training, pharmacists, pharmacy support staff and other VA personnel are expected to be able to:

1. Identify the scope of the problem of suicide among Veterans.
2. Identify the importance of suicide prevention.
3. Discuss myths and misinformation about suicide.
4. Identify a veteran who may be at risk of suicide.
5. Discuss signs and symptoms of suicidal thinking.
6. Ask questions about suicide in an objective and non-threatening way.
7. Refer a veteran for evaluation and treatment.

Outcomes of Training

Subjects are VA employees who attended Operation S.A.V.E. training and returned their evaluation forms (completed on paper at the end of training) between January 1 and September 30, 2008.

Training evaluation forms were collected by the trainers (SPCs) at the end of each Operation S.A.V.E. training session and mailed to the VISN 2 Center of Excellence at Canandaigua for data entry. Each form was entered twice and any discrepancies resolved by hand to ensure data accuracy.

Evaluation forms were anonymous. Forms included demographics (gender, age, self-described job title), hours of previous suicide prevention training, and items about satisfaction with the training, and four questions about attitudes toward suicide: [1] I know enough about suicide. [2] I am prepared to handle a suicidal veteran. [3] I am comfortable talking about suicide. [4] It is my job to help suicidal veterans. Respondents were asked to rate each item on a 4-point Likert scale ("Disagree", "Somewhat Disagree," "Mostly agree," "Completely agree"). Analyses include proportions and Z-statistics with p-values to compare the training results of pharmacists and pharmacy staff to other VA employees. To better understand differences within the pharmacy staff, we used generalized linear regression models (GLM).

The Institutional Review Board at the Syracuse VA Medical Center reviewed and approved this study.

RESULTS

Table 1. VA Pharmacists and Pharmacy Staff Indicating a confident response of "Mostly or "Completely Agree" on pre and post-tests of pharmacy training

Attitude Item	Pre-Training N=290	Post-Training N=290	Statistics (n)
"I know enough about suicide."	47 (22%)	136 (67%)	Z=12.1** (210)
"I am prepared to handle a suicidal veteran."	20 (10%)	121 (62%)	Z=13.6** (207)
"I am comfortable talking about suicide."	89 (43%)	141 (72%)	Z=8.79** (207)
"It is my job to help suicidal veterans."	134 (66%)	174 (88%)	Z=7.76** (203)

Of 7,431 subjects, 290 were pharmacists or worked in a pharmacy setting. On all measures, training was associated with a statistically significant (p<0.001) increase in the proportion of pharmacy staff "completely" or "mostly" in agreement with each of the evaluation items. (Table 1). Compared to all VA employees, a higher proportion of pharmacist and pharmacy employees reported that they "completely" or "mostly" agreed with the statements: [1] "I know enough about suicide." (68% cf. 60%) and [2] "It is my job help suicidal veterans." (88% cf. 86%) (Table 2). Yet, a lower proportion of pharmacists and pharmacy employees (compared to all other VA employees) reported "completely" or "mostly" agreeing with the statements: [1] "I am prepared to handle a suicidal veteran." (61% cf. 66%) and [2] "I am comfortable talking about suicide." (72% cf. 77%).

General linear regression modeling did not reveal any significant baseline differences in suicide knowledge by age, gender or education. Yet, after training, older age and male gender were associated with lower rates of agreement with the statement "I know enough about suicide." Women and those with prior training in suicide prevention were more likely to "completely" or "mostly" agree with the statement: "I am prepared to handle a suicidal veteran". High satisfaction with training (i.e., materials, content, trainer expertise) was associated with relatively large change scores in the 4 evaluation items.

Table 2. Post-Training Suicide Knowledge and Attitudes of VA Pharmacists and Pharmacy Staff Indicating a confident response of "Mostly or "Completely Agree" compared to All VA Staff

Attitude Item	Pharmacy Staff N = 290 N (%)	All VA Staff N = 7,431 n (%)
"I know enough about suicide."	136 (68%)	4332 (60%)
"I am prepared to handle a suicidal veteran."	121 (61%)	4333 (66%)
"I am comfortable talking about suicide."	141 (72%)	5108 (77%)
"It is my job to help suicidal veterans."	174 (88%)	5636 (86%)

DISCUSSION

Our findings are consistent with those of other studies of suicide prevention training program evaluationswhich have shown an association between training and increased confidence in dealing with suicidal people as well as increasing knowledge of suicide risk.[10-13] Some programs have also been associated with reductions in suicidal ideation, attempts and/or deaths by suicide. [14-15] Examples of gatekeeper (or "guide") training programs beyond Operation S.A.VE. include: Applied Suicide Intervention Skills, [16] Question, Persuade and Respond, [17] and Yellow Ribbon International for Suicide Prevention.[18]

Yet, among the pharmacists and pharmacy support staff studied, older age and male gender were associated with less confident responses with regard to knowledge of suicide and the ability to "handle a suicidal veteran."

Limitations

Limitations of the *Operation SAVE* are discussed elsewhere. Specific to this evaluation of *Operation SAVE* among pharmacy staff, we identified pharmacy staff by the job titles they spelled out on their assessment forms. These job titles gave little information about the specific pharmacy setting in which the staff member worked, her duties in that setting, her experience with direct patient care, or her past training and education. Nor did we have zip code or location data from which to draw conclusions about potential differences in scope of practice by geographic region. Yet, as a national system, the VA is likely to have less variation than typical pharmacy practice across states.

Educational Intervention Considerations: Pharmacy Staff

Future Operation S.A.V.E. training efforts may benefit from relating suicide prevention directly to pharmacist skills, knowledge and abilities as well as continuing professional development. For example, training materials could be designed to highlight the likelihood that a patient at risk of suicide has passed through the pharmacy in the past (a) month, (b) year, (c) pharmacist's career. Pharmacists and pharmacy employees could be asked to calculate these frequencies themselves using [1] published statistics about suicidal ideation, suicide attempt and suicide, and [2] pharmacy patient and fill volume and the number of hours per week and years the pharmacist or pharmacy support staff person expects to work. A similar method is used to educate pharmacists about the frequency of medication errors [19]

Some pharmacists and pharmacy employees may perceive suicide prevention as being beyond the skills and responsibilities of the pharmacy staff. To address this issue, trainers might review the relevance of suicide risk monitoring to the practice of traditional pharmacy skills and practices. Specifically, pharmacists are trained to monitor patients for known adverse effects of medications. Suicidal ideation and behavior are labeled adverse effects of a wide variety of high volume medications, including antidepressants, anti-epileptics, anti-psychotics, benzodiazepines, sedative-hypnotics, opiate-agonists and at least one smoking cessation agent, antibiotic and leukotriene agonist/antagonist [20]. All pharmacists currently train in patient communication and motivational interviewing, skills that will help pharmacists meet the mandated charge to assist suicidal Veterans.

Similarly, future training events might invite a discussion from pharmacists and pharmacy staff about the potential opportunities and barriers to providing suicide prevention in various VA pharmacy practice sites. Routine pharmacist duties are likely to vary widely across clinical and non-clinical settings within an institution. Similarly, among clinical pharmacists scope of practice may vary somewhat by state.

Pharmacy staff may be concerned about acting beyond their area of professional expertise by following the Operation SAVE program goals to "encourage and expedite referral." Training materials might be developed around the analogy of reporting adverse drug reactions to the Food and Drug Administration (FDA). Just as pharmacists report potential adverse effects of drugs to the FDA without knowing exactly if a particular drug caused that particular adverse effect, so the pharmacist may – and should -- refer a patient for assessment and potential treatment without knowing if he is truly in crisis or at risk for suicide.

Providing statistics of the number of patients who die by suicide without any mental health diagnosis or pharmacotherapy may enlightenpharmacy staff. Ask them to compare the frequency with which patients visit pharmacies per month to the frequency with which patients typically visit a [1] primary care provider, and a [2] mental health specialist. Discuss the time per visit and the number of problems typically addressed in each provider visit.

Finally, the Institute of Medicine's recommendations for Continuing Professional Development (CPD) will require pharmacists to take proactive and continuing efforts to enhance practice knowledge and skills.[21] Our study results suggest that those with prior suicide prevention training were more likely to agree or completely agree that they were prepared to handle a suicidal Veteran. Operation SAVE provides an example of an employer-defined knowledge and skill-based development need that may be met through a combination of mandated training and self-directed continual learning.

ACKNOWLEDGMENTS

Heather von Bergen, PhD (in memoriam) led the design of the early SAVE Program.

CONCLUSION

After Operation SAVE training, a higher proportion of pharmacy staff reported that they knew enough about suicide and that it was their job to help suicidal Veterans, compared to other VA employees. Yet, among pharmacy staff, men and older pharmacists were less likely to report that they were prepared to handle a suicidal veteran.

Future efforts to support pharmacists and pharmacy staff in meeting the VA program objectives to [1] identify, [2] counsel and [3] refer patients who may be at risk of suicide, may be even more effective if those programs tie directly to pharmacist skills, knowledge, scope of practice and continuous professional development needs. Examples include monitoring of adverse effects of drugs, patient communication and motivational interviewing.

Operation SAVE may be useful to pharmacists in other settings. To our knowledge, it is the only guide training program that is free to both students and trainers and does not require a license agreement.

REFERENCES

[1]   Centers for Disease Control and Prevention. National Suicide Statistics at a Glance: Twenty Leading Causes of Death Highlighting Suicide Among Persons Ages 10 Years and Older, United States, 2006. Last accessed on August 8, 2011 at: http:// www.cdc.gov/ViolencePrevention/suicide/statistics/leading_causes.html.

[2]   Centers for Disease Control and Prevention. Injury Prevention Research Agenda: Suicide. Last accessed on August 8, 2011 at:http://www.cdc.gov/injury/Research Agenda/pdf/Suicide-a.pdf

[3]   Centers for Disease Control. (2010) Understanding Suicide: Fact Sheet. Last accessed on August 8, 2011 at: http://www.cdc.gov/ViolencePrevention/pdf/Suicide-FactSheet-a.pdf.

[4]   Remarks by Secretary Eric K. Shinseki. Departments of Defense-Veterans Affairs. Suicide Prevention Conference Washington DC, January 11, 2010. Last accessed on August 8, 2011 at: http://www.va.gov/opa/speeches/2010/10_0111hold.asp.

[5]   Tarabay J. Suicide rivals the battlefield toll on US military. National Public Radio. June 17, 2010. Last accessed on-line on August 8, 2011 at: http://www.npr.org/templates/story/story.php?storyId=127860466.

[6]   Centers for Disease Control and Prevention. Suicide: Definitions. Last accessed on-line on August 8, 2011at: http://www.cdc.gov/ViolencePrevention/suicide/definitions.html.

[7]   VA Eastern Colorado Healthcare System. Blister Packaging Medication to Increase Treatment Adherence and Clinical Response (BP). Clinical Trials Identifier: NCT01118208. Last accessed on August 8, 2011, at: http://clinicaltrials.gov/ct2/show/NCT01118208.

[8]   Education, Training and Dissemination Core of the VISN 2 Center of Excellence, Canandiagua VA Medical Center. Suicide Prevention: Operation SAVE. Last accessed on August 2, 2011 at: http://www.mentalhealth.va.gov/docs/Suicide_Prevention_Community_Edition-shortened_version.pdf.

[9]   American Foundation for Suicide Prevention and Suicide Prevention Research Center. Operation S.A.V.E. VA Suicide Prevention Gatekeeper Training. Best Practices Registry Section III: Adherence to Standards. Last accessed on August 3, 2011 at: http://www2.sprc.org/sites/sprcs.org/files/Operation

[10]   Chagnon F, Houle J, Marcoux I, Renaud J. Control-group study of an intervention training program for youth suicide prevention. *Suicide Life Threat Behav*. 2007;37: 135-144.

[11]   Cross W, Matthieu MM, Levine D, Knox KL. Does a brief suicide prevention gatekeeper training program enahcne observed skills? Crisis. 2010;31:149-159.

[12]   Matthieu MM, Cross W, Batres A, Flora C, Knox K. Evaluation of gatekeeper training for suicide prevention in veterans. *Arch Suicide Res*. 2008;12:148-54.

[13]   Wyman P, Brown C, Inman J, Cross W, Schmeelk-Cone K, Guo J, et al. Randomized trial of gatekeeper program for suicide prevention: Year 1 impact on secondary school staff. *J Consult Clin Psych*. 2008;76:104-115.

[14]   Szanto K, Kalmar D, Hendin H, Rihmer Z, Mann J. A suicide prevention program in a region with a very high suicide rate. *Arch Gen Psych*. 2007;64:914-920.

[15]   Knox KL, Litts D, Talcott W, Feig J, Caine E. Risk of suifcide and related adverse outcomes after exposure to a suicide prevention programme in the US Air Force: Cohort Study. BMJ. 2003;327:1-5.

[16]   Living Works. Applied Suicide Intervention Skills Training (ASIST). Last accessed February 1, 2011 at: http://www.livingworks.net/page/Applied%20Suicide%20 Intervention%20Skills%20Training%20(ASIST).

[17]   QPR Institute. (1999) Institutional Suicide Risk Reduction Program. Last accessed February 1, 2011 at: http://qprinstitute.com/CommunitiesDH.htm.

[18]   Yellow Ribbon International, 2007. Be a link! Gatekeeper Training. Last accessed February 1 2011 at: http://www.yellowribbon.org/Training_Information.htm.

[19]   King DA, Von Bergen H, Knox KL, Wood J, Stephenson K, Chauncey L, Lu NJ, Kaukeinen K, Kemp JE. (2012) Operation S.A.V.E.: Suicide Prevention Training for Front-Line Employees in the Us Department of Veterans Health Affairs. In: Lavigne JE (Ed.) *Frontiers in Suicide Research: Risk, Prevention and Treatment*. Nova Science Publishers.

[20]   Warholak TL, West D, Holdford. (2009) Educating Pharmacists and Pharmacy Students to Improve Quality (EPIQ). Last accessed on August 8, 2011 at: http://www. pqaalliance. org /files/EPIQ-Flyer_MAR2010.pdf.

[21]   Lavigne JE, Au A, Jian R, Wang Y, Good CB, Glassman PA, Cunningham F. Utili-zation of prescription drugs with warnings of suicidal thoughts and behaviors in the US and the US Department of Veterans Affairs (VA), 2009. *Journal of Pharmaceutical Health Services Research. In press*.

[22]   Institute of Medicine. (2009) Redesigning Continuing Education in the Health Professions. Last accessed on August 8, 2011 at: http://iom.edu/Reports/2009/ Redesigning-Continuing-Education-in-the-Health-Professions.aspx.

In: Frontiers in Suicide Risk
Editor: Jill E. Lavigne

Chapter 13

COURT PERSPECTIVES ON ADDRESSING MENTAL HEALTH IN THE JUSTICE SYSTEM THROUGH COMMUNITY-BASED PARTICIPATORY RESEARCH

Ann Marie White,[1] Corey A. Nichols-Hadeed,
Henry J. Steadman[2] and Catherine Cerulli[1]
[1]University of Rochester Medical Center, Rochester, New York,
[2]Policy Research Associates, Inc., Rochester, New York

ABSTRACT

Little is known about how legal practitioners partner in research to promote mental health and prevent suicide in court settings. Community-based participatory research (CBPR) including action research promise to foster coordination and collaboration among community and academic sectors, and are innovative processes for improving court performance in mental health promotion and illness prevention. We report on the qualitative descriptive analysis of semi-structured interviews designed to illuminate court professionals' perspectives on community-academic collaborative research in mental health. Court-based professionals' insight into the feasibility and acceptability of expanding operations to include CBPR are presented. Although there are many barriers to successfully initiating and maintaining research partnerships in court-based settings, findings suggest that these can be overcome with proper project implantation and team building as well as the application of common partnership principles enumerated in the health-related CBPR literature.

INTRODUCTION

Courts are venues that address societal problems such as crime, family turmoil, and financial disruptions. As a result, many people coming into contact with justice systems experience extreme health burdens, including suicidal thoughts and attempts. Expanding evidence-based suicide prevention into the justice system will require active community engagement to build prevention initiatives and research [1]. Yet, little is known about whether and how legal practitioners (e.g., judges and court professionals), court consumers (e.g., defendants and victims), and stakeholders (e.g., voting constituencies or child welfare professionals), might partner in action-research and related scientific processes to promote mental health in court settings.

Methods to foster courts' adoption of evidence-based suicide prevention in higher-risk communities are needed. Mental and behavioral disorders remain unaddressed public health concerns, with noted racial and ethnic disparities in treatment seeking [2][3][4]. Courts and criminal justice systems are themselves formal community responses to drug or alcohol abuse and violence. These risk factors for mental illness and suicide are significant among adult and youth court consumers. Estimates of the proportion of children with a diagnosable mental health disorder in the juvenile justice system are as high as 70 to 100 percent [5]. Researchers have partnered with public schools to test interventions toimpart knowledge, build skills, mold the attitudes of trainees, and reduce suicide attempts and suicides [6], yet courts remain largely operationally distinct from explicit suicide prevention and related research initiatives, with a few exceptions [7].

Alignment with Court Missions. The promotion of mental health through court systems has begun to occur through the therapeutic justice movement. "Courts" are broadly defined as the civil and criminal justice court systems. While distinct in case processing and adjudication, both systems address social and public health issues, apply therapeutic justice approaches to behavioral health issues and interact with community members on a daily basis [8]. Specialty courts, such as domestic violence, drug, and mental health courts, operate with the mission to improve the quality of life of defendants, victims, and communities. Expanding research capacity in and for courts is a top priority for improving court operations, performance, and the relationships between courts and other institutions involved and affected by courts [9].

Action Research and Other Community-Based Participatory Research Approaches. Community-based participatory research (CBPR) is an umbrella concept referring to several collaborative approaches that incorporate research, action and education such as action-learning, action-research and participatory action research traditions [10]. Each draws on different intellectual traditions and emphasizes different aspects of its practice. For instance, action research and action learning are founded on the principle of cooperative inquiry, where the person owning the problem inquires about the problem with assistance from others, generating solutions and creating a wider inquiry community where broader learning benefits ensue [11][12][13]. Community may be broadly or narrowly defined, and engaged for reasons such as enhancing social equality among oppressed people or solving practical problems. In one approach, community-based organizations or groups such as churches or block clubs partner with academic researchers in selecting topics responsive to community identified priorities and in designing and disseminating research findings [14][15].

Community-based participatory research is conceptually distinct from community-partnered research. Both designs include collaborative approaches to research projects and often take place within a community (as compared to within an academic institution). The former stresses equitable and active decision-making authority across partnering community members or those affected by a study's focal topic (disease, program, policy, etc.), as well as organizational representatives and academic researchers, during all phases of the research process from inception [16]. Academic researchers adopting a community-partnered approach more often have community members in an advisory role regarding matters of science. Community needs may, as a result, be placed second to scientific needs for producing new knowledge [10][17]. See Tricket and Espino (2004) for a complete review of these research approaches.

CBPR in Court Contexts. Community-based participatory research approaches promise to foster coordination and collaboration among traditionally bifurcated community and academic sectors, and are also currently considered innovative processes for improving court performance and the quality of court programs and operations [18]. Collaborative research efforts among legal, mental health and advocacy practitioners or other court stakeholders to improve both jurisprudence and public health outcomes among court consumersexist [19], but community-based participatory research in health remains largely absent in court settings [7].

Illustrations of collaborative research approaches may be found in a variety of justice-related fields such as criminal justice,reentry, and civil rights [20][21][22]. Early examples of participatory research instruction in the U.S. undergird legendary civil rights activities that contributed to transformations in law such as Myles Horton's Highlander Center, whose trainees included Rosa Parks [23][24]. While history crystallizes CBPR's significant potential from such powerful examples, our search of legal research projects or trainings published between 2002 and 2008 in ERIC, LexisNexis, Criminal Justice Abstracts and Westlaw Campus Research yielded less than 100 total abstracts. Scarce among these were examples of CBPR in court contexts.

Research Context for the Practice of CBPR. In order for the field of community health partnerships to progress, research into community perspectives on roles and conduct of CBPR is necessary [25]. Systematic principles and guidelines for conducting successful CBPR and for evaluating CBPR partnerships in health are now emerging [16][17][26]. These efforts draw on CBPR examples across numerous fields, including environmental sciences, education, and occupational sciences [27][28][29][30]. Yet, examinations of the fit of such guidelines for CBPR in court-based contexts are lacking.

The past decade has seen the National Institutes of Health's increasing emphasis on community engagement and participatory research in clinical and translational sciences. This has both spurred and mirrored growing interest and productivity in CBPR within public health in recent years, and has begun to touch the field of suicide prevention [7]. More systematic and scientific inquiries about processes and outcomes for community engagement in health research including CBPR are now sought nationally [31][32].

Examination of educational initiatives within legal fields suggests a similar burgeoning paradigm shift, and supports further inquiry into principles for the application of CBPR in court-settings. AALS's Equal Justice Project generated many examples of community-based research courses designed to pair students and faculty researchers with community concerns and community[33]. A small number of universities and organizations have recently made commitments that increase community involvement in legal and criminal justice research to better inform legal and law enforcement policies and achieve community goals [34][35]. Scholarly activities and instruction in social and environmental justice pedagogy in legal and undergraduate education are burgeoning as well [36]. Justice pedagogy involves the study of teaching and learning processes for achieving *conscientization* [28]. In this model, active learners deepen awareness of the social and cultural realities that shape their lives and consider how to ameliorate resulting inequalities.

Although few court-specific CBPR collaborations are cited in the literature, application of CBPR principles in court-based research may produce benefits similar to those described in the health literature. [14][37]. Community-based researchers find more satisfaction when community members are fully involved in the research [38][39]. When the community is "empowered" during collaborations with researchers, results are relevant to all of the varied perspectives of everyone involved [38]. Similar feedback emerged in research involving community youth. When the roles of youth members of the community are limited, feelings of "unequal power relationships" among the collaborators result [39]. When youth became involved with all aspects of the research and participated in leadership roles, everyone reported greater success and benefits [39]. Community-based participatory research partnerships among court and academic professionals have directly led to innovative court-embedded mental health services and provider training in community-based service delivery outside of medical centers. Challenges are noted as well. For instance, incarcerated women under surveillance face difficulties in writing openly [40]. Remaining is the challenge of how to infuse CBPR principles into court improvement projects to strengthen mental health.

Aims. Our research team identified how legal practitioners engage in community collaborations that include action-research goals or CBPR in court environments. We reported on the results of a semi-structured interview process designed to illuminate court-professionals' perspectives on community and academic partnerships involving courts, CBPR principles for the conduct of mental health-related research in court-based settings, and court-based professionals' insight into the feasibility and acceptability of expanding CBPR into courts. We discuss the potential benefits of court-based health enhancement projects with CBPR principles.

METHODS

Study Design. In the fall of 2007, we identified geographically diverse urban county court systems across the country where suicide-prevention and other academic-court partnered research projects had recently been successfully implemented. From these we selected two locations in which to conduct a series of semi-structured interviews: a mid-sized Midwest county and large West Coast county., These sites were selected for their proliferation of court-based projects aimed at addressing community social problems including reentry after incarceration, child welfare, domestic violence, mental health, and substance abuse. The Midwest county had over 238,603 residents, with 80% living in its urban center [41]. The second location is among the largest cities in a heavily populated West Coast state. It is also one of the most densely populated cities in the United States, and a city noted also for its culturally diverse neighborhoods (U.S. Census Bureau, 2006).

The research team worked with consultants with whom these courts had collaborated on federal- or state-funded research projects. With assistance from academic researchers and community-based evaluators known within these two County court systems, we identified attorneys and court-based employees within departments of potential relevance to suicide prevention. We approached those nominated with phone calls and letters about participating in a semi-structured interview. We excluded court consumers from the sample selection process because our purpose was to gather input prior to the design of a brief educational workshop designed specifically for court-based professionals to introduce suicide prevention and CBPR principals and practices. After reviewing the project procedures, our Internal Review Board determined that this study was exempt from review because it did not qualify as human subject research under federal law.

Participants. Fifteen professionals agreed to participate and fourteen completed the interview process, incluidngseven from each county. Participants were employed by criminal, family and juvenile court systems as probation/diversion professionals, public defenders, prosecutorial chiefs, court-appointed advocates, and courthouse and courts systems administrators, including judges. Seven of the fourteen were audio-recorded,. Demographic information was not collected.

Data Collection. Individual semi-structured face-to-face interviews, designed to last 45-60 minutes, occurred during a single day visit to each county court location. The research teamcomprised an attorney with a PhD in Criminal Justice, and faculty members two faculty members trained in education and sociology, respectively. The entire research team interviewed each respondent at one sitting. The remaining interviews, conducted at the West Coast site were not recorded.

Interviewees granted permission to audiotape each session. We sought descriptions of professional background and their current organization's general mission, culture, and where opportunities for change in practice were occurring. None of the participants received any form of compensation for completing the interviews.

Interviews. The interviewer began each session with a brief introduction. The research team described the purpose of the interview: a) to engage in a dialogue about interviewees' views of their court's capacities in suicide prevention and research partnerships (cultural audit), including personal concerns that are rarely aired; and b) to guide the creation of an introductory curriculum module (funded by the National Institute of Mental Health (NIMH) to help courts to work with academic partners, as equals, in empirical, mental-health relevant projectsof mutual benefit..

The semi-structured interview questions required participants to reflect on their views of research and of collaboration with academic research partners. We reviewed and modified the protocol in consultation with our consultants from each study community. Participants were encouraged to discuss any research collaborations that they had been involved with and how they felt about those collaborations. We probed for attitudes about future health-related research collaborations. For instance:

1. What would facilitate your participation in health research that aims to promote programs and policies that increase the well-being and prevent adverse outcomes or illness?
2. How can we bring community driven research on suicide prevention in court systems to the forefront?

The interview questions facilitated a discussion of barriers to partnerships and strengths and assets for the conduct of partnerships. The participants were prompted to give suggestions for building strong research partnerships and lessons that could be learned in future research collaborations. We asked them to speak about any experiences with or knowledge of CBPR, and of successful curriculum or training experiences for court personnel.

Analysis. Three research team members employed a qualitative descriptive analysis [42], to tell the story from participants' viewpoints and to generate deep understanding of issues. We hand-coded responses in order to derive main themes. We independently made a preliminary list of key primary concepts linked to text, to develop what were thought to be the single ideas raised by the participants. We condensed these primary concepts into broader categories, prior to collapsing these categories into agreed upon themes.

RESULTS

The results are organized around six a-priori themes: 1) views ofresearch; 2) work environment and culture in the court setting; 3) barriers and obstacles to research partnerships; 4) strengths of forming research partnerships; 5) essential principles of a strong partnership; and 6) relevance of mental health and suicide prevention related programmatic objectives.

Views ofRresearch. Most participants were familiar with academic research models relevant to courts and could draw on varied examples. Some described less beneficial "fly-by" projects where researcher demands required court staff resources to help with file reviews and interviews. Some spoke of having been deeply involved as advisors on long-term academic projects of direct relevance to their day-to-day work, and as partners to academics truly savvy and sensitive to navigating court culture.

Individuals in the court-based settings expressed caution towards involvement in academic-partnered research, describing it as impersonal and boring or disconnected from their day-to-day work. Court professionalsreported being reluctant and distrustful participants in court-led administrative evaluation efforts, for instance to count services delivered or rates of recidivism, when these are perceived as being linked to high stakes political agendas such as de-funding programs.

However, participants reportedseeing promise in courts as site for research. All provided a balanced view and articulated practical potential benefits, such asresearch-funded resources to enable Court professionals to step away from business as usual to examine inefficiencies, to provide insight into potential solutions to daily problems, and to generate evidence of what works or does not work. Specific comments from participants included:

> "I like the idea of research because the truth is we spend too much time reacting to things rather than actually find out what is going on. And you can get into reactive mode of operations." (Participant 2)

> "If you have data it can give you a tremendous amount of information of what you have…it can drive you in many places." (Participant 7)

Some participants expressed frustration with their colleagues' hesitation to use research as a tool for making improvements. Participants reported that their colleagues failed to see the potential of research to lighten workloads, to go beyond siloed data to study complete cases that might suggest system reforms, to re-ignite lost passions, and to get a chance to go beyond routines to do something new and different. One participant felt research could be beneficial but that there needed to be more individuals open to the idea of research partnerships. Some felt that court personnel should collaborate with other outside institutions who could provide different perspectives. Participants pointed that academic researchers can contribute to innovative problem solving in the court based setting.

> "You need to be a researcher...I want to say a visionary...you really do need that kind of outlook". (Participant 5)

Participants noted that researchers can afford an opportunity to the courts, to be an outside or neutral voice to lead inquiry into the merits or policies or programs, for instance, when staff felt disempowered and unable to question these with any efficacy from within the system. Yet, some voiced reluctance to participate due to the belief that the data would be not applied well, if at all. They recognized that a large constituency of peers, including administrators, existed who still didn't see the value of data or measurement.

> It kind of seems like you hit a brick wall when you get to the level of the worker. (Participant 6)

Court-based Working Environment and Culture. Court-based cultures may present hurdles to those interested in research collaborations. Interviewees described a "daily grind" of time-sensitive, high volume caseloads and handled by a relatively small staff.

> "There is a lot of frustration from just the caseload". (Participant 2)

> "We are extremely overwhelmed, how are we expected to take on more than we already do?"(Participant 1)

In addition to time-economy limitations presented by court work environments, fiscal resource limitations and burnout were quoted as being commonplace in the court-based work environment.

> "We gave up the idea of fixing problems a long time ago." (Participant 2)

Despite the descriptions of court cultures as being high-paced, stressful, intractable to change, and hierarchical, participants recognized that many of their colleagues did have positive intentions and were often looking for ways to better manage programming and policy.

> "The system is flawed...but you have genuinely good people working in the system who wan to improve the situation and the lives of the people they can help." (Participant 1)

One common area of frustration among employees was a feeling of ineffectiveness due to a lack of feedback from clients.

> "The problem with working in the court is you never know if you are making an impact or not. It is easy to burn out when you are not getting feedback." (Participant 1)

A theme from respondents was eliciting feedback from and responding directly to various consumers and clients, including youth. For instance, some respondents noted the presence of a vocal body of "crusty" workers in the system who would not listen, as equals, to consumers who they saw as unable to "figure out their own lives." Some spoke passionately about past work experiences that engaged the community directly, and saw these as innovations worth backing. For instance, one participant spoke of being, early in her career, at the vanguard of a national community prosecution movement that placed prosecutors in partnerships with neighborhood residents to help neighborhood blocks deal effectively with quality of life problems as well as criminal complaints. Another participant spoke of the value of new approaches, led by outsiders, to engage adjudicated youth through the arts and other innovative approaches.

Some participants described their working environments as being comprised of several cultures all working together, which can also be statutorily driven as in the case of prosecutors being placed in an adversarial position to defendants.

"Although we get along very well, there are different cultures within the office" (Participant 2)

Yet, some participants also recognized that positional power can drive a new, uniform culture by infusing practice standards that all staff under them must conform to in order to successfully maintain their employment.

Barriers and Obstacles to Research Collaborations. Specific barriers to successful research collaboration in court-based settings were identified. A lack of contact with academics and a mutual lack of outreach were noted frequently. An overwhelming feeling that the criminal justice system is generally resistant to change was also frequently reported.

"The criminal justice system does not change easily or quickly." (Participant 5)

The most frequently cited obstacle was the lack of trust between agencies that might collaborate on research. Policy burdens were often cited as an obstacle to forming successful relationships.

"Program and policy drives so much of how we operate." (Participant 4)

The politics found in the court-based setting left some feeling that research partnership decisions were at the sole discretion of administrators and that other members of the court staff would have little say, if any, in regards to research.

"It (the partnership decision) is usually a decision made in a vacuum." (Participant 1)

As noted in the previous section, court personnel expressed that time restrictions would be a significant barrier to establishing a strong partnership and conducting research activities. Yet, while discussing major hurdles, some were hopeful collaboration was not impossible.

"Time, time away…but it is not undoable." (Participant 4)

Confidentiality was another key issue that participants saidcould create a significant challenge to research conducted in a court setting. One participant cited "keeping names confidential" as their biggest concern with research collaboration.

"Here we have many cases where files are kept non-public." (Participant 6)

Strengths of Research Collaborations/ Elements of a Strong Partnership. Participants felt that research collaborations were beneficial for a variety of reasons. Many felt that programs could be developed more efficiently with input from research. Research results could be used to validate changes in policy and programming. One participant felt that although policy changes would be more difficult to achieve, collaborative research could creatively influence court-based programming.

"Policy is pretty constricted; here is how you have to behave. Programming can be much more creative and driven by research." (Participant 4)

The following ideas about what makes a strong research partnership were described by participants:Trust and experience with court partners, having proximity and familiarity with court ways of doing business, and being engaged in high quality research. Some participants had experience with research partnerships and shared lessons from their experiences. Communication was mentioned repeatedly as the most critical element of a strong partnership. For instance, providing clear communication about research operations and specifying the time needed for communication among partners are valued principles. There was an emphasis on ensuring that there was balanced representation among all involved, that the researcher was timelyand current about court systems needs, and designed research likely to strengthen court effectiveness.

"If you are going to have a plan as a group, each one of you has to have a plan too...so tell us what you got". (Participant 7)

Court-based employees felt that everyone involved should have complete transparency with the other partners so that research objectives and procedures were clear. In addition, all partners would have to have a strong knowledge base and complete understanding of the research goals and procedures. One participant reflected on critical initial steps to collaborating with academic researchers. When researchers presented collaborative ideas, specific requirements were considered.

"When they [researchers] present it to you as: A. We are not going to take too much time from staff...very little imposition on us; and B. the ultimate goal, what are they trying to do, how is it going to help us...are we really trying to break the cycle of violence, they are going to give us insight as to what is really happening."(Participant 5)

An emerging theme was that only with open communication, proper training, and clear mutual benefitwill court-based research initiatives would benefit all partners. Respondents experienced with academic-court research partnerships reported a positive change in attitudes and perspectives over the course of the research. Those who participated in the research came to understand that more "good" could be accomplished if they knew more about themselves as a group. Although it took some time, participants reflected that the academic research teams and the community partners realized the benefits gained from the collaborations.

Relevance of Mental Health and Suicide Prevention Research Objectives. A common theme among participants was the recognition that mental health burdens are present among adult court consumers. Yet, common also were acknowledgements that while present, addressing mental health needs were often beyond their scope of practice, training and explicit public missions. Rather, mental heatlh was perceived asrequiring interventions by psychiatrists and other health professionals. Some exceptions were noted such as mental health courts, and acute mental illness during prosecutions,parole or probation reentry planning.

Community-academic-court partnerships were frequently cited as a means for court-linked systems to better address mental health of client concerns, for instance, through the provision of research-validated screening tools to be applied in casework, or via access to gatekeeper training opportunities to prevent suicide. Community-based organizations (CBOs) and academic partners are sources of infrastructure building for courts in this arena. For instance, one participant spoke of the academic-court-CBOs partnership to develop electronic information systems to enable the transfer of medical records to other clinics during community reentry from prisons and jails.

Suicide specifically, was relevant in a number of ways to court professionals' day-to-day work. Its relevance varied across professional roles. For instance, a completed suicide is as an administrative cause for case closure against a perpetrator, a risk to consider when prosecuting on a victim's behalf. For respondents workingwith adjudicated youth, suicide was cited as the worst possible outcome.

> "The second worse thing that can happen here is – kid escapes. The first worst is – we've had one suicide here in the history of this building. I wasn't here for it but I keep the file of the kid right in my desk drawer so I can be reminded". (Participant 4)

CONCLUSION

Communities rely on court systems to manage community mental health– frequently defined as one's ability to adequately adjust to the demands of life. Findings suggest that communities might consider using CBPR principles in court improvement projects to address consumer health. Although there are many barriers to successfully initiating and maintaining research partnerships in court-based settings, our findings include barriers that may be overcome with proper project implantation and team building, and the application of common-ground principles of effective partnerships enumerated in the health-related CBPR literature [16][43].

Action-research and other CBPR methods may also provide a means to catalyze related suicide prevention for court-involved consumers, as well as other court innovations, so courts may better improve community health in responding to their mission to strengthen communities' quality of life. A key step in action research is to identify the driving and restraining forces for organizational change [44]. Our court-based interviews identified agents within court settings who can see the benefit of engaging in outcomes-driven and action-research projects, who articulate challenges that they see as surmountable or worth trying, and who seek information about future trainings in CBPR to build supportive networks and practices. This research helped assess feasibility and acceptability of mental health and research partnerships among operational heads of county family, juvenile and criminal court-involved systems.

Court-systems have several dualities. Courts both empower and are highly empowered community institutions. Supporting the rights of one person may come at the cost of another. Courts are structures that also have the potential to be a negative point of contact for health by perpetuating social inequalities that contribute to health disparities. In addition to being a means for catalyzing system and community capacity changes [43], evidence supports the hypothesis that CBPR is a means to address health disparities among populations via empowerment processes [45][46][47]. Therefore, CBPR may provide immediate benefit to participants. Traditional methods of investigator-driven research place the researcher as the expert and the community member as the novice. This can reinforce problems of inequality experienced by court-based community members in everyday life (e.g., victims who have been marginalized by a perpetrator) and negatively affect health, and can undermine research by overlooking community experiences and cultures that can affect the relevancy and validity of the investigator-driven research. CBPR, an approach that empowers all partners in the research including community stakeholders, may offer vehicle to buttress the role of courts in improving the health and as well as the quality of life of communities. Several factors known to influence the pace of innovation [48] may apply to integrating CBPR into courts. Yet, even the most basic of CBPR principles, such as knowing "who the community is", can pose a challenge . Prosecutors may define the community as comprising the citizens whom they protect. Public defenders may view their community as the defendants they represent. Family court judges may view the court community as the children who reside in the families whose cases are being adjudicated. Care must be brought to understand who the community is as well as defining the population focus of the research, in order to include those voices at the table. Our work is limited by the lack of inclusion of court consumers as interview participants. Further CBPR methods development, to move beyond engagement of court-based professionals in order to include court-consumers, in court-based CBPR and action research, is likely needed.

Understanding the strengths of research partners is also critical. One of the most significant obstacles to CBPR described by the participants was the issue of time restrictions and the large volume of work. Research partners must foster open communication and strong support among the court-based partners to overcome these perceived limitations to research. The strength of research partners may be resources, in the way of research assistants or students, who can help reduce the burden of research on court staff. Likewise, the strength of the court partner may be that they have the necessary expertise to design and implement the study, as well as access to the data and a unique understanding of the policy implications for the findings. Unique contributions of each research team member – both academic and practitioner – make for a successful project. All research members must be respected for their contributions, involved in all stages of the project planning. Researchers cannot expect court staff to assume data collection, coding or entering responsibilities.

Sharing of researchresponsibilities is only the beginning. It is equally important for the resources, information gained, and learning to be shared among the community partners.

Some participants shared a sense of hopelessness that the findings of research are never put into place. Community-based participatory research is a promising approach for further fostering court partnerships in health as it, by definition, demands equity among partners in all stages of the research. The desire of academics to preference epistemology, or who knows what and how, can be balanced with the engine of courts, the political enterprises focused on who pays, who saves, and at what cost.

Guidance from government agencies, such as the Agency for Healthcare Research and Quality (AHRQ), and examples of past successes, can begin to build the foundation for strong and more trusted relationships. Courts, while empowered community institutions, are not immune toexploitative research practices. Community-based participatory research, in emphasizing mutual benefit and processes that establish equity among all partners – is tailored to address court needs. Our interview results demonstrate that there are court employees who are already serving as resources to foster CBPR by identifying barriers and providing solutions. Open communication prior to commencing a research relationship will provide all partners with a strong sense of how obstacles can be approached. Feedback provided by court employees indicated a strong interest in becoming more involved in research partnerships to inform policy and programming. Results could also foster a sense of accomplishment among court personnel.

The dynamic nature of the courts provides an ideal setting for solving many problems faced in the civil and criminal systems, as well as other social and related health and health care access issues handled through the legal system [49]. Additional outreach to the courts by academic researchers will provide opportunities for conducting perhaps better, more informed research, in the courts. Many court personnel have not even considered research partners as a means to strengthening policy and programming. However, courts alone cannot accomplish their mission to improve community quality of life. Strengthening urban communities' quality of life and mental health are related trans-disciplinary phenomenon [50]. Trans-disciplinary action research models that facilitate inter-sector scientific collaborative teams [51] among community members, legal professionals and academics can be considered a practical, potentially feasible means to innovate courts in order to both maximize their mission delivery and how this system contributes to mental health in the community.

ACKNOWLEDGMENTS

This research was supported by grants from the National Institute of Mental Health (Phase II SBIR Contract No. HHS-N-271-2007-74101-C, Under NIMH Topic 045; K01MH75965; R25MH68564). We wish to thank Gerald Eisman, Adam Haim, Amanda Holbrook, Catherine Kothari, James A. Wiley, Alice Wu and Rena Wu for their support of this project.

REFERENCES

[1]   Lezine D, Reed G. Political Will: A Bridge between Public Health Knowledge and Action. *Am. J Public Health.* 2007;97(11).

[2]   Caine ED, Knox KL. New Freedom Commission on Mental Health: Preventing Suicide and Reducing the Burden of Suicidal Behaviors. 2002.

[3]   World Health Organization. The World Health Report 2001, Mental Health: New Understanding, New Hope. 2001.

[4]   Wells K, Klap R, Koike A, et al. Ethnic disparities in unmet need for alcoholism, drug abuse, and mental health care. *Am. J Psychiatry.* 2001;158(12):2027.

[5]   Cocozza JJ, Shufelt JL. Juvenile mental health courts: An emerging strategy. 2006.

[6]   Isaac M, Elias B, Katz LY, et al. Gatekeeper Training as a preventative intervention for suicide: a systematic review. *Can. J Psychiatry.* 2009;54(4):260-268.

[7]   White AM, Cerulli K. Preventing Suicide Using the CBPR Model. Presented at: Challenges to the Development and Implementation of Community-Based Participatory Research in Mental Health and Suicide Prevention, Rochester, (NY), 2008.

[8]   Daicoff S. *Law as a Healing Profession: The Comprehensive Law Movement.* Pepp.Disp.Resol.LJ. 2006;6:1.

[9]   Mahoney B, Tashiro S. *Developing an OJP Initiative on Courts and the Justice System:* Report on a Planning Group Meeting. 2001.

[10]   Trickett E, Espino S. Collaboration and Social Inquiry: Multiple Meanings of a Construct and its Role in Creating Useful and Valid Knowledge. *Am. J. Community Psychol.* 2004(34):1-69.

[11]   Marquardt M. Action Learning. Palo Alto, CA: Davies-Black Publishing; 1999.

[12]   Fisher D, Rooke D, Torbet B. Personal and Organizational Transformations Through Action Inquiry. Boston, MA: Edge/Work Press; 2001.

[13]   Reason P, Bradbury H. Handbook of Action Research. Thousand Oaks, CA: Sage; 2001.

[14]   Agency for Healthcare Research and Quality. AHRQ Activities Using Community-Based Participatory Research to Address Health Care Disparities. September 2009(AHRQ Publication No. 09-P012). Available at www.ahrq.gov/research/cbprbrief.htm.

[15]   White AM, Funchess M, Sellars C, et al. Neighborhood Natural Helpers as Community-based Participatory Research Partners - Mental Health Promotion and Violence Prevention in Urban Neighborhoods. *Presented at the Sixth World Conference on the Promotion of Mental Health and Prevention of Mental and Behavioral Disorders.* Washingon, D.C., 2010.

[16]   Israel BA, Schulz AJ, Parker EA. Review of community-based research assessing partnership approached to improve public health. *Annu Rev Public Health.* 1998;19:173-174-202.

[17]   Viswanathan M, Ammerman A, Eng E, et al. Community-based participatory research: assessing the evidence. 2004.

[18]   Remple M, Rossman SB. Action Research: Using Research to Improve your Drug Court. New York: Center for Court Innovation; 2005.

[19]   Ballou M, Tabol C, Liriano D, et al. Initial development of a psychological model for judicial decision making in continuing restraining orders. *Family Court Review.* 2007;45(2):274-286.

[20]   Parsons ML, Warner-Robbins RC. Formerly incarcerated women create healthy lives through participatory action research. *Holist Nurs Pract.* 2002;16(2):40.

[21]   Freudenberg N. Adverse Effects of US jail and prison policies on the health and well-being of women of color. *Am J Public Health.* 2002;92:1895-1899.

[22]   Puckett J, Harkavy I. The action research tradition in the United States: Towards a strategy for revitalizing the social sciences, the University, and the American city. In: Greenwood DJ, ed. Action research: From practice to writing in an international action research development program. Philadelphia, PA: John Benjamins Publishing Company; 1999:147-168.

[23]   Adams F, Horton M. Unearthing seeds of fire: The idea of Highlander. John F. Blair Publisher; 1975.

[24]   Highlander Research and Education Center. A brief survey of Highlander's history, philosophy, and links to the field of adult education. Available at http://www.paulofreireinstitute.org/Documents/highlander-1.html.

[25]   Tandon SD, Phillips K, Bordeaux B, et al. A vision for progress in community health partnerships. Progress in Community Health Partnerships: Research, Education, and Action. 2007;1(1):11-30.

[26]   Ahmed SM, Palermo AGS. Community Engagement in Research: Frameworks for Education and Peer Review. *Am J Public Health.* 2010;100(8):1380.

[27]   Kinney PL, Aggarwal M, Northridge ME, et al. Airborne concentrations of PM (2.5) and diesel exhaust particles on Harlem sidewalks: a community-based pilot study. Environ Health Perspect. 2000;108(3):213.

[28]   Freire P. *Pedagogy of the Oppressed.* New York: Herder and Herder. 1970.

[29]   Pless-Mulloli T, Dunn CE, Bhopal R, et al. Is it feasible to construct a community profile of exposure to industrial air pollution? Occup Environ Med. 2000;57:542-549.

[30]   Wing S, Cole D, Grant G. Environmental injustice in North Carolina's hog industry. Environ Health Perspect. 2000;108(3):225.

[31]   Cook J. Improving Health WITH Communities: The Role of Community Engagement in Clinical and Translational Research. 2009;Natcher Conference Center, National Institutes of Health May 14-15, 2009. Available at http://www.ncrr.nih.gov/clinical_research_resources/clinical_and_translational_science_awards/publications/Improving_Health_WITH_Communities_The_Role_of_Community_Engagement_in_Clinical_and_Translational_Research.pdf.

[32]   Alving B, Bonham A, Norris K. Partnering to Improve Health: The Science of Community Engagement. Presented at: 3rd Annual Conference of the Association for Prevention Teaching and Research. May 13-14, 2010. http://www.aptrweb.org/prof_dev/ce_presentations.html.

[33]   Smith A, Christopher S, McCormick AKHG. Development and implementation of a culturally sensitive cervical health survey: a community-based participatory approach. Women Health. 2004;40(2):67-86.

[34]   University of California, Berkeley School of Law. Courses at Boalt. Available at http://www.berkeley.edu/courses/coursePage.php?cD=5934. Updated 2007. Accessed June 1, 2010.

[35]   Tri-State Regional Community Policing Institute, Course Descriptions. Available at http://www.tri-statercpi.org. Accessed January 7, 2008.

[36]   Ansley F, Cochran C. Going On-Line with Justice Pedagogy: Four Ways of Looking at a Website. 2005;50:875.

[37] Blanck P, Ritchie H, Schmeling JA, et al. Technology for Independence: A Community-Based Resource Center. Behav Sci Law. 2003;21(1):51-62.

[38] Reardon KM. Promoting Community/University Partnerships That Work: Lessons from the East St. Louis Action Research Project (ESLARP). Conference on Clinical Legal Education Web site. Available at http://www.aals.org/profdev/clinical2002/reardon.html. Published 2002. Updated 2002. Accessed January 3, 2008.

[39] Harvard Family Research Project. Juvenile Justice Evaluation Project. The Evaluation Exchange, V(1). Available at http://gse.harvard.edu/hfrp/eval/issue13/pp2.html. Published 1999. Updated 1999. Accessed January 3, 2008.

[40] Fine M, Torre ME, Boudin K, et al. Participatory action research: From within and beyond prison bars. *Working method: Research and social justice.* 2004:95–119.

[41] U.S. Bureau of the Census. Statistical Abstract of the United States: 2000. 2000;120th Ed(Washington, DC: US Bureau of the Census).

[42] Sandelowski M. Whatever happened to qualitative description? *Res Nurs Health.* 2000;23(4):334-340.

[43] Wallerstein N, Oetzel J, Duran B, et al. What predicts outcomes in CBPR. Community Based Participatory Research for Health: Process to Outcomes.2nd ed.San Francisco, CA: Jossey-Bass. 2008:371–392.

[44] Lewin K. Action research and minority problems. *J Soc Iss.* 1946;2(4):34-46.

[45] Wallerstein N. Evidence on Effectiveness of Empowerment in Reducing Health Disparities. Geneva: Health Evidence Network, World Health Organization. 2006. www.euro.who.int/HEN.

[46] Wallerstein N. Commentary: challenges for the field in overcoming disparities through a CBPR approach. *Ethnicity and Disease.* 2006;16(1):1.

[47] Wallerstein N, Duran B. Using Community-Based Participatory Research to Address Health Disparities. *Health Promot Prac.* 2006;7:312-23.

[48] Rogers EM. A prospective and retrospective look at the diffusion model. *J Health Commun.* 2004;9:13-19.

[49] Tenenbaum C. The Role of Lawyers in Improving Access to Care. *J Health Care Poor Underserved.* 2007;18:6-11.

[50] Rosenfeld PL. The potential of transdisciplinary research for sustaining and extending linkages between the health and social sciences. *Soc Sci Med.* 1992;35:1343-1357.

[51] Stokols D. Toward a science of transdisciplinary action research. *Am. J Community Psychol.* 2006;38(1):63-77.

THE ECONOMICS OF SUICIDE
AND SUICIDE PREVENTION

In: Frontiers in Suicide Risk
Editor: Jill E. Lavigne

ISBN 978-1-62081-373-7
©2012 Nova Science Publishers, Inc.

Chapter 14

Determinants of Suicidal Ideation and Behavior, Economic Theories of Suicidal Behavior and the Economics of Prevention

Alper Altinanahtar and Nazmi Sari

Department of Economics, Yeditepe University, Istanbul, Turkey
Department of Economics, University of Saskatchewan, Canada

ABSTRACT

Suicide dates back to the earliest historical records of humankind. In 2010, almost one million people committed suicide, which corresponds to a mortality rate of 16 per 100,000 people. There are also significant numbers of suicide attempts for every completed suicide, especially for young people. The economics literature documents a substantial cost of suicide. These costs include ambulance services, hospitalization, autopsy services and other healthcare and mental health services for the person who dies by suicide as well as family members, friends and significant others. Additional economic costs include the value of the life lost and productivity loss.

Economists have started to study suicide, including its economic determinants and the economic evaluation of suicide prevention programs. In this chapter, we provide a brief review of these two areas. Lessons learned and directions for further research are highlighted.

1. INTRODUCTION

Suicide occurs among people of all ages, educational and socio-economic backgrounds. The phenomenon dates back to the earliest historical records of humankind. Currently, almost one million people died from suicide each year, or about 16 per 100,000 people. This amounts to one death every 40 seconds. More than half of the people who die by suicide are ages 15 to 44 (WHO 2011).

Suicide rates vary significantly by culture and country. Rates in Jamaica, Syria, Egypt, Honduras, and Haiti are among the lowest (0.0 to 0.1 per 100,000). The average rate in

Europe is 13.9 per 100,000 with the highest rates in the Commonwealth of Independent States (21.4 per 100,000) followed by the new European Union countries (13.8 per 100,000). With a 30.7 per 100,000 people, Lithuania has the highest suicide rate followed by Hungary (21.5 per 100,000), Finland (18.5 per 100,000), and Slovenia (18.4 per 100,000) (WHOEurope 2011). On the eastern side of the world, Pakistan has the lowest suicide rate (<3 per 100,000), while China, Japan, the Republic of Korea, and Sri Lanka all have suicide rates above 20 per 100,000 population (WHO 2008). According to 2007 statistics, suicide is the 11th leading cause of death for all ages, all races and both sexes in the U.S., and it is the 2nd leading cause of death for those aged 25 to 34 (CDC 2007).

It is likely that reported rates underestimate the actual suicide rate. As indicated by several researchers, suicide has been misclassified in death records. For instance, Rockett and McKinley (1999) state that suicide is commonly classified as unintentional poisoning, drowning, or undetermined death, while Douglas (1967) indicates that suicides are also classified as accidents or homicides. A potential correlation between vehicle accidents and suicide deaths has also been documented (Peck and Warner 1995). As a result of misclassification, underestimation of suicide rates is likely. In fact, under reporting may be by as much as 10 to 20% (Kleck 1988). Suicide rates also exclude attempts, and for every death by suicide there are likely several attempts (Goldsmith et al. 2002; Farberow and Shneidman 1961). The number of attempts has been estimated at 100 to 200 attempts for every completed suicide among people aged 15 to 24. (Goldsmith et al. 2002).

The relatively high rate of suicide and suicidal behavior across the world has important cost implications for society. The cost of a suicide or a suicide attempt includes ambulance services, hospitalization, autopsy services and other healthcare and mental health services due to pain and suffering for the individual who attempted suicide as well as his/her family members, friends and significant others. Relevant costs also include the value of the life lost and productivity loss.

Economists have begun to study suicide, particularly its economic determinants and the economic evaluations of various suicide prevention programs. In this chapter, we provide a review of this literature, including risk factors for suicide based on the empirical literature and economic theories of suicidal behavior. Finally, we describe suicide prevention programs in various countries, and examine economic evaluation methods for suicide prevention programs and policies.

2. SOCIAL AND ECONOMIC DETERMINANTS OF SUICIDE

2.1. Health Behavior and Medical Risk Factors

The most commonly cited risk factor associated with suicide are mental disorders, which may be accompanied by symptoms of hopelessness, impulsivity, loneliness, anxiety or even psychosis (i.e., separation from reality). Most suicides involve psychiatric illness, 48.5% of which are mood disorders (Pompili et al. 2011). Other studies have found that mental disorders are associated with about 60% of completed suicides (Mann et al. 2005; Stoudemire et al. 1986; Wood, Harrington and Moore 1996). Although depression is strongly associated with suicide, it is neither a necessary nor sufficient cause of suicide. Many depressed individuals do not attempt suicide, and non-depressed individuals are known to exhibit suicidal behaviors. For example, women have a higher prevalence of diagnosed depression but a lower suicide rate than men (Ross, Yakovlev and Carson 2010). Mitra and Shroff (2008) explain this by women's effectiveness in expressing their emotions compared to men. Steen and Mayer (2003), on the other hand, claim that women are more likely to hold religious beliefs and negative attitudes towards suicides. Finally, men generally tend to adopt violent and assured suicide methods which are more likely to end individual's life whereas women adopt gentler methods which often prove to be unsuccessful in completing the task (Mitra and Shroff 2008).

Suicidal behavior may be triggered by physical problems, such as infertility. Using panel data from 15 European countries, Andrés (2005) showed that besides economic growth and alcohol consumption, infertility rates are significantly associated with male and female suicide rates (Also see Mäkinen 1997; Mathur and Freeman 2002; Chen, Choi and Sawada 2008). In a recent Danish study Andrés and Halicioglu (2010) confirm this association.

Heavy alcohol consumption causes lack of social integration and also increases the probability of committing violent acts (such as dying by suicide) during states of acute intoxication (Neumayer 2003; Rodriguez 2005). According to the CDC (2009), in a study of 16 US states using Blood Alcohol Concentration (BAC) tests, 72.5% of all subjects who died by suicide were tested for BAC and 33.3% tested positive for intoxication. Of those who tested positive, 56.3% had BAC levels greater than 0.08mg/dL alcohol which is above the limit of intoxication. According to the NVDRS, of the 72.5% of suicide decedents in 16 states tested for substances, one-third had alcohol in their blood system when they died and almost 20% had evidence of narcotic drugs (CDC 2009).

2.2. Economic, Social and Socio-Environmental Risk Factors

While economic studies have identified numerous determinants of suicide, causality remains unclear. Most studies assume that the reason for a major depression or suicide attempt is loss of income, unemployment or bankruptcy. For example, it has been argued that unemployment leads to a reduced level of psychological well-being (Ezzy 1993), hence it is associated with an increase in completed or attempted suicide (Platt 1984; 1986). Alternatively, suicide could be because of mental illness, unemployment or not being able to run business smoothly due to mental and psychiatric problems. Hence the validity of causality arguments should be examined in future studies.

Failure to carefully study causality has resulted in a literature about the social and economic determinants of suicide that provides contradictory evidence. For instance, the literature on the impact of economic booms and depressions provides mixed results. Durkheim (1897/2002) predicted that suicide rates would rise during both economic booms and depressions while Viren (1999), Rodriguez (2005), and Barstad (2008) claim that suicide rates should increase only during economic booms. Other studies predict that suicide rates should increase only during economic depressions (Hammermesh and Soss 1974; Neumayer 2003; Yamamura 2010; Altinanahtar and Halicioglu 2009).

The impact of female labor market participation on suicide rates is also unclear. Burr, McCall and Powell-Griner (1997) found a positive relationship between the level of female labor force participation among married women with small children and the male suicide rate based on data from 1970. Yet, when they used data from 1980, they found the opposite. Yang (1992) reported a negative relationship between both white and non-white female suicide rates and female labor force participation but a positive relationship between non-white male suicide rate and female labor force participation. Similar to Yang (1992)'s cross-state study of the U.S., Chuang and Huang (1997) do not find any significant effect of female labor force participation on Taiwan's female or male regional suicide rates. However, in a time-series context, both Yang et al. (1992) and Chuang and Huang (1995) found a significant effect of female labor force participation on total male, and female suicide rates over time. In Neumayer (2003), the effect is positive in one model which uses a small sample, but it is insignificant in the second model based on a large sample. Using data from 17 European countries, Mäkinen (1997) reports a positive relationship between female labor participation and suicide. Newman, Whittemore and Newman (1973) also suggest that female labor participation is positively associated with suicide rates of the census tracts in both Atlanta and Chicago. In another study, Stack (1987) reports a negative association for the U.S. during 1948-1980.

The association between suicide and its social and economic determinants such as income, divorce rates, urbanization, unemployment and bankruptcy has been studied by various researchers. Rather than reviewing each factor in detail, we provide a summary of these findings in Table 1.

Other social and socio-environmental factors have been shown to be associated with suicide. For instance, Koivumaa-Honkanen et al. (2001) show that personal happiness protects one against a suicide attempt. Yet, a recent paper by Daly et al. (2011) finds that the happiest places tend to have the highest suicide rates. Using micro data for more than 1 million Americans on well-being and suicide, Daly et al. (2011) argue that the level of others' happiness is a risk factor for suicide. As shown by Daly and Wilson (2009), and Daly, Wilson and Johnson (2007) when less fortunate individuals in the society begin to compare their incomes with fortunate ones' (i.e., interpersonal income comparison), the probability of dying by suicide may increase. Similarly, Jungeilges and Kirchgassner (2002) note that income redistribution, which equalizes people in a rigid way, provides disincentives to work. Eventually, this frustrates people who work harder due to insufficient returns to their efforts. In this context, personal unhappiness may worsen when compared to those who are relatively more pleased with their lives.

Intelligence may also be associated with suicidal behavior. Using data from 48 Eurasian countries, Voracek (2005) found a strong correlation between suicide rates and the national average IQ in most of the countries surveyed. Voracek argues that the higher rate of Western suicide could be because people are, on average, more intelligent. For instance, Jamaica with a low average IQ of 72 has suicide rates of 0.5 for men and 0.2 for women, while Japan with an average IQ of 102 has suicide rates of 25 for men and 12 for women per 100,000 people. One may think this positive correlation arises as a result of socioeconomic factors and urbanization or other economic factors. However Voracek (2005) insists that even when these factors are controlled, there is still a positive correlation between IQ and suicide. His findings are similar to those of Voracek (2004) and Lester (2003).

Most recently, Hansen and Lang (2011), contrary to the previous evidence, find that when school is not in session there is a significant decrease in youth suicide. However, their finding is contradictory to the previous suicide summary data provided in the National

Violent Death Reporting System (NVDRS). According to the NVDRS, out of 8,599 suicides in 16 states during 2006, the monthly suicide rate varied little throughout the year, ranging from 0.8 to 1.0 suicide per 100,000 population (CDC 2009).

Table 1. Summary of Effects of Selected Factors on Suicide Rates

	Estimation Method	Main findings by selected independent variables			
		Y	D	U	BU
Quinney (1965)	DS			+	
Hammermesh and Soss (1974)	CS, TS	-			
Platt (1984; 1986)	CS, TS				+
Kowalski, Faupel, Starr (1987)	OLS			+	
Stack (1989)	OLS, TS		+		+
Yang and Lester (1992; 1994)	OLS, TS				+
Rossow (1993)	TS		+		
Yang and Lester (1995)	TS				+
Lester and Yang (1998)	TS		+		
Viren (1999)	OLS, TS, CS	+		+	+
Ruhm (2000)	IV, TS				+
Gerdtham and Johannesson (2003)	DS, PR				+
Neumayer (2003)	PD	-	+	+	
Rodriguez (2005)	PD	+	+		+
Granados (2008)	TS	-			+
Barstad (2008)	TS	+	+		-
Suzuki (2008)	TS				-
Yamamura (2010)	PD	-	+		-
Koo and Cox (2008)	TS, PD, OLS		+		+
Jungeilges and Kirchgassner (2002)	CS, LG,	+			
Altinanahtar and Halicioglu (2009)	TS	-		+	+
Andrés (2005)	TS,PD	-	+		+
Andrés and Halicioglu (2010)	TS	-		+	
Mäkinen (1997)			+		
Chen, Choi and Sawada (2010)	IV		+		
Chen, Choi and Sawada (2009)	CS	-			
Stevenson and Wolfers (2006)	PD, OLS		+*		
Blakely, Collings and Atkinson (2003)	LR				+
Singh and Mohammad (2002)	MR, PR			-	
Minoiu and Andrés (2008)	PD		+		+
Inagaki (2010)					+
Lewis and Sloggett (1998)	TS, LR				+
Chuang and Huang (1997)		-	+		+

Abbreviations in the table are as follows.

Variables: Y: per capita income, D: divorce, U: urbanization, BU: bankruptcy/unemployment.

Estimation methods: OLS: Ordinary Least Squares, IV: Instrumental Variables, TS: Time Series, CS: Cross Section, PD: Panel Data, DS: Descriptive Statistics, PR: Probit Regression, LG: Logit Regression, MR: Multiple Regression, PR: Poisson Regression.

Note: This table is a revised and expanded version of the summary table presented in Altinanahtar and Halicioglu (2009). We provide selected findings from each study. * indicates positive relationship between divorce rates and suicide rates for women only.

3. SUICIDE THEORIES: A BRIEF REVIEW OF THE ECONOMICS LITERATURE

Hammermesh and Soss (1974) were among the first to develop "an economic theory of suicide on the basis of the argument that much of the variation in aggregate suicide rates is due to economic decision making and, therefore, such variation can be explained by using economic models" (Molina and Duarte 2006, p.407). In this section, we provide a very brief overview of economic theories of suicide. Interested readers can find detailed reviews of this literature elsewhere (Chen et al. 2011; Lester 1989, 2004; Lester and Yang 1997).

3.1. Cost-Benefit Theories of Suicide

A rational individual (as defined in consumer theory in economics), uses a simple cost-benefit principle to choose a "consumption bundle" from among all of the available goods and services to buy and actions to take. By comparing the net benefit (i.e., net satisfaction) derived from competing alternatives, individuals make choices to maximize their net benefit given resource constraints and the information available to them. This simple principle can be applied to a decision to take a vacation, to start a business or to pursue higher education. It can even be applied to a decision to attempt suicide or to die by suicide.

Based on this cost-benefit principle, an individual will choose to die by suicide if her expected benefits from ending his/her life exceed the costs associated with the action. In a simplified version, Hammermesh and Soss (1974) suggest that a suicidal person would compare his/her expected lifetime utility to the utility from committing suicide. In other words, an individual's expected benefit from living the remaining life is compared to the benefit from ending it.

According to Yeh and Lester (1987) and Lester and Yang (1997), costs associated with committing suicide include monetary values and physical effort spent in the procurement of necessary information and means of suicide. Since the suicidal individual will no longer generate future income, expected future earnings should be considered as a part of the cost of committing suicide. The committed individual must also consider the physical pain and fear of death associated with the attempt. Given that most of the major religions of the world condemn suicide, individuals will also consider any expected punishment after death. Finally, there are the opportunity costs of any expected foregone enjoyment from living.

The benefits from suicide, on the other hand, include avoiding further physical or mental pain, anticipation of the impact of the individual's death on others (i.e. guilt or increase in their wealth through life insurance payments (see Chen, Choi and Sawada 2008)), or restoring one's public image (i.e. traditional suicide (see Chen, Choi and Sawada 2009)). In addition, as suggested by Lester and Yang (1997), suicide action may be enjoyable. Especially after the beginning of the 21st century, extreme sports became very popular all around the world. One of the reasons these activities became so popular is the amount of adrenaline and other hormones released during the activity that provide a natural "high". Similarly, an individual contemplating suicide may consider as a benefit the natural "high" they may experience from the action of taking her life.

One can easily argue that the cost and benefit of suicide may not be clear to prior to a suicide attempt. The decision involves uncertainty. Individuals will not know with certainty the impact of their action on others or even themselves. Therefore, economic theory related to suicidal behavior must be studied using the theory of consumer behavior under uncertainty, an area of economics studied extensively during recent decades.

Using the cost-benefit principle, Lester and Yang (1997) developed a theory of the variation in probability of commiting suicide among individuals with similar characteristics. Their theory is based on a demand and supply framework with the probability of dying by suicide explicitly included as part of the model. In this framework, the probability of committing suicide is placed on the horizontal axis while the price and cost of committing suicide are placed on the vertical axis. As opposed to a regular demand and supply model, the demand in their framework has a positive slope. As the amount of benefit expected from suicide increases, the probability of an individual committing suicide also increases. On the other hand, when the cost of suicide from suicidal individual's point of view increases, the individual will be less likely to commit suicide. These costs include loss of life, time spent gathering information about means and time and other resources spent procuring the necessary means of suicide. Hence, the supply curve has a negative slope. The supply and demand for suicide intersect at a point where the probability of committing suicide is the same for both the equilibrium level of distress and the corresponding cost of committing suicide.

This model implies that individuals with the same level of distress may have different probabilities of dying by suicide due to differences in other characteristics including personality, education, age, sex, family background, and social environment (Lester 1983). These other factors determine the demand curve. On the supply side, there are time costs to obtain information about suicide as well as finding means of suicide, and emotional costs that include loved ones' sorrow after the individual's death, plus any pain and fear experienced during the suicide (Rosenthal 1993, Lester and Yang 1997, Sari et al. 2008). Compared to the determinants of demand, the determinants of supply are more flexible and most of them are endogenous. Any restrictions or regulations related to these determinants that make suicide more costly will decrease the probability of dying by suicide.

3.2. Suicide Theory Based on a Signaling Game

Rosenthal (1993) formulated the suicidal behavior of an individual in a game theoretical framework. In his model, there are two players; a sender and a receiver. The sender is the individual who is planning on committing suicide to manipulate the receiver's behavior in a way favorable to himself. Here the suicide attempt can be seen as a signal to the receiver. The sender may be in one of the two psychological states - depressed or normal. The sender's psychological state is unknown to the receiver and the receiver's possible response to the sender's signal is unknown to the sender. The sender can determine the strength of his signal, which may result in survival (i.e., a suicide attempt) or death (i.e., suicide).

Although the receiver may have two strategies, either to respond sympathetically or unsympathetically, Rosenthal assumes that the receiver prefers to respond sympathetically to the depressed sender but unsympathetically to the healthy sender. Naturally, both types of senders would be expected to prefer a sympathetic response. In this model, Rosenthal examines the Nash-equilibrium solution and suggests two hypotheses. First, he claims that a suicidal individual will be unlikely to engage in gambling-type suicidal behavior if he strongly demands a sympathetic response. Second, if the receiver is very likely to give a sympathetic response, the depressed sender is less likely to engage in gambling-type suicidal behavior. These findings suggest which suicide prevention methods are most likely to work.

Marcotte (2003) confirmed Rosenthal's expected outcome of the signaling game. Marcotte concludes that individuals who attempt suicide but survive report higher monetary incomes than those who considered suicide but never attempted. Notably, the magnitude of the increase in income is positively associated with the severity of the suicide attempt. The improved income of the individual may be a result of the amount of tremendous stress the individual endured during and after the suicide attempt. This may make the individual more determined or more risk-taking in his work environment than before. Marcotte also suggests that this large and immediate effect is consistent with family and friends helping the suicide attempt survivor through income transfers, care or treatment. Similarly, Rosenthal argues that individuals may use suicide attempt as a signal to others in order to get favorable treatments. Although these scenarios differ from each other, the economic outcomes of the individual who attempts suicide tend to increase in both cases.

3.3. Application of Labor Force Participation Models to Suicide

According to Huang (1997) suicidal behavior can be studied using a model derived from the labor force participation model. A labor force participation model explains how an individual decides whether to enter or exit the labor market. Similarly, a suicidal individual decides to stay or leave the "life market." In a labor force participation model, an individual supplies his labor in return for a certain market wage, and uses this wage to acquire things that increase his satisfaction. However, the individual also derives satisfaction from not working (i.e. leisure). As a result, an individual faces a tradeoff given that he has limited time. On the other hand, an individual may have other sources of income (i.e., allowances, government transfers, returns on investment). The determining factors in this utility maximization problem are the market wage and the individuals' non-labor income. In this model, the individual enters the labor market, choosing the optimum combination of work and leisure as long as the expected wage rate is greater than his/her reservation wage. If individual's reservation wage increases above the market wage due to an increase in non-labor income, then the individual chooses to leave the labor market.

Huang argues that the "life market" participant also attempts to maximize utility by remaining in the life market to earn positive returns. Here, Huang incorporates income with all dimensions of the value of life (i.e., love, health, respect, security, power, youth, and prestige) and non-labor income with parental love and endowed fortune. To earn labor income, an individual has to forgo other enjoyments such as heavy drinking or drugs, and has to face stress and pressure to achieve financial and professional goals. More importantly the individual has to forgo his leisure. Finally, the market wage rate is interpreted as the perceived opportunity or ability to earn life income for a unit of life effort.

There are two possible outcomes: the individual will choose to live (interior solution) if the perceived wage exceeds the reservation wage, otherwise the individual will choose suicide (i.e., to exit the life market) (corner solution). The corner solution may be preferable due to a reduction in the expected wage which may be a result of a number of extreme events (such as loss of a loved one, divorce, or disgrace) or due to an increase in the reservation wage that may be attributable to the increase in non-labor income. Huang suggests that as an individual gets wealthier and more famous, his utility from life wealth diminishes and as a result of his boredom he may pursue other experiences and may find the corner solution (i.e. suicide) more desirable. Labor market and life market participation theories have some similarities, however an individual who leaves the "life market" can of course never change his mind or reverse his course and return to the life market as one can return to the labor market.

4. SUICIDE PREVENTION METHODS AND THE ECONOMIC ANALYSIS OF SUICIDE PREVENTION

Here we present prevention methods implemented in various countries. Some of these programs can be implemented with minimal cost while others require substantial time, effort, and money. In the second subsection, we provide economic evaluations of suicide prevention programs with specific reference to cost benefit analysis.

4.1. Suicide Prevention Programs

The complexity and multi-factorial nature of suicide determinants and risks requires a multi-dimensional approach to prevention. Improving antidepressant medications and psychotherapy techniques, educating therapists in new and advanced techniques of identifying and treating patients, involving mass media in the education of individuals about suicidal behavior, and opening more suicide prevention centers and clinics are all necessary means of reducing suicide rates (Yaniv 2001).

Strategies proven to reduce suicide rates include increasing the cost of committing suicide by either restricting access to methods (i.e., firearms and pesticides), or making them less effective (Lester and Yang 1997). The falling toxicity of car exhaust in new vehicles also leads to lower rates of suicide (Lester and Yang 1997). Declining suicide rates in England and Wales have also been attributed to the new catalytic converter technology (Kendell 1998). In England, Florentine and Crane (2010) show that due to the reduced toxicity of domestic gas, suicide rates in all age groups and for both sexes declined by almost 30 percent. Similar results are reported for Switzerland, Ireland, Scotland, Japan (Lester and Abe 1989) and the U.S. (Lester 1990). Similarly, restricting access to firearms has reduced suicide rates in Canada, the U.S., Australia, and the U.K. (See Florentine and Crane 2010). After banning a few pesticides from the market, the total suicide rate in Sri Lanka decreased by more than 50% (Gunnell et al. 2007).

Antidepressant medications are one of the most common treatments for mental illness, a risk factor for suicide (Wood, Harrington and Moore 1996). Increasing sales of antidepressants have been associated in population-level studies with declining suicide rates (Marcotte and Norberg 2009). Yet, some antidepressant therapies have been associated with the emergence of suicidal ideation and behavior, particularly at the onset of treatment (Isacsson 2000).

Many countries, including the U.S., have created national suicide prevention programs that utilize a variety of strategies. The first comprehensive national suicide prevention strategy was developed by Finland. Australia started the "Here for Life Youth Initiative" in 1995 and in 1999 extended its suicide prevention strategies across the age spectrum. National suicide prevention strategies have also been established by Norway (1994), Denmark (1998), England (2002), and Canada (2004) (for more information see the CASP National Suicide Prevention Strategy). Other countries implemented different policies. For instance, the "Reaching Young Europe" program, also called "Zippy's Friends", is offered by the partnership for children in different European countries. The purpose of the program is to help young children develop coping and social skills. The program also develops resources for parents and teachers to help young children deal with complicated circumstances, such as grief, separation and divorce. Currently the program is running in primary schools and kindergartens in 19 countries, helping more than 400,000 children.

In the U.S., the Los Angeles Suicide Prevention Center was among the first suicide prevention centers when it was established in 1958. In time, many other suicide prevention programs were adopted. School-based suicide prevention programs comprise suicide education programs, peer support programs, and school-based general education programs (see King 2001 for a review of comprehensive prevention programs). Numerous national and international professional associations for suicide prevention have been established, as well as several professional journals have started to publish articles primarily about suicide. The first U.S. suicide prevention strategy, the National Strategy for Suicide Prevention: Goals and Objectives for Action, was published in 2001.

Around the globe, countries have adopted various suicide prevention policies and programs. In Japan, community based suicide prevention programs were introduced for the first time in Akita prefecture in 2000 (Motohashi, Kaneko and Sasaki 2004) followed by a report of national suicide prevention strategies in 2002. Community based suicide prevention programs have been recognized by Yamamura (2010) for the important informal social ties they generate and their social environments which are conducive to preventing suicides in Japan. Japan implemented the Basic Act of Suicide Prevention in 2006. Among many preventive measures implemented in Japan, Chen, Choi and Sawada (2009) describe the installation of large mirrors in one of Tokyo's subways as the most creative suicide prevention strategy.

4.2. Economic Evaluations of Suicide Prevention Programs

Economics deals with the efficient allocation of scarce resources. This approach in economics is also useful for economic analysis of suicide prevention methods. There are multiple economic evaluation methods used in the literature. These methods can be grouped under cost effectiveness (CEA) and cost benefit analysis (CBA). Both methods use the same costing methods to estimate the costs, for example, of suicide prevention programs. The method for measuring outcomes varies by method. CEA measures program outcomes in non-monetary units such as the number of averted suicide attempts, life years saved or the number of quality adjusted life years saved. CBA measures both costs (input) and benefits (outcome) in monetary terms.

The CBA approach has been widely used in the economics literature for evaluations of public policies and programs including suicide prevention (i.e. Sari et al. 2008). In this section, we will focus on the CBA method as it is applied to suicide prevention strategies (for comprehensive reviews of the CEA methods, see Drummond et al. 1997).

4.2.1. Costs of Suicide Prevention Programs

In order to perform an economic evaluation of a suicide prevention program, we must first identify the relevant costs of the program. Cost estimates may be available from similar programs implemented in other locations or contexts, or for different population groups. For instance, in their economic evaluations of two suicide prevention programs for college age youth in Florida, Sari et al. (2008) obtained the cost of peer support and suicide education programs from existing prevention programs (i.e. the California School Suicide Prevention Program (CSSPP) implemented in California). The CSSPP is a statewide youth suicide prevention program for high schools in California. Given that California has a large school district similar to the Florida school district, where the population is also composed of a large number of minority groups, Sari and his colleagues estimated the cost of a suicide education program for Florida using cost figures from California. This approximation would be plausible if the economic circumstances of an existing program are similar to the ones for the proposed program.

There are prevention strategies which can be implemented with minimal cost. For instance, regulations to restrict access to common methods of suicide such as firearms or toxic substances like pesticides are low-cost methods proven to be effective in preventing suicide. Others as mentioned in the previous section would be to adjust the toxicity of toxic substances, car exhaust or domestic gas.

4.2.2. Benefits of Suicide Prevention Programs

Suicide prevention programs create benefits to society by avoiding the direct and indirect costs associated with suicide. Direct costs include healthcare costs such as ambulance services (including in-ambulance pharmaceutical and travel costs), hospitalization and autopsy services. In addition to healthcare costs for the individual who committed suicide, it is likely that his/her family members, friends and significant others may also require mental health services due to pain and suffering. Other non-healthcare related costs associated with suicide are money and time spent in obtaining both the necessary information on how to commit suicide and the means of committing suicide (e.g., guns, poison).

Indirect costs include the lost economic value of the person who died by suicide (measured as foregone future earnings, for example), as well as the monetized value of the suffering of any family members and friends. After a suicide, family members, friends and significant others may experience productivity losses due to reduced productivity at work, sick days or leaves of absence from work. In addition to negative labor market outcomes, suicide creates additional costs in the form of pain, psychological fear of death, expected punishment after death, and forgone expected enjoyment from the future.

There are some estimates available in the literature for the costs of suicide. Stoudemire et al. (1986) estimated the indirect cost of major depressive illness at US$ 4.2 billion. Given that only 60% of suicides are as a result of a major depressive illness, one can estimate the total cost of suicides through lost lifetime earnings to be around US$ 7 billion. In a more recent study in Japan, Chen et al. (2009) suggest that the costs associated with suicides are around US$197 million in 2006 alone even if some costs such as psychological counseling are excluded. Estimates for European countries are similar to cost estimates in the U.S. and Japan. For instance, total costs are shown to be € 2.04 million in Ireland (Kennelly, Ennis and O'Shea 2005), and € 1.88 million in Scotland (McDaid et al. 2007). Another study completed in New Brunswick, Canada estimates the average direct and indirect cost per suicide at $850,000 (Clayton and Barcelo 1999).

Cost of suicide estimates may be inflated if they fail to account for cost-savings in health care and other societal expenses that would have otherwise been incurred by the person who died by suicide (Lester 1995). Similarly, cost estimates assume that the labor productivity of those who die by suicide is similar to those who do not. Sensitivity analyses should be included in economic studies of prevention programs to take into account this issue.

Although these estimates suggest that the cost of suicide is significant, this does not imply that the benefit from a suicide prevention program would be equally substantial. Any benefit from a suicide prevention program will depend on the effectiveness of any program in preventing suicide. For instance, effect rates for the general education and peer support programs are about 57 and 60 percent respectively (de Castro et al. 2004). Therefore, at best the benefit from one of these programs would be in the range of 57 to 60 percent of the costs of suicide presented above.

Estimating benefits from a prevention program for savings in direct costs such as ambulance services, hospitalization and autopsy services are relatively easy to obtain. However, remaining cost estimates especially those related to the value of life lost are not straightforward. They involve multiple parties and require estimating the forgone earnings due to suicide for both the individual who committed suicide, and the others.

There are various methods to estimate the value of life or forgone earnings due to a suicide. The human capital approach is one of the most common methods used in the literature. In this method, the monetary value of each life is estimated using the market value of the expected output produced by an individual during his/her expected lifetime (Mishan 1971; Giles 2003). This approach measures the monetary value of life using the discounted value of future earnings resulting from an improvement or extension of life. There are, however, other monetary and non-monetary benefits that must be taken into account. Additional benefits, although non-monetary in nature, may include improved social functioning, higher educational achievement, reduced personal and family stress, better household management, improved social support, improved mental health, fewer social and emotional adjustment problems, improved physical health, fewer injuries, and improved social functioning. It is likely that an economic evaluation of prevention program using the human capital approach underestimates net benefit since it does not capture these additional benefits (Sari et al. 2008).

Additional non-monetary benefits can be included by using alternative methods for measuring the value of life, one of which is the willingness-to-pay approach. In this approach, estimates represent society's willingness to pay to avoid the death or injury. Although the human capital approach depends only on the market value of contributions to the production process by each individual (as measured by earnings and paid benefits), the willingness-to-pay approach measures the total value of life by including both the forgone earnings and the non-market value received from life and good health. Net benefit estimates based on the willingness-to-pay approach will be higher than those generated by the human capital approach. For instance, at a 4 percent discount rate, the value of life estimate based on the human capital approach is less than $1.54 million in 2000 dollars (Sari et al. 2008) while Viscusi (1993) reports that the willingness-to-pay estimates for value of life range between $3 million and $7 million in 1990 dollars. In Miller (1990), it is higher than $3.4 million in 1995 dollars. The lower limits from these studies using the willingness-to-pay approach are $3.95 million and $3.84 million in 2000 dollars respectively. It is, therefore, essential that future studies of economic evaluation of suicide prevention programs consider these alternative methods.

CONCLUSION

Suicide has been a great concern for many scientists from various fields for decades. Although economists joined this group relatively recently, they have spent a great deal of time and effort to identify its economic and socio-economic determinants. While some economists applied economic models to study suicidal behavior, others studied prevention methods and their economic evaluations. This chapter has provided an overview of the literature on theories of suicide primarily derived from the economics literature followed by literature on economic, social, socio-environmental, and medical determinants of suicide. Finally, we focused on existing prevention programs in various countries, provided an overview of the economic evaluation of suicide prevention strategies, and highlighted areas for further research.

As well-established in the literature, suicide involves a complex wide-ranging network of risk factors which makes it a multi-dimensional puzzle. Although a mental health disorder is the most commonly cited risk factor for suicide, economic, social, and environmental factors also contribute to risk. Suicide risk research and prevention therefore requires the attention of various clinicians and scientists, including social scientists such as economists, sociologists and psychologists. Multi-disciplinary teams should collaborate to design studies and programs to deter suicide, including a greater emphasis on the economic evaluation of such suicide prevention programs.

REFERENCES

Altinanahtar, A.,and Halicioglu, F. (2009). A dynamic econometric model of suicides in Turkey. *Journal of Socio-Economics, 38*, 903-907.

Andrés, A. R., and Halicioglu, F. (2010). Determinants of suicides in Denmark: evidence from time series data. *Health Policy, 98*, 263-269.

Andrés, A.R. (2005). Income inequality, unemployment, and suicide: a panel data analysis of 15 European countries. *Applied Economics, 38*, 903-907.

Barstad, A. (2008). Explaining changing suicides rates in Norway 1948-2004: the role social integration. *Social Indicators Research, 87*, 47-64.

Blakely, T.A., Collings S.C.D., and Atkinson J. (2003). Unemployment and suicide. Evidence for a causal association?. *Journal of Epidemiology and Community Health, 57*, 594-600.

Burr, J.A., McCall, P.L.,and Powell-Griner, E. (1997). Female labor force participation and suicide. *Social Science and Medicine, 44(12),* 1847-1859.

CDC. (2007). 11 Leading Causes of Death, United States. http://webappa.cdc.gov/cgi-bin/broker.exe (accessed July 26th, 2011).

CDC. (2009). Surveillance for Violent Deaths-National Violent Death Reporting System, 16 States, 2006. *MMWR, 58(01),* 1-44.

Chen, J., Choi, Y. J., Mori, K.,Sawada, Y., and Sugano, S. (2009). Those who are left behind: an estimation of the number of family members of suicide victims in Japan. *Social Indicators Research, 94,* 535-544.

Chen, J., Choi, Y. J., Mori, K.,Sawada, Y., and Sugano, S. (2011). Socio-economic studies on suicide: a survey. *Journal of Economic Survey*, doi: 10.1111/j.1467-6419.2010.00645.x

Chen, J., Choi, Y.J., and Sawada, Y. (2009). How is suicide different in Japan? *Japan and The World Economy, 21,* 140-150.

Chen, J., Choi, Y.J., and Sawada, Y. (2008). Suicide and life insurance. http://www.cirje.e.u-tokyo.ac.jp/research/dp/2008/2008cf558ab.html.

Chuang, H.L., and Huang, W.C. (1995). A comparison of the economic and social correlates of yearly suicide rates between the U.S. and Taiwan, 1952-1994. Unpublished manuscript.

Chuang, H.L., and Huang, W.C. (1997). Economic and social correlates of regional suicide rates: a pooled cross-section and time-series analysis. *Journal of Socio-Economics, 26(3),* 277-289.

Clayto, D., and Barcelo, A. (1999). The cost of suicide mortality in New Brunswick. *Chronic Diseases in Canada, 20(2),* 85-95.

Daly, M.C., Wilson, D.J.,and Johnson, N.J. (2007). Relative status and well-being: evidence from U.S. suicide deaths, *Federal Reserve Bank of San Francisco,* working paper.

Daly, M.C., and Wilson, D.J. (2009). Happiness, unhappiness, and suicide: an empirical assessment. *Journal of the European Economic Association, 7,* 539-549.

Daly, M.C., Oswald, A.J., Wilson, D. and Wu, S. (2011). Dark contrasts: The paradox of high rates of suicide in happy places. *Journal of Economic Behavior and Organization*, doi: 10.1016/j.jebo.2011.04.007.

de Castro, S., Mils, G., Sari, N., and Newman, F.L. (2004). Using meta analysis to generate a cost-benefit analysis to two suicide prevention programs for the middle and high school age population in Florida. *Session on Mental Disorders Among Children: Epidemiology and Prevention.* Washington, DC: American Public Health Association Meeting.

Douglas, J. (1967). *The social meaning of suicide.* Princeton, N.J.: Princeton University Press.

Drummond, M.F., O'Brien, C.P., Stoddart, G.L., and Torrance, G.W. (1997). *Methods for the economic evaluation of health care programmes.* New York: Oxford University Press.

Durkheim, E. (1897/2002). *Suicide: A Study in Sociology.* London: Routledge.

Ezzy, D. (1993). Unemployment and mental health. *Social Science and Medicine, 37,* 41-52.

Farberow, N.L., and Shneidman, E.S. (1961). *The cry for help.* New York: McGraw Hill.

Florentine, J. B., and Crane, C. (2010). Suicide prevention by limiting access to methods: a review of theory and practice. *Social Science and Medicine, 70,*1626-1632.

Gerdtham, U., and Johannesson, M. (2003). A note on the effect of unemployment on mortality. *Journal of Health Economics, 22,* 505-518.

Giles, M. (2003). The Cost of Road Crashes: A Comparison of Methods and Recent Australian Estimates. *Journal of Transport Economics and Policy, 37(1)*, 95-110.

Goldsmith, S.K., Pellmar T.C., Kleinman, A.M., and Bunney, W.E. (2002). *Reducing suicide: a national imperative.* Washington (DC): National Academy Press.

Granados, J. A. (2008). Macroeconomic fluctuations and mortality in postwar Japan. *Demography, 45(2),* 323-342.

Gunnell, D., Fernando, R., Hewagama, M., Priyangika, W. D. D., Konradsen, F., and Eddleston, M. (2007). The impact of pesticide regulations on suicide in Sri Lanka. *International Journal of Epidemiology, 36,* 1235-1242.

Hammermesh, A. S., and Soss, N.M. (1974). An Economic Theory of Suicide. *Journal of Political Economy,82,* 83-98.

Hansen, B., and Lang, M. (2011). Back to school blues: Seasonality of youth suicide and the academic calendar. *Economics of Education Review*, doi:10.1016/j.econedurev.2011.04.012.

Huang, W. C. (1997). A Life Force participation perspective of suicide. In Lester, D. and Yang, B (Ed.), *The Economy and Suicide: Economic Perspectives on Suicide*, (83-89). New York: Nova Science Publishers, Inc.

Inagaki, K. (2010). Income inequality and the suicide rate in Japan: Evidence from cointegration and LA-VAR. *Journal of Applied Economics, 13(1),* 113-133.

Isacsson, G. (2000). Suicide prevention: a medical breakthrough? *Acta Psychiatrica Scandinavica, 102(2),* 113-115.

Jungeilges, J., and Kirchgassner, G. (2002). Economic welfare, civil liberty, and suicide: an empirical investigation. *Journal of Socio-Economics, 31,* 215-231.

Kendell, R. E. (1998). Catalytic converters and prevention of suicides. *Lancet, 352,* 1525.

Kennelly, B., Ennis, J., and O'Shea, E. (2005). *Reach out National Strategy for Action on Suicide Prevention 2005-2014: Economic cost of suicide and deliberate self harm.* Ireland: Department of Health and Children.

King, K.A. (2001). Developing a comprehensive school suicide prevention program. *Journal of School Health, 71(4),* 132-137.

Kleck, G. (1988). Magnitude of underreporting of suicide. *Suicide and Life Threatening Behavior, 18(3),* 219-236.

Koivumaa-Honkanen, H., Hokanen, R., Viinama, H. H., Heikkila, K. K., Kaprio, J., and Koskenvuo, M. (2001). Life Satisfaction and Suicide: a 20-year follow-up study. *American Journal of Psychiatry, 158,* 433-439.

Koo, J., and Cox, M. W. (2008). An economic interpretation of suicide cycles in Japan. *Contemporary Economic Policy, 26(1),* 162-174.

Kowalski, G.S., Faupel, C.E., and Starr, P.D. (1987). Urbanism and suicide: a study of American counties. *Social Forces, 66(1),* 85-101.

Lester, D. (1983). *Why do people kill themselves.* Springfield: Charles Thomas.

Lester, D. (1989). *Suicide from a sociological perspective.* Springfield, IL: Charles Thomas.

Lester, D. (1990). The effects of detoxification of domestic gas on suicide in the United States. *American Journal of Public Health, 80,* 80-81.

Lester, D. Estimating the true economic cost of suicide. *Perpetual and Motor Skills* 80 (1995): 746.

Lester, D. (2003). National estimates of IQ and suicide and homicide rates. *Perceptual and motor skills, 97(1),* 206.

Lester, D. (2004). *Thinking About Suicide: Perspectives on Suicide.* New York: NOVA Science Publishers.

Lester, D., and Yang, B. (1998). *Suicide and homicide in the 20th century. Changes over time.* New York: NOVA Science Publishers.

Lester, D., and Yang, B. (1997). *The Economy and Suicide: Economic Perspectives on Suicide.* New York: NOVA Science Publishers.

Lester, D., and Abe, K.(1989). The effect of restricting access to lethal methods for suicide: study of suicide by domestic gas in Japan. *Acta Psychiatrica Scandinavia, 80,* 180-182.

Lewis, G., and Sloggett, A. (1998). Suicide, deprevation, and unemployment: record linkage study. *British Medical Journal, 317(7168),* 1283-1286.

Ludwig, J., Marcotte, D.E, and Norberg, K. (2009). Anti-depressants and suicide. *Journal of Health Economics, 28,* 659-676.

Mäkinen, I. (1997). Are there social correlates to suicide? *Social Science and Medicine, 44,* 1919-1929.

Mann, J.J., Apter, A., Bertolote, J., Beautrais, A., Currier, D., Haas, A., Hegerl, U., Lonngvist, J., Malone, K., Marusic, A., Mehlum, L., Patton, G., Phillips, M., Rutz, W., Rihmer, Z., Schmidtke, A., Shaffer, D., Silverman, M., Takahashi, Y., Varnik, A., Wasserman, D., Yip, P., and Hendin, H. (2005). Suicide prevention strategies. A systematic review. *Journal of The American Medical Association, 294,* 2064-74.

Marcotte, D.E. (2003). The economics of suicide. Revisited. *Southern Economic Journal, 69(3),* 628-643.

Mathur, V.K., and Freeman, D.G. (2002). A theoretical model of adolescent suicide and some evidence from US data. *Health Economics, 11,* 695-708.

McDaid, D., Halliday, E., McKenzie, M., MacLean, J., Maxwell, M., McCollam, A., Platt, S., and Woodhouse, A. (2007). *Issues in the economic evaluation of suicide prevention strategies: practical and methodological challanges.* London: Personal Social Services Research Unit.

Miller, T.R. (1990). The plausible Range for the Value of Life – Red Herrings among the Mackerel. *Journal of Forensic Economics, 3,* 17-39

Mishan, E.J. (1971). Evaluation of Life and Limb: A Theoretical Approach. *Journal of Political Economy, 79(4),* 687-705.

Minoiu, C., and Andrés, R.A. (2008). The effect of public spending on suicide: evidence from U.S. state data. *Journal of Socio-Economics, 37,* 237-261.

Mitra, S., and Shroff, S. (2008). What suicides reveal about gender bias. *Journal of Socio-Economics, 37,* 1713-1723.

Molina, J.A., and Duart, R. (2006). Risk determinants of suicide attempts among adolescents. *American Journal of Economics and Sociology, 65,* 407-434.

Motohashi, Y., Kaneko, Y., and Sasaki, H. (2004). Community based suicide prevention program in Japan using a health promotion approach. *Health and Preventive Medicine, 9,* 3-8.

Neumayer, E. (2003). Are socioeconomic factors valid determinants of suicide? Controlling for national cultures of suicidewith fixed-effects estimation. *Cross-Cultural Research, 37(3),* 307-329.

Neumayer, E. (2003). Socioeconomic Factors and Suicide Rates at Large-unit Aggreagate Levels: A Comment. *Urban Studies, 40(13),* 2769-2776.

Newman, J., K. (1973). Whittemore, and H. Newman. Women in the labor force and suicide. *Social Problems, 21,* 220-230.

Peck, D.L., and Warner, K. (1995). Accident or Suicide? Single-vehicle car accidents and the intent hypothesis. *Adolescence Sum, 30(118),* 463-472.

Platt, S.D. Parasuicide and unemployment. *British Journal of Pscyhiatry* 149 (1986): 401-405.

Platt, S.D. (1984). Unemployment and suicidal behavior. *Social Science and Medicine, 19,* 93-115.

Pompili, M., Girardi, P., Lester, D., and Tatarelli, R. (2011). *Antidepressants Therapy and Risk of Suicide among Patients with Major Depressive Disorders.* New York: Nova Publishers.

Quinney, R. (1965). Suicide, Homicide, And Economic Development. *Social Forces, 43(3),* 401-406.

Rockett, I. R., andMc Kinley, T.B. (1999). Reliability and sensitivity of suicide certification in higher income countries. *Suicide and Life-Threatening Behavior, 29(2),* 141-149.

Rodriguez, A.A. (2005). Income Inequality, Unemployment, and Suicide: A Panel Data Analysis of 15 European Countries. *Applied Economics, 37,* 439-451.

Rosenthal, R.W. (1993). Suicide attempts and signaling games. *Mathematical Social Sciences, 26,* 25-33.

Ross, J.M., Yakovlev, P.A., and Carson, F. (2010). Does state spending on mental health lower suicide rates? *Journal of Socio-Economics,* doi: 10.1016/j.socec.2010.10.005.

Rossow, I. (1993). Suicide, alcohol, and divorce: aspects of gender and family integration. *Addiction,88,* 1659-1665.

Ruhm, C. J. (2000). Are recessions good for your health. *Quarterly Journal of Economics, 22,* 617-650.

Sari, N., de Castro, S., Newman, F.L., and Mills, G.(2008). Should we invest in suicide prevention programs? *Journal of Socio-Economics, 37,* 262-275.

Singh, G. K., and Mohammad, S.M. (2002). Increasing rural urban gradients in U.S. suicide mortality. *American Journal of Public Health, 92(7),* 1161-1167.

Stack, S. The effect of female participation in the labor force on suicide: a time series analysis, 1948-1980. *Sociological Forum* 2 (1987): 257-277.

Stack, S. (1989). The impact of divorce on suicide in Norway, 1951-1980. *Journal of Marriage and The Family, 51,* 229-238.

Steen, M.D., and Mayer, P. (2003). Patterns of suicide by age and gender in the Indian states: a reflection of human development? *Archives of Suicide Research, 7,* 247-264.

Stevenson, B., and Wolfers, J. (2006). Bargaining in the shadow of the law: divorce law and family distress. *Quarterly Journal of Economics, 121,* 267-288.

Stoudemire, A., Frank, R., Hedemark, N., Kamlet, M., and Blazer, D. (1986). The economic burden of depression. *General Hospital Psychiatry, 8,* 387-394.

Suzuki, T. (2008). Economic modeling of suicide under income uncertainty: for better understanding of middle-aged suicide. *Australian Economic Papers, 47(3),* 296-310.

Viren, M. (1999). Thesting the Natural Rate of Suicide Hypothesis. *International Journal of Social Economics, 26(12),* 1428-1440.

Viscusi, W.K. (1993). The Value of Risks to Life and Health. *Journal of Economic Literature, 31,* 1912-1946.

Voracek, M. (2004). National intelligence and suicide rate: An ecological study of 85 countries. *Personality and Individual Differences, 37,* 543-553.

Voracek, M. (2005). National Intelligence, Suicide Rate in The Elderly, and a Threshold Intelligence For Suicidality: An Ecological Study of 48 Eurasian Countries. *Journal of Biosocial Science, 37,* 721-740.

WHO. (2011). http://www.who.int/features/factfiles/mental_health/ mental_health_facts /en/index2.html. (accessed April 22, 2011).

WHO. (2008). *Suicide and suicide prevention in Asia.* Geneva: WHO Department of Mental Health and Substance Abuse.

WHO Europe. (2011). *Facts and figures.* http://www.euro.who.int/en/what-we-do/health-topics/noncommunicable-diseases/mental-health/facts-and-figures. (accessed May 2, 2011).

Wood, A., Harrington, R., and Moore, A. (1996). Controlled trial of a brief cognitive-behavioral intervention in adolescent patients with depressive disorders. *Journal of Child Psychology and Psychiatry, 37(96),* 737-746.

Yamamura, E. (2010). The Different Impacts of Socio-economic Factors on Suicide between Males and Females. *Applied Economic Letters, 17(10),* 1009-1012.

Yang, B. (1992). The economy and suicide: a time-series study of the USA. *American Journal of Economics and Sociology, 51(1),* 87-99.

Yang, B., and Lester, D. (1996). Conceptualizing suicide in economic models. *Applied Economic Letters, 3,* 139-143.

Yang, B., and Lester, D. (1994). Crime and unemployment. *Journal of Socio-Economics, 23,* 215-222.

Yang, B., and Lester, D. (1992). Suicide homicide and unemployment: a methodological note. *Psychological Reports, 71,* 844-846.

Yang, B., and Lester, D. (1995). Suicide, homicide and unemployment. *Applied Economic Letters, 2,* 278-279.

Yang, B., Lester, D., and Yang, C. (1992). Sociological and economic theories of suicide: a comparison of the USA and Taiwan. *Social Sciences and Medicine, 34(2),* 333-334.

Yaniv, G. (2001). Suicide intention and suicide prevention: an economic perspective. *Journal of Socio-Economics, 30,* 453-468.

Yeh, B.Y., and Lester, D. (1987). An economic model for suicide. In D. Lester (Ed.), *Suicide As a Learned Behavior* (51-57). Spring.

INTERNATIONAL PERSPECTIVES ON CLINICAL APPROACHES TO SUICIDE PREVENTION

In: Frontiers in Suicide Risk
Editor: Jill E. Lavigne

ISBN 978-1-62081-373-7
©2012 Nova Science Publishers, Inc.

Chapter 15

SUICIDE: RISK FACTORS AND PREVENTION

*Barbara Schneider**

Psychiatry and Psychotherapy, Specialist in Psychiatry and Psychotherapy,
Abteilung Abhängigkeitserkrankungen, LVR-Klinik Köln, Germany

ABSTRACT

Across different cultures and countries the most important risk factors for suicide are psychiatric disorders; particularly affective disorders, substance use disorders, schizophrenia, and personality disorders are associated with a highly elevated suicide risk. Somatic disorders, social factors like unemployment, life events, such as financial loss or loss of significant others, previous suicide attempts, male gender, older age, and firearms are also risk factors for suicide. Unfortunately there are only few results about the impact of several risk factors on suicide and about differences in risk constellations in different regions and cultures. However, it is clear that suicide rarely occurs in the absence of mental disorder. Therefore, prevention, early identification, and appropriate treatment of mental disorders have to be the main components for suicide prevention; that would reduce suicide rates worldwide. Another target of suicide prevention is suicide prevention in the general population including media reporting. The media can play a major role in reducing stigma and discrimination associated with suicidal behaviours and mental disorders.

FINDINGS OF COHORT STUDIES AND CONTROLLED PSYCHOLOGICAL AUTOPSY STUDIES ON RISK FACTORS FOR COMPLETED SUICIDE

A risk factor is defined as "an aspect of personal behaviour or lifestyle, environmental exposure, or inborn or inherited characteristic, which, on the basis of epidemiologic evidence, is known to be associated with a health-related condition considered important to prevent". Risk factors differ from other factors such as concomitants or consequences of the observed outcome by the important characteristic of precedence. Information about risk factors for

---

* Tel. +492218993400, Telefax: +492218993486 , E-mail: B.Schneider@em.uni-frankfurt.de

suicide can be obtained by population-based cohort studies and by controlled psychological autopsy studies with living control persons. Suicide is a complex phenomenon with psychological, social, biological, cultural and environmental factors involved. As shown by cohort studies and controlled psychological autopsy studies (Cavanagh, Carson, Sharpe, and Lawrie, 2003; Harris and Barraclough, 1997; Schneider, 2008), suicide risk is highly increased in almost all mental disorders, particularly in affective disorders, substance use disorders, schizophrenia, and personality disorders. Affective disorders are the psychiatric disorders most often found in suicide victims (Bertolote and Fleischmann, 2002). Furthermore, in Asian countries impulsiveness may play an important role for suicide risk (World Health Organisation, 2010).

In controlled psychological autopsy studies, psychoactive substance use disorders were associated with an up to sevenfold increased suicide risk (Foster, Gillespie, McClelland, and Patterson, 1999). Harris und Barraclough (1997) and Wilcox et al. (2004) found an increased suicide risk in alcohol use disorders compared to the general population. Furthermore, most controlled psychological autopsy studies repeatedly identified alcoholism as a risk factor for suicide (see (Schneider, 2003; Kõlves, Värnik, Tooding, and Wasserman, 2006)). Nicotine use was also associated with an increased suicide risk (Harris and Barraclough, 1997; Schneider et al., 2010). Several authors (Harris and Barraclough, 1997; Angst, Stassen, Clayton, and Angst, 2002) reported that in cohort studies suicide risk was about 20 times higher in patients with unipolar depression than in the general population. In controlled psychological autopsy studies, suicide risk was also elevated for unipolar and bipolar disorders (e. g. (Schneider et al., 2006)). In schizophrenia and with a slower decline in affective disorders, a high percentage of people committed suicide soon after onset of the disease; in alcoholism the percentage of suicides showed only slight variation over the life of the cohort (Inskip, Harris, and Barraclough, 1998). Co-morbid mental disorders and substance abuse also preceded suicide in more cases than in controls; co-morbid affective disorders and substance use disorders were associated with very highly increased suicide risk (Cheng, 1995). Other risk factors for suicide are somatic disorders, such as kidney diseases, cancer, and various neurologic disorders. These are associated with an increased risk for suicide (Schneider, 2008). With respect to social factors, unmarried state, childlessness, unemployment, manual social class, some professions, such as farmer, and negative life events are associated with increased suicide risk. (Schneider, 2003). Furthermore, suicide risk is increased in immigrants and in individuals with former suicide attempts (Schneider, 2003).

The cause of a complex outcome like a suicide consists of a constellation of components that act together and vary from one individual to another. Psychiatric disorders, such as substance use disorders, depression, and emotional instable personality disorder, inpatient psychiatric treatment, and discharge from hospital were identified as independent risk factors for suicide (Cheng, Mann, and Chan, 1997; Cheng, 1995). However, in multivariate analysis, estimation of risk of the different factors is not precise due to wide confidence intervals.

PROBLEMS

Although there are well-established universal risk factors for suicidal behaviour, the prediction of suicide in individual cases remains difficult. Unfortunately, there are no models that can accurately predict or prevent suicide in any individual. Furthermore, risk constellations and the quantitative meaning of the different risk factors in different cultures are not clarified yet. The extent of risk associated with suicide seems to vary for different regions of the world; however, there are too few studies to compare the height of the risk. Furthermore, studies from Africa and South America are still lacking. Despite of this extensive literature replicating risk factors for suicide, there is still little empirical knowledge of which preventive interventions may be effective in high risk groups or in the population in general.

DIRECTIONS AND AIMS OF SUICIDE PREVENTION

Prevention, early identification, and treatment of mental disorders are therefore one of the main components for suicide prevention. The treatment of the most frequently associated disorders with suicide would reduce suicide rates worldwide. The treatment of schizophrenia, alcohol use disorders, and depression, the three disorders most frequently found in association with suicide, would reduce suicide rates of about 20.5% from 15.1 per 100,000 to 12 per 100,000 (Bertolote, Fleischmann, De Leo, and Wasserman, 2004).

According to the WHO, restriction of access to means of suicide, such as toxic substances and firearms, identification and management of persons suffering from mental and substance use disorders, improved access to health and social services, and responsible reporting of suicide by the media are effective strategies for the prevention of suicide. The World Health Organization (WHO) and the United Nations have drafted strategy proposals for the work on suicide prevention. There are currently several national programmes for suicide prevention in existence. The WHO has published a series of documents on how to prevent suicide in psychiatric and general practice settings, in schools, prisons, and in survivors of suicide, as well as documents on how to report suicide in the media (World Health Organisation, 2010). The WHO worldwide initiative include aims, such as raising awareness of the magnitude of the problem, identifying cost-effective strategies for training workers in health, proposing cost-effective strategies for the reduction of methods of suicide, promulgating cost-effective interventions for the management of people at risk of suicidal behaviours and identifying relevant partners across sectors (Saraceno, 2010).

FUTURE OUTLOOK: WHICH QUESTIONS ARE STILL OPEN AND WHAT MUST BE DONE?

The following salient questions are still unanswered and must be explored (Schneider, 2010; Berman, 2011): the role of co-morbidity and strategies for risk formulation, particularly in different countries and cultures, research on suicide risk and risk factors in the general population, definition of sensitive "markers" for acute risk of suicide, continuation of development of theoretical concepts, such as "thwarted belongingness" und "burdensomeness", development of new interventions and treatment strategies, evaluation of implemented suicide prevention programs, and reduction of risk factors for suicidal behavior and mental disorders in the general population. Research on several of these yet-unanswered questions is costly and time-consuming and does not seem very profitable. However, we should have in mind, that almost one million people die from suicide every year, i.e. a "global" mortality rate of 16 per 100,000, or one death every 40 seconds (World Health Organisation, 2010).

REFERENCES

Angst, F., Stassen, H. H., Clayton, P. J., and Angst, J. (2002). Mortality of patients with mood disorders: follow-up over 34-38 years. *J Affect.Disord., 68,* 167-181.

Berman, A. L. (2011). Perspectives in Suicide Research and Prevention. A commentary. In M.Pompili and R. Tatarelli (Eds.), *Evidence-based Practice in Suicidology* (1 ed., pp. 351-369). Göttingen/Cambridge,MA: Hogrefe.

Bertolote, J. M. and Fleischmann, A. (2002). Suicide and psychiatric diagnosis: a worldwide perspective. *World Psychiatry, 1,* 181-185.

Bertolote, J. M., Fleischmann, A., De Leo, D., and Wasserman, D. (2004). Psychiatric diagnoses and suicide: revisiting the evidence. *Crisis, 25,* 147-155.

Cavanagh, J. T., Carson, A. J., Sharpe, M., and Lawrie, S. M. (2003). Psychological autopsy studies of suicide: a systematic review. *Psychol.Med., 33,* 395-405.

Cheng, A. T. (1995). Mental illness and suicide. A case-control study in east Taiwan. *Arch.Gen.Psychiatry, 52,* 594-603.

Cheng, A. T., Mann, A. H., and Chan, K. A. (1997). Personality disorder and suicide. A case-control study. *Br.J.Psychiatry, 170,* 441-446.

Foster, T., Gillespie, K., McClelland, R., and Patterson, C. (1999). Risk factors for suicide independent of DSM-III-R Axis I disorder. Case-control psychological autopsy study in Northern Ireland. *Br.J Psychiatry, 175,* 175-179.

Harris, E. C. and Barraclough, B. (1997). Suicide as an outcome for mental disorders. A meta-analysis. *Br.J.Psychiatry, 170,* 205-228.

Inskip, H. M., Harris, E. C., and Barraclough, B. (1998). Lifetime risk of suicide for affective disorder, alcoholism and schizophrenia. *Br.J Psychiatry, 172,* 35-37.

Kõlves, A., Värnik, A., Tooding, L. M., and Wasserman, D. (2006). The role of alcohol in suicide: a case-control psychological autopsy study. *Psychol.Med., 36,* 923-930.

Saraceno, B. (2010). The World Health Organization's role in suicide prevention. In D.Wasserman and C. Wasserman (Eds.), *Oxford Textbook of Suicidology and Suicide Prevention* (1 ed., pp. 723-725). Oxford: Oxford University Press.

Schneider, B. (2010). [Rauchzeichen aus dem DGS-Vorstand. Wo steht die Suizid-forschung?]. *Suizidprophylaxe, 143,* 134-135.

Schneider, B. (2003). *Risikofaktoren für Suizid.* Regensburg: Roderer.

Schneider, B. (2008). Risikofaktoren für Suizid. In M.Wolfersdorf, T. Bronisch, and H. Wedler (Eds.), *Suizidalität. Verstehen - Vorbeugen - Behandeln.* (pp. 119-128). Regensburg: Roderer.

Schneider, B., Baumert, J., Schneider, A., Marten-Mittag, B., Meisinger, C., Erazo, N. et al. (2010). The effect of risky alcohol use and smoking on suicide risk: findings from the German MONICA/KORA-Augsburg Cohort Study. *Soc.Psychiatry Psychiatr Epidemiol..*

Schneider, B., Wetterling, T., Sargk, D., Schneider, F., Schnabel, A., Maurer, K. et al. (2006). Axis I disorders and personality disorders as risk factors for suicide. *Eur.Arch.Psychiatry Clin.Neurosci., 256,* 17-27.

Wilcox, H. C., Conner, K. R., and Caine, E. D. (2004). Association of alcohol and drug use disorders and completed suicide: an empirical review of cohort studies. *Drug Alcohol Depend., 76 Suppl,* S11-S19.

World Health Organisation (2010). Suicide Prevention. World Health Organisation [On-line]. Available: *http://www.who.int/mental_health/prevention/suicide/country_reports/en/index.htm*l

World Health Organisation (2010). Suicide prevention (SUPRE). World Health Organisation [On-line]. Available: *http://www.who.int/mental _health/prevention /suicide /suicide prevent/en/index.htm*l.

In: Frontiers in Suicide Risk
Editor: Jill E. Lavigne

ISBN 978-1-62081-373-7
©2012 Nova Science Publishers, Inc.

Chapter 16

SUICIDE ATTEMPTERS TRANSFERRED BY AMBULANCE: PREVENTION OF RECURRENT SUICIDE ATTEMPTS

Kaoru Kudo, Kotaro Otsuka and Akio Sakai

Department of Neuropsychiatry,
Iwate Medical University, Japan

ABSTRACT

In Japan, suicide deaths have exceeded 30,000 per year since 1998. Iwate prefecture, where our hospital is located, has a markedly higher number of suicide deaths than other areas in Japan, with about 240 suicidal individuals presenting to our emergency department each year. Since 2002, we have staffed Iwate Prefectural Advanced Critical Care and Emergency Center with psychiatrists around the clock to provide suicidal individuals with psychiatric treatment along with treatment by emergency physicians immediately after their arrival. The most common method of suicide was "hanging" for both men and women, followed by "suffocation by carbon monoxide poisoning using briquette coal, etc." for men. It should be noted that in Japan, the number of suicide attempts by carbon monoxide poisoning has been increasing since 2003 and "group gas suicide using briquette coal" has repeatedly occurred. Suicide attempts using hydrogen sulfide have also gradually emerged since 2007 and have been rapidly increasing since 2008. For both of these emerging means of suicide, increased availability of information through the internet and mass media has led to an increased number of cases in chain-reaction and copycat fashion. This indicates that people in the press/media should also be more aware of the importance of suicide prevention. Evaluation of psychiatric symptoms and patient backgrounds should be performed immediately after the arrival of the patient in the emergency room. In our hospital, for example, we request intervention by a psychiatric social worker for patients who have made suicide attempts due to economic or family issues, for the period encompassing their arrival through to the time after their discharge from the hospital. In cases of completed suicide, there are increased needs for psychosocial support and provision of information to bereaved relatives. Support to bereaved relatives is provided through a multidisciplinary team in our hospital.

The purposes of this chapter is to describe the backgrounds and status of suicidal individuals encountered through emergency care in a region with high suicide rate and the actual care provided to them, and to comprehensively discuss the prevention of recurrent suicide attempt from the standpoint of emergency care.

INTRODUCTION

In Japan, the annual number of suicide deaths has exceeded 30,000 since 1998. To cope with this situation, the Japanese government is making a strong effort to promote suicide prevention. Despite this effort, the suicide rate in Japan is still among the highest of developed countries. The Northern Tohoku district of Japan, including Iwate Prefecture, where Iwate Medical University Hospital is located, has a higher number of suicide deaths than other areas in Japan, with about 240 suicide attempters presenting to the emergency department of our hospital annually. In emergency rooms, hospital admission is usually based on physical condition. Therefore even patients with a serious psychological condition may be sent home in the absence of a serious physical injury. However, these patients may repeat suicide-related behavior unless a mental/social assessment or intervention is made to identify the reason for the suicide attempts. Providing a continuous treatment environment by transferring patients from emergency to psychiatric departments is considered an effective strategy for the prevention of recurrent suicide attempts. Yet, in Japan, coordination between emergency and psychiatric departments to ensure that patients immediately receive psychiatric treatment has not been well established.

Under these circumstances, since 2002 we have staffed Iwate Prefecture Advanced Emergency and Critical Care Center (hereinafter, referred to as "the emergency center") with at least one psychiatrist around the clock. These psychiatrists, together with emergency physicians, treat psychiatric patients and suicide attempters immediately after their arrival. In an emergency room, while performing close physical examination and treatment, physicians evaluate patients' psychiatric severity, collect information such as patient background and motive for suicide, and comprehensively assess the physical, mental and social well-being of the patient to determine the optimal treatment strategy. For example, patients in a mentally and physically serious condition are admitted to the emergency center and transferred to the psychiatry department after they have physically recovered while those in a physically satisfactory but mentally serious condition may be admitted direclty to the psychiatric department [1].

In this chapter we describe the backgrounds and status of suicide attempters who presented to the emergency center of our hospital and the actual care provided to them. Specifically, we discuss suicide attempt risk factors and care to be given at an emergency room to prevent recurrent suicide attempts, based on the data collected in our system.

BACKGROUND AND CHARACTERISTICS OF SUICIDE ATTEMPTERS

1) Gender and Age

There is a worldwide trend that more women than men attempt suicide, but men are more likely to use serious methods in their suicide-related behavior and complete the suicide [2]. According to suicide statistics compiled by the National Police Agency of Japan, men account for about 70% of all suicide deaths [3]. Meanwhile, about 70% of all suicide attempters transferred by ambulance to our hospital are women.

Previous studies on the gender difference in suicide risk factors have suggested that being a man is a risk factor for suicide attempt. Other risk factors include, for men, serious methods of suicide attempt, repeated suicide attempt, and presence of major depression for men, and, for women, being 50 years of age or older, presence of strong suicide ideation, major depression, and psychiatric history [4].

The higher frequency of suicide attempts among women can be explained by the concept of parasuicide. Psychologically speaking, not all suicide-related behaviors are intended to result in death. Rather, some behaviors function as an unconscious signal for help. These recurrent help-seeking behaviors are collectively termed "parasuicides" and are frequently observed in young women [5] [6]. Many of these individuals have conditions that are mild in physical severity and they exhibit impulsive behavior as triggered by mild stress, such as difficulties in interpersonal relationships. In many of these cases, intention of suicide is unclear. Therefore, after being given emergency treatment, they are often instructed to consult a psychiatrist and are sent home. In our hospital, more than 80% of these patients had similar outcomes [1]. The details of care provided at an outpatient clinic will be described below.

Men tend to have severe psychiatric symptoms and strong suicide ideation, and make suicide attempts using serious methods. This results in physically serious consequences and high rates of completed suicide and hospitalization after presentation to emergency rooms [7]. In our investigation, more patients were admitted to the emergency center than were admitted to the psychiatric department [1]. It is likely that, compared to women, men do not consult with people around them prior to suicide attempt and often refuse to see a psychiatrist, even when people around them encourage them to do so [8]. Therefore, men, tend to have too much stress themselves and develop psychological tunnel vision [9]. In these situations, men seek a reliable way to die and thus tend to have physically serious consequences.

In terms of age, a higher suicide rate among the elderly than other age groups is a tendency common to developed countries [10]. The suicide statistics by the National Police Agency also show that suicide deaths are most frequent among those in their 50s, followed in order by the 60s, 40s and 30s [3]. Among the those who have presented to our hospital for suicide attempt, the majority are in their 20s. Frequency decreases as age advances to the 50s. In relation to the outcome of the suicide attempt, those admitted are older than those sent home and those who complete suicide are older than those admitted [7]. Among those admitted, those admitted to the emergency center tend to be older than those admitted to the psychiatric department [1]. This might be explained by the increasing prevalence of physical comorbidities with increasing age, which is further complicated by physical injury caused by suicide attempt, resulting in increased physical severity in older age groups. Another possible explanation is that increased exposure to stress events, such as experiencing loss, and pain associated with illness, contributes to increased risk of depression.

2) Primary Psychiatric Diagnosis (ICD-10) and Psychiatric Symptoms

Approximately 90% of suicide attempters are believed to have some kind of psychiatric disorder [11]. A multinational survey conducted by the World Health Organization (WHO) showed that mood disorders were the most commonly observed among those who died by suicide (30%), followed by substance-related disorder (including alcoholism), schizophrenia, and personality disorder [12]. Among the elderly depression is suggested to be a factor for suicide attempt [13]. With regard to the diagnoses given to the suicide attempters presenting to the emergency department of our hospital, anxiety disorder and mood disorder spectra each accounted for 30% and schizophrenia and personality disorder each accounted for about 10% of all diagnoses.

Our previous investigation showed that compared to anxiety disorder, mood disorder was more frequently associated with an important life event, advanced age, male gender and use of more lethal means at the initial suicide attempt [14]. Hawton et al. identified the following risk factors for suicide among individuals with bipolar mood disorder: family history of suicide, onset at a young age, degree of depressive symptoms, presence of mixed state, rapid cycling and alcohol/drug abuse [15]. It has also been suggested that coexistence of mood disorder and anxiety disorder is associated with an increased risk of suicidal ideation and attempt [16].

Suicide attempt associated with schizophrenia is committed by relatively younger individuals than that associated with mood disorder and is reported to occur commonly between 8 and 10 years after onset of schizophrenia. Its risk factors include male sex, repeated flare-ups and remissions, history of attempted suicide, history of depression, unrest/restlessness and anosognosia. Reported causes of suicide include extraordinary experiences, such as hallucination/delusion, and depression resulting social life problems [17] [18]. A previous study has shown that schizophrenic patients, although less frequently compared to those with mood disorder, tend to use more lethal methods of suicide, such as burning and poisoning [19], which is consistent with our findings. In cases of schizophrenic patients, compared with other psychiatric patients, even if they show obvious signs of suicidal tendency, such as attempting suicide or telling others of their intention to commit suicide, especially around 12 months before the occurrence of completed suicide, these signs are often overlooked as part of their psychiatric symptoms and not recognized as signs of suicidal tendency [20].

A previous study reported that, although a majority of suicide attempters had mental problems prior to suicide attempt, only about 20% of them received psychiatric treatment and a large majority had received almost no treatment [12]. Our previous study also showed that those consulting a psychiatrist for the first time and those attempting suicide for the first time tended to use serious methods and have physically serious consequences. [19] An underlying question is whether the presence of the underlying psychiatric condition was indentified but not treated or whether it was never identified. To prevent suicide, we must raise awareness in the community of the importance of preventing suicide and the early detection of psychiatric disorders.

CURRENT STATUS AND ISSUES RELATED TO METHODS OF SUICIDE ATTEMPT

In Japan, where the possession of guns is strictly regulated, the most common method of suicide is hanging for both men and women, followed by "suffocation by carbon monoxide poisoning using charcoal briquettes, etc." for men and jumping for women, according to 2009 statistics [3]. The selection of the method of suicide attempt is influenced by various factors, such as cultural/social background, intensity of suicide ideation, and simplicity and accessibility of the method. It is assumed that those with stronger suicide ideation choose more serious methods. Means such as burning, gassing, hanging, poisoning, and jumping from a height of ten meters or more are closely related to completed suicide [21]. In contrast, in cases of parasuicide, the majority of the methods used were of low fatality, such as drug overdose and impulsive wrist cutting on the skin surface [19].

Yet, trends in suicide means are changing. In Japan, suffocation by carbon monoxide poisoning using charcoal briquettes is the second most common method of suicide among men after hanging. The mortality rate of acute carbon monoxide poisoning has been reported to be about 30% [22], which, taken together with serious sequela of intermittent carbon monoxide poisoning, suggests that inhalation of carbon monoxide is an effective method of suicide. An increased occurrence of carbon monoxide poisoning for the purpose of suicide was first noted in the 1970s. As a countermeasure to this problem, improvements were made to reduce the carbon monoxide content of utility gas and vehicle emissions. Subsequently, the number of cases of carbon monoxide poisoning gradually decreased, but rates again began to increase in 2003. There are underlying social and physical factors behind this increase. In terms of social factors, media coverage has spread news of both the multiple occurrences of "group gas suicide using charcoal briquettes" driven by internet incitement of suicide and information about this particular means of suicide. Physical factors include easy access to charcoal briquettes in Japan and the simplicity of the method [23].

Suicide attempts using hydrogen sulfide have also gradually emerged since 2007 and have been rapidly increasing since 2008, with the annual number of cases exceeding 4000. This was likely also influenced by the dissemination of specific methods through the Internet and other media coverage. The knowledge that hydrogen sulfide can be generated by simply mixing two easily obtained materials was disseminated through the Internet. Initial media reports also included statements that appeared to suggest "hydrogen sulfide is easy to produce" or "it is easy to die using this method," statements that allowed people to easily identify product names, statements that introduced messages posted on Internet message boards as if creating an interest in this method of suicide, and statements that described the details of the method [24]. Hydrogen sulfide is highly toxic and, if generated in a residential area, may harm not only the person who attempts suicide but also the people who discover the suicidal person, family members, rescuers, or people living in the neighborhood. Hydrogen sulfide has therefore become a major social problem [25]. Both carbon monoxide and hydrogen sulfide are more often used by younger people than older ones and one attempt can produce multiple poisoning deaths [26].

To deter the incitement to suicide by media coverage and access to information about means, the WHO and the International Association for Suicide Prevention released suicide coverage guidelines for the media in 2008, which define what should and should not be done by the media when reporting suicide cases [27]. Japanese newspaper publishers independently revised their guidelines for coverage and now present a list of call centers that provide information for suicide prevention [24]. The government has also established laws and an environment to prevent incitement to commit suicide through the Internet, such as reinforcement of the criminal liability of those who encourage suicide through websites and strengthening oversight of website administrators for regulating harmful information on the Internet [28].

Given easy access to many items that can harm humans, new methods of suicide are likely to emerge in the future. The high affinity of young people to new information and trends is also identified as a problem. The government, press and media, and educational institutions should actively implement suicide prevention measures.

CARE TO BE GIVEN AT EMERGENCY ROOMS FOR PREVENTION OF RECURRENT SUICIDE ATTEMPTS

1) Guidelines for the Handling of Suicide Attempters

Suicide attempters are generally transported to emergency centers for physical reasons. The quality of intervention provided at the emergency center substantially affects the prevention of recurrent suicide attempts. To prevent newly discharged patients from attempting suicide upon their release, the Japanese Society for Emergency Medicine has developed guidelines that incorporate psychiatric factors for the handling of suicide attempters for those working in emergency rooms, emergency departments, and emergency centers [29].

The guidelines summarize the flow of treatment and interventions to be provided to those who have attempted suicide, and define "what should be done," including listening to the patient, being sympathetic and receptive, identifying the presence or absence of suicide ideation and the reason for the suicide attempt, introduction of psychiatric care and eliciting a promise from the patient not to attempt suicide again. The guidelines also specific "what should not be done," including encouraging the patient thoughtlessly, persuading from one's own point of view and, criticizing or denying.

The Japanese Association for Emergency Psychiatry has also developed separate guidelines for psychiatric professionals to prevent recurrence in suicide attempters [30]. These guidelines have been developed based partially on experiences in our hospital. Here we describe actual practices performed in our hospital for the prevention of recurrent suicide attempts.

After a patient suspected to have attempted suicide has been transported by ambulance, while physical examination and treatment are performed, the emergency psychiatrists will collect information from the ambulance crew, the patient, and his or her family members. When doing this, it is important to give the patient and family a sense of security so that subsequent treatment can be performed smoothly. We confirm that the patient actually attempted suicide while identifying the method of the attempt and evaluating the patient's physical severity.

Severely injured patients will be admitted for treatment, but where the patient is admitted should take into account his or her mental state. For example, if the patient is conscious with strong suicidal ideation, then it may be difficult to manage the patient in the general ward. The timing of the development and intensity of suicide ideation and planning and concreteness of suicide commitment should be determined through repeated and sincere talks with the patient. Clinicians should remember that patients may deny active suicidal ideation.

If the patient has been admitted to a department providing physical treatment, psychiatric treatment should be given as soon as his or her physical status has been improved. For those with minor physical injury, whether they should be admitted to the psychiatric department should be determined based on the presence or absence of general risk factors for suicide. In our hospital we request intervention by a psychiatric social worker until after discharge for patients who have made suicide attempts due to social problems, such as financial or family issues.

Psychiatric social workers will contact relevant consultation services and social resources available in the community and will make arrangements for solving problems on a case-by-case basis. When the patient is discharged, an effort should be made to elicit a promise from the patient not to attempt suicide again. Patients need to receive a psychiatric follow-up after being discharged from the hospital. If the patient has no regular psychiatrist, he or she should be instructed to be sure to see a psychiatrist preferably on the following day and a referral letter to a psychiatrist should be provided.

2) Differential Handling of Suicide Attempters Depending on Their Characteristics

Patients with repeated episodes of suicidal behavior tend to be sent home after being given mental and physical treatment at an emergency room [1]. Medical staff and family members may tend to underestimate the danger of suicide attempt in these patients. However, in view of the possibility that their suicide ideation is temporarily weakened by a post-attempt cathartic effect [31] and that they may engage in a fatal suicide action after repeated suicide attempts, and given the previous studies suggesting that a suicide attempt itself is a risk factor for completed suicide [32] [33] [34], these patients should be handled carefully, without disregard for the danger of suicide attempts.

Specifically, we encourage the patient to explain the reason for the suicide attempt in detail so that problems can be identified. Healthcare professionals should evaluate the intensity of suicide ideation and share the information with the patient's family members. When it has been decided that the patient can be sent home, family members should be informed of the possibility that the patient's mental status is temporarily stable due to a cathartic effect and that suicidal ideation may reemerge.

Clinicians should elicit a promise from the patient and her family that she will see a psychiatrist in the next few days. The availability of psychotherapeutic interventions to improve the ability to cope with stress should be explained as well as support systems for solving specific problems within a short period of time.

In contrast, middle-aged to elderly men tend to be in a biopsychosocially severe condition and often commit suicide without prior psychiatric history [1]. These patients should thus be referred to a psychiatrist immediately after emergency treatment has been given.

Specifically, every possible intervention should be made immediately after the arrival of the patient in the emergency room, such as the introduction of psychiatric interventions and the evaluation of physical severity as well as psychiatric symptoms, assessment of the patient's background, motives for suicide, and types of support systems available to the patient. To provide this level of care, it is essential for emergency medical care, psychiatric care, and community mental health services to work hand-in-hand.

3) Completed Suicide Cases

If a person attempts or completes suicide, it is said that at least five of the person's family members and friends will suffer serious psychological effects [12]. Bereaved family members and friends have a great need for information, psychological and social support. However, since bereaved family members are usually unable to talk or listen to others calmly immediately after the arrival of the person to the emergency room, postventions such as debriefings should be performed one to two weeks after the occurrence of suicide [35].

After a completed suicide has been confirmed in the emergency room, support to bereaved relatives is provided through a psychiatric team in our hospital. Specifically, immediately after the arrival of the patient, the psychiatric team asks family members if they had noticed anything abnormal so that motives for the suicide attempt and the presence or absence of psychiatric symptoms can be determined. After the declaration of death has been made, a staff member stays close to bereaved family members uses a leaflet to explain the psychological changes they will experience. They are also told to contact the person in charge of bereaved family support if any difficulties arise. Families that have given consent are contacted by telephone in about one month to check on their condition. The person in charge of bereaved family support calls or has an interview with bereaved family members to evaluate their mental status and identify problems, encourages them to see a psychiatrist if deemed necessary, and provides other support, such as assisting in coping with legal or financial issues by introducing consultation services available in the community.

CONCLUSION

We described the characteristics of suicide attempters transported by ambulance and provided examples of interventions that can be made in emergency rooms for the prevention of recurrent suicide attempts. In Japan, there is almost no precedent for a system in which psychiatrists are available around the clock in an emergency center. It is considered increasingly important for psychiatrists to participate in interventions to prevent suicide attempts from an early stage and provide psychiatric care on a case-by-case basis.

Those who have attempted suicide have an especially high risk of a subsequent completed suicide. To prevent recurrent suicide attempts, patients should be encouraged to access consultation services and social resources through a psychiatric social worker during their stay in an emergency center or psychiatric department or immediately after returning home. We believe that coordination among physical treatment professionals and psychiatrists at the emergency center, psychiatric social workers, and social resources available in each community plays an important role in the prevention of recurrent suicide attempts and the reduction of the suicide rate.

REFERENCES

[1] Kudo K, Otsuka K, Endo J, Yoshida T, Isono H, Yambe T , Nakamura H , Kawamura S, Koeda A, Yagi J, Kemuyama N, Harada H, Chida F, Endo S, Sakai A.BMC Psychiatry.Study of the outcome of suicide attempts: characteristics of hospitalization in a psychiatric ward group, critical care center group, and non-hospitalized group,2010, 10:4.

[2] Oda S, Higashi T. J.Nahl.Inst.Public Health. Current status of research on suicide and suicide prevention in foreign countries,2003, 52.Community Safety Planning Division, Community Safety Bureau, National Police Agency. Summary data on suicide cases in 2010. 2011.Available from:http://www.npa.go.jp/safetylife/seianki/H22jisatsuno gaiyou.pdf.

[4] Skogman K, Alsen M, Öjehagen A. *Soc Psychiatry Psychiatr Epidemiol*. Sex differences in risk factors for suicide after attempted suicide—a follow-up study of 1052 suicide attempters,2004,39,113-20.

[5] Suzuki H: *Journal of clinical and experimental medicine*.The realities of attempted suicides at the emergency service of a university hospital,2003,55-58.

[6] Okamoto K, Sakata Y, Shimokawa K, Takahashi H, Shigena S, Endo K, Monou H. In Proceedings of the Japanese society of psychosomatic medicine. On sexual difference of help-seeking behavior, 2002,42(10).

[7] Matsuishi K. Japanese journal of molecular psychiatry. Self-harm and suicide attempts in emergency and critical care center, 2007,293-294.

[8] Iwato S, Otsuka K, Nakamura H, Fujiwara E, Sasaki C, Nakamura H. The journal of the iwate medical association, Depression in working people in suicide-prone districts: Study of current conditions and risk factors,2009,1-15.

[9] Schnaideman ES. *Suicide as psychache a clinical approach to self-destructive behavior.* London: Rowanand Littelefield publishers;1993.

[10] Takahashi Y. Geriatric Medicine. Senile depressionand suicide,2002,40(4),477-479.Cho Y. From the front line of advanced medical care: 3. New era of depression: For the understanding and total care of depression. Tokyo: Heibonsha Limited, Publishers; 2010.

[12] Takahashi Y. Suicide risk management procedures to be followed by medical professionals. 2nd Edition. Tokyo: Igaku Shoin Ltd.; 2006.

[13] Takahashi Y. Geriatric Medicine.Senile depressionand suicide, 2002,40(4),477-479.

[14] Isono H, Otsuka K, Hoshi K, Yambe T, Endo J, Nakamura H, Endo S. The journal of the iwate medical association. A comparative study between Patients with mood disorder and with neurotic disorder who exhibited suicide-related behaviors,2008, 151-162.

[15] Hawton K, Sutton L, Haw C, Sinclair J, Harriss L. *J Clin Psychiatry*.Suicide and attempted suicide in bipolar disorder: a systematic review of risk factors,2005,66, 693-704.

[16] Sareen.J, Cox BJ, Afifi TO, de Graaf R, Asmundson GJ, Ten Have M, Stein MB. Arc Gen Psychiatry .Anxiety disorders and Risk for Suicidal Ideation and Suicide Attempts, 2005,62,1249-1257.

[17] Asukai N. *Journal of Japanese* association of psychiatric hospitals .Actual situation of suicide caused by mental disorders, 2001,20,13-16.

[18] Hawton K, Sutton L, Haw C, Sinclair J, Deeks JJ. *Br J Psychiatry*. Schizophrenia and suicide: systematic review of risk factors,2005,187,9-20.

[19] Endo J, Otsuka K, Yoshida T, Nakamura H, Yambe T, Isono H, Chida F.The Journal of the Japanese Association for Emergency Psychiatry.On factors related to risk to life in attempted suicides: comparison between absolutely and relatively dangerous suicides in emergency and critical care center,2009,12,60-73.

[20] De Leo.D, Klieve.H . Int J Ment Health Syst.Communication of suicide intent by schizophrenic subjects: data from the Queensland Suicide Register, 2007,1,6.

[21] Asukai N. *Psychiatry Clin Neurosci*. Suicide and mental disorders,1995,49,91-97.Taki K. *Journal of Japanese* Association for Clinical Hyperbaric Oxygen and Diving Medicine. Evaluation of hyperbaric oxygen therapy (HBOT) for carbon monoxide poisoning – Acute carbon monoxide poisoning cases in Japan -, 2009,6,7-12.

[23] Hitosugi M. Current Review of Clinical Pathology. Suicide by carbon monoxide poisoning –Current trend and preventative measures—, 2008,141,40-44.

[24] Nakamura M. The Japanese *Journal of Toxicology*. How should the media report suicide cases using easily accessible toxic chemicals? 2009.22,320-324.

[25] Yamamoto I. The Japanese *Journal of Toxicology*. Crisis management system against hydrogen sulfide poisoning; From the analysis of group suicide cases, 2009,22,19-24.

[26] Ishizawa F., Norimine E. and Honda K. The Japanese *Journal of Toxicology*. Changing trend in gas poisoning as influenced by the internet, 2011,24,3-8.

[27] WHO,IASP.Preventing Suicide-A Resource for Media Professionals. Geneve:WHO Document Production Services;2008.

[28] Koike R. The Japanese Journal of Toxicology. The relationship between internet and suicide, 2009,22,325-329.

[29] Japanese Society for Emergency Medicine. Handling of suicide attempters; Guidance for medical professionals working in emergency rooms, emergency departments and emergency centers. 2009.

[30] The Japanese Association for Emergency Psychiatry. Psychiatric Emergency Care Guidelines 2009 "Handling of suicide attempters". 2009.

[31] Matsuishi K, Kitamura N, Sato M, Nagai K, Huh SY, Ariyoshi K, Sato S, Mita T . Psychiatry Clin Neurosci.Change of suicidal ideation induced by suicide attempt,2005,59,599-604.

[32] Jenkins GR, Hale R, Papanastassiou M, Crawford MJ, Tyrer P. *BMJ*.Suicide rate 22 years after parasuicide: *cohort study*,2002,325,1155.

[33] Suokas J, Suominen K, Isometsä E, Ostamo A, Lönnqvist J . *Acta Psychiatr Scand*. Long-term risk factors for suicide mortality after attempted suicide—findings of a 14-*year follow-up study*, 2001,104,117-21.

[34] Suominen K, Isometsä E, Suokas J, Haukka J, Achte K, Lönnqvist J. *Am J Psychiatry.* Completed suicide after a suicide attempt: a 37-year follow-up study, 2004,161,562-3.Takahashi Y. and Fukuma S. Postvention of suicide; Mental care for people bereaved by suicide. Tokyo: Igaku Shoin Ltd.; 2004.

In: Frontiers in Suicide Risk
Editor: Jill E. Lavigne

ISBN 978-1-62081-373-7
©2012 Nova Science Publishers, Inc.

Chapter 17

SUICIDAL SYNDROME RATHER THAN PROCESS RELATED TO SUICIDE IN SEVERE DEPRESSION: EVIDENCE FROM A CONTROLLED LONGITUDINAL CASE STUDY OF 100 PEOPLE WHO DIED BY SUICIDE

Louise Bradvik and Mats Berglund

Department of Clinical Sciences, Division of Psychiatry,
Lund University, Sweden

ABSTRACT

Major Depressive Disorder (MDD) with melancholic and/or psychotic features is associated with an increased risk of suicide compared to MDD without such features. The former diagnosis also appears to predominate among completed suicides.

Suicide attempt is the risk factor with the greatest impact on accomplished suicide in depression and for other diagnoses. The progression of suicide potential from more innocent to more dangerous behaviour has been postulated as the suicidal process. This starts with suicidal thoughts, evolving through more concrete plans and suicide attempts, which are often recurrent and may show increasing levels of suicidal intent and lethality of methods used, through to completed suicide. In contrast, other investigators have proposed that suicidal behaviour may be independent of depression. Attempts have been made to delineate this syndrome on a phenomenological level by describing core symptoms, such as hopelessness, etc. which appeared to be independent of illness. Biological findings have also supported this view.

In a long-term investigation into suicidal behaviour we have found evidence of a suicidal syndrome rather than a process in severe depression with melancholic and psychotic features. The data were based on multiaxial ratings performed on all in-patients at the Department of Psychiatry on discharge in the 1950s and 1960s. The sample has been monitored to 2009. The case records of 100 suicides were compared with matched controls in a blind evaluation. This gave us prospective as well as pseudo-prospective data. The present chapter is a review of several studies on this sample in an attempt to put suicidal behaviour into a theoretical framework.

There were no differences between suicides and controls concerning severity of depression, such as number of episodes and psychomotor retardation. Suicide attempt was the major predictor for suicide, but there was no further predictive value of severity, violence of method or repetition of attempt. Life events had little impact on suicide attempts in future suicides. Contemplation of suicide and actual plans appeared to have no impact, while ego-dystonic ideation (beyond one's own will) was associated with an increased suicide risk in bipolar patients and psychotic men. In the present sample, female future suicides were found to make severe attempts early in the suicidal career, while their controls made severe attempts later. A process of behavioural sensitisation was found in future suicides, where new episodes were related to an increased risk of attempt. There was a switch between different methods of suicide attempt during the suicidal career. Half of the men and a third of the women used both violent and non-violent methods for non-fatal and fatal suicidal behaviour. A non-violent method of suicide attempt could be followed by a violent suicide in men, diminishing the predictive value of a violent attempt. The suicide risk remained for up to decades with a median of 6.7 years between first suicide attempt and completed suicide. Seasonality of completed suicide, with a peak in the autumn, was found in the male group independent of seasonality of depression. Ego-dystonic suicidal ideation and aborted suicide attempts were found during efficient antidepressant pharmacotherapy, indicating that there was not a direct relationship between depression and suicidal behaviour.

In conclusion, some depressives appeared to be more suicidal than others from early on and then intermittently during a long-term course. It appeared to be independent of severity of depressive characteristics. There were limitations in the effect on suicidal behaviour when depression was treated, so there was evidence of a suicidal syndrome rather than a process.

Identification of the syndrome seems important in the efforts to prevent suicide in severe depression with melancholic and psychotic features.

INTRODUCTION

Suicidal Behaviour in Severe Depression with Melancholic ar Psychotic Features

Major depressive disorder (MDD) is a diagnosis with a high risk of suicide [Harris and Barraclough, 1998], and the risk is clearly increased if there are severe features such as melancholia or psychosis [Helgason, 1964 Brådvik et al., 2008]. Furthermore, severe depression appears to predominate among accomplished suicide due to this high risk, despite its relative infrequency among the general population [Brådvik et al., 2010].

Suicide attempts constitute a high risk of completed suicide among depressives [Nordström et al., 1995a; Sainsbury, 1986; Goldstein, 1991; Tidemalm, 2008]. The progression of suicide potential from more innocent to more dangerous behaviour has been postulated as the suicidal process [Beck et al., 1979; Kessler, 1999]. It is used to describe the intra-individual process in reaction to a person's environment, starting with feelings of despair, then fleeting suicidal thoughts, and evolving through more concrete plans and suicide attempts, which are often recurrent and may show increasing levels of suicidal intent and lethality of methods used, to completed suicide [van Heeringen, 2000]. In retrospective psychological autopsies, many suicides were found to have suffered from depression at suicide, and a correlation between depression and suicide has been assumed [Barraclough, 1974; Arsenault-Lapierre et al., 2004; Bertolote et al., 2004]. It has even been stated that depression is a necessary factor for suicidality [Isacsson, 2006]. However, other investigators have proposed that suicidal behaviour may be independent of depression. Attempts have been made to delineate this syndrome on a phenomenological level by describing core symptoms, such as hopelessness, etc. which appeared to be independent of illness [Ahrens and Linden, 1996; Ahrens et al., 2000]. Biological findings have also supported this view [Åsberg et al., 1996].

This chapter discusses findings from several longitudinal studies on suicidal behaviour in severe depression, in order to delineate the relation between depression and suicidal behaviour. The findings will be discussed in relation to the two theories of suicidal process and syndrome.

METHODS

The Sample

In the 1950s and 1960s, all in-patients at the Department of Psychiatry, University Hospital, Lund, Sweden, were rated on a multiaxial diagnostic schedule on discharge [Essen-Möller and Wohlfahrt, 1947]. This database enabled selection of patients with a prospectively rated severe depression/melancholia for an investigation into suicide. The design of the sampling procedure is presented in a flow diagram (Figure 1). The very long-term follow up (to 2010) enabled investigation of a fairly high number of deaths by suicide.

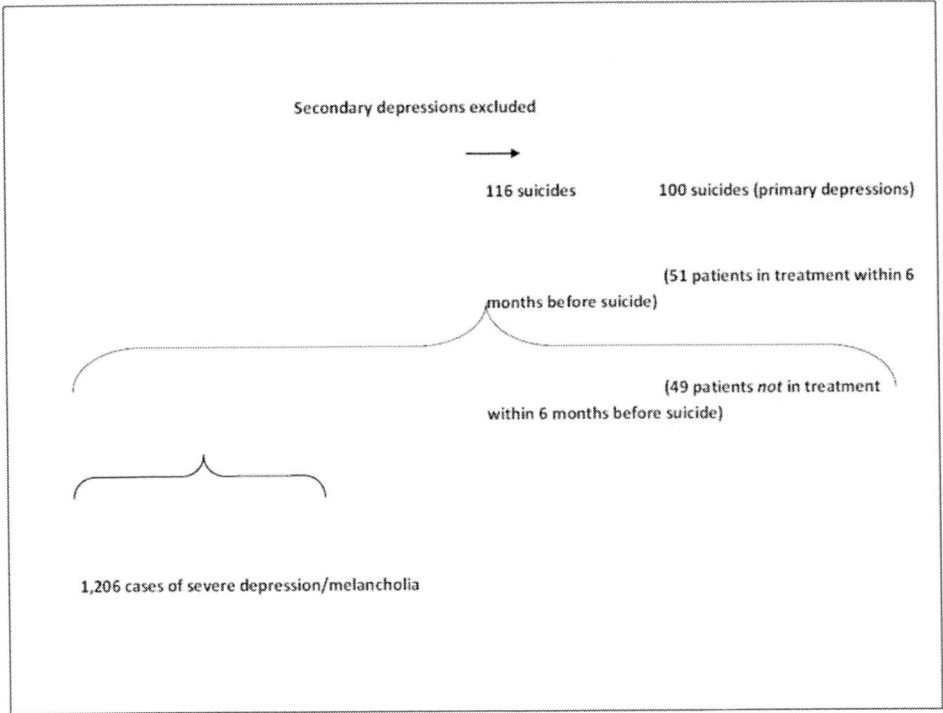

Figure 1. Design of Sampling Procedure.

A total of 1,206 patients received the diagnosis severe depression/melancholia (506 men and 700 women). Their mortality was followed-up in three sessions: to January 1, 1984 [Berglund and Nilsson, 1987], to January 1, 1998 [Brådvik and Berglund, 2001], and to February 15, 2010 [Brådvik and Berglund, 2011]. There were 116 suicide victims up to 2010. Of these, 103 had taken their lives up to 1984, another 11 up to 1998, and 2 more up to 2010.

The case records of those who died by suicide and matched controls [Brådvik and Berglund, 1993] were evaluated in detail. The researcher was unaware of the suicidal outcome and a similar procedure was carried out at second and third follow-up. A blind procedure allowed us to avoid the usual bias inherent in the retrospective evaluation. Secondary depressions, mainly alcoholism, were excluded according to Research Diagnostic Criteria [Spitzer and Endicott, 1978].

We obtained 100 deaths by suicide, 44 men and 56 women, with a primary severe depression. Matched controls, one for each suicide, were selected (from the total sample of 1,206 former in-patients of the Department of Psychiatry) using the criteria of diagnosis, gender, year of birth, and index admission year. The controls were chosen on the basis of being alive at the suicide death of the persons they matched and they were monitored up to the time of death, so the length of follow-up was the same for both suicides and controls.

A retrospective diagnosis according to DSM-IV [APA, 1994] was performed, based on the symptoms reported in the records. It turned out that 91% of the patients met the criteria for major depressive disorder with melancholic or psychotic features when in a depressive phase. Though the case records were carefully written and very informative, individual symptoms might have been underreported, so the actual number was probably higher. Both the suicide group and the control group contained 20 patients who, at some time, had at least one episode of elevated mood, indicating bipolarity. There were 57 suicides and 57 controls that had an episode of psychotic depression at some time.

There has also been a follow-up of survivors with severe depression through personal interviews by telephone in 2006-2010, including those who were born in the 1920s, 1930s, 1940s and one born in 1951 [Crona and Brådvik, 2009; Mossberg and Brådvik, 2011]. Of the total of 467, 196 had died, 106 could not be traced in the various follow-ups, and 19 could not participate due to dementia or physical illness. Of the remaining 150 asked to participate, 75 agreed. Among those there were 29 who had made at least one suicide attempt that was related to course of depression. Case records were read when possible.

Several articles have been published on many aspects of depression, suicidality, and treatment in a long-term perspective, with gender taken into consideration. To the best of our knowledge, few studies deal with completed suicide in severe depression, a high-risk group for suicide and a major contributor to suicide death. The follow-up of suicide deaths compared to controls that were still alive at the time enables a description of pathways to accomplished suicide and not only suicide attempts. Though suicide attempt is a major risk factor for suicide, and attempters resemble completers in many ways, it should be kept in mind that most attempters are survivors and therefore it is easy to miss out the actual risk factors in those who die by suicide. An important limitation is that the follow-up is based on case records.

The present chapter is a review of these papers with focus on different aspects of suicidal behaviour and severe depression in the light of a suicidal process or a suicidal syndrome as a theoretical framework.

THE IMPACT OF PSYCHIATRIC ILLNESS ON SUICIDE

Severity of Depression in Severe Depression

The definition of melancholic and psychotic feature specifiers of a major depressive disorder [APA, 1994] may indicate that they are on a continuum of the same disorder, a unitary view. Some investigators, however, have argued that major depression and melancholia are two different disorders, a binary view [Parker and Hadzi-Pavlovic, 1996]. According to the latter study, psychomotor disturbances were regarded as the core symptom, while in the DSM IV [APA, 1994] the essential feature is loss of interest or pleasure in activities or a lack of reactivity to usually pleasurable stimuli. Likewise, psychotic features could be seen as a continuum of the melancholic entity or as a separate disease.

As mentioned above, severe depression with melancholic and/or psychotic features inherits an increased risk of suicide as compared to MDD only. This fact may indicate that a more severe depression means increased hopelessness and more suicidal ideation, which more easily starts a suicidal process, a view of a continuum. On the other hand there may be a distinct quality in melancholia/psychosis that increases the risk of suicide or risky suicidal behaviour, which may even be a distinct symptom in some severely depressed patients.

More severe course of depression that involves recurrence of episodes has also been related to an increased risk of accomplished suicide [Barraclough and Pallis 1975; Waern et al., 2002].

We found no evidence that severity of depression was related to an increased risk of suicide within the severe depression group. There were a similar number of depressive episodes in suicides and controls when followed for a similar length of time (average 4 episodes and median 3). Furthermore, the rate of psychotic features was the same in suicides and controls [Brådvik and Berglund, 2010] and rates of psychomotor retardation were similar [Brådvik and Berglund, 1993].

Consequently, the risk of completed suicide in severe depression did not seem to be increased with more episodes or with the severe traits measured. Progress towards more severe form of depression does not appear to increase the suicide risk, and suicidality seems to be independent of severity within the severe depression group, i.e. a syndrome rather than a process.

Co-Morbidity and Risk of Suicide

Co-morbidity with alcohol dependence was not found to discriminate between suicides and controls in the present sample. There were only four patients in the suicide group and four in the control group who developed secondary alcohol dependence after inclusion in the study. Co-morbid obsessional-compulsive symptoms blindly scored in the case records in the first follow-up did not significantly differentiate between suicides and controls (13% vs. 8%). Anxiety prospectively scored on the multiaxial ratings did not differentiate either (35% vs. 33%). However, brittle/sensitive personality was more common among suicide victims in the male group [Brådvik and Berglund, 1993]. This type of personality has also been found to be related to suicide among males with alcohol dependence [Berglund, 1984], so is unrelated to the diagnosis of depression. In addition, those alcoholics with "brittle and sensitive" personality who committed suicide did so during drinking, in contrast with other alcoholics [Berglund et al., 1987]. In the depressed sample, three of the 16 future suicides with this diagnosis, but none of the controls, had made spontaneous reports that they were too cowardly to kill themselves, which concurs with the finding that alcoholics have been drinking before suicide if they use alcohol [Brådvik and Berglund 2010]. Some common mechanism could be present in alcoholism and depression in males.

This factor has also a strong similarity with dependent personality disorder, as has been suggested by Bolton and co-workers [2008]. Dependent personality disorder was strongly related to a high rate of male attempted suicide in the NESARC study [Bolton et al., 2008]. It was the mental disorder most strongly correlated with suicide attempt among all Axis I and Axis II disorders with an almost four-fold increase in the probability of suicide attempt.

Again, as it was related to suicide in depression as well as alcohol dependence, it seems to be a sign of a suicidal syndrome independent of depression.

THE IMPACT OF SEVERITY OF SUICIDAL BEHAVIOUR

Suicidal Ideation As a Precursor of Suicide

By definition suicide is always preceded by ideation. However, suicidal ideation is far more frequent than suicide. A correlation between ideation and accomplished suicide has been found by some investigators [Brown et al., 2000; Goldstein et al., 1991; Wolfersdorf et al., 2000], while others have failed to find a relation with accomplished suicide among in-patients [Beck et al., 1985]. However, according to another study [Fawcett 1990], it was a predictor of late suicide, within 2-10 years after examination. Those studies did not deal with depression as a separate entity.

In the present sample of severely depressed people we could apply the Beck's SSI [Scale of Suicidal Ideation, 1979], as life-weariness, contemplation of suicide, and plans were frequently reported in the case records. In addition there were reports of less rational suicidal ideation, such as suicidal ideation beyond one's own will, a feeling of not being worthy of living, and imperative suicidal ideation. Non-rational suicidal ideation has previously been described as ego-dystonic by Ringel [1969]. According to the Beck's SSI, the overall suicidal ideation (ego-syntonic ideation) did not differentiate between suicides and controls [Brådvik and Berglund, 2000]. The vast majority of the controls (85%) as well as suicides (92%) had experienced suicidal ideation at some time during their illness, indicating that suicidal ideation may be closely related to the experience of depression among those severely depressed patients. (Those who had made suicide attempts were excluded from the calculation, as the attempts were probably preceded by some kind of suicidal ideation.)

On the other hand, "suicidal ideation beyond one's own will" or ego-dystonic ideation was associated with accomplished suicide in bipolar patients and psychotic men.

These findings indicate that rational ego-syntonic contemplation of suicide is related to depression with no further relation to suicide, while ego-dystonic suicidal ideation is a risk factor for suicide and may also be related to psychosis rather than depression. Consequently, there may be a suicidal syndrome, which is related to suicide independent of depression.

Severity of Suicide Attempt and Suicide

A suicide attempt is an important predictor for accomplished suicide in depression (Sainsbury, 1986; Goldstein, 1991; Nordström, 1995; Tidemalm, 2008), so the characteristics of suicide attempts have been extensively studied. Serious suicide attempts have been shown to be predicative for suicide more than non-severe attempts [Rosen, 1976] and such attempts are sometimes referred to as "failed suicides". Other authors failed to find a relationship between severity of attempt and accomplished suicide [Nielsen et al. 1990]. Furthermore, other investigators have found an increased risk of suicide after violent suicide attempts [Hawton, 1996; Runeson et al., 2010].

The present study confirms the association between suicide attempt and completed suicide. In the suicide group 60% had made a suicide attempt versus 34% in the control group. However, there were similar rates of serious suicide attempts among attempters (32% in suicides versus 26% in controls). There were also similar rates of violent attempts (41% in suicides versus 50% in controls).

Consequently, less serious suicidal behaviour also showed similar rates in suicides and controls. A substantial minority (33% in suicides versus 32% in controls) made aborted suicide attempts, as described by Marzuk [1997], a type of suicidal behaviour which has achieved little attention in suicide research, though it has been shown to be related to actual suicide attempts [Barber, 1998]. A suicidal act with little appeal and chance of rescue, often intended to be violent, is initiated by the subject. However, the subject seems to change his/her mind and interrupts the behaviour without causing much harm. Finally, suicidal gestures, where intent to die is unclear also showed similar rates (25% in suicides versus 26% in controls).

It appears that a suicide attempt is a risk factor for suicide independent of severity and/or violence. This in turn means that there is no indication of a suicidal process with increasingly severe attempts but rather the attempt may be a syndrome/symptom of a suicide risk.

The Suicidal Career in Severe Depression

Repetition is common among suicide attempters [Haukka et al., 2008], and repeated suicidal behaviour may increase the risk of subsequent suicide [Christiansen and Jensen, 2007], although the association between repetition and completed suicide is not consequent in the literature [Nielsen et al., 1990].

In the present sample we did not find repetition to be more common among future suicides; 45% in suicides and 41% in controls [Brådvik and Berglund 2009], nor was there a higher average number of suicide attempts among the repeaters (3.7 in suicides and 4.0 in controls). Several authors have suggested that there is a suicidal progress, as severe attempts appear to occur later in the course among depressed patients [Roy-Byrne et al., 1988; Duggan, 1991; Malone, 1995]. However, in contrast, we found that severe attempts were more common as a first attempt in the suicidal career among women who later committed suicide than among female controls [Brådvik and Berglund, 2002]. No such pattern could be detected in the male group. Previous studies dealt with suicide attempters, and these are compatible with controls in the present sample, as most attempters survive. In describing them, there is always a risk of finding characteristics of survivors rather than of suicides.

Furthermore, the suicidal career in severe depression may be different from other suicidal careers with severe suicidality from the very beginning.

Another aspect of seriousness of attempts is the violence of the method chosen for attempted suicide. Men used violent methods more often than women, or if they used non-violent methods there was more often a switch from non-violent suicide attempts to a violent accomplished suicide [Brådvik, 2007]. In the female group there was a bimodal distribution, some died in a first violent suicidal act, and some made repeated suicide attempts and finally died by a non-violent completed suicide. Some women even switched from violent attempts to a non-violent completed suicide. Consequently there was no uniform process, and the most striking finding was a common switch between violent and non-violent suicidal acts.

In conclusion, there was no uniform progress towards more severe or violent suicide attempts. These findings support the view of suicidal syndrome independent of violence and severity of method.

THE TEMPORAL ASPECT OF SUICIDAL BEHAVIOUR

Long-Term Course of Depression and Suicide Attempt

Over the long-term course of depression, the onset of depressive episodes may become increasingly autonomous and less related to life-stressors [Kessing et al., 2000; Kessing et al., 2004]. This pattern has been hypothesised to result from a sensitisation process analogous to an animal electrophysiological model called "the kindling hypothesis" [Post et al., 1986; Kendler et al., 2000; Kessing, 2008], or a behavioural sensitisation where every new episode gives rise to negative thinking patterns [Teasdale, 1983; Teasdale, 1988]. Those models may be applicable to suicidal behaviour as well as depression, and a cognitive processing for suicidal behaviour has been proposed [Lau, 2004].

As mentioned above there were an equal number of episodes, indicating a similar course, in the suicide and the control group. (Had there been a sensitisation of depression related to suicidal outcome, future suicides would have been expected to have more episodes within the same time span.) Consequently no sensitisation of course of depression could be shown to be related to a suicidal outcome. However, more depressive episodes *including* suicide attempts appeared to be related to suicide [Brådvik and Berglund, 2010]. This was found for unipolar depression.

Patterns of repetition of attempts also differed between suicides and controls with a unipolar depression. During the first episode there was no significant difference in the occurrence of suicide attempts between suicides and controls [Brådvik and Berglund, 2011]. However, controls more often than suicides repeated suicide attempt early in the course, while future suicide victims repeated attempts throughout the episodes. This finding is compatible with a behavioural sensitisation of attempts across the depressive episodes, which is found in the suicide group only and therefore related to a suicidal outcome. Apart from a similar number of episodes there were also similar rates of adequate treatment, as well as improvement, in both groups [Brådvik and Berglund, 2006]. Consequently, the difference does *not* appear to be secondary to a more severe course of depression with more frequent episodes in the suicide group, *or* secondary to less adequate treatment. There seemed to be a sensitisation of suicide attempts that was apparently unrelated to a sensitisation of depression.

Repeated suicide attempts occurred during the early episodes of depression in controls. Repetition has also been shown to be more often related to distressing life events in controls, a fact that may explain a shorter and more intense suicidal career in controls [Brådvik and Berglund, 2002; Brådvik and Berglund, 2011].

In a very long-term follow-up of severe depression (37-53 years) suicide attempt among survivors could be related to the long term of depression [Mossberg and Brådvik, 2011]. They made single or repeated suicide attempts early in the course of depression but often continued to have depressive episodes for a long time after the last suicidal event. The time after the last suicide attempt was significantly longer than the time before the first attempt. The median time from first episode to first suicide attempt was two years and there were eight years between the last suicide attempt and last depressive episode. For twelve percent of the patients the first suicide attempts occurred after more than ten years and the time span after the last attempt was more than ten years for 52 percent (40 percent more than twenty years). In addition to the above, this second study indicates that there are often more depressive episodes after the suicide attempts and they also sometimes continue for a very long time, sometimes decades, after the suicidal career.

In conclusion depression often appears to continue after the period of suicide attempts in survivors, with several episodes as well as for many years after the suicidal career. These findings support the view of independent processes for depression and suicide attempt, indicating a suicidal syndrome.

Life Course and Suicide Attempt

Repetition and severity as such did not appear to differentiate between suicides and controls. Some studies have shown that increasing age at the suicide attempt is a risk factor for accomplished suicide [Hawton and Fagg, 1988; Reith et al., 2004]. A gender difference in suicide risk after attempt related to age has often been observed, but findings have been inconsistent. The risk has been shown to be increased with old age for women [Nordström et al.,1995b; Skogman et al., 2004], for men [Suokas and Lönnqvist, 1991; Iribarren et al., 2000] and young women [Iribarren et al., 2000]. However, in the present sample repeated attempts were significantly more common in older female suicides than controls, indicating that repetition in older age groups was predictive for suicide in women. On the other hand, serious suicide attempts differed between suicides and controls in the male group, being more common in older male suicides.

According to several studies, completed suicide often occurs soon after the first suicide attempt [Hawton and Fagg, 1988; Tidemalm, 2008], but others have found an increased risk even after several decades [Suominen, 2003]. In the present sample 50% of the suicide attempts occurred after more than 6.7 years, including 38% after more than 10 years and 14% after more than 20 years [Brådvik, 2003]. If the two suicides that occurred in the follow-ups after this publication are added, 10/60 or 17% of the suicides occurred after more than 20 years. Furthermore, the median time from a first suicide attempt to accomplished suicide was increased for men who had shown psychomotor retardation. The median survival in this group was 13.7 years as compared to 3.8 years among non-retarded male suicides. It appears that the suicidal process, once it has started, is delayed in men with psychomotor retardation. The time of survival was neither reduced by severity or violence of the attempt nor by repetition of attempt. Alternatively, a combination of psychomotor retardation and several episodes may be related to a progressively severe form of depression (or suicidal behaviour) with late suicide. Furthermore, an increased risk of suicide remained in a late follow-up 15 to 42 years after index admission, more so in men [Brådvik and Berglund, 2001], though there had been a similar risk in the earlier follow-up [Berglund, 1987]. This again indicates a long-standing, probably intermittent, risk of suicide.

In conclusion, the suicide risk is higher for attempts in older age (severe for men and repeated for women) and also appears to be long-lasting or rather intermittent for a very long time.

Seasonality of Completed Suicide and Depression

In an early review by Morselli in 1879 [Massing and Angermeyer 1985] a steady increase in suicide rates was noted from the beginning of the year, with a peak in June and then a decrease until the end of the year. This unimodal distribution of suicide with spring peaks has later been shown in an extensive review by Massing and Angermeyer [1985] and by others in the Northern and Southern Hemisphere [Parker and Walter, 1982] for people with and without mood disorder [Postolache et al., 2010].

Nevertheless, a second less clearly-defined peak in the autumn was found in one-fifth of the studies according to Massing's review [1985]. A bimodal distribution with two peaks has sometimes been found, mostly for females [Lester and Frank, 1988; Altamura et al., 1999]. As depression sometimes shows a seasonal pattern [APA, 1994] the occurrence of depression has been correlated to the seasonality of suicide. A coincidence between depression and suicide in the spring and autumn [Eastwood and Peacock, 1976], spring and winter [Maes et al., 1993b], or spring in females [Parker and Walter, 1982] has been shown.

In the present sample of depressives, there was a suicide peak in the autumn in the male group (October/November). In all 41%, almost half, of the male suicides occurred during these months. In contrast, a seasonal distribution of depression was rather rare and there was no correlation between autumn depression and autumn suicide. Furthermore, suicide did not occur more often early in the course of depression.

These findings support the view of a suicidal syndrome, as suicide appeared to be independent of the occurrence of depressive disorder.

EFFECT OF TREATMENT ON DEPRESSION AND SUICIDAL BEHAVIOUR

The Impact of Treatment

After the publication of Rouillon's investigation on the effect of maprotiline [Rouillon et al., 1989], it has been speculated that antidepressants may exert a different effect on depression and suicidal acts. It was found that maprotiline had a good effect on depressive symptoms, but it may also induce suicide attempts in some people.

In the present sample, in investigating the long-term course and treatment of severe depression, seriousness of suicide attempt appeared to be reduced in those with at least four weeks of antidepressant medication treatment [Brådvik and Berglund, 2006]. The suicide attempts at this point of treatment were actually often interrupted by the attempter. This may be an indication that the urge to act on suicidal feelings was reduced but not extinguished, when antidepressant therapy has relieved depressive symptoms.

In concordance with this finding, a certain type of suicidal ideation, namely ego-dystonic (suicidal ideation beyond one's own will) was more common during efficient antidepressant therapy as compared to ego-syntonic ideation [Brådvik and Berglund, 2011].

Men who committed suicide during adequate antidepressant therapy more often reported ego-dystonic suicidal ideation earlier in their lives compared with those who were not treated, also indicating that this type of ideation shows a reduced response to antidepressant therapy. As mentioned, suicidal ideation was very common in both suicides and among those who survived.

Perhaps ego-syntonic ideation is part of a depressive disorder and consequently reduced when there is a relief of depression. On the other hand ego-dystonic ideation, which appears to show a poor response, may be independent of depressive symptoms.

Both of these findings on suicidal ideation and suicide attempt indicate that suicidal behaviour tend to occur independent of antidepressant therapy; in other words relief of depression does not automatically mean relief of suicidality. These findings support the view of a suicidal syndrome.

Gender

In general, the well-known gender difference in non-fatal and fatal suicidal behaviour [Canetto and Sakinovski, 1998] was not found in the present sample of severely depressed former in-patients. The suicide rates were 11% for men and 9% for women. The rate of suicide attempts was 57% for men and 63% for women.

However, there were several gender differences in the pathways to suicide (presented in table 1). Brittle/sensitive personality was related to suicide in men only. Ego-dystonic suicidal ideation was related to suicide in psychotic men but not women. Severe attempts occurred early in the suicidal career in female suicides only.

In the male group severe attempts were related to suicide in men of the older age groups. On the other hand repeated attempts were related to suicide in elderly women. Psychomotor retardation is related to delayed suicide after suicide attempt in men only. Seasonality of suicide was found in men only.

The progress from non-violent suicide attempt to violent completed suicide was found in men only. The female group displayed a significant linear trend for non-violent completed suicide after one suicide attempt, and even more significantly, after repeated attempts.

Consequently, there are many gender differences, for which we have no clear explanation. But we can conclude that it is important to take gender into consideration in the prediction of suicide in severe depression.

Table 1. A summary of risk factors related to suicide by gender

	MEN		WOMEN
	Positive correlation	Negative correlation	Positive correlation
Co-morbidity	Brittle/sensitive personality		
Suicide attempt and psychomotor retardation (pmr)	Suicide delayed in men with pmr		
Suicidal ideation	Life-weariness in brittle/sensitive personality. Ideation "beyond one's own will" in psychotic depression		
Suicidal process	Violent 1st Violent to violent Non-violent to violent		Violent 1st Non-violent to violent (Violent to non-violent) Severe attempt early in the career.
Old age	Serious attempt		Repeated attempt
Seasonality	Autumn in men		No correlation
Suicide	Lower increased risk of suicide late in the course - higher than for women		Lower increased risk late in the course

CONCLUSION

Severe depression with melancholic or psychotic features has an increased risk of suicide. These diagnoses are also more common than MDD without such features among completed suicides. This might be seen as an indication of severity of depression being related to an increased risk of suicide; the more depressed, the more suicidal. However, when we had the opportunity to study severe depression in relation to suicide, we did not find any further evidence of increased risk of suicide by severity measures. More frequent episodes were not found in the suicide group, or higher rates of severity symptoms, such as psychosis or psychomotor retardation. Instead there may be a distinct quality of suicidality in the severe depression group related to suicide, a suicidal syndrome. Co-morbidity with brittle/sensitive personality was related to suicide in the male group in severe depression as well as alcohol dependence, indicating a relationship independent of diagnoses.

Suicidal ideation, such as death wish, contemplation and plans, was very common in both suicides and controls and so appeared to be related to depression rather than suicide. However, ego-dystonic suicidal ideation (beyond one's own will) was associated with an increased suicide risk in patients with a bipolar disorder and men with a psychotic depression. This type of ideation did not appear to be related to depression in the first place.

Suicide attempt per se was related to suicide, but severity did not appear to increase the risk, unless it was a first attempt in women or an attempt that occurred late in life in men. Violent suicidal behaviour did not appear to be predicative as such. Instead there was a switch of methods during the suicidal career. In agreement with the finding of little impact of severity or violence, the patients seemed to be suicidal with the conception or urge of carrying out a suicidal act without regard to severity or violence, again in agreement with the theory of suicidal syndrome rather than a process.

In the present sample we did not find repetition to be more common among future suicides. However, we found that severe attempts were more common as a *first* attempt in the suicidal career among women who later committed suicide than among female controls. Consequently suicidal behaviour did not seem to develop but was rather a long-standing risk, a fact that supports the view of a suicidal syndrome independent of depression.

Furthermore, suicide attempts appeared to occur early in the course of depression in both suicides and controls, so were not a result of more depressive episode. More episodes were related to accomplished suicide only if there also were suicide attempts and there was a unipolar depression. Though the first suicide attempt occurred early in course for both suicides and controls, and repeated attempts were about equally common in suicides and controls, the repeated attempts showed different patterns. Repetition occurred early and was related to life events in controls, indicating a suicidal crisis. In contrast, repetition all through the depressive episodes was more common in future suicides, indicating a behavioural sensitisation or may be a suicidal syndrome. After the initial suicide attempt the accomplished suicide may occur long after an initial attempt, sometimes decades (median 6.7 years). Psychomotor retardation appeared to delay rather than prevent suicide in the male group. This means that the suicide risk remained over a long time in suicides. There was also still an increased risk of suicide late in life, indicating a long-term risk.

Seasonality of completed suicide in men appeared to be independent of seasonality of depression, indicating that seasonality of suicide was *not* secondary to a seasonality of depression and so not secondary to depression itself.

Finally, suicidal ideation and suicide attempts did not appear to automatically vanish with the treatment of depression. Ego-dystonic ideation occurred despite adequate treatment and was more frequently reported previously in life for men who committed suicide despite adequate antidepressant treatment. Suicide attempts that occurred after the effect of antidepressant pharmacotherapy was achieved tended to be aborted rather than extinguished, so there appeared to be only a partial effect with antidepressant treatment. Depression may be relieved but an urge to initiate suicidal behaviour remains, indicating a suicidal syndrome independent of depression.

In conclusion, there was major evidence of a suicidal syndrome in severe depression, as there appeared to be no direct causal relationship between depression and suicide, neither in severity of depression, occurrence of suicidal ideation or severity or violence of suicide attempt. Only suicide attempt as such appeared to predict suicide. Suicide does not appear to be an endpoint of depression but rather of suicidality. Suicide attempt may be severe early in the course (as in women) and attempts may occur intermittently during the very long-term course of depression as a suicidal syndrome, where depression appears to be a mediating factor rather than a direct cause of suicide.

REFERENCES

Ahrens, B., and Linden, M. (1996). Is there a suicidality syndrome independent of specific major depressive disorder? Results of a split half multiple regression analysis. *Acta Psychiatrica Scandinavica*, 94, 79-86.

American Psychiatric Association [APA]. (1994). *Diagnostic and Statistical Manual of Mental Disorders (DSM-IV)* (4th ed). Washington, DC: APA.

Arsenault-Lapierre, G., Kim, C., and Turecki, G. (2004). Psychiatric diagnoses in 3275 suicides: a meta-analysis. *BMC Psychiatry, 4,* 37.

Åsberg, M., Nordström, P., and Träskman-Bendz, L. (1986). Cerebrospinal fluid studies in suicide. An overview. *Annals of the New York Academy of Sciences, 487*, 243-255.

Barber, ME, Marzuk, PM, Leon, AC, and Portera, L. (1998) Aborted suicide attempts: a new classification of suicidal behavior. *American Journal of Psychiatry, 155*, 385-389.

Barraclough, B, Bunch J, Nelson B, Sainsbury P. (1974). A hundred cases of suicide: Clinical aspects. *British Journal of Psychiatry* 125, 355-73.

Barraclough, B, Pallis, D. (1975). Depression followed by suicide: a comparison of depressed suicides with living depressives. *Psychological Medicine*, 5, 55-61.

Beck, AT, Kovacs, M, Weissman A (1979). Assessment of suicidal intention: The Scale for Suicide Ideation. *Journal of Consulting and Clinical Psychology* 47, 343-352.

Bertolote, J.M., Fleischmann, A., De Leo, D., and Wasserman, D. (2004). Psychiatric diagnoses and suicide: revisiting the evidence. *Crisis, 25,* 147-155. Review.

Bolton, J.M., Belik, S., Enns, M.W., Cox, B.J., and Sareen, J (2008). Exploring the correlates of suicide attempts among individuals with major depressive disorder: Findings from the national epidemiologic survey on alcohol and related conditions. *Journal of Clinical Psychiatry, 69,* 1139-1149.

Brådvik L. and Berglund M. (2011). Antidepressant therapy in severe depression may have different effects on ego-dystonic and ego-syntonic suicidal ideation. *Depression Research and Therapy*, Article ID 896395.

Brådvik L., and Berglund M. (2011). Repetition of suicide attempts across episodes of severe depression. Behavioural sensitisation found in suicide group but not in controls. *BMC Psychiatry* 2011, 11:5.

Brådvik L., and Berglund M. (2010). Depressive episodes with suicide attempts in severe depression. Suicides and controls differ only in the later episodes of unipolar depression. *Archives of Suicide Research*, 14: 363-367.

Brådvik L., Mattisson C, Bogren M, Nettelbladt P. (2010). Mental disorders in suicide and undetermined death in the Lundby study. The contribution of severe depression and alcohol dependence. *Archives of Suicide Research* 2010, 14: 266-275.

Brådvik L., and Berglund M. (2009). Repetition and severity of suicide attempts across the life cycle. A comparison by age-groups between suicide victims and controls with a severe depression. *BMC Psychiatry* 2009, 9:62.

Brådvik L., Mattisson C, Bogren M, Nettelbladt P. (2008). Long-term suicide risk of depression in the Lundby cohort 1947-1997 – severity and gender. *Acta Psychiatrica Scandinavica* 2008, 117:185-191.

Brådvik L. (2007). Violent and non-violent method in suicide. Different patterns may be found in men and women with severe depression. *Archives of Suicide Research*, 11: 255-264.

Brådvik L. and Berglund M. (2006). Long-term treatment and suicidal behaviour in severe depression. ECT and antidepressant pharmacotherapy may have different effects on the occurrence and seriousness of suicide attempts. *Depression and Anxiety* 2006, 23: 34-41.

Brådvik L. and Berglund M. (2005). Suicide in severe depression related to treatment. Depressive characteristics and rate of antidepressant overdose. *European Archives of Psychiatry and Clinical Neuroscience*, 255: 245-50.

Brådvik L. (2003). Suicide after suicide attempt in severe depression: A long-term follow-up. *Suicide and Life-Threatening Behavior*, 33: 381-388.

Brådvik L. and Berglund M. Seasonal distribution of suicide in alcoholism. (2002). *Acta Psychiatrica Scandinavica*, 106: 299-302.

Brådvik L. (2002). The occurrence of suicide in severe depression related to the months of the year and the days of the week. *European Archives of Psychiatry and Clinical Neuroscience*, 252: 28-32.

Brådvik L. and Berglund M. (2002). Aspects of the suicidal career in severe depression. A comparison between attempts in suicides and controls. *Archives of Suicide Research* 2002, 6: 339-349.

Brådvik L. and Berglund M. (2001). Late mortality in severe depression. *Acta Psychiatrica Scandinavica*, 103: 111-116.

Brådvik L. and Berglund M. (2000). Suicidal ideation in severe depression. *European Archives of Psychiatry and Clinical Neuroscience*, 250: 139-144.

Brådvik L. and Berglund M. (1993). Risk factors for suicide in melancholia. A case record evaluation of 89 suicides and their controls. *Acta Psychiatrica Scandinavica* 1993, 87: 306-311.

Brådvik L. and Berglund M. (2010). The overlap between depression and suicidal behaviour: implication for the preventative effect of antidepressant pharmacotherapy. In: *Antidepressants: Types, Efficiency and Possible Side Effects*. Nova Science Publishers, Inc., Hauppauge, NY, 2010.

Brown GK, Beck AT, Steer RA, and Grisham JR. (2000). Risk factors for suicide in psychiatric out-patients: A 20-year prospective study. *Journal of Consulting and Clinical Psychology* 68, 371-377, 2000.

Canetto, S.S., and Sakinofsky, I. (1998). The gender paradox in suicide. *Suicide and Life-Threatening Behavior*, 28, 1-23.

Corcoran P, Keeley HS, O'Sullivan M, Perry IJ. (2004). The incidence and repetition of attempted suicide in Ireland. *European Journal of Public Health*, 14:19-23.

Christiansen E and Jensen BF. (2007). Risk of repetition of suicide attempt, suicide or all deaths after an episode of attempted suicide: a register-based survival analysis. *The Australian and New Zealand Journal of Psychiatry, 41*, 257-265.

Crona L., Brådvik L (2009) Long-term course of severe depression. Late remission and recurrence may be found in a follow-up of 37-53 years. Manuscript (elective research paper).

De Leo D, Padoani W, Scocco P, et al. (2001). Attempted and completed suicide in older subjects: results from the WHO/EURO multicentre study of suicidal behaviour. *International Journal of Geriatric Psychiatry*, 16:300-10.

Duggan CF, Sham P, Lee AS, and Murray RM. (1991). Can future suicidal behaviour in depressed patients be predicted? *Journal of Affective Disorders* 22, 111-118.

Eastwood MR, and Peacocke J (1976). Seasonal Patterns of Suicide, Depression, and Electroconvulsive Therapy. *British Journal of Psychiatry* 129:472-5.

Essen-Möller E, and Wohlfart S (1947). Suggestions for the amendment of the official Swedish classification of mental disorder. *Acta Psychiatrica Neurologica et Scandinavica* 22 Suppl. 47:551-55.

Goldstein RB, Black DW, Nasrallah A, and Winokur G. (1991). The prediction of suicide. Sensitivity, specificity, and predictive value of a multivariate model applied to suicide among 1906 patients with affective disorders. *Archives of General Psychiatry* 48, 418-422.

Fawcett J, Scheftener WA, Fogg L, Clark DC, Young MA, Hedeker D, and Gibbons R. (1990). Time-related predictors of suicide in affective disorders. *American Journal of Psychiatry* 147, 1189-1194.

Harris EC, and Barraclough B. (1998). Excess mortality of mental disorder. *British Journal of Psychiatry* 173, 11-53.

Haukka J., Suominen K., Partonen T., and Lönnqvist J. (2008). Determinants and outcomes of serious attempted suicide: a nationwide study in Finland 1996-2003. *American Journal of Epidemiology*, 167, 155-163.

Hawton K, and Fagg J. (1988). Suicide, and other causes of death, following attempted suicide. *British Journal of Psychiatry*, 152:359-66.

Hawton, K. Suicide and attempted suicide. In Paykel ES (ed). A Handbook of Affective Disorders. Edinburgh, Churchill and Livingstone, pp 635-650, 1992.

Hawton K, and Harriss L. (2006). Deliberate self-harm in people aged 60 years and over: characteristics and outcome of a 20-year cohort. *International Journal of Geriatric Psychiatry*, 21:572-81.

Helgason T. (1964). Epidemiology of mental disorders in Iceland. A psychiatric and demographic investigation of 5395 Icelanders. *Acta Psychiatrica Scandinavica*, 40:SUPPL 173:258.

Hepple J, and Quinton C. (1997). One hundred cases of attempted suicide in the elderly. *British Journal of Psychiatry*, 171:42-6.

Hjelmeland H, Stiles TC, Bille-Brahe U, Ostamo A, Salander Renberg E, and Wasserman D. (1998). Parasuicide: The value of future suicidal intent and various motives as predictors of future suicidal behaviour. *Archives of Suicide Research*, 4:209-25.

Holley HL, Fick G, and Love EJ. (1998). Suicide following an inpatient hospitalization for a suicide attempt: a Canadian follow-up study. *Social Psychiatry and Psychiatric Epidemiology*, 33:543-51.

Iribarren C, Sidney S, Jacobs DR Jr, and Weisner C. (2000). Hospitalization for suicide attempt and completed suicide: epidemiological features in a managed care population. *Social Psychiatry and Psychiatric Epidemiology*, 35:288-96.

Isacsson G. (2006). Depression is the core of suicidality--its treatment is the cure. *Acta Psychiatrica Scandinavica* 114:149-50.

Kendler KS, Thornton LM, and Gardner CO. (2000). Stressful life events and previous episodes in the etiology of major depression in women: an evaluation of the "kindling" hypothesis. *American Journal of Psychiatry*, 157: 1243-51.

essing LV, Andersen EW, and Andersen PK. (2000). Predictors of recurrence in affective disorder - analyses accounting for individual heterogeneity. *Journal of Affective Disorders*, 57: 139-45.

Kessing LV, Hansen MG, Andersen PK, and Angst J: The predictive effect of episodes on the risk of recurrence in depressive and bipolar disorders - a life-long perspective. *Acta Psychiatrica Scandinavica* 2004, 109: 339-44.

Kessing LV. (2008). Severity of depressive episodes during the course of depressive disorder. *British Journal of Psychiatry*, 192: 290-3.

Kessler RC, Borges G, and Walters EE. (1999). Prevalence of and risk factors for lifetime suicide attempts in the National Comorbidity Survey. *Archives of General Psychiatry*, 56: 617-26.

Kreitman N, and Foster J. (1991). The construction and selection of predictive scales, with special reference to parasuicide. *British Journal of Psychiatry*, 159:185-92.

Lester D, and FrankML (1988) Sex differences in the seasonal distribution of suicides. *British Journal of Psychiatry* 153:115-7.

aes M, Meltzer HY, Suy E, and De Meyer F (1993) Seasonality in severity of depression: relationships to suicide and homicide occurrence. *Acta Psychiatrica Scandinavica* 88:156-61.

Malone KM, Haas GL, Sweeney JA, and Mann JJ. (1995). Major depression and the risk of attempted suicide. *Journal of Affective Disorders* 34, 173-185, 1995.

Marzuk, P.M., Tardiff, K., Leon, A.C., Portera, L., and Weiner, C. (1997) The prevalence of aborted suicide attempts among psychiatric in-patients. *Acta Psychiatrica Scandinavica*, 96, 492-496.

Massing W, and Angermeyer MC (1985) The monthly and weekly distribution of suicide. *Social Science and Medicine* 21:433-41.

Merrill J, and Owens J. (1990). Age and attempted suicide. *Acta Psychiatrica Scandinavica*, 82:385-8.

Mossberg A., and Brådvik L. (2011). The suicidal career in long term survivors of severe depression. A follow-up after 37-53 years. Manuscript (elective research paper in medical education).

Nielsen B, Wang AG, and Bille-Brahe U. (1990). Attempted suicide in Denmark. IV. A five-year follow-up. *Acta Psychiatrica Scandinavica* 81, 250-254.

Nimeus A, Alsen M, and Träskman-Bendz L. (2000). The suicide assessment scale: an instrument assessing suicide risk of suicide attempters. *European Psychiatry*, 15:416-23.

Nordentoft M, Breum L, Munck LK, Nordestgaard AG, Hunding A, and Laursen Bjaeldager PA. (1993). High mortality by natural and unnatural causes: a 10 year follow up study of patients admitted to a poisoning treatment centre after suicide attempts. *BMJ*, 306: 1637-41.

Nordström P, Åsberg M, Åberg-Wistedt A, and Nordin C. (1995a). Attempted suicide predicts suicide risk in mood disorders. *Acta Psychiatrica Scandinavica* 92, 345-350.

Nordström P, Samuelsson M, Åsberg M. (1995b). Survival analysis of suicide risk after attempted suicide. *Acta Psychiatrica Scandinavica*, 91:336-40.

Parker G, Hadzi-Pavlovic D. Melancholia: A Disorder of Movement and Mood. Cambridge University Press, New York, 1996.

Parker G, Walter S (1982) Seasonal Variation in Depressive Disorders and Suicidal Deaths in New South Wales. *British Journal of Psychiatry* 140:626-32.

Platt S, Bille-Brahe U, Kerkhof A, et al. (1992). Parasuicide in Europe: the WHO/EURO multicentre study on parasuicide. I. Introduction and preliminary analysis for 1989. *Acta Psychiatr Scandinavica*, 85:97-104.

Post RM, Rubinow DR, and Ballenger JC. (1986). Conditioning and sensitisation in the longitudinal course of affective illness. *British Journal of Psychiatry*, 149:191-201.

Postolache TT, Mortensen PB, Tonelli LH, Jiao X, Frangakis C, Soriano JJ, and Qin P. (2010). Seasonal spring peaks of suicide in victims with and without prior history of hospitalization for mood disorders. *Journal of Affective Disorders* 121:88-93.

Reith DM, Whyte I, Carter G, MCPherson M, and Carter N. (2004). Risk factors for suicide and other deaths following hospital treated self-poisoning in Australia. *Austalian and New Zeeland Journal of Psychiatry*, 38:520-5.

Ringel E, "Selbstmordverhütung". Verlag Hans Huber Bern Stuttgart. Wien, Österreich. 1969.

Rosen D. (1976). The serious suicide attempt. Five-year follow-up study of 886 patients. *Journal of American Medical Association*, 235, 2105-2109.

Rouillon F, Phillips R, Serrurier D, Ansart E, and Gérard MJ. (1989). Rechutes de dépression unipolaire et efficacité de la maprotiline. *L'Encéphale* XV, 527-534.

Roy-Byrne PP, Post RM, Hambrick DD, Leverich GS, and Rosoff AS. (1988). Suicide and course of illness in major depressive disorder. *Journal of Affective Disorders* 15, 1-8.

Rygnestad T. (1997). Mortality after deliberate self-poisoning. A prospective follow-up study of 587 persons observed for 5279 person years: risk factors and causes of death. *Social Psychiatry and Psychiatric Epidemiology*, 32:443-50.

Sainsbury P. Depression, suicide and suicide prevention. In Roy A (ed). Suicide. William and Wilkins, Baltimore, pp 73-88, 1986.

Sakinofsky I, and Roberts RS. (1990). Why parasuicides repeat despite problem resolution. *British Journal of Psychiatry*, 156:399-405.

Schmidtke A, Bille-Brahe U, DeLeo D, et al. (1996). Attempted suicide in Europe: rates, trends and sociodemographic characteristics of suicide attempters during the period 1989-1992. Results of the WHO/EURO Multicentre Study on Parasuicide. *Acta Psychiatrica Scandinavica*, 93: 327-38.

Skogman K, Alsen M, and Öjehagen A. (2004). Sex differences in risk factors for suicide after attempted suicide - a follow-up study of 1052 suicide attempters. *Social Psychiatry and Psychiatric Epidemiol*, 39:113-20.

Spitzer R, Endicott J, and Robins E. (1978). Research diagnostic criteria. Rational and reliability. *Archives of General Psychiatry* 35, 773-782.

Suokas J, and Lönnqvist J. (1991). Outcome of attempted suicide and psychiatric consultation: risk factors and suicide mortality during a five-year follow-up. *Acta Psychiatrica Scandinavica*, 84:545-9.

Suominen K, Isometsä E, Suokas J, Haukka J, Achte K, and Lönnqvist J. (2004). Completed suicide after a suicide attempt: a 37-year follow-up study. *American Journal of Psychiatry* 161:562-3.

Teasdale JD. (1983). Negative thinking in depression: Cause, effect, or reciprocal relationship? *Advances in Behaviour Research and Therapy*, 5:3-25.

Teasdale JD. (1988). Cognitive vulnerability to persistent depression. *Cognition and Emotion* 2:247-74.

Tidemalm D, Långström N, Lichtenstein P, and Runeson B. (2008). Risk of suicide after suicide attempt according to coexisting psychiatric disorder: Swedish cohort study with long term follow-up. *BMJ* 18;337:a2205.

van Heeringen K, Hawton K, and Williams JMG. Pathways to suicide: An integrative approach In Hawton K, Van Heeringen K (eds). The International Handbook of Suicide and Attempted Suicide. John Wiley and Sons Ltd, Chichester, pp 223-234, 2000.

Waern M., Runeson B.S., Allebeck P., et al. (2002). Mental disorder in elderly suicides: a case-control study. *American Journal of Psychiatry, 159,* 450-5.

In: Frontiers in Suicide Risk
Editor: Jill E. Lavigne

ISBN 978-1-62081-373-7
©2012 Nova Science Publishers, Inc.

Chapter 18

EXECUTIVE FUNCTIONING IN BORDERLINE PERSONALITY DISORDER WITH AND WITHOUT SELF-HARMING BEHAVIORS

Laurence Claes[1,,†], Frederique Van den Eynde[2,3,†],*
Sébastien Guillaume[3,4], Caroline Vogels[5] and Kurt Audenaert[2]

[1]University of Leuven, Department of Psychology, Leuven, Belgium
[2]University Hospital Ghent, Department of Psychiatry, Ghent, Belgium
[3]King's College London, Institute of Psychiatry, London, United Kingdom
[4]University Montpellier; Academic Hospital Montpellier; Montpellier, France
[5]Psychiatric Hospital Sint-Camillus, Sint-Denijs-Westrem, Belgium

ABSTRACT

In this study we compared borderline (BPD) patients with and without self-harm with respect to self-reported impulsiveness and executive functioning. Our sample consisted of 41 BPD patients (7 males, 34 females), of whom 68.3% (N=28) performed at least one act of self-harm (non-suicidal or suicidal in nature). Patients completed the Barrett Impulsiveness Scale, the Beck Depression Inventory and several executive function tasks. Self-harming patients reported significantly higher levels of depression. With respect to impulsiveness, self-harming patients had higher scores on motor and non-planning impulsiveness compared to patients without self-harm, also after controlling for depression. However, we did not find significant between-group differences on executive function tasks. These results are in line with previous studies that could not replicate findings of self-reported impulsiveness in self-harming patients by means of performance-based tasks.

Keywords: Borderline personality disorder; self-injury; suicide; impulsivity; executive functions

---

[*] Corresponding author. Tiensestraat 102, 3000 Leuven; E-mail: laurence.claes@psy.kuleuven.be; Phone:+32-16-32.61.33;Fax:+32-16-32.59.16.
[†] Laurence Claes and Frederique Van den Eynde have equally contributed to the manuscript.

INTRODUCTION

The majority of patients with borderline personality disorder (BPD) engage in self-harming behavior with or without a suicidal intent. Studies estimate that 40% to 85% of BPD patients carry out suicide attempts (Oumaya et al., 2008); 69% to 75% of BPD patients engage in non-suicidal self-injury (Fertuck et al., 2006; Ludäscher et al., 2009) and approximately 50%-70% of patients with a history of non-suicidal self-injury attempt to commit suicide at some point (Janis and Nock, 2009).

Symptoms of BPD are, at least partially, associated with problems in basic neuro-cognitive processes (Fertuck et al., 2006). Several authors have reported on impairments in a range of neurocognitive domains, including executive functioning (e.g., Arntz et al., 2000; Dinn et al., 2004); however, others could not replicate these findings (e.g., Kunert et al., 2003; Sprock et al., 2000). A meta-analysis shows that BPD is associated with poor executive functioning, in particular 'planning' and 'cognitive flexibility' (e.g., Ruocco et al., 2005). Those who have executive function deficits may comprise a subgroup of patients with BPD (Bustamante et al., 2009; Sprock et al., 2000).

In the present study, we will investigate whether BPD patients with (suicidal and/or non-suicidal) self-harm, show more cognitive deficits compared to patients without self-harm. According to Fertuck et al. (2006), cognitive and motor disinhibition may be strong predictors of suicidal and non-suicidal behavior in BPD patients. Burgess (1991), for example, found that suicidal self-harm was associated with neurocognitive impairment, but not with depression severity. Jollant et al. (under revision) showed that suicide attempters - independent of concomitant psychiatric disorders - showed higher attention to specific emotional stimuli, impaired decision-making, poorer problem solving abilities and reduced verbal fluency. This suggests that executive functions deficits may help to identify BPD patients at a high risk of self-harming (Fertuck et al., 2006). Few studies have compared neurocognitive impairments in patients with versus without non-suicidal self-harm. Janis and Nock (2009), for example, found that non-suicidal self-injurers had higher levels of self-reported impulsiveness compared to non-injurious controls; however, no between-group differences were observed with regard to performance on neurocognitive tasks that assess aspects of impulsivity (motor inhibition and decision-making). Others investigated executive functioning (shifting, updating/memory and inhibition) in adolescents with and without non-suicidal self-injury (NSSI) (Fikke et al., 2011). The high-severity NSSI group showed more memory deficits, while the low-severity NSSI group showed more impaired inhibitory control compared to adolescents without NSSI.

The aim of the present study was to investigate whether BPD patients who engage in self-harm (both non-suicidal and/or suicidal) have higher levels of self-reported impulsiveness and perform worse on tasks that assess executive functions, compared to BPD patients who do not self-harm. In addition, we explored whether four groups (no self-harm; non-suicidal self-injury only; suicidal self-injury only; both non-suicidal and suicidal self-injury) can be differentiated by means of self-reported impulsiveness and executive function tasks. Based on the existing literature (Burgess, 1991; Fikke et al., 2011; Janis and Nock, 2009), we hypothesized that BPD patients with self-harm would report higher levels of self-reported impulsiveness. The available data on executive functioning are heterogeneous; we hypothesized that patients with BPD with self-harm behavior would perform worse on these behavioral tasks.

METHOD

Subjects

Forty-one in- and outpatients (7 males and 34 females; Mage=26.56 years, SD=9.01) with a DSM-IV diagnosis of BPD were recruited. The BPD diagnosis was based on the results of the Structured Clinical Interview for DSM-IV Axis II personality disorders (SCID II), Dutch version (Weertman, Arntz, and Kerkhofs, 2000) and a score of 7 or higher on the Diagnostic Interview for Borderline Personality Disorder, Dutch version (Derksen, 1988). Patients with a co-morbid diagnosis of schizophrenia, dementia, and substance dependence were excluded. Patients on a stable dose of selective serotonin/norepinephrine reuptake inhibitor for at least 2 weeks before the study were allowed to enter the study. Co-morbid DSM-IV Axis I diagnoses (SCID I) were: post-traumatic stress disorder (n=3), eating disorder not otherwise specified (n=3), body dysmorphic disorder (n=2) and social anxiety disorder (n=1) (Van den Eynde et al., 2008, 2009 for a detailed description of the sample).

Instruments

At enrollment, patients completed an informed consent form, the Barratt Impulsiveness Scale, version 11 (BIS-11; Patton, Stanford, and Barratt, 1995) to measure three aspect of impulsiveness (motor, attentional and non-planning impulsiveness) and the Beck Depression Inventory-II (Van der Does, 2002). In addition, patients performed neurocognitive tasks assessing different aspects of executive functioning:

The Trail Making Test (TMT; Reitan, 1955) consists of two parts in which the time to track a number sequence (TMT-A) or a sequence of alternating numbers and letters (TMT-B) is measured. The time to complete the TMT-B minus the time to complete TMT-A is a measure of set-shifting or mental flexibility.

The Wisconsin Card Sorting Task (Heaton and Goldin, 2003) requires patients to sort cards by varying decision rules. The main outcome used in this study is the number of perseveration errors. A higher number of perseveration errors indicates poorer set-shifting abilities.

In the Verbal Fluency (Benton and Hamsher, 1976) task, patients are instructed to name as many words as possible in 1 minute starting with a specific letter (N, A, K) or belonging to a category (animals, professions). The total numbers of words generated is the outcome measure of verbal fluency used here.

The Tower of London (Berg and Byrd, 2002) requires patients to rearrange balls on a series of pegs to match a predetermined pattern in as few movements as possible. The total time to complete the 10 trials provides a measure of speed of performance and planning.

In the Stroop Color Word Task (Stroop, 1953) patients complete different types of 100-item card. On card II, rectangular colored boxes are depicted. Patients are instructed to name the colors of the boxes correctly and as quickly as possible. Card III contains incongruent word stimuli (e.g. the word 'red' is written in blue ink). Patients are instructed to name the color of the ink in which the word was written correctly as quickly as possible. The main outcome variable is the interference score, calculated as the difference (in sec) between the times to complete cards II and III.

The Iowa Gambling Task (Bechara, et al., 1994) evaluates decision making under conditions of uncertainty. Patients are required to make 100 picks from four identical-looking decks of cards (A, B, C, D). The objective is to win as much money as possible. Decks A and B are the 'disadvantageous' decks (higher rewards, but also greater losses). Decks C and D are the 'advantageous' decks (small gains, but also rare small losses). The outcome score used is the net score of advantageous choices (C+D). Impulsive patients show the tendency to choose more cards from the disadvantageous decks than from the advantageous decks.

RESULTS

Based on the self-harm item of the SCID-II, we were able to investigate the life-time prevalence of self-harm in our sample. Twenty-eight (68.3%) patients had a history of engaging in at least one form of self-harm behavior. Further, we were able to differentiate between non-suicidal (NSSI) and suicidal self-injury (SSI) by asking the participant about the intent of their self-harm. Thirteen patients (31.7%) had no history of self-harm (no self-harm), 9 (22%) engaged only in NSSI (NSSI-only), 9 (22%) only in SSI (SSI-only) and 10 patients (24.3%) engaged in both NSSI and SSI (NSSI+SSI).

We found no significant differences between BPD patients with and without self-harm with respect to gender [$\chi_{(1)}$=0.038, ns], age [$F_{(1,\ 39)}$=0.647, ns] and antidepressant use [$\chi_{(1)}$=0.545, ns]. However, those with self-harm (M=42.33; SD=9.05) reported significant higher depression symptom levels compared to patients without self-harm (M=34.77; SD=10.93) [$F_{(1,\ 38)}$=5.35, $p<0.05$]. Therefore, we controlled for depression symptom levels in the following analyses. With regard to self-reported impulsiveness, we found that self-harming BPD patients reported significant higher levels of attentional, motor and non-planning impulsiveness compared to patients without self-harm. However, after controlling for depression symptom levels (Table 1), only motor and non-planning impulsiveness remained significantly higher in the self-harming BPD group. Further, we compared executive functioning between these two groups (Table 1). Although the BPD with self-harm group performed worse than those without self-harm on some executive function tasks, no significantly differences emerged. We found no significant associations between self-reported impulsiveness and executive function tasks.

To address our second research question, we split our BPD population in four subgroups based on the presence/absence of non-suicidal (NSSI) and suicidal self-injury as described above (no self-harm: n=13; NSSI-only: n=9; SSI-only: n=9; NSSI+SSI: n=10).

Table 1. Means and standard deviations of self-reported impulsiveness and executive function tasks of BPD patients without and with self-harm behaviors controlled for depression level

	No Self-Harm (N=13)		Self-Harm (N=27)		F
	M	SD	M	SD	
BIS-11 Attentional	22.23	3.03	24.70	2.59	3.85
BIS-11 Motor	25.85	4.33	31.44	3.86	15.91***
BIS-11 Non-planning	25.69	4.59	32.70	4.44	14.48***
BIS-11 Total	73.77	9.81	88.85	7.78	20.42***
TMT B - TMT A	49.00	27.42	60.89	56.51	0.96
WCST - % Perseveration Errors	9.58	2.23	11.62	5.13	0.38
TOL – Total Time	492.54	279.67	436.56	235.78	0.19
WF Phonological	29.46	9.58	26.67	9.01	0.58
WF Semantic	35.6	13.0	35.52	8.74	0.11
SCWT Card3 – Card2	47.50	27.00	43.42	18.02	0.49
IGT – Good last 50 trials	25.46	6.15	27.96	7.07	1.67
IGT – Total Good	48.77	9.47	51.93	8.93	1.35

BIS-11 = Barratt Impulsiveness Scale (11 items); TMT = Trail Making Test; WSCT = Wisconsin Card Sorting Test; TOL = Tower of London; WF = Word Fluency; SCWT = Stroop Color Word Task; IGT = Iowa Gambling Task.

* $p < 0.05$, ** $p < 0.01$, *** $p < 0.001$.

We found no significant differences between the four patient groups with respect to gender, age and antidepressant use. However, those with SSI-only reported significant higher depression symptom levels compared to the other three groups. With respect to self-reported impulsiveness, the BPD without self-harm group scored significantly lower on all subscales compared to the three other groups. Furthermore, patients with SSI-only scored significantly higher on motor impulsiveness compared to the other groups. We did not find significant between-group differences on any of the executive function tasks.

DISCUSSION

In this study, we investigated differences in BPD patients with and without self-harming behaviors with respect to self-reported impulsiveness and executive functions. In line with previous research, 68.3% of our sample reported at least one type of self-harm (Ludäscher et al., 2009; Fertuck et al., 2006). After controlling for depression, BPD patients who self-harm reported significantly higher levels of motor and non-planning impulsiveness compared to patients without self-harm. Self-harming BPD patients experience more difficulties in controlling their behaviors and in planning activities compared to BPD without self-harm. In addition, we compared BPD patients with and without self-harm by means of different executive function tasks. In contrast to our hypotheses (i.e. patients with self-harm will show more executive functioning problems), performance was similar in both groups. Similarly,

Janis and Nock (2009) found that self-harming patients reported more impulsiveness but did not score differently on two performance-based tasks. However, other authors (Doughterty et al. 2004; Jollant et al., 2005) found significant differences between suicidal and non-suicidal patients on behavioral measures of impulsiveness.

While comparing patients without self-harm and three different group of self-harming patients (NSSI-only, SSI-only, NSSI and SSI), we found that the three groups of self-harming patients scored significantly higher on the three aspects of impulsiveness compared to BPD patients without NSSI. Furthermore, BPD patient with SSI-only scored significantly higher on motor impulsiveness than the other three groups. With respect to executive functioning we did not find significant differences between the four groups. These results are in line with previous studies that do not show significant associations between self-report and performance based measures of similar constructs (Janis and Nock, 2009).

To the best of our knowledge, this is the first study to compare BPD patients with and without different types of self-harm by means of a battery of executive function tasks. To differentiate between BPD patients with and without self-harm we made use by reliable and valid instruments (SCID-II, DIB) and we measured different aspects of executive functioning. However, this study has also limitations. The number of patients is rather small. Further, it is conceivable that differences in executive functioning between groups may only reveal themselves under stressful situations; therefore mood induction strategies or testing patients in more stressful situations can reveal more pronounced differences between patient groups (Janis and Nock, 2009), as well as the use of specific emotional stimuli (e.g., Stroop with suicide-related words). Finally, including a subgroup of age- and gender-matched controls could also help us to find out whether (specific groups of) with BPD differ from healthy controls on the executive function tasks. Thus, further cross-sectional and prospective studies are needed to improve our understanding of the impulsive nature of BPD patients engaging in self-harming behaviors.

REFERENCES

Arntz, A., Appels, C., and Sieswerda, S. (2000). Hypervigilance in borderline disorder: a test with the emotional Stroop paradigm. *Journal of Personality Disorders*, *14*, 366-373.

Bechara. A., Damasio, A.R., and Damasio, H. (1994). Insensitivity to future consequences following damage to human prefrontal cortex. *Cognition. 50*, 7-15.

Benton, A.L., and Hamsher, K. (1976). *Multilingual Aphasia Examination.* Iowa City, Iawo, AJA Associates.

Berg, K., and Byrd, D. (2002). The Tower of London spatial problem-solving task: enhancing clinical and research implementation. *Journal of Clinical and Experimental Neuropsychology*, 24, 586-604.

Burgess, J.W. (1991). Relationship of depression and cognitive impairment to self-injury in borderline personality disorder, major depression, and schizophrenia. *Psychiatry Research, 38*, 77-87.

Bustamante, M.L., Villarroel, J., Francesetti, V., Rios, M., Arco-Burgos, M., Jerez, S., et al. (2009). Planning in borderline personality disorders: Evidence for distinct subpopulations. *The World Journal of Biological Psychiatry, 10*, 512-517.

Derksen, J.L.L. (1988). *Het diagnostisch interview voor borderline patiënten: handleiding (DIB)*. Lisse, Netherlands: Swets Test Services (STS).

Dinn, W.M., Harris, C.L., Aycicegi, A., Green, P.B., Kirkley, S.M.,and Reilly, C. (2004). Neurocognitve function in borderline personality disorder. *Progress in Neuropsychoparmacology and Biological Psychiatry, 28*, 329-341.

Dougherty, D.M., Mathias, C.W., Marsh, D.M., Papageorgiou, T.D., Swann, A.C.,and Moeller, F.G. (2004). Laboratory measured behavioral impulsivity relates to suicide attempt history. *Suicide and Life-Threatening Behavior, 34*, 374–385.

Fertuck, E.A., Lenzenweger, M.F., Clarkin, J.F., Hoermann, S., and Stanley, B. (2006). Executive neurocognition, memory systems, and borderline personality disorder. *Clinical Psychology Review.26*, 346-375.

Fikke, L.T., Melinder, A., and Landro, NI. (2011). Executive functions are impaired in adolescents engaging in non-suicidal self-injury. *Psychological Medicine, 41*, 601-610.

Heaton, R.K., and Goldin, J.N. (2003). *Wisconsin Card Sorting Test®: Computer Version 4– Research Edition*. Lutz, FL: PAR.

Janis, I.B., and Nock, M.K. (2009). Are self-injurers impulsive? Results from two behavioral laboratory studies. *Psychiatry Research, 169*, 261-267.

Jollant, F., Bellivier; F., Leboyer, M., Astruc, B., Torres, S., Verdier, R., et al. (2005). Impaired decision making in suicide attempters. *American Journal of Psychiatry, 162*, 304–310.

Jollant, F., Lawrence, N.L., Olié, E., Guillaume, S., and Courtet, P. (in revision). The suicidal mind and brain: a review of neuropsyhological and neuroimaging studies. *World Journal of Biological Psychiatry*.

Kunert, H.J., Druecke, H.W., Sass, J., and Herpertz, S.C. (2003). Frontal lobe dysfunctions in borderline personality disorder? Neuropsychological findings. *Journal of Personality Disorders, 17*, 497-509.

Ludäscher, P., Greffrath, W., Schmahl, C., Kleindienst, N., Kraus, A., Baumgärter, U., et al. (2009). A cross-sectional investigation of discontinuation of self-injury and normalizing pain perception in patients with borderline personality disorder. *Acta Psychiatrica Scandinavica, 120*, 1-9.

Oumaya, M., Friedman, S., Pham, A., Abou Abdallah, T., Guelfi, J.D., and Rouillon, F. (2008). Borderline personality disorder, self-mutilation and suicide: literature review. *Encephale, 34*, 452-458.

Patton, J.H., Stanford, M.S., and Barratt, E.S. (1995). Factor structure of the Barratt Impulsiveness Scale. *Journal of Clinical Psychology, 51*, 768-774.

Reitan, R.M. (1955). The relation of the trail making test to organic brain damage. *Journal of Consulting Psychology, 19*, 393-394.

Ruocco, A.C. (2005). The neuropsychology of borderline personality disorder: a meta-analysis and review. *Psychiatry Research, 137*, 191-202.

Sprock, J., Rader, T.J., Kendall, J.P., and Yoder, C.Y. (2000). Neuropsychological functioning in patients with borderline personality disorder. *Journal of Clinical Psychology, 56*, 1587-1600.

Stroop, J.R. (1935) Studies of interference in serial verbal reactions. *Journal of Experimental Psychology, 18*, 643-661.

Van den Eynde, F., De Saedeleer, S., Naudts, K., Day, J., Vogels, C., van Heeringen, C., and Audenaert, K. (2009). Quetiapine treatment and improved cognitive functioning in borderline personality disorder. *Hum Psychopharmacology: Clinical and Experimental, 24*, 646-649.

Van den Eynde, F., Senturk, V., Naudts, K., Vogels, C., Bernagie, K., Thas, O., van Heeringen, C., and Audenaert, K. (2008). Efficacy of Quetiapine for impulsivity and affective symptoms in borderline personality disorder. *Journal of Clinical Psychopharmacology, 2*, 147-155.

Van der Does, A.J.W. (2002). *De Nederlandse versie van de Beck Depression Inventory (2nd edition).* Lisse, Netherlands: Swets Test Publishers.

Weertman, A., Arntz, A., and Kerkhofs, M.L. (2000). *Gestructureerd klinisch interview voor DSM-IV As II Persoonlijkheidsstoornissen, SCID-II.* Lisse, Netherlands: Swets Test Publishers.

INDEX

A

abstraction, 102
abuse, x, 16, 23, 24, 25, 26, 27, 29, 30, 31, 85, 98, 99, 112
access, 36, 42, 49, 59, 60, 61, 70, 72, 101, 103, 131, 166, 167, 168, 172, 173, 186, 192, 196, 197, 212, 213, 214, 229, 231, 234, 236, 243, 251, 252, 254
accessibility, 27, 74, 251
accounting, 58, 139, 273
acetaminophen, 60
acetic acid, 10
acid, 28
action research, 203, 204, 212, 213, 214, 215, 216, 217
actuality, 124
adaptation, 79, 158
adaptive functioning, 102
adhesion, 9
adjustment, 5, 46, 232
administrative support, 117
administrators, x, 117, 207, 209, 210, 252
adolescents, 4, 14, 15, 21, 72, 73, 87, 93, 97, 128, 135, 140, 142, 154, 155, 236, 278, 283
adrenaline, 5, 226
adult education, 216
adulthood, 7, 124, 134, 157
adults, 4, 42, 52, 53, 60, 61, 71, 87, 93, 97, 113, 118, 123, 124, 125, 126, 129, 130, 131, 132, 133, 134, 136, 140, 173, 177, 180, 196
adverse effects, ix, 29, 35, 36, 41, 42, 43, 44, 45, 46, 200, 201
advocacy, 205
affective disorder, 7, 8, 17, 18, 21, 62, 63, 140, 241, 242, 244, 272, 273
Afghanistan, 97, 110, 111, 113, 169, 180, 181
Africa, 243
African Americans, 9

African-American, 167
age, 1, 66, 74, 97, 100, 101, 123, 124, 128, 129, 130, 133, 134, 168, 188, 190, 198, 199, 227, 229, 230, 231, 234, 237, 241, 248, 249, 250, 265, 266, 267, 268, 270, 280, 281, 282
agencies, ix, 106, 131, 210, 214
aggregation, 140, 142
aggression, 7, 10, 19, 20, 97, 100, 112, 142
aggressiveness, 4, 156
agonist, 24, 25, 26, 200
agoraphobia, 66
agriculture, 166
AIDS, 174, 179
Air Force, 167, 176, 177, 182, 187, 192, 202
Alaska, 166, 169, 170, 173
alcohol abuse, 66, 99, 115, 204, 223
alcohol dependence, 18, 121, 261, 262, 268, 270
alcohol use, 115, 119, 242, 243, 244
alcoholism, 90, 92, 116, 215, 242, 244, 250, 260, 262, 271
algorithm, 43
allele, 3, 5, 6, 7, 15, 18
alternative drug products, 24
ambivalence, 79, 80, 83, 88, 168
American Psychiatric Association, 54, 113, 270
American Psychological Association, 113, 134
amino, 6
amphetamines, 99, 116
amygdala, 4
analgesic, 26, 72, 74
anger, 13, 102, 103, 113, 130
anterior cingulate cortex, 4
antibiotic, 200
anticonvulsant, 43, 60
antidepressant, 10, 19, 43, 52, 192, 229, 258, 267, 269, 271, 280, 281
antidepressant treatment, 10, 19, 269
antidepressants, ix, 10, 16, 43, 135, 200, 229, 266
antipsychotic, 28, 29, 32, 57, 71, 72

antisocial behavior, 20, 154

anxiety, 2, 3, 5, 9, 10, 17, 19, 21, 36, 58, 98, 102, 141, 222, 250

anxiety disorder, 2, 250

AOC, 96

APA, 260, 261, 266, 270

aripiprazole, 46, 47

arthritis, 42, 52

Asian countries, 242

assessment, 63, 64, 65, 68, 69, 72, 73, 74, 96, 98, 99, 101, 102, 103, 104, 106, 108, 109, 110, 112, 113, 130, 131, 133, 147, 186, 199, 200, 234, 248, 253, 273

assets, 177, 207

asymmetry, 15

attitudes, 4, 18, 133, 134, 142, 185, 195, 198, 204, 207, 211

audit, 207

authorities, 64

authority, 177, 204

autonomy, 80, 84, 85, 86, 87, 88

autopsy, 14, 100, 116, 119, 120, 125, 133, 141, 143, 155, 221, 222, 231, 232, 242, 244

awareness, 98, 172, 174, 175, 177, 179, 205, 243, 250

axons, 9

B

BAC, 223

bandwidth, 172

bankruptcy, 223, 224, 225

barriers, 24, 106, 107, 181, 200, 203, 207, 208, 210, 212, 214

basal ganglia, 21

base, 3, 66, 116, 139, 141, 146, 177, 191, 211

Beck Depression Inventory, 277, 279, 284

behavior therapy, 115, 116, 119, 120, 178

behavioral change, 89

behavioral disorders, 89, 204

behavioral sciences, 91

behaviors, x, 2, 8, 28, 41, 45, 52, 56, 58, 61, 62, 66, 80, 86, 89, 92, 101, 105, 117, 118, 119, 120, 128, 129, 131, 134, 135, 141, 156, 157, 183, 202, 223, 249, 255, 281, 282

Belgium, 277

beneficiaries, 32

benefits, 32, 41, 47, 48, 49, 70, 110, 168, 169, 183, 204, 206, 212, 226, 231, 232

benzodiazepine, 5, 18, 20

bias, 236, 260

bioavailability, 23, 26, 27

biological markers, 3

biomarkers, 1, 12

bipolar disorder, 5, 12, 14, 21, 27, 28, 32, 35, 36, 41, 42, 43, 45, 46, 47, 52, 140, 242, 255, 269, 273

bleeding, 42

blood, 1, 42, 75, 223

bonds, 166, 171

borderline personality disorder, 91, 116, 119, 120, 140, 278, 282, 283, 284

boredom, 229

bottom-up, 118

bowel, 42, 102

brain, x, 3, 4, 5, 7, 9, 11, 12, 13, 14, 15, 17, 19, 20, 21, 96, 99, 109, 110, 111, 112, 132, 283

brain damage, 111, 283

brain functioning, 7, 96, 99

brainstem, 13, 14

Broadband, 173, 181

bulimia, 172, 179

burdensomeness, 104, 105, 243

Bureau of Labor Statistics, 179

burn, 209

burnout, 209

by-products, 28

C

calcium, 11

call centers, 251

cancer, 57, 74, 90, 242

capsule, 23, 24, 25

car accidents, 237

carbamazepine, 48, 60, 71

carbon, 18, 51, 59, 247, 250, 251, 256

carbon monoxide, 51, 59, 247, 250, 251, 256

cardiovascular disease, 57

aregivers, 163

Caribbean, 167

catecholamines, 6

catfish, 166

Caucasians, 5

causal inference, 148, 153

causal relationship, 146, 147, 269

causality, 141, 223

causation, 140, 141, 145

C-C, 45, 157

CDC, 96, 123, 124, 127, 128, 133, 140, 170, 196, 222, 223, 225, 234

cell phones, 174, 177

Census, 164, 165, 169, 173, 179, 184, 206, 217

central nervous system, 111

cerebrospinal fluid, 10, 17

certificate, 50

certification, 237

CFI, 151, 152

challenges, 43, 65, 74, 100, 107, 132, 134, 167, 178, 213, 217

chemicals, 71, 256

childhood, 7, 9, 16, 19, 140

childhood sexual abuse, 7

children, 4, 14, 73, 86, 96, 154, 204, 213, 224, 230

China, 222

chromosome, 5

chronic diseases, 44, 182

chronic obstructive pulmonary disease, 57

cigarette smoking, 146

circulation, 25, 29

city(ies), 206, 282

citizens, 213

civil rights, 205

clarity, 129

classes, ix, 24, 36, 118

classification, 142, 270, 272

classroom, 195, 197

clients, 66, 79, 80, 81, 82, 83, 84, 85, 86, 87, 88, 89, 134, 178, 209, 210

climate, 166

clinical application, 113

clinical assessment, 130

clinical interventions, 87

clinical psychology, 181

clinical risk assessment, 101

clinical trials, 30, 41, 62, 63, 79, 116

closure, 212

clozapine, 36, 43, 46, 47, 48

clustering, 140, 141

CNS, 24, 30, 52

coal, 59, 247

Coast Guard, 167

cocaine, 4, 89, 99, 116, 119, 120

coding, 80, 188, 191, 213

codominant, 7

codon, 7

cognition, 7

cognitive deficit(s), 102, 278

cognitive dissonance, 89, 90

cognitive function, 18, 100, 124, 142, 283

cognitive impairment, 99, 104, 113, 282

cognitive process, 100, 102, 264

cognitive therapy, 116

cognitive-behavioral therapy, 82, 115, 116

collaboration, 84, 176, 203, 205, 207, 210, 211

collaborative approaches, 204

collateral, 102

color, 216, 280

combination therapy, 41

commercial, 42, 167

Commonwealth of Independent States, 222

communication, 81, 90, 97, 105, 169, 171, 172, 173, 174, 175, 176, 177, 178, 179, 200, 201, 211, 213, 214

communication systems, 172, 178

communities, x, 163, 164, 166, 167, 169, 171, 176, 177, 192, 204, 212, 213, 214

community, ix, x, 41, 63, 89, 103, 104, 105, 107, 119, 129, 131, 140, 162, 163, 166, 169, 176, 177, 179, 180, 184, 188, 192, 203, 204, 205, 206, 207, 210, 212, 213, 214, 215, 216, 230, 250, 253, 254

comorbidity, 49, 120

Comparative Fit Index, 151

compensation, 207

complexity, 42, 83, 151, 229

compliance, 23, 27, 28, 29, 63, 70, 74, 76

complications, 57

computer, 4, 64, 103, 176, 179

conception, 269

conceptual model, 144, 145, 153

conceptualization, 130

concordance, 267

concreteness, 252

concussion, 97

conduction, 157

conference, ix, 187

confidentiality, 64, 85, 86

conflict, 162, 174

confrontation, 81, 87

Congress, 96, 192, 196

consciousness, 96

consensus, ix, 46, 53, 54, 110

consent, 64, 73, 254

consolidation, 107

construct validity, 69, 75

construction, 174, 273

consulting, 250

consumers, 179, 181, 204, 206, 210, 212, 213

consumption, 226

control group, 6, 57, 117, 260, 261, 263, 264

Controlled Substances Act, 25

controlled trials, 41, 120

controversies, 110

cooperation, 81

coordination, 103, 117, 203, 205, 248, 254

COPD, 74

coping strategies, 105, 106, 107, 183

oronary artery bypass graft, 42

correlation, 1, 143, 144, 145, 148, 188, 222, 224, 258, 262, 266, 268

correlation analysis, 144

correlations, 143, 145, 158

cortex, 6, 14

corticotropin, 14, 21

cortisol, 9, 21

cost, 76, 80, 146, 178, 179, 213, 214, 221, 222, 226, 227, 229, 230, 231, 232, 234, 235, 243

cost benefit analysis, 229, 230

cost-benefit analysis, 234

counsel, 201

counseling, 64, 187, 232

Cox regression, 143

criminal justice system, 204, 210

criminal system, 214

crises, 61, 79, 103, 117, 162

crops, 166

Cross-national, 18

CSA, 25, 26

CSF, 16, 22

cues, 107

cultural beliefs, 142

culture, 73, 164, 165, 207, 208, 210, 221

cure, 272

curriculum, 117, 118, 119, 197, 207

customer loyalty, 173

cycles, 235

cycling, 43, 45, 48, 250

cytochrome, 10

D

daily living, 103, 113

danger, 85, 96, 253

dangerous behaviour, 257, 258

data collection, 213

data distribution, 188

data gathering, 66, 67

data set, ix

database, 16, 259

deaths, 45, 59, 60, 61, 66, 73, 75, 100, 109, 116, 119, 125, 126, 139, 140, 142, 161, 163, 171, 187, 196, 199, 222, 234, 247, 248, 249, 251, 259, 260, 271, 274

decision trees, 102

defendants, 204, 210, 213

deficit, 96

degradation, 6, 28, 65

delusion, 250

demand curve, 227

dementia, 18, 113, 260, 279

demographic data, 165

demographic factors, 95

denial, 81, 87

Denmark, 154, 230, 233, 273

Department of Agriculture, 164

Department of Commerce, 179

Department of Defense, ix, 36, 41, 52, 58, 70, 196

Department of Health and Human Services, xi, 2, 53

Department of Labor, 179

dependent personality disorder, 262

dependent variable, 143, 146

depressants, 24, 43, 58, 236

depressive disorders, 1, 2, 4, 6, 130, 238

depressive symptoms, 8, 12, 121, 130, 131, 250, 266, 267

despair, 258

detectable, 101

detection, 3, 36, 250

detoxification, 121, 235

developed countries, 24, 248, 249

developmental psychopathology, 155

dexamethasone in suppression tests (DST), 8

dexamethasone suppression test, 14, 21

diabetic patients, 41, 57

Diagnostic and Statistical Manual of Mental Disorders, 54, 270

diagnostic criteria, 274

Diagnostic Statistical Manual, 46

diastolic blood pressure, 57

diathesis-stress model, 140, 141, 142, 144, 145, 146, 148, 149, 153

diet, 80

diffusion, 217

diluent, 28

diplopia, 97

direct costs, 232

disability, 97, 104, 108, 125, 126, 178

disclosure, 81, 131

discrimination, 241

diseases, 35, 41, 238, 242

disequilibrium, 17

disorder, 1, 2, 5, 6, 14, 17, 18, 35, 36, 41, 46, 52, 63, 64, 67, 71, 99, 110, 119, 140, 141, 158, 172, 181, 184, 204, 233, 244, 249, 250, 255, 258, 261, 266, 267, 273, 275, 279, 282

disposition, 141

dissonance, 83

distress, 55, 65, 69, 87, 93, 99, 103, 227, 237

distribution, 11, 15, 19, 20, 24, 153, 167, 172, 179, 264, 266, 271, 273

divorce rates, 170, 224, 225

dizziness, 97

DNA, 8

DOC, 179

domestic violence, 204, 206

donations, 167

dopamine, 4, 5, 6, 11, 12, 17, 20

dopamine metabolite homovanillic acid, 4

dopaminergic, 11, 15

dorsolateral prefrontal cortex, 6
dosage, 24, 26
dosing, 29, 44, 65
DRD4 gene, 4
drug abuse, 23, 24, 25, 30, 43, 82, 89, 92, 215, 250
drug delivery, ix, x, 23, 24, 30
Drug Enforcement Administration, 31
drug interaction, 29
drug reactions, 200
drug release, 24, 26, 28, 29
drug safety, ix, xi, 30, 45
drug treatment, 28, 42, 69
drugs, xi, 23, 24, 29, 36, 41, 42, 43, 44, 46, 52, 53, 58, 65, 71, 74, 76, 99, 200, 201, 223, 228
DSM, 46, 261
DSM-IV-TR, 54
dumping, 29
dynamic risk factors, 125, 126
dysphoria, 130
dysthymia, 66

E

earnings, 226, 231, 232
economic evaluation, 221, 222, 229, 230, 231, 232, 233, 234, 236
economic growth, 223
economic status, 167
economic theory, 226, 227
economics, ix, 221, 226, 227, 230, 231, 233, 236
education, x, 53, 100, 108, 118, 183, 186, 198, 199, 204, 205, 207, 227, 229, 230, 231, 273
educational institutions, 252
EEG, 99
Egypt, 221
elaboration, 88
Electroconvulsive Therapy, 272
electronic communications, 171
emergency, 55, 56, 58, 65, 69, 73, 97, 109, 117, 140, 163, 169, 196, 247, 248, 249, 250, 252, 253, 254, 255, 256
emergency physician, 247, 248
emotional distress, 178
emotional stimuli, 278, 282
emotionality, 131
empathy, 81, 84, 92
empirical studies, 69
employees, x, 49, 188, 191, 195, 197, 198, 200, 201, 206, 209, 211, 214
employment, 106, 124, 180, 188, 210
empowerment, 106, 213
encoding, 8, 15
encouragement, 163, 177

England, 61, 143, 229, 230
enrollment, 65, 68, 171, 279
environment, 12, 80, 142, 145, 154, 166, 171, 172, 174, 209, 248, 251, 258
environmental factors, 3, 144, 145, 224, 233, 242
environmental variables, 145
environments, 9, 14, 206, 210
enzymatic activity, 7
enzyme, 3, 5, 11
epidemiologic, 157, 178, 241, 270
epidemiology, ix, 123, 155, 181
epilepsy, 99
epinephrine, 6
epistemology, 214
equality, 204
equilibrium, 227, 228
equity, 214
ester, 29, 227
ethnicity, 66, 120, 123, 124, 126, 170
etiology, 3, 10, 145, 146, 272
Europe, ix, 222, 230, 238, 274
European Union, 222
everyday life, 162, 213
evolution, 129
examinations, 126, 205
exclusion, 41
execution, 176
executive function(s), 97, 100, 102, 103, 108, 142, 277, 278, 279, 280, 281, 282
executive functioning, 97, 100, 102, 103, 142, 277, 278, 279, 280, 281, 282
expertise, 42, 169, 188, 191, 198, 200, 213
exposure, 24, 25, 41, 45, 46, 104, 105, 127, 128, 129, 182, 192, 202, 216, 241, 249
externalizing behavior, 155
extraction, 24, 26
extracts, 49

F

Facebook, 171, 173
family members, 10, 100, 106, 129, 162, 163, 173, 175, 176, 177, 186, 221, 222, 231, 234, 251, 252, 253, 254
farmland, 165, 166
Food and Drug Administration (FDA), ix, xi, 25, 26, 28, 29, 30, 31, 35, 36, 41, 43, 45, 46, 53, 157, 200
FDA approval, 36
fear, 83, 85, 104, 127, 135, 136, 226, 227, 231
Federal Communications Commission, 179
federal government, 42, 171
federal law, 207
Federal Reserve, 234

feelings, 81, 83, 87, 100, 104, 105, 140, 172, 187,
    197, 206, 258, 267
femininity, 135
fidelity, 116
fillers, 28
films, 27
financial, 100, 103, 168, 203, 228, 241, 253, 254
financial support, 100, 103
Finland, 58, 111, 222, 230, 272
firearms, 100, 127, 131, 133, 186, 196, 229, 231,
    241, 243
first generation, 25
fish, 166
fishing, 166
flexibility, 100, 102, 103, 125, 187, 279
fluctuations, 235
fluid, 26, 129, 270
fluoxetine, 48
focus groups, 118
food, 103
force, 163, 224, 228
forebrain, 22
France, 72, 277
freedom, 85, 87, 151
frontal cortex, 4
frontal lobe, 100
funding, 208
family history, 6, 43, 66, 101, 250
formation, 9, 28
families, 17, 35, 140, 141, 162, 163, 164, 166, 169,
    171, 173, 175, 176, 178, 213

G

GABA, 5, 12, 18
gambling, 91, 128, 135, 228
gastrointestinal bleeding, 42
gender differences, 124, 125, 126, 129, 132, 135,
    169, 267
gender role, 126, 131
gene expression, 3, 6, 11, 15, 20
gene promoter, 17
gene silencing, 12
general education, 230, 232
general practitioner, 183, 193
generalized anxiety disorder, 67, 183
genes, 3, 6, 8, 9, 12, 15, 142
genetic predisposition, 141, 157
genetics, 3, 15, 17, 18, 157
genotype, 3, 7, 17
geography, 164
Georgia, 155, 170
gestures, 263

glial cells, 15
globus, 3
glucocorticoid, 8, 9, 22
glucose, 57
goal-directed behavior, 100
goods and services, 226
grades, 44
grading, 53
grants, 214
graph, 124
gray matter, 12
group characteristics, 145
growth, 7, 9, 80, 171, 183
guidance, 9, 35
guidelines, 36, 41, 43, 46, 47, 52, 53, 88, 96, 101,
    113, 116, 152, 205, 251, 252
guilt, 12, 226
Gulf of Mexico, 166

H

habituation, 105, 127, 129
Haiti, 221
haplotypes, 14
happiness, 224
head injuries, 109
head injury, 96, 110
health care, 28, 32, 55, 110, 181, 186, 214, 232, 234
health care professionals, 186
health condition, 140
health information, 174, 179
health problems, 140, 168, 181
health promotion, 174, 203, 236
health services, 167, 168
health status, 69, 126
heavy drinking, 228
height, 59, 100, 243, 251
hemispheric asymmetry, 13
heroin, 119
heterogeneity, 273
HHS, 119, 214
high blood pressure, 57, 70
high school, 231, 234
higher education, 226, 232
hippocampus, 7, 19
hiring, 187
history, 8, 16, 23, 43, 45, 46, 49, 58, 61, 66, 68, 69,
    95, 96, 98, 99, 100, 101, 102, 105, 106, 108, 110,
    112, 116, 127, 131, 140, 141, 205, 212, 216, 249,
    250, 253, 274, 278, 280, 283
HIV, 174, 196
homicide, 196, 235, 236, 238, 273
homovanillic acid, 4

Honduras, 221

Hong Kong, 58, 71

hopelessness, 6, 21, 88, 101, 103, 104, 127, 132, 140, 213, 222, 257, 259, 261

hormone(s), 9, 12, 14, 21, 226

hospitalization, 42, 58, 61, 85, 93, 97, 140, 221, 222, 231, 232, 249, 255, 272, 274

host, 49, 144

hostility, 103, 113

HPA axis, 8, 9, 15, 16, 19

human, 4, 5, 13, 15, 16, 20, 22, 139, 140, 171, 207, 232, 237, 282

human behavior, 139, 140

human brain, 20, 22

Hungary, 222

hydrogen, 247, 251, 256

hydrogen sulfide, 247, 251, 256

hydrolysis, 10, 28, 29

hydrops, 110

hygiene, 102

hyperactivity, 9, 16

hyperbaric oxygen therapy, 256

hyperglycemia, 44

hypertension, 47, 196

hypothalamic–pituitary–adrenal (HPA), 8

hypothesis, 6, 59, 83, 148, 150, 152, 153, 213, 237, 264, 272

I

IASP, 256

iatrogenic, 90

ibuprofen, 51

Iceland, 272

ideal, 68, 88, 214

identification, 1, 101, 108, 156, 241, 243

identity, 100

illicit drug use, 99, 120

imagination, 16

immediate situation, 117

immigrants, 242

immunoreactivity, 13, 14, 15

impairments, 97, 103, 278

improvements, 208, 251

impulses, 59, 103

impulsive, 3, 4, 15, 59, 60, 121, 125, 128, 133, 136, 140, 141, 142, 156, 249, 251, 282, 283

impulsiveness, 242, 277, 278, 279, 280, 281, 282

impulsivity, 4, 13, 100, 101, 105, 125, 128, 141, 146, 222, 278, 283, 284

in vitro, 26

in vivo, 13, 103

incarceration, 206

incidence, 2, 27, 45, 74, 96, 98, 140, 162, 169, 180, 196, 271

income, 223, 224, 226, 228, 229, 237

income transfers, 228

increased access, 24, 25

independence, 147, 148, 217

independent variable, 146, 150, 225

indirect effect, 147, 148, 150, 163

individual characteristics, 126, 145

induction, 26, 282

industry, 42, 216

ineffectiveness, 209

inequality, 213, 233, 235

inferences, 188

infertility, 223

inflammation, 132

informed consent, 63, 64, 73, 279

infrastructure, 176, 177, 212

ingest, 61

ingestion, 26, 59, 61

inhibition, 103, 278

inhibitor, 16, 279

initiation, 100, 102, 191

injections, 26, 28, 29, 30, 32

injuries, 45, 96, 97, 109, 111, 112, 196, 232

injury, 2, 42, 50, 56, 68, 83, 85, 95, 96, 97, 98, 99, 100, 105, 108, 109, 110, 111, 133, 136, 155, 166, 169, 201, 232, 248, 249, 253, 278, 280, 282, 283

injury mechanisms, 110

insertion, 3

institutions, 204, 209, 213, 214

integration, 102, 237

integrity, 92

intellect, 16

intelligence, 182, 238

intensive care unit, 65

interference, 280, 283

internal consistency, 69, 93

internal validity, 41, 43

International Classification of Diseases, 2

interpersonal interactions, 145, 172

interpersonal relationships, 105, 249

intervention, 56, 57, 61, 72, 74, 79, 80, 83, 89, 92, 99, 101, 105, 108, 115, 117, 118, 120, 125, 126, 146, 163, 177, 178, 180, 182, 183, 186, 192, 202, 215, 238, 247, 248, 252, 253

intervention strategies, 147

intoxication, 223

intramuscular injection, 23, 29

intrinsic motivation, 80

intron, 5

investment, 171, 228

iodine, 17

Iowa, 280, 281, 282
Iraq, 97, 110, 111, 113, 117, 169, 180, 181, 184
Iraq War, 117
Ireland, 229, 232, 235, 271
isolation, 85, 102, 105, 107, 126, 132, 140, 148, 149, 161, 162, 163, 164, 170, 171, 184
Israel, 215
issues, 27, 56, 73, 74, 87, 91, 131, 143, 154, 156, 163, 167, 168, 169, 171, 174, 204, 208, 214, 247, 253, 254

J

Jamaica, 221, 224
Japan, ix, 222, 224, 229, 230, 232, 234, 235, 236, 247, 248, 249, 250, 251, 254, 256
jumping, 59, 100, 166, 251
juvenile justice, 204

K

Karl Pearson, 143
Kenya, 182
kidney, 42, 242
kill, 87, 88, 196, 235, 262
kindergartens, 230
Korea, 222

L

labor force, 224, 228, 234, 237
labor market, 223, 228, 229, 231
laboratory studies, 2, 12, 283
lactic acid, 28
language barrier, 166
later life, 133, 134
law enforcement, 205
laws, 251
lead, 9, 12, 26, 28, 29, 103, 104, 105, 132, 141, 142, 209
leadership, 206
learners, 191
learning, 21, 107, 200, 204, 205, 213
learning disabilities, 21, 205
legislation, 59, 60, 61, 72, 73
leisure, 228
lens, 136
level of education, 66
liberty, 235
life course, 158
life cycle, 270
life experiences, 141

life satisfaction, 56
lifetime, 9, 13, 66, 67, 98, 100, 105, 112, 116, 120, 156, 226, 232, 273
ligand, 4
light, 11, 105, 260
Likert scale, 80, 188, 198
limbic system, 9, 18, 20, 22
linear model, 193
lithium, 5, 37, 38, 39, 43, 44, 45, 48
Lithuania, 222
litigation, 85
liver, 11, 60
liver transplant, 60
livestock, 166
living conditions, 166
living environment, 163
localization, 11, 20
locus, 5, 10, 13, 15, 19, 21
loneliness, 131, 222
longitudinal study, 112
loss of consciousness, 96
Louisiana, 166, 169
love, 228
LSD, 99

M

magnitude, 70, 228, 243
major depression, 4, 5, 13, 14, 17, 18, 19, 20, 22, 61, 91, 110, 133, 134, 135, 223, 249, 261, 272, 282
major depressive disorder, 6, 11, 15, 260, 261, 270, 274
majority, 58, 59, 62, 66, 96, 99, 124, 130, 140, 162, 166, 173, 174, 176, 249, 250, 251, 262, 278
malaria, 57
maltreatment, 9, 21
man, 124, 126, 249
management, ix, 3, 24, 31, 32, 36, 46, 47, 52, 58, 63, 73, 75, 101, 102, 103, 108, 110, 111, 116, 130, 178, 182, 232, 243, 256
mania, 36, 37, 43, 46
manic, 19, 36, 42, 66
manic-depressive illness, 19
marijuana, 99, 157
Marine Corps, 181
marine fish, 166
marital status, 66
married women, 224
Maryland, 180
masculinity, 132, 134
mass, 229, 247
mass media, 229, 247

materials, 31, 117, 118, 187, 188, 191, 198, 199, 200, 251
matrix, 25, 26, 44, 45, 47, 53
measurement, ix, 45, 71, 75, 209
media, 26, 126, 171, 173, 174, 241, 243, 247, 251, 252, 256
median, 6, 13, 258, 261, 265, 269
mediation, 146, 147, 148, 149, 150, 151, 152, 153
Medicaid, 32
medical, x, 28, 32, 35, 36, 42, 45, 47, 49, 55, 57, 58, 62, 63, 64, 65, 66, 67, 69, 80, 96, 97, 103, 107, 112, 125, 131, 141, 167, 176, 183, 188, 197, 206, 212, 233, 235, 253, 255, 256, 273
medical care, 96, 131, 253, 255
Medicare, 42, 49, 50, 51
medication, 25, 27, 28, 32, 36, 41, 46, 47, 55, 56, 57, 58, 59, 62, 63, 64, 65, 67, 68, 70, 71, 75, 76, 80, 103, 132, 196, 200
medication compliance, 71, 80
medication counts, 27
medicine, ix, 36, 41, 44, 143, 255
membership, 143
memory, 9, 15, 16, 96, 97, 102, 107, 278, 283
mental disorder, 2, 16, 20, 75, 90, 115, 120, 135, 140, 141, 146, 154, 155, 168, 181, 222, 241, 242, 243, 244, 255, 256, 262, 272
mental health professionals, 167, 182
mental illness, 57, 62, 120, 126, 166, 167, 180, 181, 186, 204, 212, 223, 229
messages, 174, 175, 176, 179, 251
meta-analysis, 7, 10, 13, 14, 16, 17, 82, 90, 91, 93, 110, 120, 135, 155, 157, 244, 270, 278, 283
metabolic pathways, 28
metabolism, 10, 21
metabolites, 17, 22
methadone, 27, 32
methodology, 63, 70, 89, 139, 143
methyl group, 6
methylation, 8, 16
Mexico, 167
mice, 3, 9, 10, 11, 21
Microsoft, 176
microspheres, 28
midbrain, 4, 14
military, 58, 64, 66, 75, 95, 96, 97, 99, 100, 118, 127, 133, 136, 161, 166, 167, 168, 169, 177, 181, 182, 187, 196, 201
mineralocorticoid, 8, 21
minority groups, 231
miscommunication, 107
mission(s), 204, 207, 212, 214
misuse, 23, 24, 25, 26, 27, 29, 30, 99, 196
mixing, 251

mobile communication, 173
mobile phone, 174, 182
models, 42, 127, 139, 141, 143, 145, 146, 150, 152, 153, 154, 155, 176, 177, 183, 208, 214, 226, 233, 238, 243, 264
moderates, 8
modifications, 68
modules, 187, 197
mold, 204
molecules, 9
monomers, 28
Montana, 169
mood disorder, 2, 5, 11, 15, 16, 17, 19, 21, 22, 67, 98, 116, 142, 146, 154, 157, 222, 244, 250, 255, 266, 273, 274
mood states, 35
morbidity, 55, 58, 59, 60, 61, 139, 140, 184, 243, 261, 268
morphine, 23, 24, 25, 26
morphology, 20
mortality, 42, 49, 53, 55, 58, 59, 60, 61, 75, 140, 169, 183, 186, 193, 221, 234, 235, 237, 244, 251, 256, 260, 271, 272, 273, 274
mortality rate, 58, 186, 221, 244, 251
motivation, 9, 81, 82, 83, 84, 85, 88, 92, 195
motor skills, 235
MRI, 96
mRNA, 6, 8, 11, 13, 17, 20, 22
mucosa, 27
multiple factors, 145
multiple regression, 42, 143, 270
multivariate analysis, 242
muscular tissue, 28
myocardial infarction, 42
MySpace, 173

N

narcotic, 25, 223
narratives, 87
national community, 210
national culture, 236
National Institute of Mental Health, ix, 123, 207, 214
National Institutes of Health, 110, 205, 216
National Strategy, 177, 184, 230, 235
National Survey, 184
natural gas, 59
nature of time, 158
negative attitudes, 223, 224
negative emotions, 87
nerve, 11, 60
nervous system, 9
Netherlands, 283, 284

networking, 174
neurobiology, 17
neurodegeneration, 7
neuroimaging, 99, 283
neuroleptics, 10
neurons, 4, 5, 9, 11
neuropsychology, 283
neurotoxicity, 9
neurotransmission, 5
neurotransmitter, 3, 5, 17
neurotransmitter alterations, 3
neutral, 209
New England, 42, 181
New South Wales, 273
New Zealand, 183, 192, 271
next generation, 178
nodes, 146
nodules, 28
non-opioid dependent abusers, 27
norepinephrine, 6, 279
normal distribution, 147, 153
North America, 133
Northern Ireland, 244
Norway, 58, 171, 180, 230, 233, 237
novelty seeking, 4
nuclei, 6, 13
nucleus, 3, 4, 12, 14
null, 148, 150, 152
nurses, 180, 186, 187, 188, 197
nursing, ix

O

obesity, 47
objectivity, 2
obstacles, 208, 213, 214
Office of the Inspector General, 186, 187, 193
oil, 28
OJP, 215
Oklahoma, 169
olanzapine, 44, 45, 46, 47, 48
old age, 265
openness, 125
openness to experience, 125
Operation Enduring Freedom, 95, 168
Operation Iraqi Freedom, 95, 168
operations, ix, 203, 204, 205, 208, 211
opiates, 116
opioids, 29, 31, 53
opportunities, x, 30, 47, 107, 166, 200, 207, 212, 214
opportunity costs, 226
organ, 41

outpatient, 42, 44, 49, 55, 62, 64, 76, 86, 111, 113, 117, 118, 174, 180, 188, 249
outpatients, 52, 57, 65, 66, 71, 73, 83, 89, 90, 178, 279
outreach, 171, 210, 214
outreach programs, 171
overlap, 45, 271
oversight, 252
OxyContin®, 25

P

Pacific, 166
pain, 23, 24, 25, 28, 31, 42, 53, 57, 60, 74, 83, 88, 100, 104, 105, 126, 127, 129, 132, 135, 162, 163, 222, 226, 227, 231, 249, 283
pain perception, 283
pain tolerance, 105, 127
Pakistan, 222
palliative, 90
panic disorder, 10, 66, 172, 183
paradigm shift, 205
parallel, 162
paralysis, 97
parents, 145, 182, 230
parole, 212
paroxetine, 3
participants, 49, 62, 63, 64, 65, 66, 68, 116, 126, 129, 146, 185, 186, 187, 188, 190, 191, 207, 208, 209, 210, 211, 212, 213
pathology, 147
pathophysiology, 5, 6, 12, 110
pathways, 6, 10, 12, 15, 80, 139, 144, 145, 146, 152, 260, 267
patient care, 199
PBMC, 8, 11
pedagogy, 205
peer support, 180, 230, 231, 232
per capita income, 225
peripheral blood, 8, 17, 20
peripheral-type benzodiazepine receptor (PBR), 5
permission, 207
personality, 2, 14, 16, 19, 21, 61, 62, 93, 125, 142, 157, 227, 241, 242, 245, 250, 261, 262, 267, 268, 278, 279, 283
personality disorder, 21, 61, 62, 125, 241, 242, 245, 250, 262, 278, 279, 283
personality traits, 14, 19, 125, 157
pesticide, 235
PET, 4
pharmaceutical, 42, 231
pharmacological treatment, 52
pharmacotherapy, x, 43, 45, 196, 200, 258, 269, 271

phenotype, 3, 11
Philadelphia, 216
photon emisson computer tomography, 4
physical health, 30, 69, 124, 140, 232
physicians, 108, 177, 179, 183, 186, 188, 248
physicochemical properties, 29
physiology, 132
pilot study, 216
pipeline, 31
placebo, 42, 43, 52
plasma levels, 21
plasticity, 7
platelets, 5
platform, 174, 175
pleasure, 261
poison, 231
polar, 29, 52
police, x, 186
policy, 95, 155, 180, 181, 182, 204, 209, 210, 211,
    213, 214
politics, 210
pollution, 216
polymer, 23, 28
polymorphism(s), 3, 4, 5, 6, 7, 8, 10, 13, 14, 15, 16,
    17, 18, 19, 20, 22, 154
population density, 172
population group, 231
positive attitudes, 196
positive correlation, 143, 224
positive relationship, 223, 225
positron, 4, 15, 18, 19
positron emission tomography, 4, 18, 19
posttraumatic stress, 14, 110, 140, 181
post-traumatic stress disorder, 1, 36, 168, 172, 181,
    182, 279
potential benefits, 30, 58, 206, 208
power relations, 206
prefrontal cortex, 7, 11, 142, 282
preparation, 103, 136, 187
prescription drugs, ix, 24, 30, 35, 41, 202
preservation, 135
prestige, 228
primacy, 174
primary function, 10
primary school, 230
principles, 63, 79, 86, 90, 145, 203, 205, 206, 208,
    211, 212, 213
prisons, ix, 212, 243
probability, 42, 223, 224, 227, 262
problem drinking, 79, 92
problem-solving, 85, 102, 106, 107, 108, 209, 278,
    282
product attributes, 27

product design, 24, 25, 26, 29
professional development, 199, 201
professionals, 97, 106, 108, 168, 203, 204, 206, 207,
    208, 212, 213, 214, 252, 253, 254, 255, 256
program outcomes, 230
programming, x, 209, 211, 214
project, 60, 67, 69, 71, 91, 178, 203, 207, 212, 213,
    214
proliferation, 206
promoter, 3, 8, 13, 14, 16, 22
protective factors, 32, 72, 74, 101, 102, 103, 107,
    108, 112, 135, 136, 139, 141, 142, 145, 180
protein family, 11
protein kinases, 15
protein level, 3
proteins, 10, 19
psychiatric diagnosis, 36, 112, 244, 249
psychiatric disorders, 5, 7, 20, 95, 98, 99, 100, 109,
    111, 112, 125, 134, 140, 168, 241, 242, 250, 278
psychiatric hospitals, 255
psychiatric illness, 2, 8, 15, 56, 98, 99, 144, 222
psychiatric patients, 7, 22, 69, 70, 112, 140, 154,
    156, 248, 250
psychiatrist, 248, 249, 250, 253, 254
psychiatry, 248, 255
psychological distress, 55
psychological states, 227
psychological well-being, 223
psychology, 141
psychometric properties, 68, 69
psychopathology, 62, 100, 110, 142, 155
psychoses, 14, 44, 48, 50, 111
psychosis, 11, 45, 98, 110, 111, 222, 258, 261, 262,
    268
psychosocial stress, 8
psychosocial support, 247
psychosomatic, 255
psychotherapy, 90, 91, 132, 167, 179, 181, 229
psychotic symptoms, 56, 98
psychotropic drugs, 16
PTSD, 1, 11, 20, 36, 66, 97, 98, 99, 102, 111, 168,
    169, 171, 180, 184
public health, ix, 1, 70, 135, 139, 140, 161, 174, 177,
    182, 204, 205, 215
punishment, 226, 231

Q

qualifications, 82
quality improvement, 63

quality of life, 69, 75, 99, 100, 169, 204, 210, 212, 213, 214
Queensland, 256
query, 133
questionnaire, 65, 67, 69, 76, 188
quetiapine, 47, 48

R

race, 123, 124, 126, 167
racism, 166
radius, 42
rating scale, 36, 67, 81, 92
reactions, 283
reactivity, 8, 15, 21, 261
reading, 188
reality, 30, 70, 222
reasoning, 102
receptors, 3, 4, 8, 10, 11, 12, 13, 17, 20
recidivism, 208
recognition, 70, 80, 117, 176, 212
recommendations, 53, 73, 101, 133, 157, 176, 200
recovery, 61, 83, 96, 112, 181
recurrence, 43, 52, 252, 261, 271, 273
redistribution, 224
reforms, 208
regions of the world, 243
Registry, 202
regression, 43, 143, 144, 145, 146, 149, 153, 155, 156, 198
regression model, 43, 143, 149, 198
regulations, 227, 231, 235
rehabilitation, 97, 108
reinforcement, 251
relapses, 85
relatives, 162, 176, 177, 247, 254
relevance, 101, 102, 142, 178, 200, 206, 208, 212
reliability, 69, 73, 129, 153, 274
relief, 267
religious beliefs, 223
remission, 2, 41, 42, 43, 44, 47, 271
rent, 140, 141, 142
repackaging, 65
repair, 7
replication, 70
repression, 12
requirements, 176, 211
researchers, x, 2, 49, 56, 58, 75, 79, 80, 82, 95, 130, 153, 204, 205, 206, 209, 211, 214, 222, 224
resilience, 183
resistance, 8, 26, 81
resolution, 274

resources, 53, 62, 70, 108, 147, 167, 173, 177, 208, 213, 214, 216, 227, 230, 254
response, 5, 8, 9, 12, 19, 21, 22, 41, 46, 48, 66, 104, 127, 135, 143, 149, 172, 177, 198, 199, 227, 267
responsiveness, 11
restrictions, 72, 210, 213, 227
retardation, 257, 261, 265, 266, 267, 268, 269
retention rate, 171
rewards, 280
rights, 205, 213
risk assessment, 75, 96, 101, 102, 103, 104, 105, 106, 108, 112, 113, 130, 141, 157, 193
risk management, 31, 91, 117, 131, 255
risks, 41, 48, 56, 70, 169, 171, 229
risperidone, 23, 28, 29, 32, 45, 46, 47, 48
RMSEA, 151, 152
role playing, 197
Rouleau, 17, 20, 133
routes, 26
routines, 208
rules, 85, 103, 279
rural areas, 59, 161,163, 164, 165, 166, 167, 168, 169, 170, 172, 173, 174, 176, 177, 178, 179
rural women, 169

S

sadness, 130
safety, x, 28, 29, 32, 35, 41, 42, 44, 46, 47, 52, 53, 58, 63, 71, 96, 103, 105, 106, 107, 108, 117, 119, 120, 131, 162
SAS, 49, 50, 150, 153, 188, 193
savings, 232
Scandinavia, 154, 192, 193, 236
scarce resources, 230
schizophrenia, 2, 11, 14, 15, 16, 17, 18, 20, 27, 28, 29, 32, 36, 43, 46, 52, 56, 62, 70, 71, 74, 140, 141, 241, 242, 243, 244, 250, 279, 282
school, ix, 21, 100, 102, 182, 193, 202, 224, 230, 231, 235, 243
science, ix, xi, 143, 155, 205, 216, 217
scientific knowledge, x
scope, 91, 101, 117, 197, 199, 200, 201, 212
scripts, 30
seasonality, 258, 266, 269
second generation, 28, 36, 41, 44, 47
secretion, 15
security, 105, 174, 188, 228, 252
sedative(s), 58, 200
selective serotonin reuptake inhibitor, 10
self-assessment, 102, 107
self-destructive behavior, 135, 255
self-efficacy, 117, 187

self-injury, 2, 68, 104, 278, 280, 282, 283
self-regulation, 66, 100
SEM model, 151, 152, 153
semi-structured interviews, 203, 206
sensation, 97, 128, 136
sensation seeking, 128, 136
sensitivity, 45, 49, 68, 127, 130, 237
September 11, 169
serotonin, 3, 4, 6, 10, 11, 13, 14, 15, 16, 17, 18, 19,
    20, 21, 142, 279
serum, 8, 11
service provider, 167
services, 56, 65, 75, 89, 92, 95, 140, 167, 168, 169,
    172, 173, 174, 176, 180, 181, 184, 206, 208, 221,
    222, 231, 232, 253, 254
severity levels, 97
sex, 49, 123, 126, 128, 227, 250
shape, 172, 205
showing, 42, 95, 117, 146, 174
sibling(s), x, 163
side effects, 28, 46
signs, 36, 101, 102, 103, 105, 106, 108, 113, 118,
    186, 197, 250
simulation, 151
skin, 3, 251
small communities, 166
smoking, 146, 147, 200, 244
smoking cessation, 200
SMS, 180
snorted, 25
SNP, 6, 22
social anxiety, 67, 279
social environment, 227, 230
social exchange, 171
social group, 145
social inequalities, 213
social integration, 183, 223, 233
social life, 250
social network, 173
social norms, 129, 146
social problems, 206, 253
social sciences, 216, 217
social security, 49, 103
Social Security Administration, 49
social services, 243
social skills, 230
social structure, 171
social support, 28, 101, 102, 103, 105, 106, 107, 142,
    171, 181, 183, 232, 254
social workers, 187, 188, 197, 253, 254
socialization, 128, 129
society, 105, 143, 174, 222, 224, 231, 232, 255
sociology, 207

software, 64, 153, 173
solution, 28, 228
South Africa, 174, 179
South America, 167, 243
South Dakota, 169
spending, 107, 236, 237
spirituality, 102
Spring, 238
Sri Lanka, 222, 229, 235
SSI, 262, 280, 282
staff members, 64, 195
stakeholders, 204, 205, 213
standard deviation, 281
standard error, 151, 152
state, 28, 29, 59, 142, 167, 170, 181, 200, 206, 222,
    224, 227, 236, 237, 242, 250
states, 20, 27, 35, 66, 120, 127, 166, 169, 170, 199,
    223, 225, 237
statistics, 42, 133, 140, 142, 152, 192, 193, 198, 200,
    201, 222, 249, 251
stigma, 85, 131, 161, 169, 180, 241
stimulus, ix
stratification, 43, 45
stress, 7, 8, 9, 19, 21, 63, 141, 142, 146, 150, 154,
    157, 168, 171, 172, 184, 228, 232, 249, 253
stress response, 7, 8
stressful life events, 2, 8, 9, 141, 143, 181
stressors, 124, 264
stroke, 42
structure, 15, 88, 91, 156, 177, 283
style, 100
subgroups, x, 280
subscribers, 171
substance abuse, 36, 55, 62, 67, 83, 90, 98, 99, 108,
    111, 117, 118, 119, 120, 125, 172, 206, 242
Substance Abuse and Mental Health Administration
    (SAMHSA), 117, 178
substance use, x, 2, 30, 56, 62, 80, 85, 100, 101, 106,
    115, 116, 119, 128, 130, 140, 142, 144, 149, 186,
    241, 242, 243
substitution, 3, 5, 6, 7, 60
substrates, 10, 11, 15, 112
SUD, 115, 116, 117, 118, 119
suicidal ideation, ix, x, 1, 2, 11, 18, 24, 35, 36, 41,
    42, 43, 45, 46, 66, 87, 89, 95, 98, 100, 101, 107,
    127, 131, 132, 140, 178, 184, 187, 196, 199, 200,
    230, 250, 252, 253, 256, 258, 261, 262, 267, 268,
    269, 270
suicide attempters, 3, 4, 5, 7, 13, 16, 19, 21, 61, 100,
    112, 116, 128, 136, 180, 248, 249, 250, 252, 253,
    254, 255, 256, 263, 273, 274, 278, 283
suicide rate, 36, 59, 62, 70, 74, 123, 124, 126, 127,
    129, 157, 169, 170, 186, 187, 193, 196, 202, 222,

223, 224, 225, 226, 229, 234, 235, 237, 238, 241, 243, 247, 248, 249, 254, 266, 267

sulfate, 31

supervision, 28, 117

supplementation, 29

supply curve, 227

support staff, 197, 199, 200

suppression, 8, 9, 16

surveillance, 71, 206

survival, 7, 143, 227, 265, 271

survivors, 16, 112, 162, 243, 260, 263, 265, 273

susceptibility, 5, 6, 10

Sweden, 10, 12, 75, 192, 257, 259

Switzerland, 113, 229

symptoms, 21, 36, 55, 56, 69, 87, 91, 97, 98, 99, 101, 102, 108, 110, 111, 125, 130, 161, 162, 168, 177, 181, 184, 197, 222, 247, 249, 250, 253, 254, 257, 259, 260, 261, 268, 284

syndrome, 135, 257, 258, 259, 260, 261, 262, 263, 264, 265, 266, 267, 268, 269, 270

synthesis, 5

Syria, 221

T

T cell, 19

Taiwan, 59, 74, 224, 234, 238, 244

target, xi, 30, 46, 125, 169, 177, 196, 241

TBI, 58, 95, 96, 97, 98, 99, 100, 101, 102, 103, 104, 105, 106, 107, 108, 110, 113

teachers, 230

team members, 208

teams, 176, 212, 214, 233

techniques, x, 70, 79, 81, 82, 84, 87, 88, 229

technology(ies), x, 23, 26, 29, 31, 172, 178, 179, 182, 229

telephone, ix, 63, 65, 92, 103, 131, 171, 172, 175, 176, 180, 183, 254, 260

temperament, 3, 21

testing, 62, 65, 69, 73, 74, 83, 103, 146, 147, 152, 153, 171, 172, 282

test-retest reliability, 68

text messaging, 174, 175, 178, 180

theft, 166, 174

therapeutic effects, 146

therapeutic process, 85

therapeutic relationship, 81, 82, 84, 93

therapist, 89, 92, 182

therapy, 28, 29, 32, 42, 43, 46, 81, 88, 89, 92, 115, 119, 120, 135, 163, 174, 179, 267, 270

thoughts, x, 2, 41, 45, 52, 66, 81, 84, 86, 87, 101, 105, 106, 117, 118, 119, 120, 131, 196, 202, 203, 257, 258

threatening behavior, 157

threats, 66

time series, 233, 237

tissue, 11

tobacco, 146, 147, 148, 149, 153

total costs, 232

toxic substances, 231, 243

toxicity, 71, 229, 231

trade, 44

traditions, 204

trainees, 188, 191, 204, 205

training, ix, x, 57, 63, 91, 92, 108, 115, 117, 118, 119, 177, 185, 186, 187, 188, 190, 191, 192, 193, 195, 196, 197, 198, 199, 200, 201, 202, 206, 207, 211, 212, 243

training programs, 186, 187, 188, 191, 193, 197, 199

traits, 13, 19, 112, 125, 133, 140, 142, 261

trajectory, 127, 158

transcription, 5

transcripts, 11

transformations, 205

transmission, 17, 141, 142

transparency, 211

transplant, 60

transport, 4, 102

transportation, 103, 168

trauma, 8, 9, 16, 19, 101

traumatic brain injury, 58, 66, 72, 108, 109, 110, 111, 112, 114, 168, 169

traumatic events, 1

treatment venue, 115, 116, 118, 119

trial, 32, 33, 43, 46, 52, 63, 67, 75, 82, 89, 90, 92, 118, 119, 120, 178, 180, 181, 182, 183, 193, 202, 238

triggers, 142

tryptophan, 3, 6, 13, 14, 15, 17, 18, 22

tuberculosis, 3

Tucker-Lewis Index (TLI), 151

tundra, 166

Turkey, 221, 233

turnover, 174

type 2 diabetes, 75

tyrosine, 5, 12, 15, 16, 19

Tyrosine, 5, 13, 15, 19

tyrosine hydroxylase, 5, 12, 16, 19

U

United Kingdom (UK), 59, 60, 61, 72, 73, 75, 134, 154, 277

ultrarapid metabolism, 10, 21

undergraduate education, 205

underlying mechanisms, 79

unhappiness, 224, 234
United, xi, 1, 2, 31, 49, 55, 59, 60, 69, 70, 72, 73, 75, 92, 95, 109, 120, 123, 134, 139, 140, 155, 171, 179, 180, 181, 182, 184, 201, 206, 216, 217, 234, 235, 243, 277
United Nations, 155, 243
United States (US), xi, 1, 2, 23, 31, 35, 49, 55, 60, 69, 70, 75, 92, 95, 109, 120, 123, 134, 139, 140, 171, 179, 180, 181, 182, 184, 201, 206, 216, 217, 234, 235, 238
urban, 59, 62, 65, 116, 164, 166, 167, 168, 169, 170, 172, 173, 179, 180, 181, 183, 184, 206, 214, 237
urban areas, 59, 164, 167, 169, 172, 173
urbanization, 224, 225
US Department of Health and Human Services, 177, 184
USDA, 164, 165

V

vacuum, 210
validation, 43, 45, 72, 76, 148
valine, 6, 7
variables, 49, 66, 85, 87, 91, 126, 134, 143, 144, 145, 146, 149, 151, 152, 153, 155
vehicles, 177, 229
verbal fluency, 278, 279
victims, 2, 6, 8, 12, 13, 14, 15, 16, 19, 20, 22, 111, 120, 133, 166, 204, 213, 234, 242, 260, 261, 264, 270, 274
Vietnam, 168, 171, 181, 182
violence, 17, 21, 55, 56, 58, 59, 61, 62, 65, 70, 71, 96, 107, 204, 211, 258, 263, 264, 266, 269
viscosity, 25, 26
vision, 97, 216, 249
volatilization, 26
voting, 204
vulnerability, 5, 6, 8, 141, 157, 274

W

wage increases, 228
Wales, 61, 71, 229
war, 58, 110, 111, 113, 168, 181
Washington, 72, 109, 110, 111, 113, 120, 134, 166, 201, 217, 234, 235, 270
water, 23, 26, 29, 166
wealth, 226, 229
web, 113, 145, 175, 182
websites, 251
weight gain, 44
welfare, 204, 206, 235
well-being, 207, 216, 224, 234, 248
Western countries, 126
wildlife, 166
Wisconsin, 279, 281, 283
work environment, 208, 209, 228
workers, 166, 167, 210, 243, 262
workforce, 178, 180
World Health Organization (WHO), 71, 76, 104, 113, 123, 136, 140, 154, 158, 180, 186, 193, 215, 217, 221, 222, 238, 242, 243, 244, 245, 249, 251, 256, 271, 274
worldwide, 112, 139, 140, 241, 243, 244, 248

Y

young adults, 91, 184
young people, 166, 221, 252
young women, 249, 265

Z

zinc, 5
ziprasidone, 43, 46, 47, 48, 52